Contrastive Corpus Linguistics

Corpus and Discourse

Series Editors: Michaela Mahlberg (University of Birmingham, UK) and Gavin Brookes (Lancaster University, UK)

Consulting Editor: Wolfgang Teubert (University of Birmingham, UK)

Editorial Board

Paul Baker, Lancaster University, UK
Frantisek Čermák, Charles University, Prague
Susan Conrad, Portland State University, USA
Matteo Fuoli, University of Birmingham, UK
Maristella Gatto, University of Bari, Italy
Dominique Maingueneau, Université de Paris XII, France
Christian Mair, University of Freiburg, Germany
Alan Partington, University of Bologna, Italy
Charlotte Taylor, University of Sussex, UK
Elena Tognini-Bonelli, University of Siena, Italy
Ruth Wodak, Lancaster University, UK
Ruihua Zhang, Tianjin University of Science and Technology, China
Feng Zhiwei, Institute of Applied Linguistics, Beijing, China

Language is ubiquitous. As never before, it is now commonly understood how crucial language is for human interaction, for negotiating and shaping our material and ideational reality. In the digital age, the speed, scale and diversity of forms of communication and language use have grown rapidly. The increasing amount of language data that influences attitudes, decision-making and relationships highlights how the methodology of corpus linguistics together with the explanatory power of discourse analysis are indispensable for deciphering the world around us.

Situated at the interface of corpus linguistics and discourse studies, the *Corpus and Discourse* series publishes innovative research where humanities and social sciences come together to understand the relationship between discourse and society in an increasingly digital world.

Titles in the Series:

Academic Vocabulary in Learner Writing, Magali Paquot
Corpus Approaches to the Language of Sports, edited by Marcus Callies and Magnus Levin

Corpus-Based Approaches to English Language Teaching, edited by Mari Carmen Campoy, Begona Belles-Fortuno and Maria Lluisa Gea-Valor
Corpus, Discourse and Mental Health, Daniel Hunt and Gavin Brookes
Corpus Linguistics and 17th-Century Prostitution, Anthony McEnery and Helen Baker
Corpus Linguistics and World Englishes, Vivian de Klerk
Corpus Linguistics in Literary Analysis, Bettina Fischer-Starcke
Corpus Stylistics in Heart of Darkness *and its Italian Translations*, Lorenzo Mastropierro
The Discursive Construction of Economic Inequality, edited by Eva M. Gomez-Jimenez and Michael Toolan
Evaluation and Stance in War News, edited by Louann Haarman and Linda Lombardo
Historical Corpus Stylistics, Patrick Studer
Investigating Adolescent Health Communication, Kevin Harvey
Keywords in the Press, Lesley Jeffries and Brian Walker
Learner Corpus Research, Vaclav Brezina and Lynne Flowerdew
Multimodality and Active Listenership, Dawn Knight
New Trends in Corpora and Language Learning, edited by Ana Frankenberg-Garcia, Guy Aston and Lynne Flowerdew
The Prosody of Formulaic Sequences, Phoebe Lin
Representation of the British Suffrage Movement, Kat Gupta
Rethinking Idiomaticity, Stefanie Wulff
Sadness Expressions in English and Chinese, Ruihua Zhang
Web as Corpus, Maristella Gatto

Contrastive Corpus Linguistics

Patterns in Lexicogrammar and Discourse

Edited by
Anna Cermakova, Hilde Hasselgård, Markéta Malá
and Denisa Šebestová

BLOOMSBURY ACADEMIC
LONDON • NEW YORK • OXFORD • NEW DELHI • SYDNEY

BLOOMSBURY ACADEMIC
Bloomsbury Publishing Plc, 50 Bedford Square, London, WC1B 3DP, UK
Bloomsbury Publishing Inc, 1359 Broadway, New York, NY 10018, USA
Bloomsbury Publishing Ireland, 29 Earlsfort Terrace, Dublin 2, D02 AY28, Ireland

BLOOMSBURY, BLOOMSBURY ACADEMIC and the Diana logo are trademarks
of Bloomsbury Publishing Plc

First published in Great Britain 2024
Paperback edition published 2026

Copyright © Anna Cermakova, Hilde Hasselgård, Markéta Malá, Denisa Šebestová
and Contributors, 2024, 2025

Anna Cermakova, Hilde Hasselgård, Markéta Malá, Denisa Šebestová and Contributors have asserted
their right under the Copyright, Designs and Patents Act, 1988, to be identified as Authors of this work.

For legal purposes the Acknowledgements on p. vii constitute an extension of this copyright page.

Cover design: Elena Durey
Cover image © Azri Suratmin/Getty

All rights reserved. No part of this publication may be: i) reproduced or transmitted in
any form, electronic or mechanical, including photocopying, recording or by means of
any information storage or retrieval system without prior permission in writing from the
publishers; or ii) used or reproduced in any way for the training, development or operation
of artificial intelligence (AI) technologies, including generative AI technologies. The rights
holders expressly reserve this publication from the text and data mining exception as
per Article 4(3) of the Digital Single Market Directive (EU) 2019/790.

Bloomsbury Publishing Plc does not have any control over, or responsibility for, any third-party websites
referred to or in this book. All internet addresses given in this book were correct at the time of going
to press. The author and publisher regret any inconvenience caused if addresses have changed or sites
have ceased to exist, but can accept no responsibility for any such changes.

A catalogue record for this book is available from the British Library.

Library of Congress Cataloging-in-Publication Data

Names: Cermakova, Anna, 1972- editor. | Hasselgård, Hilde, editor. | Malá, Markéta, 1967- editor. |
Šebestová, Denisa, editor.
Title: Contrastive corpus linguistics : patterns in lexicogrammar and discourse / edited by Anna
Cermakova, Hilde Hasselgård, Markéta Malá and Denisa Šebestová.
Description: London ; New York : Bloomsbury Academic, 2024. | Series: Corpus and discourse | Includes
bibliographical references and index. | Summary: "Marking 30 years of contrastive corpus linguistics,
this volume provides a state-of-the-art of the field, charting its development over time and pushing the
boundaries of the discipline. By exploring the application of complex multi-genre multilingual data sets
and expanding the horizons of contrastive studies, it demonstrates how a juxtaposition of cross-linguistic
and register variation can deepen our insight into language variation and use"–Provided by publisher.
Identifiers: LCCN 2023048303 (print) | LCCN 2023048304 (ebook) | ISBN 9781350385931 (hardback) |
ISBN 9781350385979 (paperback) | ISBN 9781350385955 (epub) | ISBN 9781350385948 (ebook)
Subjects: LCSH: Corpora (Linguistics) | Contrastive linguistics. | Discourse analysis. | LCGFT: Essays.
Classification: LCC P128.C68 C636 2024 (print) | LCC P128.C68 (ebook) | DDC 410.188–dc23/
eng/20231226
LC record available at https://lccn.loc.gov/2023048303
LC ebook record available at https://lccn.loc.gov/2023048304

ISBN: HB: 978-1-3503-8593-1
PB: 978-1-3503-8597-9
ePDF: 978-1-3503-8594-8
eBook: 978-1-3503-8595-5

Series: Corpus and Discourse

Typeset by Deanta Global Publishing Services, Chennai, India

For product safety related questions contact productsafety@bloomsbury.com.

To find out more about our authors and books visit www.bloomsbury.com
and sign up for our newsletters.

Contents

List of figures	ix
List of tables	xi
List of contributors	xiv

Introduction *Hilde Hasselgård, Anna Cermakova, Markéta Malá and Denisa Šebestová*   1

1   The Present Status and Recent Trends in Corpus-Based Contrastive Linguistics *Karin Aijmer*   11

Part I Lexicogrammar in Contrast

2   Seeing Through Languages and Registers: A Closer Look at the Cognates SEE and SE *Signe Oksefjell Ebeling*   29

3   Periphrastic Genitive Constructions in English and Norwegian *Hilde Hasselgård*   62

4   Double Object Constructions in English and Norwegian: Verbs of SENDING, BRINGING, LENDING and SELLING *Thomas Egan*   87

5   Prepositional Patterns in English and Czech Newspaper Discourse *Denisa Šebestová and Markéta Malá*   108

6   A Cross-Linguistic Study of Journalistic Phraseology *Jiajin Xu, Guying Zhou, Xinlu Liu, Yuanyuan Wei, Ruchen Yu and Suhua Zhang*   132

7   Corpus-Based Contrast in Audiovisual Customization: A Pilot Study on *Can/Could* and Subject Pronouns in Spanish Dubbing *Camino Gutiérrez-Lanza and Rosa Rabadán*   157

Part II Discourse in Contrast

8   The Social Functions and Linguistic Patterns of *Please* and Its Norwegian Correspondences *Stine Hulleberg Johansen and Kristin Rygg*   183

9   Discourse Connectives in English and French: A Contrastive Study on Political Discourse *Diana Lewis*   204

10 Reporting Verbs in English, Czech and Finnish *Anna Cermakova and Lenka Fárová* 236

11 From Dashes to Dashes? – A Contrastive Corpus Study of Dashes in English, German and Swedish *Jenny Ström Herold and Magnus Levin* 260

Index 285

Figures

3.1	Dispersion of the Norwegian *til*-genitive and the English *of*-genitive	69
3.2	Possessive relations in periphrastic genitives	70
3.3	Animacy of possessor (N2)	72
3.4	Congruent and noncongruent translation correspondences	75
3.5	Distribution of congruent translations (*til* = *of*) across corpus texts	76
3.6	Percentages of animate and inanimate possessors in congruent and noncongruent translations between Norwegian and English	78
4.1	Percentages for the ditransitive and prepositional dative with the eight verbs in the original texts in the ENPC	92
4.2	Percentages of syntactically congruent and divergent translations of the eight verbs	92
4.3	Extent of semantic overlap between the verbs of sending, selling, lending and bringing in double object constructions	101
6.1	Density plots of variability and predictability across five languages	141
6.2	Mosaic plot of functional characteristics across five languages	144
7.1	*Can* (STs) > *poder* (TT1s and TT2s)	166
7.2	*Poder* < *can*: TT1s, TT2s and STs (Es)	169
7.3	*Could* (STs) > *poder* (TT1s and TT2s)	170
7.4	*Poder* < *could*: TT1s, TT2s and STs (Es)	172
7.5	Subject pronouns in Spanish: TT1s, TT2s and STs (Es)	173
9.1	Token frequency of connectives that occurred at least once in the comparable corpus	215
9.2	Main functions of *alors*, *then* and *puis* in the interviews data	219
9.3	Distribution of *then*, *alors* and *puis* in the data (excluding *alors que*)	227
9.4	Comparison of distribution of *alors* and *then* in a conversational comparable corpus and in the political interviews comparable corpus	228
10.1	*With*-PP: Congruency of verb translations (Czech and Finnish)	249
10.2	*Without*-PP: Congruency of verb translations (Czech and Finnish)	250
11.1	Structure of the Linnaeus University English-German-Swedish corpus (LEGS)	263
11.2	Dashes in English, German and Swedish originals in LEGS per 10,000 words	267

11.3	Frequencies of dashes and brackets in originals per 10,000 words	268
11.4	Functional categories of dashes in the LEGS material	268
11.5	Proportions of primary functions of dash-introduced text	270
11.6	Primary functions of dash-introduced versus bracket-introduced text	270
11.7	Sub-categories of content-oriented and interpersonal functions of dash-introduced text per 10,000 words	271
11.8	Positions of clauses and phrases introduced by dashes	273
11.9	Frequencies per 10,000 words of dashes in originals and translations	275
11.10	Proportions of retained dashes in translations	276
11.11	Real numbers for added dashes	276
11.12	Replacements from dashes: proportions of 'non-dash' correspondences in translations	279
11.13	Replacements into dashes: proportions of 'non-dash' correspondences in originals	279

Tables

2.1	Token counts in the ENPC original texts: dialogue vs. narrative	37
2.2	Distribution of the verb forms in raw numbers after disambiguation	39
2.3	Occurrences of *see* and *se* in the sub-corpora	41
2.4	Complementation patterns of *see* and *se* in the different sub-corpora	43
2.5	Semantic classification of *see* and *se* (according to SFG process types)	47
2.6	Overview of Premier League and *Eliteserie* clubs represented in the ENMaRC	60
2.7	Overview of authors and texts in the ENPC used in this study	61
3.1	Expressions of possessive relations in English and Norwegian	63
3.2	Size and structure of the English-Norwegian Parallel Corpus	66
3.3	Possessive meaning relations	68
3.4	Frequencies of periphrastic genitives in English and Norwegian fiction and nonfiction	69
3.5	Most frequent meaning relations with animate and inanimate possessors	73
3.6	Meaning relations and congruence	77
3.7	Noncongruent translation correspondences of the periphrastic genitive	78
3.8	Prepositions corresponding to *of/til* in noncongruent translations of the periphrastic genitive	80
4.1	Number of double object examples in the ENPC original language texts	91
4.2	Verbs used in congruent and divergent translations of *send* and *sende*	93
4.3	Verbs used in congruent and divergent translations of *sell* and *selge*	96
4.4	Verbs used in congruent and divergent translations of *lend* and *låne*	97
4.5	Verbs used in congruent and divergent translations of *bring* and *bringe*	99
4.6	Mutual correspondence of pairs of verbs in double object constructions	101
5.1	Corpora and tools used in the present study	110
5.2	Frequencies of the prepositional n-grams analysed	112
5.3	Position of the prepositions *IN* and *V* in the n-grams	113

5.4	Structural classification of prepositional n-grams	114
5.5	Complex prepositions containing *v* sorted by frequency	119
5.6	Complex prepositions with *in* ordered by frequency	122
6.1	Top 5 p-frames in the five languages	138
6.2	Examples of discourse-pragmatic functions of p-frames in the five languages	139
6.3	Summary of the 100 top 3–5-word p-frames of the five languages	140
6.4	Median variability and median absolute deviation of the 100 top p-frames across the five languages	141
6.5	Median predictability and median absolute deviation of the 100 top p-frames across the five languages	142
6.6	Mean predictability of the 100 top p-frames across five languages	144
7.1	*Poder < Can*: Verification of dubbese (TRACEci-CORPES XXI)	168
7.2	*Poder < Could*: Verification of dubbese (TRACEci-CORPES XXI)	171
7.3	Subject pronouns: Verification of dubbese (TRACEci-CORPES XXI)	174
7.4	*Yo*: Verification of dubbese by function (TRACEci-CORPES XXI)	174
7.5	*Usted*: Verification of dubbese by function (TRACEci-CORPES XXI)	175
7.6	*Él-ella(s)*: Verification of dubbese by function (TRACEci-CORPES XXI)	175
8.1	Summary of types of situations and interaction types in the ENPC	191
8.2	Patterns of *please* in English original and translated texts in the ENPC	192
8.3	Correspondences of *please* in ENPC	193
8.4	Typical translations from *please* to Ø in the ENPC	198
9.1	Comparable corpus	206
9.2	Normalized frequencies of coherence-marking expressions occurring more than five times per 100,000 words (*que* = que/qu')	216
9.3	Usage of *then, alors* and *puis* in the interview data	226
10.1	English fiction corpus	240
10.2	Translation corpus	240
10.3	Distribution of *said* in the English fiction corpus	242
10.4	Distribution of the lexicogrammatical patterns modifying reporting *said*	243
10.5	Frequency distribution of *with-* and *without-*PP	247
10.6	Translation solutions of *with-PP* in verb congruent translations (Czech)	251
10.7	Translation solutions of *without-PP* in verb congruent translations (Czech)	251

10.8	Translation solutions of *with-PP* in verb congruent translations (Finnish)	252
10.9	Translation solutions of *without-PP* in verb congruent translations (Finnish)	253
10.10	Translation solutions of *with-PP* in verb-divergent translations (Czech)	255
11.1	Word counts for the LEGS sub-corpora	263

Contributors

Karin Aijmer is Professor Emerita at the University of Gothenburg, Sweden. Her research is mainly in pragmatics and discourse with conversational English and modality as special foci of interest. She was among the pioneers in establishing corpus-based contrastive linguistics in the 1990s, co-directing the compilation of the English-Swedish Parallel Corpus together with Bengt Altenberg. Some of her recent contributions are within the field of corpus pragmatics, including the recent subfield of corpus-based contrastive pragmatics.

Anna Cermakova is Senior Research Associate at the Department of Linguistics and English Language and ESRC Centre for Approaches to Social Science at Lancaster University, UK. She is an active researcher in the field of corpus linguistics and education with a longstanding research interest in corpus-based contrastive linguistics. She has recently edited two volumes in the area: *Time in Languages, Languages in Time* (2021) and the special issue of the BeLLS journal (*Bergen Language and Linguistics Studies*) 'Analysing Complex Contrastive Data' (2021).

Thomas Egan is Professor Emeritus at Inland Norway University of Applied Sciences. His research interests encompass topics within the areas of corpus linguistics, contrastive linguistics, cognitive linguistics and historical linguistics. He has published some forty academic articles, as well as a monograph on complementation, entitled *Non-Finite Complementation: A Usage-Based Study of Infinitive and -ing Clauses in English* (2008). He wrote the chapter on coordination and subordination in the *Oxford Handbook of English Grammar* (2020) and is a member of the editorial board of the journal *Languages in Contrast*.

Lenka Fárová teaches Finnish language, linguistics and translation at the Faculty of Arts at Charles University, Czechia. She has published several articles on corpus linguistics and corpus stylistics, especially contrasting Czech, Finnish and English, as well as some on translation and teaching Finnish as a foreign language. At present, she is co-ordinating the Finnish sub-corpora of the synchronic parallel corpus InterCorp and is a member of the research project Fiction as a Promoter of the Finnish Language Learning among Adults with

Im/migrant Background run by the University of Turku, Finland. She has also translated fiction from Finnish.

Camino Gutiérrez-Lanza is Associate Professor at the Department of Modern Languages at the University of León in Spain. Her areas of interest include descriptive translation studies, (re)translation and censorship, and audiovisual translation. She has contributed to *Target, Meta, Across Languages and Cultures* and *Lingue e Linguaggi*, among other journals, and in a number of scholarly volumes.

Hilde Hasselgård is Professor of English Language at the University of Oslo, Norway. She holds a PhD from the same institution. She has done corpus-related work on issues of English grammar and discourse, learner corpus research and corpus-based contrastive analysis. Her research foci are grammar, phraseology and discourse analysis, as evidenced by numerous publications. She has co-authored several textbooks on English grammar and usage for Norwegian students of English at secondary and tertiary levels. She has also co-edited a good number of books and special issues on contrastive linguistics in the past and has acted as general editor of *Languages in Contrast*.

Stine Hulleberg Johansen has a PhD in English linguistics from the Department of Literature, Area Studies and European Languages at the University of Oslo, Norway. Her areas of interest are corpus linguistics, pragmatics and learner language. She is currently employed as a post-doctoral researcher in the MULTIWRITE project funded by the Norwegian Research Council at the University of Oslo.

Magnus Levin is Associate Professor of English Linguistics at Linnaeus University, Sweden. He has done research on change and variation in English, and more recently has focused on English in contrast with German and Swedish. He is the co-compiler of the Linnaeus University English-German-Swedish corpus (LEGS) with Jenny Ström Herold.

Diana Lewis is Associate Professor of English Linguistics (retired) at the University of Aix Marseille and LPL Research Centre, France. Her main research interests are in semantic and morphosyntactic change from Early Modern to Present-Day English, discourse coherence, discourse prominence relations and English-Romance contrastive linguistics, and she has published studies in these areas within a functionalist and corpus-based framework. Recent publications include the co-edition with Karin Aijmer of *Contrastive Analysis of Discourse-Pragmatic Aspects of Linguistic Genres* (2017).

Xinlu Liu is Professor of Arabic Language and Culture, and Dean of the School of Arabic Studies, Beijing Foreign Studies University, China. His research interests are Arabic language and culture and Arab area studies.

Markéta Malá is Associate Professor of English language and linguistics at the Faculty of Education, Charles University, Prague. The main focus of her work is on contrastive corpus-assisted approaches to phraseology, academic English and the language of children's literature.

Signe Oksefjell Ebeling is Professor of English Language at the University of Oslo, Norway. Her research interests include corpus-based contrastive analysis with a focus on lexicogrammar. Her previous publications include *Patterns in Contrast* (co-authored with Jarle Ebeling) and several cross-linguistic case studies, as well as articles on contrastive methods. She has been involved in the compilation of several corpora for contrastive research.

Rosa Rabadán is Professor at the Department of Modern Languages at the University of León in Spain. Her areas of interest include corpus-based contrastive grammar English-Spanish, translation and writing applications. Her publications have appeared in *Languages in Contrast*, *Meta*, *Babel*, *Linguistica Pragensia* and *BeLLS*, among other journals, and in a number of scholarly volumes.

Kristin Rygg is Associate Professor at the Norwegian School of Economics, in the Department of Professional and Intercultural Communication. Her research areas include socio-pragmatics with a special focus on politeness theory and intercultural business communication with a special interest in the East Asian and Scandinavian regions.

Denisa Šebestová is Lecturer in the Department of English Language and ELT Methodology at Charles University, Czechia. She focuses on contrastive corpus linguistics. Her most recent research project was her PhD dissertation, adopting a corpus-driven approach to identifying phraseological sequences, comparing these between different registers as well as cross-linguistically between English and Czech.

Jenny Ström Herold is Senior Lecturer in German linguistics at Linnaeus University, Sweden. She has worked in contrastive linguistics since her PhD, focusing mostly on syntax. She is the co-compiler of the Linnaeus University English-German-Swedish corpus (LEGS) with Magnus Levin.

Yuanyuan Wei is Lecturer at the School of African Studies, and she is a leading scholar of Swahili language in China. She obtained her PhD at Beijing Foreign Studies University. Her research interests are Swahili language, comparative literature and cross-cultural communication.

Jiajin Xu is Professor of Linguistics at the National Research Centre for Foreign Language Education, Beijing Foreign Studies University, China, as well as secretary general of the Chinese Society of Corpus Linguistics. He obtained his PhD, specialized in corpus-based discourse studies, from Beijing Foreign Studies University. From 2008 to 2009, he was post-doctoral researcher in the Department of Linguistics and English Language at Lancaster University. He has published English papers in international journals including *Across Languages and Cultures*, *Corpora*, *Corpus Linguistics and Linguistic Theory*, *ICAME Journal*, *International Journal of Corpus Linguistics* and *Language Sciences*. He has developed over twenty corpora over the last ten years and maintained the BFSU CQPweb Multilingual Corpus Portal, which hosts over 150 corpora.

Ruchen Yu is an MA student at the National Research Centre for Foreign Language Education, Beijing Foreign Studies University, China. He is a native Chinese speaker and near-native in Italian and English. His research interests are corpus-based sociolinguistics and contrastive linguistics.

Suhua Zhang is Senior Lecturer at the School of Asian Studies and Head of the Malay Department of Beijing Foreign Studies University, China. Her research interest is in Malay language and culture.

Guying Zhou is a PhD candidate at the National Research Centre for Foreign Language Education at Beijing Foreign Studies University, China. She is a native Chinese speaker and near-native in German and English. Her research interests are corpus pragmatics, discourse studies, German linguistics and contrastive linguistics.

Introduction

Hilde Hasselgård, Anna Cermakova, Markéta Malá
and Denisa Šebestová

Editors' introduction

Marking thirty years of contrastive corpus linguistics, this volume takes stock of the developments in the field so far and, at the same time, aims to push the discipline forward. The first plans for a new and innovative sentence-aligned bidirectional translation corpus were presented at the ICAME conference in 1993 in Zürich, namely the English-Norwegian Parallel Corpus (ENPC) (Johansson and Hofland 1994). No such corpus was yet in existence, but advances had been made in corpus technology to make an aligned and searchable parallel corpus conceivable (see Johansson and Hofland 1994; Ebeling and Ebeling 2013 and Ebeling 2016). In the audience were, among others, Karin Aijmer and Bengt Altenberg, who were immediately excited by the idea and soon after initiated the project 'Text-based contrastive studies in English' at Lund University (Aijmer, Altenberg and Johansson 1996b). The English-Swedish Parallel Corpus (ESPC) and the ENPC were developed in close cooperation from 1994, sharing many of the English original texts (Altenberg and Aijmer 2000: 18). Both corpora were completed a few years later (the ENPC in 1997 and the ESPC about 1999; Johansson 2007; Altenberg and Aijmer 2000), and a new branch of corpus linguistics was born (Ebeling 2016).

Since then, the field of contrastive corpus linguistics has been firmly established, and much has been achieved. As observed by Aijmer and Altenberg:

> The use of corpora for contrastive analysis has led to new insights into the languages compared. These insights, whether corpus-driven or corpus-informed, have resulted in more realistic, detailed and empirically sound comparisons of languages, both in terms of their structure and use. (Aijmer and Altenberg 2013b: 3)

In addition, the field has been expanding in terms of available multilingual corpora, languages compared and methods for investigating them (Aijmer and Altenberg 2013b: 3), and the growth is still ongoing (Hasselgård 2020).

Most of the chapters in this volume were first presented at the workshop 'Crossing Language and Discipline Boundaries through Corpora' held at the ICAME 42 conference in Dortmund in 2021, convened by the editors of this volume. This was the tenth ICAME workshop of its kind, thus forming another milestone in the history of contrastive corpus linguistics. The first contrastive ICAME workshop was convened by Karin Aijmer and Bengt Altenberg in Oslo in 2011.[1] The title of that workshop was simply 'Corpus-based contrastive analysis', and it served as a consolidation of the field, while at the same time exploring new avenues such as corpus-driven approaches and closer attention to genre than had been common practice (see Aijmer and Altenberg 2013a). The following year, Karin and Bengt organized another contrastive workshop at ICAME 43 in Leuven (Altenberg and Aijmer 2013). While the first workshop was organized in order to honour Stig Johansson's work, the second was the start of a tradition. The ICAME contrastive workshops have indeed become an important forum for innovations in the field. This is also where the editors of this volume have got to know each other and where, in many ways, the history of the field has been (and is) shaped. The workshops are strongly linked to the Scandinavian research tradition connected with the ENPC and ESPC. The Scandinavian vision has influenced the developments in the field elsewhere and other corpus centres followed suit, for example, in Prague, the work on large multilingual corpus *InterCorp* began in 2008 (Čermák and Rosen 2012).

It is, therefore, with deep gratitude that we dedicate the present volume to Karin Aijmer and Bengt Altenberg in recognition of their pivotal work in the area of contrastive corpus linguistics. Following the lead of Stig Johansson, they have decisively shaped the discipline from its very beginnings, pioneering research practice in multilingual corpus compilation and research and thus laying the foundation for this rich field of scholarly activity (see, e.g., Aijmer, Altenberg and Johansson 1996a). Karin, Bengt and Stig have not only had a profound impact on the field but also influenced generations of linguists as the editors of this volume can testify. We come from different perspectives and places, but we have all learnt from Karin and Bengt. Markéta met Karin and Bengt for the first time at the ICAME conference and workshop in Leuven in 2012. Anna met Karin for the first time at ICAME in Santiago de Compostela in 2013, fondly remembering the long afternoon walk where Karin patiently answered all her questions. Denisa, though joining the ICAME community a bit later, also felt the welcoming atmosphere with regard to PhD students. Hilde's story, of course, goes much further back, having worked closely with Stig Johansson at the University of Oslo and enjoyed Bengt and Karin's company in academic as well as social settings since the 1990s. We have all benefited from their generosity in sharing their insights and including young scholars in the community.

We can only outline a few of the ways in which Karin Aijmer and Bengt Altenberg have influenced contrastive corpus linguistics, starting with their much-quoted, rather programmatic, summary of the potential of multilingual corpora:

- They give new insights into the languages compared – insights that are likely to be unnoticed in studies of monolingual corpora;
- They can be used for a range of comparative purposes and increase our knowledge of language-specific, typological and cultural differences, as well as of universal features;
- They illuminate differences between source texts and translations, and between native and non-native texts. (Aijmer and Altenberg 1996: 12)

An important contribution to contrastive corpus-linguistic methodology was Altenberg's idea and operationalization of *mutual correspondence* (MC), that is, a formula for calculating – on the basis of data from a bidirectional translation corpus – 'the frequency with which different (grammatical, semantic, and lexical) expressions are translated into each other' (Altenberg 1999: 254). For example, English *instead* is translated into Swedish *i stället* 80 per cent of the time, while *i stället* becomes *instead* 78 per cent of the time, giving an MC of 79 per cent (Altenberg 1999: 256). Other comparisons may be less symmetrical, showing good correspondence in only one of the translation directions. Altenberg calls this 'translation bias' (Altenberg 1999: 258). These two measures can certainly uncover subtle and sometimes unexpected differences between the linguistic items compared, for example when the cognates *therefore* and *derför* differ in frequency and areas of use in spite of similar meanings, revealing that *derför* is wider in its scope and stylistically more neutral (Altenberg 2007).

Among Karin Aijmer's many merits in contrastive corpus linguistics over the years, the field of contrastive corpus pragmatics stands out (e.g. Aijmer 2020). It is closely linked to her interest in epistemic modality and pragmatic markers as well as in conversational routines (Aijmer 1996). However, the focus of pragmatic studies 'on the use of lexical elements or grammatical structures in their linguistic, social and cultural context' (Aijmer 2020: 29) requires detailed qualitative attention to individual instances to understand what these 'linguistic elements are doing in the communicative situation' (Aijmer 2020: 29). Aijmer's suggested technique for investigating the multifunctionality of pragmatic markers is to examine all their translations into another language. For example, in a study of *well* compared with its correspondences in Swedish and French, Aijmer observes that the translation perspective, even though pragmatic markers are notoriously difficult to translate, reveals the meaning potential of *well*: 'A meaning which is selected by the translator is potentially a part of its meaning potential' (Aijmer 2015: 225).

The influence of Karin Aijmer and Bengt Altenberg's work on the present volume is visible in its attention to the continuum from lexicogrammar to discourse and furthermore in the number of papers that make direct reference to them. For example, Chapter 2 (Ebeling) makes reference to work by Altenberg on diverging polysemies and Aijmer's on the perception verb SEE. Chapter 3 (Hasselgård) quotes Altenberg's work on mutual correspondence as well as on the English genitive construction. Chapters 8 (Johansson and Rygg) and 9 (Lewis) draw on Aijmer's work on discourse markers and contrastive pragmatics; Lewis furthermore refers to Altenberg's work on connectors. It is fitting that the opening chapter of this volume is by Karin Aijmer herself. She reflects on the current breadth and future prospects of research in the area while pointing to emergent trends, especially within contrastive corpus pragmatics, with an insight that only she can offer. Furthermore, she discusses new types of corpora for contrastive studies, including multimodal and genre-based ones, which represent a step forward in contrastive corpus linguistics.

The bulk of the volume is divided into two parts: Lexicogrammar in Contrast (I) and Discourse in Contrast (II). Both parts represent a diversity of methods and approaches to language comparison, using both comparable and translation corpora, and explore a broad range of language registers from newspaper reporting and spoken political discourse to film scripts, fiction and football match reports. While English is the pivot language for all the studies, the volume offers contrastive bilingual and multilingual perspectives on a number of languages, including Czech, Finnish, French, German, Norwegian, Spanish, Swedish, Chinese, Swahili, Arabic and Malay. The number and typological variety of languages that are offered in contrastive perspective to English and the variety of genres studied are an important feature of the volume and entirely in line with Johansson's advice for future contrastive corpus studies that 'we need to widen the range of languages, including the variety of texts' and 'we need multi-register corpora' (2012: 64). The gain of juxtaposing cross-linguistic and register variation contributes to deepening of our insight into language variation and use.

The chapters in Part I, Lexicogrammar in Contrast, focus on both frequent and less frequent cross-linguistic patterns that contribute to the shape of the discourse in that particular language. In Chapter 2, Signe Oksefjell Ebeling studies a pair of very frequent perception verbs in Norwegian and English, the cognates *se* and *see*. Through explorations of comparable corpora in three registers (fictional narrative, fictional dialogue and football match reports), she finds that the cognates have both overlapping and diverging polysemies. Moreover, the registers differ as regards both the frequency of the verbs and their preferred syntactic patterns. The football match reports differ more between the languages than the fictional registers do, and the difference between the fictional and nonfictional registers is greater in English. Ebeling therefore suggests that the genre of football match reports is more established as a separate register in English.

Using data from the English-Norwegian Parallel Corpus, Hilde Hasselgård (Chapter 3) discusses how English and Norwegian have similar-looking devices for the genitive relation (morphological and periphrastic) but, apparently, rather different systems for selecting one or the other. Her focus is on the periphrastic genitive, and she finds that the *of*-genitive is much more frequent and more general in meaning than the Norwegian *til*-genitive. In English, the periphrastic genitive is more common in nonfiction than in fiction, but in Norwegian it is the other way around. An important finding is that the animacy of the possessor favours the *til*-genitive but disfavours the *of*-genitive. Translations are therefore often noncongruent in both directions of translation, with the *s*-genitive occurring as a frequent correspondence in both languages, while Norwegian uses a greater variety of prepositions than English to express possession.

A third comparison of English-Norwegian contrasts is presented by Thomas Egan in Chapter 4, again drawing on the English-Norwegian Parallel Corpus. He studies a set of ditransitive verbs from both languages and, like Ebeling, works with pairs of cognates: *send/sende, bring/bringe, lend/låne* and *sell/selge*, all of which express transfer and can occur in two double object constructions, the ditransitive and prepositional dative. Egan examines to what extent these verbs are translated between English and Norwegian using a congruent construction. His results show that the degree of translation congruence varies considerably: while the *sell* verbs are almost always translated congruently, for the other verbs the translations vary. He suggests this may be due to formality differences, or because their semantic fields do not fully correspond across the two languages, also considering potential translation effects. The findings of this study will therefore be of interest to linguists as well as translation scholars and translators.

Moving to a comparison of English and Czech, Markéta Malá and Denisa Šebestová study prepositional patterns in newspaper discourse in Chapter 5. Their study draws on n-grams comprising the prepositions *in* and its Czech counterpart *v* to explore how the communicative purposes of the register interact with the phraseology of typologically distinct languages. Apart from meanings associated with the informational function of newspapers, the prepositional patterns were found to serve text-structuring functions and carry evaluative semantic prosodies. The study also shows the limitations of using the n-gram-based method to compare the phraseology of an analytic and highly inflectional language.

The most multilingual and linguistically diverse study in this collection is found in Chapter 6, where Jiajin Xu, Guying Zhou, Xinlu Liu, Yuanyuan Wei, Ruchen Yu and Suhua Zhang examine salient recurrent units of meaning in journalistic texts in English, Chinese, Swahili, Arabic and Malay. In comparing five typologically different languages, this chapter raises a number of interesting typological questions. The study is data-driven, based on a comparison of frequent discontinuous phrase frames with one variable word slot (p-frames) operationalized as units of meaning. Jiajin Xu and colleagues compare the p-frames across the languages for the predictability, variability and discourse functions. They present cross-linguistic clines in variability and predictability, showing that Arabic and Swahili statistically differ from the other languages the most. Their analysis also shows, for example, statistically significant differences in the use of stance-marking expressions, with English being the language most relying on stance-marking.

The first part of the volume is concluded by a chapter drawing on a rather novel corpus type, namely one of English original film scripts and their Spanish translations linguistically customized to favour isochrony in dubbing. Camino Gutiérrez-Lanza and Rosa Rabadán look at glocalization processes in the dubbing industry by studying how English subject pronouns and the modals *can/could* are rendered in Spanish dubbing. The authors suggest that an 'audiovisual mode dialect' has formed in Spanish, in which mistransferred uses of *poder*, stemming from *can, could* are regularly used with meanings and patterns that differ from non-translated audiovisual Spanish. Subject pronouns turn out to be overused in audiovisual translation as an adjusting tool, and they occur in contexts where they are not needed in a pro-drop language such as Spanish, causing unwanted emphasis. The authors suggest that applying corpus-based results to customizing routines could mean more realistic orality in audiovisual Spanish.

Part II, Discourse in Contrast, contains four chapters which offer a variety of topics: politeness and pragmatics (English and Norwegian), rhetorical style (English and French), translation of reporting verbs in fiction (English, Czech and Finnish) and punctuation stylistics (English, Swedish and German).

In Chapter 8, Johansen and Rygg take inspiration from Karin Aijmer's study of *please* and its correspondences in Swedish (Aijmer 2009) in their comparison of *please* and its Norwegian correspondences. They analyse the social functions as well as the linguistic patterns of the politeness markers, distinguishing between 'standard' and 'non-standard' situations. As expected, the functions and patterns of *please* are more diverse than any of its twelve Norwegian translation correspondences (in the English-Norwegian Parallel Corpus). *Please* is very often left untranslated in Norwegian, but the most common overt correspondence is *vær så snill* ('be so kind'), which occurs in both standard and non-standard situations. However, it is often found to strengthen the illocutionary force of a request rather than functioning as a softening politeness marker.

Diana Lewis (Chapter 9) studies coherence in English and French spoken political discourse based on a small comparable corpus of interviews. She starts with a broad overview of discourse coherence and connective usage in both languages. She then maps and categorizes connective devices in her data and zooms in, based on frequency, on the French connective markers *alors* and *puis* and English *then*, which all originate as temporal expressions. Lewis finds a greater number of connective types in French, which she attributes to 'an aesthetic preference for rhetorical variation' but also a greater density of the connective usage. In contrast, English heavily relies on only several types of connectives.

Chapter 10 takes a trilingual perspective on reporting verbs in typologically different languages: English, Czech and Finnish. Using a small translation corpus of fictional prose, Anna Cermakova and Lenka Fárová explore the frequently occurring lexicogrammatical patterns of the reporting verb *said* in English fiction. In a case study of *said with/without* (e.g. *said with a shrug*), they identify the ways in which these patterns are translated into Czech and Finnish and whether they are perceived as patterns by the translators. They find that Czech translators avoid the repetitive nature of the English *said* and tend to use a variety of reporting and other verbs to translate *said*, while Finnish translators largely stick to a similarly style-neutral verb (*sanoi*). For the *with/without* pattern, they identify a main translation correspondence in Czech while the categorization of the Finnish translations is less straightforward due to typological differences.

Finally, in Chapter 11, Jenny Ström Herold and Magnus Levin present an investigation of punctuation in translation between English, German and Swedish using the LEGS corpus. Building on a previous study of brackets (Levin and Ström Herold 2021), the chapter looks at the function, placement and translation of dash-introduced text. In original texts, dashes are most frequent in German and least frequent in English. Dash-introduced text serves a variety of discourse functions that can be characterized as content-oriented and interpersonal; the former is more common in all three languages. Translators copy the punctuation of the original in 50–90 per cent of the cases. The highest number of changes are found in translations into English, and the lowest in Swedish ones. The most common non-dash correspondences are commas and zero punctuation in all the translation pairs.

The great variety of topics, languages and analysed text types presented in this volume testify to the vitality of the field of contrastive corpus linguistics as well as to its continuing development and growth. The demonstrated breadth of corpus types, approaches, search methods and objects of study is possibly wider than the founders of the field, Stig Johansson, Karin Aijmer and Bengt Altenberg, dared to imagine in the early 1990s when they started to combine contrastive analysis with the methods and approaches of corpus linguistics. We are lucky to have benefited from their inspirational work and hope that this collection – in the spirit of Karin and Bengt – will stimulate further investigation into the similarities and differences between languages and their ways of piecing together patterns of lexicogrammar and discourse. Thank you, Karin and Bengt.

Note

1 With a single exception, contrastive corpus linguistics workshops have been held at ICAME conferences every year since then.

References

Aijmer, K. (1996), *Conversational Routines in English: Convention and Creativity*, London: Longman.

Aijmer, K. (2009), 'Please: A Politeness Formula Viewed in a Translation Perspective', *Brno Studies in English*, 35 (2): 63–77.

Aijmer, K. (2015), 'Well in an English–Swedish and English–French Contrastive Perspective', in K. Beeching and H. Woodfield (eds), *Researching Sociopragmatic Variability. Perspectives from Variational, Interlanguage and Contrastive Pragmatics*, 201–29, Basingstoke: Palgrave Macmillan.

Aijmer, K. (2020), 'Contrastive Pragmatics and Corpora', *Contrastive Pragmatics*, 1 (1): 28–57. https://doi.org/10.1163/26660393-12340004

Aijmer, K. and B. Altenberg (1996), 'Introduction', in K. Aijmer, B. Altenberg and M. Johansson (eds), *Languages in Contrast. Papers from a Symposium on Text-based Cross-linguistic Studies*, 11–16, Lund: Lund University Press.

Aijmer, K. and B. Altenberg, eds (2013a), *Advances in Corpus-based Contrastive Linguistics. Studies in Honour of Stig Johansson*, Amsterdam: John Benjamins.

Aijmer, K. and B. Altenberg (2013b), 'Introduction', in K. Aijmer and B. Altenberg (eds), *Advances in Corpus-based Contrastive Linguistics. Studies in Honour of Stig Johansson*, 1–6, Amsterdam and Philadelphia: John Benjamins.

Aijmer, K., B. Altenberg and M. Johansson, eds (1996a), *Languages in Contrast. Papers from a Symposium on Text-based Cross-linguistic Studies*, Lund: Lund University Press.

Aijmer, K., B. Altenberg and M. Johansson (1996b), 'Text-based Contrastive Studies in English', in K. Aijmer, B. Altenberg and M. Johansson (eds), *Languages in Contrast. Papers from a Symposium on Text-based Cross-linguistic Studies*, 73–86, Lund: Lund University Press.

Altenberg, B. (1999), 'Adverbial Connectors in English and Swedish: Semantic and Lexical Correspondences', in H. Hasselgård and S. Oksefjell (eds), *Out of Corpora. Studies in Honour of Stig Johansson*, 249–68, Amsterdam and New York: Rodopi.

Altenberg, B. (2007), 'The Correspondence of Resultive Connectors in English and Swedish', *Nordic Journal of English Studies*, 6 (1): 1–26.

Altenberg, B. and K. Aijmer (2000), 'The English-Swedish Parallel Corpus: A Resource for Contrastive Work', in C. Mair and M. Hundt (eds), *Corpus Linguistics and Linguistic Theory*, 15–34, Amsterdam and New York: Rodopi.

Altenberg, B. and K. Aijmer, eds (2013), *Text-based Contrastive Linguistics*. Special issue of *Languages in Contrast*, 13 (2), Amsterdam and Philadelphia: John Benjamins.

Čermák, F. and A. Rosen (2012), 'The Case of InterCorp, a Multilingual Parallel Corpus', *International Journal of Corpus Linguistics*, 17 (3): 411–27.

Ebeling, J. (2016), 'Contrastive Linguistics in a New Key', *Nordic Journal of English Studies*, 15 (3): 7–14.

Ebeling, S. O. and J. Ebeling (2013), 'From Babylon to Bergen: On the Usefulness of Aligned Texts', *Bergen Language and Linguistics Studies*, 3 (1): 23–42. https://doi.org/10.15845/bells.v3i1.359

Hasselgård, H. (2020), 'Corpus-based Contrastive Studies. Beginnings, Developments and Directions', *Languages in Contrast*, 20 (2): 184–208.

Johansson, S. (2007), *Seeing through Multilingual Corpora. On the Use of Corpora in Contrastive Studies*, Amsterdam and Philadelphia: John Benjamins.

Johansson, S. (2012), 'Cross-linguistic Perspectives', in M. Kytö (ed.), *English Corpus Linguistics: Crossing Paths*, 45–68, Amsterdam and New York: Rodopi.

Johansson, S. and K. Hofland (1994), 'Towards an English-Norwegian Parallel Corpus', in U. Fries, G. Tottie and P. Schneider (eds), *Creating and Using English Language Corpora*, 25–37, Amsterdam and New York: Rodopi.

Levin, M. and J. Ström Herold (2021), 'On Brackets in Translation (or How to Elaborate in Brackets)', in A. Čermáková, S. Oksefjell Ebeling, M. Levin and J. Ström Herold (eds), *Crossing the Borders: Analysing Complex Contrastive Data, Bergen Language and Linguistics Studies*, 11 (1): 121–44.

1

The Present Status and Recent Trends in Corpus-Based Contrastive Linguistics

Karin Aijmer

1.1 Introduction

'New' contrastive linguistics uses corpora to describe the similarities and differences between languages from a theoretical and applied perspective in contrast to the earlier applied approach to contrastive linguistics where the differences between the languages are used to predict learners' difficulties (see e.g. Taboada, Doval Suárez and González Álvarez 2013: 1). Another new development is that contrastive analysis is now studying language from a functional and discourse perspective. As a young discipline, corpus-based contrastive linguistics is developing at a fast rate, broadening its scope to new linguistic areas. Egan and Dirdal (2017) mention the growth of lexical phenomena that are now analysed based on contrastive corpora. Thus, for example, prepositions and connectors are being investigated in more detail, and the contrastive study has been extended to new types of verbs (Egan and Dirdal 2017: 8). Moreover, lexical studies using corpora also incorporate phraseology (see e.g. Ebeling and Ebeling 2013).

Another recent trend, and the main focus of this chapter, is the rapprochement between contrastive corpus linguistics and pragmatics. Contrastive corpus pragmatics is a field of research 'characterised by the joint approaches of pragmatics, corpus linguistics and contrastive analysis for describing the similarities and differences between languages' (Aijmer 2020: 28). The focus is on the description of pragmatic phenomena such as pragmatic markers (e.g. Aijmer and Simon-Vandenbergen 2006), coherence relations and speech acts across languages using contrastive corpora and corpus-linguistic techniques (see Aijmer and Rühlemann 2017 for a fuller illustration of pragmatic features that can be analysed using corpora). The recent developments can be traced to the availability of spoken contrastive corpora and corpora incorporating translations into many different languages.

The chapter is organized as follows. The topic of Section 1.2 is the different types of contrastive corpora that are (becoming) available and how they can be used for different theoretical and applied purposes. Section 1.3 is concerned with the insights that can be gained from the translation of pragmatic markers and connectives, focusing on both their translation equivalents in language and their omission in the translation. Section 1.4 discusses the opportunities created by the cross-fertilization between contrastive studies of pragmatic elements and genre analysis. Section 1.5 deals with new ways of using contrastive corpora to study speech acts. Section 1.6 summarizes the preceding discussion.

1.2 Types of corpora for contrastive studies

1.2.1 Parallel and comparable corpora

Contrastive corpus linguistics relies on the use of contrastive corpora and corpus-linguistic methods to study similarities and differences between languages. A distinction can be made between parallel corpora and comparable corpora. The typical parallel corpus contains original texts in one language and their translations into another language. If the corpus is bidirectional, it contains comparable original texts in both languages with their translations into the other language (Hasselgård 2020: 188). Such a corpus is well suited for contrastive studies since the translation relation can provide a *tertium comparationis* for the language comparison. Thus, according to Johansson (2001: 584), 'the advantage of a corpus of original texts and their translations is that the translation is intended to express the same meaning as the original text'. Although considered by many to be the best *tertium comparationis* (e.g. James 1980; Johansson 2007), translation correspondences may not always be considered a satisfactory *tertium comparationis*. For example, the translation of a lexical element into another language may be a mismatch, and there are cases where the lexical element in the original text is omitted in translation. Moreover, the methodology is not associated with a particular theory of semantics or translation, and the results may be applied in different ways (see also Ebeling and Ebeling 2020; Hasselgård 2020: 190).

Both parallel and comparable corpora are used for comparing languages. Comparable corpora consist of texts in two languages that are similar with respect to genre, length, time of composition etc. They contain both spoken and written genres (popular science, book reviews, letters to editors, letters to shareholders, research articles) that have not been translated into another language. These corpora are often small and compiled by a researcher for a special purpose. However, it is worth mentioning that, by default, a parallel bidirectional corpus contains a comparable corpus.

1.2.2 A new generation of parallel corpora

Since many pragmatic phenomena are more frequent in spoken than in written language, interest is now directed to finding authentic spoken language that also has been translated into other languages. The new types of parallel corpora have in common that they offer the opportunity to investigate the translations of pragmatic phenomena such as pragmatic markers across many different languages starting with spoken language in the source language. An example is the European Parliament Proceedings Parallel Corpus (the Europarl Corpus), which consists of the proceedings of the European Parliament in the official languages of the EU member nations (https://opus.nlpl.eu/Europarl-v3.php). The texts in the Europarl Corpus concern political issues and are generally formal, which makes them less ideal for investigating pragmatic features typical of informal spoken language. However, an opportunity to use informal spoken language is offered by corpora containing subtitles of film dialogues in different languages. A large number of subtitle texts in many languages are, for instance, available in the Open Parallel corpus (The OPUS corpus – parallel and free http://logos.npl.eu/). Another multilingual parallel corpus suitable for comparing lexical expressions and grammatical structures across many languages is TED Talks (with English as the source language). TED (Technology, Entertainment, Design) Talks bring together public speeches and academic oral speeches on a variety of topics with subtitles in other languages. The new parallel corpora have above all been used to study underspecification (especially omission) in translation across different languages. See Section 1.3.2.

1.3 The translation of pragmatic markers

1.3.1 The definition of pragmatic markers

Pragmatic markers are elusive elements that have been difficult to define in an unambiguous manner (see e.g. Brinton 2017; Beeching 2016).[1] However, there is some consensus that pragmatic markers are words or phrases separated syntactically and prosodically from the utterance where they belong. Another observation is that pragmatic markers do not contribute to the propositional meaning but function as signals guiding the hearer to the interpretation of the utterance. Importantly, they have both interactional and interpersonal functions and occur most frequently in spoken language.

The contrastive study of pragmatic markers is now a key area in corpus-based contrastive pragmatics. Corpora offer a possibility to study their multifunctionality in actual communication and can contribute to the theoretical discussion of polysemy. Pragmatic markers are being investigated from a contrastive perspective in both parallel and comparable corpora. Starting with the assumption that there is a relationship between translation and function, Aijmer and Simon-Vandenbergen (2003) investigated the translations of *well* for Swedish in the English-Swedish Parallel Corpus, and for Dutch, in the Oslo Multilingual Corpus. *Well* is associated with a 'translation paradigm' rather than a single translation where the translation choices represent the possible readings of the pragmatic marker. Based on the translations of *well* into Swedish and Dutch, Aijmer and Simon-Vandenbergen argued that *well* has a broad spectrum of functions and that the different functions of *well* could be derived from a core meaning (Aijmer and Simon-Vandenbergen 2003). Depending on which language is the target for the translation, new properties of *well* may be highlighted as shown by its translations into multiple languages. Thus, in a more recent study (Aijmer 2015), it was shown that the translations of *well* into French add new meanings or implicatures, confirming the semantic analysis based on the translations into other languages.

The contrastive analysis can reveal both similarities and differences between pragmatic markers in the compared languages. Hasselgård (2006) was interested in comparing the temporal *now* and its Norwegian counterpart *nå*. The theoretical issue was whether they have developed similar functions as discourse markers. Using the English-Norwegian Parallel Corpus, Hasselgård investigated the translations of *nå* and *now* into the other language. Surprisingly, the results from the translations showed that 'the discourse marker functions of *nå/now* were even more different in the two languages than expected, so that *nå* and *now* can hardly ever be each other's translation' (Hasselgård 2006: 110).

The contrastive analysis makes it possible to distinguish between universal tendencies and functions that are specific to a particular language or culture. Arguably, grammaticalization (or pragmaticalization) provides the theoretical framework explaining the similarities and differences between pragmatic markers in different languages (Lauwers, Vanderbauwhede and Verleyen 2010). Specifically, it is possible to draw conclusions about the extent to which pragmatic markers have grammaticalized in the compared languages based on the similarities or differences between the languages. See, for instance, the article by Lansari (2017) comparing *I was going to say* and *j'allais dire* in contemporary English and French. Lansari showed that in both languages, the expressions had pragmatic functions as reformulation markers or hedges corresponding to different degrees of pragmaticalization.

As a result of grammaticalization/pragmaticalization, pragmatic markers can also be expected to have different functions depending on their position. Translations can show whether this is the case across languages. Ruskan and Carretero (2021) investigated the modal adverbs *obviously* and *then* and their correspondences in Lithuanian and Spanish in different positions on the basis of comparable corpora. Their analysis revealed that, in the compared languages, the adverbs were most frequent in the utterance-final position and that they were restricted to certain speech acts and functions in that position. (See also Johansen and Rygg, this volume.)

1.3.2 Parallel corpora and underspecification

The translation of pragmatic markers is associated with methodological and theoretical problems. The problems are reflected in the omission in translation and strategies used by the translators to render the meaning of pragmatic markers that do not have a direct counterpart in translation. However, in a study of omission (i.e. zero correspondences) in the English-Swedish Parallel Corpus, Aijmer and Altenberg (2002: 22) showed that the omission of a word is a frequent translation strategy. For example, the pragmatic marker *well* is easily omitted in the translation from English into other languages since it does not contribute to the propositional meaning of the utterance. Pragmatic markers expressing discourse relations (connectives) in translation are other optional elements that are often left untranslated. As shown by the following example, the relationship can often be inferred from the context, and a connection is therefore not needed: *Mary was ill. (So) she couldn't come to the party.*

In the study by Aijmer and Altenberg (2002), the cases of omission of a connective marker were shown to be governed by the type of discourse relation, the clarity of the context and language-specific conventions restricting its use.

The new generation of contrastive corpus linguists has used innovative methodologies and corpora to study the omission and other types of translation mismatch. The transcripts from the proceedings in the European Union have been used by Rozumko (2021) in an English-Polish parallel corpus to study different types of underspecification in the translations of Polish modal adverbs into English. Likewise, Crible et al. (2019) analysed the translation equivalents, functions and omissions of the pragmatic markers *and*, *but* and *so* in their translations into Czech, French, Hungarian and Lithuanian based on a sample of TED Talks. The findings suggested that the omission of the pragmatic marker was mainly governed by the semantic type of relationship (the type of discourse marker) rather than by the language of the translation. The study is methodologically innovative since the starting point was not a pre-selected list of pragmatic markers, but the markers were identified on the basis of a bottom-up analysis involving reading the original texts. The pragmatic markers that were the object of study were further annotated with respect to their function in the context. Using this technique, it was possible for the authors to describe precisely the influence of the semantic type and function of the pragmatic marker on its omission. The observation that certain discourse relations are more likely to be implicit than others has been confirmed by other studies using discourse annotation. Hoek et al. (2017) proposed that expectedness (based on the complexity of coherence relations) should make coherence relations more likely to be conveyed implicitly and tested this hypothesis by means of a parallel corpus study where they analysed the coherence relations expresssed by *but* and *because* in Dutch, German, French and Spanish in Europarl Corpus.

1.3.3 Studies based on multimodal corpora

Another recent trend is the compilation of multimodal corpora combining speech with video and audio recordings. Such corpora may also be exploited for contrastive research although cross-linguistic studies based on multimodal corpora are still infrequent. Callies and Levin (2018) collected comparable corpora of live TV football commentaries in English, German and Swedish with the purpose of exploring dislocation as a genre-specific feature. Dislocated structures are characterized by the fact that a definite noun phrase occurs in either the left periphery or in the right periphery of the sentence with a co-referential pronoun filling the slot of the noun phrase. Right dislocation is, for instance, illustrated by *they had a rocky few minutes, Germany*. The findings of the study indicated that right dislocation was more frequent than left dislocation in all three languages, thus confirming the authors' hypothesis that dislocation was functionally motivated regarding the relation between the action unfolding on the TV screen and the verbal commentary where the commentator reactivates the referent in the discourse to avoid ambiguity. The authors found no differences in this regard between the English, German and Swedish TV commentaries.

Corpus-based contrastive studies have also been influenced by the increasing multimodality of spoken and written texts on social platforms (Hasselgård 2020: 200). Multimodality is now also addressed in cross-linguistic studies. In a study by Isosävi and Vecsernýes (2022), the material consisted of comparable Finnish, French and Hungarian corpora of YouTube videos containing messages to imagined recipients. The authors were particularly interested in investigating the gestures used by the YouTubers accompanying the initial sequences of the messages where they performed addresses and greetings. The results showed that the YouTubers were influenced by the genre, but the comparison also indicated that different cross-cultural practices play a role.

Above all, pragmatic phenomena have been studied contrastively in audio-visual translation. Dubbed or subtitled texts have the advantage that they contain many features characteristic of natural spoken language. For that reason, Cuenca (2008) used the Catalan and Spanish dubbed versions of the film *Four Weddings and a Funeral* in order to study the multifunctionality of *well*. However, recently more attention has been paid to the hybrid nature of subtitling and dubbing, namely that they have features characteristic of both spoken and written language. Arguably, subtitling can therefore be regarded as a genre with its own norms, which can be compared with other genres across languages. Specifically, subtitling is constrained by temporal and spatial factors necessarily leading to a reduction in the amount of text in the subtitles. According to Diaz Cintaz and Anderman, '[t]he most distinctive feature of subtitling is the need for economy of translation' (Diaz Cintaz and Anderman 2009: 14).

From this perspective, it is interesting to investigate the potential effects of the genre of subtitling on the translations of pragmatic markers compared with authentic conversation. Mattsson (2010) compared the translations of the pragmatic marker *you know* into Swedish in a self-collected collection of US films with their subtitles with the objective of investigating what types of meaning of the marker were most frequently omitted. The findings showed that *you know* was treated differently depending on its meaning and that it was most frequently omitted in the interpersonal function where it could also be translated as having a textual function. See also de Linde (1995), who claims that reductions in subtitling are not random but systematic.

1.4 Genre-based contrastive analysis

Language needs to be interpreted in its social and cultural context. Analysing genre means studying lexical and pragmatic phenomena 'in the context of institutionalized textual artefacts in the context of specific institutional and disciplinary practices, procedures and cultures' (Bhatia 2002: 6; quoted from Aijmer and Lewis 2017a: 2). Genre-based analysis can fruitfully be combined with a cross-linguistic analysis using corpora (see e.g. Aijmer and Lewis 2017b). A challenge for such an approach is to find equivalent genres in two (or several) languages since only a restricted number of genres have been translated. Fortunately, at least a few parallel corpora include several genres (or text types). Among the linguistic expressions that have been investigated contrastively across genres are pragmatic markers. In an interesting study, Buysse (2017) extracted the translations of *so* into Dutch in five different text types in the Dutch Parallel Corpus (Buysse 2017: 3). The text type analysis revealed that *so* and *dus* tended to occur with different frequencies in the different types of text in both languages. In a similar study, Martinková and Janebová (2017) studied the Czech modal particle *prý* in three different genres of the Czech InterCorp Corpus: fiction, journalistic texts and subtitling.

In many cases, comparable corpora need to be used instead of parallel corpora for studying pragmatic phenomena across genres. A genre that may be expected to have counterparts in other languages is book reviews. The reason for comparing book reviews across languages may be to find out how evaluation or criticism is expressed across cultures. Diani (2015) compared English and Italian academic book reviews with the aim of investigating how politeness (mitigated criticism) is realized in different cross-cultural contexts. Arguably, book reviews in several languages belong to the same genre if they are structured in a similar way, have the same purpose (expressing criticism) and are addressed to the same type of audience.

In Diani's study, corpora were important for identifying the patterns of usage in their different contexts across languages. The analysis focused on how mitigated criticism was expressed in the two language groups rather than on direct criticism. In the first stage of the investigation, word lists were created for each national corpus from which the types of lexically based mitigated criticism could be derived manually. In the second stage, concordances were compiled, and the cases of mitigated criticism were distinguished from those expressing direct criticism. Finally, corpus tools were used to automatically retrieve the lexical expressions conveying mitigated criticism. The analysis revealed that these expressions had different frequencies and that they were not used in the same way in the two groups of book reviews pointing to culture-specific preferences in English and Italian (Diani 2015).

As shown by recent contrastive corpus-based research, corpora and corpus-linguistic tools can also be helpful for researchers to describe the generic structure of a particular genre. Chik and Taboada (2020) wanted to compare the generic structure and rhetorical relations in online book reviews in English, Japanese and Chinese. The methodology they proposed involved an analysis of both the generic structure of the online review and the rhetorical relations (such as Elaboration, Concession or Contrast) that were expressed lexicogrammatically. The analysis showed that, on the global level, the review was constituted by predictable stages (such as Evaluation and Recommendation) and that the stages and their ordering were the same across the languages they investigated. The differences between the languages were mainly found at the local level where they could be explained as cross-linguistic preferences. Most notably the Japanese book reviews did not contain a special Recommendation component.

A similar example illustrating how it is important to identify the move structure characteristic of the genre is given by Rojas-Lizana (2015). Rojas-Lizana analysed politeness strategies containing the intention of thanking an explicit addressee in a corpus consisting of 'letters to the editor in the local newspaper' in Australian English and Chilean Spanish. The comparison involved both the generic structure of the letters and the politeness strategies performed. The results of her study indicated that there were differences between the groups in terms of both the number of moves and the strategies used to express thanks.

Johansen (2021) proposed an innovative approach to retrieve examples of hedging in English and Norwegian corpora of informal conversation without searching for these directly. She hypothesized that hedging structures, which are typically aimed at avoiding face threats, would be found in the vicinity of the adversative *but* or *men* (but) in the compared texts. *But* and *men* were then used as 'probes' to extract the comparable speech situations in which hedging could be expected.[2] In a second step, similar functional categories were used to classify the hedges in English and Norwegian, and a fine-grained comparison was made of hedges in the two languages.

Summing up, contrastive corpus-based analysis enables a deeper analysis of features such as evaluation or mitigation characteristics of the review genre (and other related genres including informal conversation). In the future, we can also expect that more attention will be given to the macro structure of genres and that pragmatic features will be analysed with respect to what they are doing at different stages of the discourse. It must be kept in mind that genre-based contrastive corpus analysis meets many challenges. The extent to which corpora can be helpful for the analysis is still limited. Moreover, the corpora used for corpus-based contrastive research of genres are often fairly small and only exist for certain genres. Finally, the identification of the patterns fulfilling a particular function such as evaluation or hedging is not easy and may be time-consuming since the patterns must be identified manually. However, corpus-linguistic techniques may be useful once the patterns have been identified, and the functional analysis may be facilitated by annotation.

1.5 The contrastive corpus-based study of speech acts

Multilingual corpora are appropriate for the purpose of comparing conventionalized forms of speech acts across languages. To illustrate, an apology often has a fairly fixed form such as *(I'm) sorry*, whose correspondences can be investigated across languages using contrastive corpora. The conventionalized forms of speech acts (conversational routines) can be assumed to provide a rich field of contrastive research. In an early study, Coulmas (1981) showed that speech acts such as apologizing and thanking tended to be realized with routine formulae and that they were used differently by English and Japanese speakers. In contrastive pragmatic research, Kadár and House's (2020) recent analysis of speech acts as routinized expressions deserves attention. Specifically, the authors proposed a theoretical framework for describing the relationship between conventionalized expressions, speech acts and standard situations (situations characterized by obligations and rights), and used this framework to show comparatively how *please* and its Chinese counterpart *qing* are deployed in different standard situations.

However, we also need to go beyond the conventionalized types of speech acts. It is well known that speech acts are often realized in indirect and non-conventional ways, which makes it difficult to search for them using the corpus tools made available by contrastive corpora. Researchers interested in comparing speech-act realizations across languages have therefore generally chosen discourse completion tests (DCTs) rather than natural spoken language in corpora as a methodology. In a discourse completion test, a speech-act situation is described (in writing), leaving a gap for the informant to produce a speech act (Blum-Kulka, House and Kasper 1989). A drawback is, however, that the language produced may differ from natural spontaneous language.

Recently, initiatives have been taken to use a function-to-form analysis to investigate speech acts. Arguably, such an approach must consider the contexts in which a certain speech-act utterance may occur. Fetzer (2011) has suggested that in order to investigate the forms of challenges in political interviews in English and German, it is necessary to take into account the contextual configuration of a challenge.

On the assumption that there would not be a direct relationship between the function and form of a speech act, Fetzer proposed that the speech act of challenging had to be defined functionally in such a way that the definition could serve as the *tertium comparationis* for the contrastive analysis. Three contextual conditions needed to be fulfilled for a speech act to count as a challenge (rejection, denial): (i) the conversational contribution would be a response, (ii) there would be an explicit or implicit anaphoric reference to a proposition or speech act that is challenged and (iii) the challenge needs to contain a contrastive device or stance marker (e.g. *I think*). The formal realizations of challenges were then compared in the British and German data. The results indicated that the linguistic realizations differed both with respect to frequency and use.

The benefits of Fetzer's analysis are that it can identify a large number of lexical or grammatical realizations of challenges (rejection, denial) by an extended analysis of the speech act taking into account the existence of words or constructions having a contrastive meaning and its relationship to the preceding context. In the future, we can expect that researchers will also resort to annotating the functions of the speech-act utterances. Another way forward to identify pragmatic meaning, especially if the material is spoken, is to use prosody and gestures to analyse illocutionary meaning. The analysis of challenges may be facilitated by the fact that Fetzer studied challenges in a particular genre where the speech act is frequent. However, interestingly, there were considerable linguistic differences between the languages.

1.6 Conclusion

Corpus linguistics and contrastive studies can profit from each other. This is evidenced, for example, by the extension of corpus-linguistic methods to new areas in contrastive pragmatics. In the first phase of corpus-based contrastive pragmatic studies, elements were primarily investigated using a form-to-function approach. Contrastive corpora are well suited for using a particular form as the starting point for the analysis of its functions in the discourse, and, consequently, a large number of pragmatic expressions have been studied from this perspective. A new generation of researchers interested in contrastive studies of pragmatic phenomena are now also focused on exploring how corpora and corpus methodologies can be extended to study topics central to pragmatics such as (im)politeness, hedging, evaluation or speech act forms that cannot be searched for directly in a corpus.

The linguistic realizations associated with such pragmatic notions must be retrieved in an indirect way by first identifying the forms and the functions they have in the context. As has been illustrated above, an innovative feature is to annotate the pragmatic elements identified in the contrastive (parallel or comparable) corpus with respect to function and other features playing a role in how the particular element is interpreted. We can then compare how a particular notion such as hedging is realized in different ways in corpora from different languages.

Much progress in the domain of contrastive corpus-based pragmatics is associated with the availability of spoken parallel and comparable corpora. Moreover, current research draws attention to the context of genre and the necessity to distinguish between differences that are genre-based and those due to the cross-linguistic perspective. The genres studied in contrastive corpora are spoken, written and multimodal. A new trend is the use of social media such as YouTube to study multimodal language use contrastively.

More attention has also been given recently to the practical and theoretical problems of translating pragmatic markers and connective elements across languages, which may have implications for contrastive studies. An area that has attracted the interest of many researchers is underspecification (in particular, omission) in translation. From a theoretical perspective, it has been shown that omission does not depend on the lack of a translation equivalent in the other language but, arguably, reflects typological differences between languages.

Notes

1 Pragmatic markers have also been referred to as discourse markers or discourse particles. In this chapter, I have used the term 'pragmatic marker' also when a researcher uses the term 'discourse marker'.
2 See also Johansen (2019) on the use of 'probes'.

References

Aijmer, K. (2015), 'Well in an English-Swedish and English-French Contrastive Perspective', in K. Beeching and H. Woodfield (eds), *Researching Sociopragmatic Variability. Perspectives from Variational, Interlanguage and Contrastive Pragmatics*, 201–29, Houndmills, Basingstoke, New Hampshire: Palgrave Macmillan.

Aijmer, K. (2020), 'Contrastive Pragmatics and Corpora', *Contrastive Pragmatics*, 1 (1): 28–57.

Aijmer, K. and B. Altenberg (2002), 'Zero Translation and Cross-linguistic Equivalence: Evidence from the English-Swedish Parallel Corpus', in L. E. Breivik and A. Hasselgren (eds), *From the COLT's Mouth . . . and Others'. Language Corpora Studies in Honour of Anna-Brita Stenström*, 19–41, Amsterdam and New York: Rodopi.

Aijmer, K. and D. Lewis (2017a), 'Introduction', in K. Aijmer and D. Lewis (eds), *Contrastive Analysis of Discourse-Pragmatic Aspects of Linguistic Genres*, 1–9, Cham, Switzerland: Springer.

Aijmer, K. and D. Lewis, eds (2017b), *Contrastive Analysis of Discourse-Pragmatic Aspects of Linguistic Genres*, Cham, Switzerland: Springer.

Aijmer, K. and C. Rühlemann (2017), *Corpus Pragmatics. A Handbook*, Cambridge: Cambridge University Press.

Aijmer, K. and A.-M. Simon-Vandenbergen (2003), 'The Discourse Particle Well and Its Equivalents in Swedish and Dutch', *Linguistics*, 41 (6): 1123–61.

Aijmer, K. and A.-M. Simon-Vandenbergen (2006), *Pragmatic Markers in Contrast*, Amsterdam: Elsevier.

Beeching, K. (2016), *Pragmatic Markers in British English. Meaning in Social Interaction*, Cambridge: Cambridge University Press.

Bhatia, V. K. (2002), 'Applied Genre Analysis: Analytical Advances and Pedagogical Procedures', in A. M. Johns (ed.), *Genre in the Classroom: Multiple Perspectives*, 279–83, Mahwah: Erlbaum.

Blum-Kulka, S., J. House and G. Kasper, eds (1989), *Cross-cultural Pragmatics: Requests and Apologies. Advances in Discourse Processes*, vol. 31, Norwoood: Ablex.

Brinton, L. J. (2017), *The Evolution of Pragmatic Markers in English. Pathways of Change*, Cambridge: Cambridge University Press.

Buysse, L. (2017), 'English *so* and Dutch *dus* in a Parallel Corpus: An Investigation into their Mutual Translatability', in K. Aijmer and D. Lewis (eds), *Contrastive Analysis of Discourse-Pragmatic Aspects of Linguistic Genres*, 33–61, Cham, Switzerland: Springer.

Callies, M. and M. Levin (2018), 'A Comparative Multimodal Corpus Study of Dislocation Structures in Live Football Commentary', in M. Callies and M. Levin (eds), *Corpus Approaches to the Language of Sports*, 253–69, London: Bloomsbury.

Chik, S. and M. Taboada (2020), 'Generic Structure and Rhetorical Relations of Online Book Reviews in English, Japanese and Chinese', *Contrastive Pragmatics*, 1 (2): 143–79.

Coulmas, F. (1981), *Conversational Routines: Explorations in Standardized Communication. Situations and Prepatterned Speech*, The Hague: Mouton.

Crible, L., Á. Abuczki, N. Burkšaitienė, P. Furkó, A. Nedoluzhko, S. Rackevičienė, G. V. Oleškevičienė and Š. Zikánová (2019), 'Functions and Translations of Discourse Markers in TED Talks: A Parallel Corpus Study of Underspecification in Five Languages', *Journal of Pragmatics*, 142 (3): 139–55.

Cuenca, M. J. (2008), 'Pragmatic Markers in Contrast: The Case of *Well*', *Journal of Pragmatics*, 40 (8): 1373–91.

De Linde, Z. (1995), '"Read My Lips": Subtitling Principles, Practices, and Problems', *Perspectives: Studies in Translatology*, 3 (1): 9–20.

Diani, G. (2015), 'Politeness', in K. Aijmer and C. Rühlemann (eds), *Corpus Pragmatics. A Handbook*, 169–91, Cambridge: Cambridge University Press.

Díaz Cintas, J. and G. Anderman (2009), 'Introduction', in J. Díaz Cintas and G. Anderman (eds), *Audiovisual Translation: Language Transfer on Screen*, 1–17, Basingstoke: Palgrave Macmillan.

Ebeling, S. O. and J. Ebeling (2013), *Patterns in Contrast*, Amsterdam and Philadelphia: John Benjamins.

Ebeling, S. O. and J. Ebeling (2020), 'Contrastive Analysis, Tertium Comparationis and Corpora', *Nordic Journal of English Studies*, 19: 97–117.

Egan, T. and H. Dirdal (2017), 'Lexis in Contrast Today', in T. Egan and H. Dirdal (eds), *Cross-linguistic Correspondences. From Lexis to Genre*, 1–33, Amsterdam and Philadelphia: John Benjamins.

Fetzer, A. (2011), 'Challenges in Contrast. A Function-to-Form Approach', in K. Aijmer (ed.), *Contrastive Pragmatics*, 73–96, Amsterdam and Philadelphia: John Benjamins.

Hasselgård, H. (2006), 'Non-correspondence between the Cognate Adverbs *Now* and *nå*', in K. Aijmer and A.-M. Simon-Vandenbergen (eds), *Pragmatic Markers in Contrast*, 93–113, Amsterdam: Elsevier.

Hasselgård, H. (2020), 'Corpus-based Contrastive Studies: Beginnings, Developments and Directions', *Languages in Contrast*, 20 (2): 184–208.

Hoek, J., S. Zufferey, J. Evers-Vermeul and T. Sanders (2017), 'Cognitive Complexity and the Linguistic Marking of Coherence Relations: A Parallel Corpus Study', *Journal of Pragmatics*, 12: 113–31.

Isosävi, J. and I. Vecsernyés (2022), 'Addressing, Greeting and Related Gestures in the Opening Sequences of Finnish, French and Hungarian YouTube Videos', *Contrastive Pragmatics*, 3 (3): 363–96.

James, C. (1980), *Contrastive Analysis*, London: Longman.

Johansen, S. H. (2019), 'Exploring the Use of Probes in a Corpus Pragmatic Study of Hedging Strategies', *Nordic Journal of English Studies*, 18 (1): 121–48.

Johansen, S. H. (2021), 'A Contrastive Approach to the Types of Hedging Strategies Used in Norwegian and English Informal Spoken Conversations', *Contrastive Pragmatics*, 2 (1): 81–105.

Johansson, S. (2001), 'The German and Norwegian Correspondences to the English Construction Type *that's What*', *Linguistics*, 39 (3): 583–605.

Johansson, S. (2007), *Seeing through Multilingual Corpora. On the Use of Corpora in Contrastive Studies*, Amsterdam: John Benjamins.

Kadár, D. Z. and J. House (2020), 'Ritual Frames. A Contrastive Pragmatic Approach', *Pragmatics*, 30 (1): 142–68.

Lansari, L. (2017), 'I was going to say/j'allais dire as Discourse Markers in Contemporary English and French', *Languages in Contrast*, 17 (2): 205–28.

Lauwers, P., G. Vanderbauwhede and S. Verleyen (2010), 'Introduction. How False Friends give True Hints about Pragmatic Markers', *Languages in Contrast*, 10 (2): 129–38.

Martinková, M. and M. Janebová (2017), 'What English Translation Equivalents can Reveal about the Czech "Modal" Particle *prý*: A Cross-register Study', in K. Aijmer and D. Lewis (eds), *Contrastive Analysis of Discourse-Pragmatic Aspects of Linguistic Genres*, 63–90, Cham, Switzerland: Springer.

Mattsson, J. (2010), 'But that's like, It's not all that I am, you know. The Swedish Subtitling of Discourse Particle you know in ten US Films', in J. Díaz Cintas, A. Matamala and J. Neves (eds), *New Insights into Audiovisual Translation and Media Accessibility*, 51–65, Amsterdam and New York: Rodopi.

Rojas-Lizana, I. (2015), '"A Very Big Thank You to . . .": Letters of Gratitude in Local Newspapers from Australia and Chile', *Languages in Contrast*, 15 (2): 251–79.

Rozumko, A. (2021), 'Underspecification in the Translation of Discourse Markers: A Parallel Corpus Study of the Treatment of Connective Functions of *indeed* in Polish Translations', *Journal of Pragmatics*, 177 (1): 122–34.

Ruskan, A. and M. Carretero (2021), 'A Cross-linguistic Look at the Right Periphery. Utterance-Final Pragmatic Markers in English, Spanish and Lithuanian', in D. Van Olmen and J. Šinkūnienė (eds), *Pragmatic Markers and Peripheries*, 415–48, Amsterdam and Philadelphia: John Benjamins.

Taboada, M., S. Doval Suárez and E. González Álvarez (2013), 'Introduction. Functional and Corpus Perspectives in Contrastive Discourse Analysis', in M. Taboada, S. Doval Suárez and E. González Álvarez (eds), *Contrastive Discourse Analysis. Functional and Corpus Perspectives*, 1–16, Sheffield and Bristol: Equinox.

Part I

Lexicogrammar in Contrast

2

Seeing Through Languages and Registers
A Closer Look at the Cognates SEE and SE
Signe Oksefjell Ebeling

2.1 Introduction and aims

Corpus-based contrastive analysis on the language pair English-Norwegian has in its almost thirty years of existence predominantly been concerned with the language of fiction, mainly due to extensive research on the fiction part of the English-Norwegian Parallel Corpus (ENPC).[1] However, in recent years, the scope has been broadened to include more research on other text types or registers.[2] This chapter follows this trend and reports on an English-Norwegian contrastive study of the cognates SEE and SE across several registers.

The cognates have previously been investigated on the basis of the ENPC by Øhman (2006) and Ebeling and Ebeling (2020a). The former investigates the polysemy of SEE in fiction and its translations into Norwegian, focusing on the extent to which SEE and SE correspond to each other. The latter draws on Øhman in an analysis of the use of the verb form *see* and its Norwegian translations in a version of the ENPC where dialogic and narrative passages have been kept apart as two sub-registers of fiction. The two studies reveal interesting differences in terms of the semantic quality and distribution of the cognates, both between the languages and the sub-registers.

The verbs are both etymological and semantic cognates, referring to the situation of perceiving with one's eyes (Aijmer 2004: 251). Nevertheless, they have developed diverging polysemies (Altenberg and Granger 2002: 22) in the sense that they have developed meanings that do not (fully) overlap. Indeed, Øhman (2006) suggests that English SEE is more commonly used in Material processes (i.e. processes expressing physical actions) than Norwegian SE, as in example (1) where the Material process of meeting someone is translated into *treffe* (meet). Using *se* in this context would not be considered idiomatic Norwegian, as *se* would rather carry the meaning of Mental perception.

(1) But then, that was the only man he had allowed her to *see*, ... (ENPC/GN1)
Men han var jo den eneste mannen han hadde gitt henne lov til å *treffe*, ... (ENPC/GN1T)

In their cross-linguistic comparison of dialogue vs. narrative in the ENPC, Ebeling and Ebeling (2020a) uncovered differences in the use of SEE between the two fictional sub-registers. While SEE was most commonly used in the prototypical Mental perception sense in narrative passages, as in example (2), there was a bias towards the Mental cognition sense in dialogue, as in example (3). Moreover, the translations into Norwegian suggested that SEE and SE are better correspondences of each other in the Mental perception sense (2) than in the Mental cognition sense of 'understand' (3).

(2) A mile to the east, you could *see* three silos that marked the northeastern corner, ... (ENPC/JSM1)
Halvannen kilometer østover kunne du *se* de tre siloene i det nordøstre hjørnet, ... (ENPC/JSM1T)
(3) 'I *see* your point', said Alice. (ENPC/DL2)
'Jeg *skjønner* hva du mener', sa Alice. (ENPC/DL2T)
(I understand what you mean, said Alice)

Against this background of differences between the cognates both across the two languages and the two sub-registers of fiction, the current study expands the object of study to include non-translated Norwegian dialogue and narrative as well as another register, namely football match reports. Thus, this chapter aims to shed further light on the verbs' lexicogrammatical features and use in a cross-linguistic comparison across registers.

The primary material for this study is culled from two different corpora representing two different languages (English and Norwegian) and three different registers (football match reports, fiction dialogue, fiction narrative). Register is understood here as 'a variety of texts associated with a particular situational context and particular linguistic features' (Egbert and Mahlberg 2020: 72).[3] With regard to fiction, it has been argued that it is a hybrid register consisting of two sub-registers – dialogue and narrative – each with its own set of specific register features (Egbert and Mahlberg 2020: 97; Ebeling and Ebeling 2020a: 311).

The investigation offers a detailed and structured analysis of both semantic and syntactic features of the verbs with the aim of pinning down with more certainty both language-specific and register-specific uses. More specifically, following an overview of the distribution of the various forms of SEE and SE in comparable data in the two languages and three registers, the study will analyse the uses of the verb forms *see* and *se* in English and Norwegian original texts in order to answer the following research questions:

i. How different/similar are the cognates in terms of lexicogrammatical behaviour?
ii. To what extent is language or register decisive for the cognates' lexicogrammatical behaviour?

The chapter is structured as follows: Section 2.2 outlines some background to perception verbs, mainly focusing on previous research on verbs of seeing and relevant classification frameworks. Section 2.3 starts with a brief introduction to the contrastive method used (2.3.1), followed by a description of the corpora (2.3.2), before the data extraction method is outlined and some preliminary observations of the material are offered (2.3.3). The detailed cross-linguistic, cross-register analysis of *see* and *se* is performed in Section 2.4, from a syntactic angle in 2.4.1 and a semantic angle in 2.4.2. Section 2.4.3 discusses the relationship between the syntactic environment and the meaning of the cognates. Finally, Section 2.5 revisits the research questions in a summary of findings, and offers some concluding remarks.

2.2 Background and previous research

Verbs of perception have received much attention in linguistic research over the years, and it is beyond the scope of this chapter to attempt a full review of this field, but see, for example, Miller and Johnson-Laird (1976); Viberg (1984, 2001, 2005); Van Putten (2020) and references therein for a detailed overview of this area of research. As the focus of this study is on one specific verb pair of perception, the current section rather restricts itself to outlining some relevant previous research on the cognates SEE and SE.

The linguistic interest in the prototypical verbs of seeing may be attributed to a number of distinctive characteristics, including their frequent use (Usoniene

2003; Aijmer 2004), their highly polysemous and syntactically versatile nature (Warnock 1974; Miller and Johnson-Laird 1976; Viberg 1984; Alm-Arvius 1993) and the more general 'complicated logic of perception' (Miller and Johnson-Laird 1976: 584). Indeed, '[i]n the actual employment of the verb "to see" there appears at first sight to be a mere chaos of constructions' (Warnock 1974: 49). While the principal sense of the cognates is that of perceiving things with the eyes, examples like (4) and (5) illustrate that 'visual perception need not be part of the descriptive content' (Alm-Arvius 1993: 344).

(4) ... and I'm glad you're beginning to see that you're wasting your time on that chap. (LOB, P02 153 7) (Alm-Arvius 1993: 344)
(5) Magnus (23) er blind og snekker. – Det gjelder å *se* muligheter. (nrk.no, 13/10/2020)
    (Magnus (23) is blind and a carpenter. – It's about *seeing* possibilities.)

Alm-Arvius (1993: 350–1) distinguishes five main senses of SEE (A–E), three of which have two or three sub-senses (B, D, E). They are as follows:

Senses		Possible paraphrases
A	see_1	perceive visually, perceive with the eyes, set (clap) eyes on
B	see_2	understand, realize, grasp, comprehend
	see_3	consider, judge, regard, view, think of
C	see_4	experience, go through
D	see_5	find out, check, ascertain
	see_6	meet, visit, consult, receive
E	see_7	make sure, attend to, ensure, look after
	see_8	escort, accompany, go with
	see_9	take leave of, send off

A different, yet partly overlapping taxonomy, is employed by Øhman (2006), who takes a Systemic-Functional Grammar (SFG) approach (Halliday 1994; Halliday and Matthiessen 2014) and classifies SEE according to the following Hallidayan process types (and subtypes):

- Mental: perception
    - E.g. ... I wanted to *see* the gloomy palace-fortress ... (ENPC/BC1)
- Mental: cognition
    - E.g. Do you *see* the point I'm making? (ENPC/JB1)
- Mental: emotion
    - E.g. ... the forms of maturity they *see* in their parents ... (ENPC/NG1)

- Material
  - E.g. I'll ask him to *see* to it at once. (ENPC/FW1)
- Relational
  - E.g. ... even if he had never *seen* the inside of one of HM prisons. (ENPC/FF1)

In addition, Øhman (2006: 123) identifies two other uses of SEE that form part of the cohesive system of CONJUNCTION, in Halliday's terms (Halliday and Matthiessen 2014: 609):

- Discourse marker
  - E.g. But I remember, *you see*. (ENPC/JB1)
- Conjunction
  - E.g. ... '*seeing* as you'll be going into this business with me one day, you've got to know ...' (ENPC/RD1)

Alm-Arvius' sense A – see_1 – corresponds to SFG's Mental perception category, senses see_2 and see_5 roughly correspond to Mental cognition, see_3 seems to be closest to Mental emotion, see_4 to Relational, and see_6, see_7, see_8 and see_9 to Material. The discourse marker and conjunction uses do not seem to be included in Alm-Arvius's framework.

According to Alm-Arvius (1993: 345), one cannot say that 'all differences in understanding among uses of SEE are due to the existence of a number of particular lexicalized uses'. Some meaning extensions rather seem to come as a result of 'pragmatic adaptation'. One such adaptation is 'pragmatic diversion', exemplified in (6), where 'the descriptive content of *see* may [...] be felt to be so relaxed or watered-down that the only thing that can be said to be really important is that the subject participant somehow learns about what is depicted in the object string' (1993: 347). This would correspond to a Relational process in the SFG framework outlined above with a meaning close to 'have', that is, a 'having attribute' (see also Halliday 1994: 132).

(6)   I would like to see a change in the law [...] (Alm-Arvius 1993: 345)

Another framework, with a typological angle based on Aktionsart and semantic roles, is proposed by Viberg (e.g. 1984). Within this framework, he distinguishes between the following uses for Swedish SE (2004/2005: 124): Activity (*se på* (look at)), Experience (*se* (see)) and Phenomenon-based (*se ... ut* (look) as a copular verb). The distribution of the various uses in Viberg's material suggests that the perceptual experience use is by far the most common for Swedish SE, accounting for 44 per cent of the cases, with perceptual activity and phenomenon-based uses accounting for 14 and 15 per cent, respectively (2004/2005: 125). The remaining 27 per cent, he adds, 'refer to cognitive uses' (2004/2005: 125). Of these, only 'experience' and 'cognitive' – roughly corresponding to Mental Perception and Mental Cognition – seem to be relevant for English SEE (cf. Viberg 1984), whereas all four may be relevant for Norwegian SE, as Swedish is even more closely related to Norwegian than to English.

Several scholars point to complementation patterns as important contributors in determining the senses of SEE, for example, Warnock (1974), Dik and Hengeveld (1991), Alm-Arvius (1993), Usoniene (2003) and Aijmer (2004). There does not, however, seem to be a one-to-one relationship between pattern and meaning at this crude syntactic level of description, albeit some clear tendencies have been noted. A case in point is *wh* clauses, which often trigger a cognitive reading of SEE, as in example (7) from Aijmer (2004: 262). This reading is further substantiated by the authentic Swedish translation into *förstår* (understand) (see also example 3 above).

(7) Do you *see* what I mean (JB1)

   Förstår ni vad jag menar?

At a finer-grained level of description, different syntactic environments of SEE/SE may give rise to different interpretations, for example within the Mental perception use, where *see*+NP+Vinf refers to an event, whereas *see*+NP+Ving refers to a process, as in *I saw him cross the street* and *I saw him crossing the street*, respectively (Aijmer 2004: 255).

Another interesting observation regarding verbs of seeing is that the actual verb form may prefer different syntactic environments and/or meanings. Aijmer (2004: 254), for instance, presents the Swedish translations of SEE according to the tense/form of SEE. One reason for doing this was that a larger proportion of the past tense form was translated into the cognition sense (*förstå* (understand)) than the other forms. Similarly, Øhman (2006) discusses the distribution of the various senses of SEE according to verb form. For example, in Øhman's material, the lemma SEE was used in the Mental perception sense in around 54 per cent of the cases (540 out of 1,001). The forms *see* and *saw* account for more than 70 per cent of these instances, with 204 and 190 occurrences, respectively. *Seen* is used 122 times, while *sees* and *seeing* are marginal with nineteen and five occurrences, respectively (Øhman 2006: 32–3).

Finally, an additional factor that seems to play a role regarding the use of SEE is register. As noted by Ebeling and Ebeling (2020a), differences emerge within the register of fiction, in that the verb form *see* in dialogic sequences is more frequently used in the Mental cognition sense than the Mental perception sense, which is the preferred use in narrative passages and thereby in fiction overall. Thus, different registers may advocate different (preferred) uses of SEE. It was further shown that this has cross-linguistic implications, as the Norwegian cognate SE seems to have a more restricted use in its cognition sense, leading to less overlap between the cognates in dialogue compared to narrative. Similarly, as suggested in Øhman's (2006) study of Norwegian SE as a translation correspondence of English SEE, other meaning extensions of SEE, for example, Material processes and the discourse marker use seem to be less natural for SE.

As will become evident, the current study draws heavily on Øhman (2006) and Ebeling and Ebeling (2020a) in that the verbs are functionally classified in accordance with Systemic-Functional Grammar and the analysis of English *see* in dialogue vs. narrative in fiction is revisited in comparison with *see* and *se* in the football match reports as well as with *se* in Norwegian dialogue vs. narrative. The study is also inspired by Aijmer (2004) and Øhman (2006) in paying particular attention to complementation patterns. The ultimate aim of this cross-linguistic, cross-register analysis is to contribute more insight into these 'familiar but mysterious verb[s]' (Miller and Johnson-Laird 1976: 583).

2.3 Material and method

This section starts with a brief outline of the contrastive method applied in this study (2.3.1), followed by a presentation of the corpora used (2.3.2). Finally, a description of the data extraction procedure, including some preliminary observations of the material, is given in Section 2.3.3.

2.3.1 The contrastive method

Some of the studies of SEE and SE referred to above have relied on unidirectional translation data, that is, data culled from original English texts with translations into, for example, Norwegian (Øhman 2006; Ebeling and Ebeling 2020a) and Swedish (Aijmer 2004). Translation correspondence thus acts as a *tertium comparationis*, in this way enabling cross-linguistic comparisons that offer some insight into the languages compared. Very often, however, bidirectional translation data are endorsed to achieve a more robust *tertium comparationis* in the form of original and translated data in both, or all, languages compared (Johansson 2011; Ebeling and Ebeling 2020b). This kind of data is not always available due to the lack of translated material in all genres or registers. The current investigation therefore relies on comparable data in two languages and three registers, where 'the types of texts in the languages compared represent a common ground suitable for comparison' (Ebeling and Ebeling 2020b: 103). Moreover, the challenge of making sure one compares like with like on the basis of texts that are not directly and explicitly linked linguistically is eliminated by the fact that SEE and SE are established cognates (Aijmer 2004; cf. *Oxford English Dictionary* and Falk and Torp 1991).

2.3.2 The corpora

The English-Norwegian Match Report Corpus (ENMaRC) is a comparable corpus of online football match reports from the English Premier League (PL) and the Norwegian *Eliteserie* (ES). They are post-match accounts written by the clubs' own reporters and posted on the clubs' respective websites. The ENMaRC currently consists of reports from four PL seasons (2016–2020) and three ES seasons (2016–2018 and 2020). The PL part holds reports from twenty-nine different clubs, amounting to just over 1.9 million running words, while the ES part is much smaller with reports from nineteen clubs and around 500,000 words. Some clubs are represented with reports from all seasons, others from only one, two or three as they were either relegated from, or promoted to, the PL/ES in one of the seasons covered. Additionally, some of the teams did not publish reports after every game, while others only published in one of the seasons covered. The length of each report also differs both between the clubs and the two leagues. These factors contribute to the notable difference in size between the English and Norwegian parts of the corpus. See Table 2.6 in the Appendix for an overview of the clubs (and their corpus identifiers) represented in the ENMaRC.[4]

The English-Norwegian Parallel Corpus (ENPC) is a bidirectional parallel corpus consisting of contemporary (late twentieth-century) original texts with their translations (Johansson and Hofland 1994). For the purpose of this study, only original texts classified as general fiction will be consulted.[5] The reason for this narrow selection is that different types of fiction have been found to behave differently with regard to the proportions of dialogic vs. narrative passages (Ebeling and Ebeling 2020a: 294). Thus, in order to ensure as homogenous a set of texts as possible, ENPC texts classified as children's fiction and detective fiction have been excluded from this study. The texts referred to as the ENPC in the remainder of this chapter include twenty English and nineteen Norwegian general fiction text extracts of 10,000–15,000 words (see the overview in Table 2.7 of the Appendix). These have been split into dialogic and narrative passages, resulting in four sub-corpora: English dialogue, English narrative, Norwegian dialogue and Norwegian narrative.

Table 2.1 gives an overview of the size of the different ENPC sub-corpora.

Table 2.1 Token counts in the ENPC original texts: dialogue vs. narrative[6]

	Number of tokens in twenty English original texts	Number of tokens in nineteen Norwegian original texts
Dialogue	51,498	31,823
Narrative	221,573	225,632
Total	273,071	257,455

The term dialogue is used for passages intended by the writer as being instances of direct speech, whereas everything else is referred to as narrative. This means that one part of the s-unit in example (8) is found in the dialogue sub-corpus (8') and one part in the narrative sub-corpus (8").[7]

(8) 'What a horror', said Aunt, gazing at it severely through narrowed eyes. (ENPC/AB1)
(8') 'What a horror', (ENPC/AB1 dialogue)
(8") said Aunt, gazing at it severely through narrowed eyes. (ENPC/AB1 narrative)

2.3.3 Data extraction and delimitation, with some preliminary observations

The corpus tool AntConc (Anthony 2019) is used to extract all forms of the lemmas SEE and SE from the corpora. Although there exist tagged versions of the corpora, searches for the individual forms and manual post-processing were considered necessary to give better precision and recall. In particular, the Norwegian past tense form *så* is problematic from an automatic tagger's point of view, as it is a homograph of the high-frequency adverb *så* 'so'. It was also deemed necessary for the purpose of this study to disambiguate the form *see* into infinitive/imperative and present and past tense (i.e. *did see*) forms. The reason for this is the direct comparison with Norwegian that will be performed. There is a skewed relationship between forms and tenses across the languages, with *se/sjå* uniquely representing the infinitive/imperative in Norwegian, which is not the case for the English base form *see*. Table 2.2 shows the distribution of the various forms of the lemma in the corpora.

As already noted in Ebeling and Ebeling (2020a: 300), the use of the form *see* is far more frequent in dialogue than in narrative. Table 2.2 hints at a similar tendency for the lemma as a whole. In fact, with a mean of 3.76 per 1,000 words in English dialogue and 2.16 in English narrative, there is a statistically significant difference ($p < 0.05$) between the two registers for the lemma SEE.[8] The distribution of the lemma SEE in the ENMaRC has the same mean – 2.16 per 1,000 words – as the narrative texts in the ENPC. However, as demonstrated in Table 2.2, the forms differ in the proportion of the lemma they account for, with the proportion of past tense *saw* being remarkably high in the match reports and the base form *see* (infinitive/imperative) being remarkably high in dialogue and remarkably low in ENMaRC. The fact that the past tense of SEE is so frequent in the English match reports is in accordance with Ebeling's (2021b) observation that there is a strong bias towards the past tense in English match reports.

A similar, yet slightly different, picture can be observed for Norwegian SE across the registers. The form *se* is proportionally more frequent in dialogue than in narrative,[9] but for the whole lemma, SE is more frequently attested in the narrative part of the ENPC, albeit not significantly so ($p=0.407$),[10] with a mean of 5.96 per 1,000 words compared to 5.17 in dialogue. With a mean of 1.85 per 1,000 words, the Norwegian ENMaRC material stands out in relation to the two Norwegian fiction registers,[11] suggesting that there are certain uses of SE found in fiction that do not feature prominently in football match reports. Similarly, in terms of proportional distribution of the forms, SE behaves differently in the Norwegian ENMaRC. Clearly, although the past tense is still the favoured verb form in the Norwegian match reports, the use of the present tense is more prominent than in the English match reports. Also the past participle is more frequently attested in the Norwegian match reports (and dialogue) compared to the English ones. This may be due to the frequent use of the fixed expression *stort sett* (on the whole; lit.: largely seen), and variations thereof.

The use of the lemmas in the two languages differs significantly in the narrative fiction texts ($p < 0.001$, according to a Wilcoxon rank sum test), but not in any of the other registers. One reason for this could be the fact that Norwegian SE may be more prone to being used in the sense of 'look' (cf. Viberg 2004/2005) in Norwegian narratives, as shown in example (9).

Table 2.2 Distribution of the verb forms in raw numbers after disambiguation[12]

SEE	ENMaRC – English	ENPC Narrative – English	ENPC Dialogue – English	ENMaRC – Norw.	ENPC Narrative – Norw.	ENPC Dialogue – Norw.	SE[13]
	Raw number (proportion of total in %)				**Raw number (proportion of total in %)**		
Infinitive/Imperative (*see*)	565 (14.9%)	172 (36.4%)	84 (48.6%)	227 (24.9%)	263 (19.6%)	59 (41.5%)	Infinitive/Imperative (*se, sjå*)
Present tense (*see, sees, does see, do see*)	49 (1.3%)	24 (5.1%)	51 (29.5%)	133 (14.6%)	405 (30.2%)	39 (27.5%)	Present tense (*ser*)
Past tense (*saw, did see*)	2,560 (67.3%)	174 (36.8%)	15 (8.7%)	375 (41.1%)	527 (39.3%)	14 (9.9%)	Past tense (*så, såg*)
Past participle (*seen*)	229 (6%)	82 (17.3%)	20 (11.6%)	178 (19.5%)	146 (10.9%)	30 (21.1%)	Past participle (*sett*)
-ing form (*seeing*)	400 (10.5%)	21 (4.4%)	3 (1.7%)	–	–	–	N/A
TOTAL	3,803	473	173	913	1,341	142	TOTAL
Mean per 1,000 words	2.16	2.16	3.76	1.85	5.96	5.17	Mean per 1,000 words

(9) Jeg *så* ut av vinduet. (ENPC/LSC2)
I *looked* out the window. (ENPC/LSC2T)

As was noted by Aijmer (2004), the different verb forms may have different preferred uses in terms of meaning and syntactic environment.[14] To avoid too many variables in the data set, the current study therefore restricts itself to an investigation of the base forms *see* and *se*, which means that results for English dialogue and narrative in Ebeling and Ebeling (2020a) provide a notion of what to expect. However, unlike Øhman (2006) and Ebeling and Ebeling (2020a), in this direct comparison with original Norwegian data, the present and past tense forms of *see* (*see* and *do/does/did see*) will be excluded from the study, since the Norwegian base form *se* only represents the infinitive and the imperative. Verb phrases with tensed catenatives, for example, past tense *began* in (10) and tensed modals (Norwegian only), for example, past tense *kunne* in (11), will be included,[15] though.

(10) The hosts <u>began</u> to *see* more of the ball, . . . (ENMaRC/AFCB)
(11) Der han stod <u>kunne</u> han *se* kuppelen på St. Paul's . . . (ENPC/EFH1)
From where he was standing, he could see the cupola on St. Paul's (ENPC/EFH1T)

Moreover, multi-word verb uses of *see* and *se* are left out of the investigation, for example, *see off* in (12) and *se ut* 'look' in (13).

(12) Marko Arnautovic's early goal was enough to *see off* the Premier League champions . . . (ENMaRC/WHU)
(13) Mamma: 'Hvorfor skal dere *se ut* som om dere går i protesttog hver dag?' (ENPC/BV2)
Mummy: Why do you all have to *look* as if you're taking part in a demonstration every day? (ENPC/BV2T)

Following this data restriction procedure of including infinitive and imperative forms only and excluding multi-word verbs with *see/se*, the material used in the more detailed analysis of this study is now both more homogeneous, more comparable and more manageable. The actual data set used for this investigation is shown in Table 2.3, where the raw numbers are slightly reduced compared to the Infinitive/Imperative row in Table 2.3 due to the exclusion of multi-word verbs.[16]

The trend noted in Ebeling and Ebeling (2020a) that the verb form *see* is more commonly used in English dialogue than in English narrative still holds

Table 2.3 Occurrences of *see* and *se* in the sub-corpora (raw numbers and mean and median per 1,000 words)

	ENMaRC-EN	ENPC-EN Narrative	ENPC-EN Dialogue	ENMaRC-NO	ENPC-NO Narrative	ENPC-NO Dialogue
	Raw numbers (mean / median per 1,000 words)[17]					
see/se	467 (0.24 / 0.22)	164 (0.73 / 0.53)	78 (1.91 / 1.42)	192 (0.4 / 0.3)	181 (0.80 / 0.83)	41 (1.10 / 0.53)

after removing present and past tense forms as well as multi-word verbs from the data set. Moreover, Table 2.3 shows a similar tendency for the Norwegian fictional sub-registers according to mean per 1,000 words. However, the median suggests that this is not a clear-cut trend, possibly due to the relatively sparse data for Norwegian dialogue (the dialogue texts are short, and one-third of them do not have any instances of *se*). Finally, by adding football match reports to the equation, it becomes clear that there are even further register differences when it comes to the frequency with which *see* and *se* are used. The football match reports in both English and Norwegian show a markedly less frequent use of *see* and *se* compared to the fiction registers. Indeed, their frequency seems very much to be dependent on the register in both English and Norwegian.

2.4 Syntactic and semantic analysis of *see/se*

In order to answer the research questions outlined in Section 2.1, the cognates will be analysed and compared across the languages and registers in terms of the following factors. A sub-section will be devoted to each of these in turn:

- Syntactic environment of *see/se*, with particular emphasis on complementation pattern
- Semantic classification of *see/se* according to SFG

A third sub-section (2.4.3) discusses the relationship between syntactic environment and semantic classification in light of the analysis in 2.4.1 and 2.4.2.

2.4.1 Syntactic environment

Based on results from Øhman's (2006) study of SEE and its Norwegian translations, it is expected that both *see* and *se* are typically followed by a simple NP, as in (14). Clausal complementation patterns are also expected to be relatively frequent; examples of an *at* 'that' clause and a *wh* clause are found in examples (15) and (16), respectively. Moreover, other patterns specifically mentioned as relatively frequent by Øhman include embedded non-finite clauses following an NP, as in (17) with *see*+NP+Vinf. Here we may expect English and Norwegian to differ as Norwegian does not have a direct counterpart to English *-ing* clauses (Hasselgård, Lysvåg and Johansson 2012: 344).

(14) West Ham left-back Masuaku could *see* <u>the number on Bernard's shirt</u>... (ENMaRC/EFC)
(15) Du kan *se* <u>at den kvinnen virkelig har levd</u>. (ENPC/BV1)
    You can *see* <u>that that woman has lived</u>. (ENPC/BV1T)
(16) Now we'll really *see* <u>what they are made of</u>. (ENMaRC/WFC)
(17) ...he loved this room above all the others – a place to *see* <u>things grow</u>. (ENPC/GN1)

Table 2.4 gives an overview of the various complementation patterns in the material. In addition to the patterns mentioned above there is one that stands out in being fairly common in some registers, that is, Zero (= no complementation) as in (18), while others are relatively infrequent overall, for example, Adverbial in (19) and NP+Adverbial in (20).[18]

(18) 'We'll wait and *see*', said Natalie, vaguely. (ENPC/FW1)
(19) Slik kan de *se* <u>rett på solen</u> uten å få øynene skadd. (ENPC/EFH1)
    ...so he can *look* <u>straight into the sun</u> without harming his eyes. (ENPC/EFH1T)
(20) ...it isn't the last time we will *see* <u>him in action</u>... (ENMaRC/MC)

Table 2.4 shows, as predicted, that a simple NP is the main complementation pattern of *see* and *se* overall. A notable exception is the English match reports, where NP+Vinf is by far the most common pattern. ENMaRC-EN also differs from the other sub-corpora in that NP+Ved is proportionally much more frequently attested.

More specifically, with regard to register variation in English, several differences can be observed. The top three complementation types are NP+Vinf > NP+Ved > NP in the match reports, NP > Zero > *that*/*wh* clause in ENPC-EN narrative, and NP > Zero > *wh* clause in ENPC-EN dialogue. While the English fictional sub-registers behave similarly at this level of description, the match reports stand out in that the preferred use of *see* is in combination with a secondary process

Table 2.4 Complementation patterns of *see* and *se* in the different sub-corpora (raw numbers and proportions %)[19]

Pattern	ENMaRC-EN	ENPC-EN Narrative	ENPC-EN Dialogue	ENMaRC-NO	ENPC-NO Narrative	ENPC-NO Dialogue
Adverbial		2	1	12 (6.3%)	23 (12.7%)	
At/that clause	1	17 (10.4%)	5 (6.4%)	16 (8.3%)	10 (5.5%)	3
Hv/wh clause	25 (5.4%)	17 (10.4%)	8 (10.2%)	11 (5.7%)	15 (8.3%)	1
Om/if clause	10 (2.1%)	8 (4.9%)	6 (7.7%)	6 (3.1%)	5 (2.8%)	3
NP	76 (16.3%)	75 (45.7%)	32 (41%)	71 (37%)	83 (45.9%)	16 (39%)
NP+A	22 (4.7%)	4 (2.4%)	2	10 (5.2%)	9 (5%)	1
NP+Ved	96 (20.6%)	7 (4.3%)	2	11 (5.7%)[20]	2	1
NP+Vinf	199 (42.6%)	7 (4.3%)	1	45 (23.4%)	10 (5.5%)	1
NP+Ving	12 (2.6%)	8 (4.9%)				
Other[21]	1	1		3	1	
Zero	25 (5.4%)	18 (11%)	21 (26.9%)	7 (3.6%)	23 (12.7%)	15 (36.6%)
TOTAL	467	164	78	192	181	41

in a non-finite clause (NP+Ved and NP+Vinf). In the case of infinitive clauses, that is, 'Object + bare infinitive complementation' (Quirk et al. 1985: 1205), the Senser sees an action performed by somebody else, as shown in example (21).

(21) Many of the United faithful were hoping to *see* <u>young prodigy Angel Gomes make an appearance</u> . . . (ENMaRC/MU)

Further, a difference between dialogue and narrative can be noted in terms of proportions. English narrative has one clearly favoured complementation pattern (NP), whereas dialogue has two (NP and Zero). As pointed out by Øhman (2006), most of these NPs have a concrete noun as head, quite a few of which refer to human beings, particularly in the dialogue part. The large proportion of Zero cases in English dialogue may be attributed to conversational turns of phrase, such as *we'll see* in example (22), which is used as an elided version of 'we'll see if I'll be able to manage all those presents'.

(22) 'Will you be able to manage all those presents?' my da yelled up the chimney.
'*We'll see*', he said back. (ENPC/RDO1)

Moving on to Norwegian register variation, we can observe a similar, albeit slightly different tendency. All three registers have NP as their preferred complement followed by NP+Vinf in the match reports and Zero in dialogue and Zero and Adverbial in narrative. In Norwegian dialogue, NP and Zero are the only patterns of any prominence, while three patterns stand out in Norwegian narrative (NP, A and Zero). In addition to the two preferred complementation patterns, the Norwegian match reports have *at* (that) clauses in third place (see example (15) above) closely followed by Adverbial in fourth place. Again the main difference is found between the match reports on the one hand and fiction on the other.

This leads us to the cross-linguistic comparison where the most conspicuous differences within each register can be summarized as follows:

Match reports:

- The use of *at* clauses and Adverbial in Norwegian match reports
- The use of NP+Ved in English match reports
- The different proportions of NP vs. NP+Vinf and NP+Ved in the match reports in both English and Norwegian

Narrative:

- The use of Adverbial in Norwegian narrative texts

Dialogue:

- The use of *wh* clauses in English dialogue

To take the use of Adverbial in two of the registers in Norwegian first: Based on the current material, this seems to be a complementation pattern that is not readily available for English *see*. The translation in example (19) above may hint at one reason for this, namely the fact that such instances often correspond to English *look*, rather than *see*. The few cases attested in the English material seem to be restricted to adjuncts of manner, as in (23).

(23)   I watch from a window, or a balcony so I can *see* better . . . (ENPC/MA1)

It is hard to explain the more frequent use of *at* 'that' clauses in ENMaRC-NO. Could it be that these in some way compensate for the more frequent use of NP+Vinf and NP+Ved in ENMaRC-EN? Compare (24) and (25), where (25) with NP+Vinf could be seen as a non-finite version of (24) with an *at* clause in the present tense.[22]

(24)   . . . det er fantastisk å *se* at flere stepper opp og tar ansvar . . . (ENMaRC/MFK)
        (it is fantastic to see that more people are stepping up and taking responsibility)
(25)   . . . det er fantastisk å *se* flere steppe opp og ta ansvar . . .
        (it is fantastic to see more people step up and take responsibility)

The Norwegian match reports also make proportionally more use of simple NPs than the English match reports. As a consequence, it may be inferred that match reporting in English carries even more emphasis on describing events/ actions performed than on static objects and people observed, although the Norwegian match reports show the same tendency when compared to the fiction registers.

Finally, the relatively high proportion of *wh* clauses sets English dialogue apart from Norwegian dialogue. As this is not a pattern that is ruled out in Norwegian, its marginal use may be partly attributed to the small size of the sub-corpus. However, this will have to be checked on the basis of more material at a later stage.

The analysis of complementation patterns suggests that both register and language have an impact on the use of *see* and *se*. This is a relevant observation regarding the second research question, but before reaching a final conclusion to this question the semantic analysis of the verbs will be carried out. The findings presented above serve as a backdrop to this analysis in Section 2.4.2, as the verbs' syntactic environment is likely to play a role in determining their meaning.

2.4.2 Semantic classification

Not surprisingly, the perception use of SEE has previously been found to be the most prominent one, at least in fiction (Øhman 2006; Ebeling and Ebeling 2020a). However, Ebeling and Ebeling (2020a) found some differences between narrative and dialogue in the use of English *see*, notably the fact that the cognitive use was more frequently attested in dialogue than in narrative. Cross-linguistically, English *see* was found to be most commonly translated into a form of SE in the Mental perception use, and less so in the Mental cognitive, Material and discourse marker uses (Øhman 2006; Ebeling and Ebeling 2020a). Thus, it can be expected that the perception use is the most prominent one in Norwegian fiction (both narrative and dialogue), even more so than in English narrative. It can also be predicted that perception is the most important category overall.

Table 2.5 gives an overview of the different senses of *see* and *se* in the material, including some interesting additions to those identified in Øhman (2006), viz. Perception/lexical metaphor, Relational/perception and Behavioural.

Table 2.5 shows that it is indeed the perception use that is the most frequent overall, but it differs proportionally according to language and register. Less general tendencies can be noted for the other uses.

To comment on the registers in English first, we can confirm the finding from Ebeling and Ebeling (2020a) that the cognition use is the most frequent category in dialogue, while perception is most frequent in narrative. Proportionally, the match reports make even more frequent use of the perception sense than narrative does (57.4 vs. 54.3 per cent, respectively). Furthermore, cognition is not as popular in the match reports as in the fiction registers; the second-most frequent use is a hybrid between Relational and Mental perception. Example (26) serves to illustrate this hybrid nature in that some ocular seeing may be involved (by observing points on the league table), but there is arguably a stronger relational connection, in that the result is that the Blues will **have** their lead cut back, that is, the possessive type of relational process (or the 'having attribute') in Halliday's (1994, 2004: 172) terms.[23]

Table 2.5 Semantic classification of *see* and *se* (according to SFG process types) (raw numbers and proportions (%) within language/register)

	ENMaRC-EN	ENPC-EN Narrative	ENPC-EN Dialogue	ENMaRC-NO	ENPC-NO Narrative	ENPC-NO Dialogue
Mental Perception	268 (57.4%)	89 (54.3%)	29 (37.2%)	144 (75%)	131 (72.4%)	21 (51.2%)
Mental Perception/ lexical metaphor	36 (7.7%)					
Mental Cognition	43 (9.2%)	44 (26.8%)	32 (41%)	22 (11.5%)	25 (13.8%)	8 (19.5%)
Relational	31 (6.6%)					
Relational/ Mental perception	85 (18.2%)	4	3	15 (7.8%)	2	1
Material	4				6 (3.3%)	3
Behavioural		24 (14.6%)	14 (18%)	11 (5.7%)	15 (8.3%)	8 (19.5%)
Evaluative		3			2	
TOTAL	467	164	78	192	181	41

(26) The Blues may *see* that lead cut back by three points tomorrow ... (ENMaRC/MC)

Two uses that are unique to the English football match reports are Perception/lexical metaphor, as in example (27),[24] and Relational, as in (28).

(27) Wilson's tenth caution of the season will *see* him receive an automatic two game ban ... (ENMaRC/AFCB)
(28) Southampton continued to *see* more of the ball ... (ENMaRC/MFC)

All instances of *see* in the Perception/lexical metaphor category resemble example (27) in that the Senser is inanimate, thus attributing human/animate qualities to, in this case, a caution that metaphorically sees Wilson receive a ban (cf. Halliday 1994: 346). Example (28) is also typical of its semantic class in the ENMaRC-EN material with the set phrase *see* + quantifier + *the ball* in the sense of having or possessing it, that is, a more clear-cut case of a 'having attribute' than the Relational/perception example discussed in (26) above.

The two fiction registers differ from the match reports in the relatively frequent use of Material processes, possibly due to the fact that this use of *see* typically has a meaning that is more natural in a fictional context, viz. *meet/visit*, as in (29).

(29) 'The last thing Harry said to me this morning was that he'd *see* me at six thirty.' (ENPC/FW1)

The absence of *see* as a discourse marker in Table 2.5 deserves a comment. The reason for this is that, formally, the form *see* as (part of) a discourse marker is generally the present tense, as in (30), and is therefore not part of this investigation.[25]

(30) My father was a sailor, *you see*. (ENPC/ABR1)

As for register differences in the Norwegian corpora, it is mainly a matter of proportions, as the top two categories are the same across the board: Perception > Cognition. However, the third most frequent category differs in that the fiction registers prefer Behavioural and the match reports Relational/Mental perception. Material is marginal in the Norwegian fiction registers and non-existent in the match reports.

The Behavioural category is interesting to compare both across the registers and languages. First, it is markedly more frequent in Norwegian dialogue than in narrative and match reports. An example of imperative *se* in this use is given in (31),[26] while example (32) demonstrates that infinitive *se* may also take on a Behavioural reading.

(31) Underforstått: '*Se*, så flinke vi har vært til å oppdra henne.' (ENPC/BV2)
Understood: *look* how well we've brought her up. (ENPC/BV2T)
(32) Vi må *se* fremover, og fokusere på neste mulighet ... (ENMaRC/KFK)
(We must look ahead, and focus on next opportunity)

Behavioural processes are 'partly like the material and partly like the mental'; the Behaver, like the Senser in a Mental process, 'is typically a human being [. . .] but the Process is grammatically more like one of "doing"' (Halliday 1994: 139). *Se* in the sense of 'look' can be classified as such a process of 'consciousness represented as forms of behaviour' (Halliday 1994: 139), an activity in Viberg's (1984) terms and 'obligatorily agentive' in Gruber's (1967: 943) terms. This use does not seem to be available for English *see*, as indicated by Viberg (1984: 149) in his framework where English *see* strictly belongs to the 'experience' category, and is obligatorily non-agentive (Gruber 1967: 943). Thus, one clear difference between the cognates lies in the Behavioural use of Norwegian *se*.

As expected, based on Øhman's (2006) and Ebeling and Ebeling's (2020a) findings for English *see* and its translations into Norwegian, there are some cross-linguistic differences in the fictional registers, notably in the categories Mental perception, Mental cognition and Material. Proportionally, the perception use is higher in Norwegian in all three registers, whereas cognition is relatively low in both English and Norwegian match reports and considerably lower in Norwegian narrative and dialogue. The more prominent cognition use in English is in line with Viberg's (1984: 157) observation that 'it seems to be fairly common that the closest equivalent to some of the cognitive verbs in English [. . .] is covered by a verb of perception through semantic extension'. Furthermore, the Material use, although fairly prominent for *see* in the English fictional registers, is marginal in Norwegian fiction and non-existent in the Norwegian match reports. Similarly, the Relational/perception use is attested for Norwegian *se*, for example (33), but it is notably less commonly used than in English, even in the match reports.

(33) Barmen skal være glad at han ikke fikk *se* sitt andre gule kort på ti sekunder ... (ENMaRC/VFK)
(Barmen should be glad that he did not get to see his second yellow card in ten seconds ...)

Moreover, the purely Relational and the Perception/lexical metaphor uses of English *see* in the match reports are not attested for *se* in the Norwegian match reports.

Apart from the cross-linguistic differences mentioned above, other notable differences have to do with preferred uses; that is, Norwegian prefers the Mental perception use to a greater extent, whereas there is more of a division of labour between Mental perception and cognition in English, at least in the fictional registers.

2.4.3 Discussion: The relationship between syntactic environment and semantic classification of *see* and *se*

In the previous two sections, similarities and differences between the registers and the languages have been revealed both regarding the syntactic environment and semantic classification of the cognates. A commonly held view in corpus linguistics is that form/pattern and meaning go together (e.g. Sinclair 1991; Hunston and Francis 2000), also in the case of verbs of perception (cf. Usoniene 2003; Aijmer 2004). Despite the observation in Section 2.2 that there does not seem to be a one-to-one pattern and meaning correspondence between *see* and *se*, this part of the study will consider the correlation between syntactic environment and semantic meaning of the two verb forms. In this respect, it is important to note that other forms of the lemma may have different preferred uses and/or may take on other uses than the ones discussed here. Indeed, the discourse marker use of English *see* appears to be correlated with the present tense in the material studied here (cf. Section 2.4.2). It is therefore important to bear in mind that the forms *see* and *se* to some extent represent different forms and functions within a verb phrase, viz. introducing non-finite infinitive clauses, main verb in finite VPs with modal auxiliaries and catenatives and imperatives.

The following list gives an overview of syntactic environments that trigger a specific sense in 100 per cent of the cases in the current material. Some are unidirectional (→) in the sense that a specific pattern results in a specific process, for example, *see/se* followed by an *if/om* clause results in a Mental cognition reading. Others are bidirectional (↔), that is, there is a one-to-one relationship between some patterns and meanings, for example, *see* as a Relational process in the English match reports always has the same syntactic environment and vice versa.

- *See/se+if/om* clause → **Mental cognition, 100 per cent**, for example:
    'I'm getting up early, to *see* if I can get hold of some money.' (ENPC/DL2)
- *See/se*+NP (human being) → **Material, 100 per cent**, for example:
    'Okay, I'll *see* you in a while', ... (ENPC/GN1)
- **Inanimate Senser+*see*+any complementation** ↔ **Perception/lexical metaphor, 100 per cent**, for example:
    A victory could *see* them move as much as five points clear ... (ENMaRC/LCFC)
- **Catenative+*see*+quantifier+*the ball*** ↔ **Relational, 100 per cent**, for example:
    ... Burnley began to *see* more of the ball as half-time approached. (ENMaRC/BFC)

The material also uncovers a unidirectional pattern-meaning relationship between a process and a specific environment: Behavioural is invariably expressed by *se* followed by either Zero or an Adverbial:

- **Behavioural** → *se*+Zero/Adv, **100 per cent**, for example:
    '*Se*', jeg peker på en eldre kvinne ... (ENPC/SL1)
    '*Look*', I point at an old woman ... (ENPC/SL1T)

    ... som trodde at han var til hjelp ved å *se* tvers gjennom ham. (ENPC/OEL1)
    ... who thought he was being helpful by *looking* right through him. (ENPC/OEL1T)

Other unidirectional and relatively strong relationships, not reaching 100 per cent, include:

- *See/se*+NP+Vinf → **Mental perception**, approx. **87 per cent** in English and **84 per cent** in Norwegian, for example:
    Aubameyang was put through on goal only to *see* Butland save again. (ENMaRC/AFC)
- *See/se*+NP (non-human) → **Mental perception**, approx. **55 per cent** in English and **85 per cent** in Norwegian, for example:
    Når de står der kan de *se* takene og pipene på mange hus ... (ENPC/BV2)
    (... see the roofs and chimneys)
- *See/se*+*wh/hva*-clause → **Mental cognition**, around **66 per cent** in English and **50 per cent** in Norwegian for example:

I looked around again in amazement; for I couldn't *see* <u>how the solid forest could become so different</u>. (ENPC/BO1)

If we compare these pattern and meaning tendencies with the overviews given in Tables 2.4 and 2.5, it seems evident that the frequency with which the syntactic patterns listed above occur contributes to the distribution of the various senses across the registers and languages. However, a strict one-to-one relationship between all patterns and meanings cannot be established, as some patterns are not tied to specific meanings and some meanings are not tied to a specific syntactic environment, notably the most frequent ones: Mental perception and Mental cognition can be expressed by *see/se* in several different syntactic environments. Conversely, the pattern *see/se*+NP (non-human) often triggers other meanings than Mental perception, particularly in English (notably Material and Mental cognition). Nevertheless, the lists illustrate some of the main tendencies, where some pattern and meaning associations are stronger than others.

2.5 Summary and concluding remarks

This study started out with an overview and discussion of the distribution of the different forms of the lemmas under investigation (see Table 2.1 and Section 2.3.3). These preliminary observations are in fact relevant to the research questions presented in Section 2.1, which address the lexicogrammatical behaviour of the cognates across registers and languages. At a glance, it became obvious that the different registers prefer different forms of the lemmas both within and across the two languages. Although not a primary concern in the current context, it was later revealed that some forms of the lemma are tied to specific uses; that is, the discourse marker use of English *see* seems to strongly prefer a present tense form (cf. Section 2.4.2). Only future studies will be able to determine how far-reaching this tendency of particular forms triggering specific uses is (but see Usoniene 2003 and Aijmer 2004 for some observations).

The investigation was delimited to a closer inspection of the forms *see* and *se*, and tendencies similar to those for the lemmas were uncovered with regard to frequency. According to the mean per 1,000 words (Table 2.3) they are least frequent in the match reports in both languages and most frequent in dialogue in both languages; however, the very limited data set in Norwegian dialogue, in particular, should be kept in mind in this comparison.

In the more detailed account of syntactic environment (Section 2.4.1), it was found that the match reports are clearly different from the two fictional registers in both languages, thus illustrating the impact of register, but at the same time the English and Norwegian match reports differ in their preferred complementation patterns, thus demonstrating a language effect as well. Narrative and dialogue are relatively similar both within and across the languages in terms of preferred syntactic environment, but the proportional distribution differs; thus, register has an impact on proportions. As far as the semantic classification is concerned (Section 2.4.2), it is particularly the English match reports that stand out, as two unique uses of *see* are recorded (Perception/lexical metaphor and Relational) and the second-most frequent use (Relational/perception) is markedly more common in the English match reports than in any of the other sub-corpora. In fact, proportional differences between the semantic categories are found between all registers both within and across the languages. Moreover, there is a marked difference between the two languages in that Norwegian *se* has a Behavioural use which is not readily available for English *see* (at least not in these registers).

In Section 2.4.3 it was shown that some patterns and meanings are more prone to being associated than others. This is reflected to some extent in the summary above, particularly when it comes to the English match reports where the two special senses are bidirectionally associated with specific syntactic environments. The lack of a one-to-one correspondence, either uni- or bidirectionally, between the more frequent processes and specific syntactic environments underlines the importance of analysing the syntactic and semantic features separately.

The answer to the first research question – How different/similar are the cognates in terms of lexicogrammatical behaviour? – is first of all that they enter into a very similar number of syntactic environments. The only pattern not available for Norwegian is NP+Ving, as expected. A more detailed analysis, referred to in Section 2.4.3, also uncovered two environments that were not recorded in the Norwegian material, namely *see* with an inanimate Senser and *see* followed quantifier+*the ball*. These are directly linked to the two senses that were only found in the English match reports. The number of senses attested for *see* and *se* is also similar but with two that are unique to the English material and one to the Norwegian material.

The second research question – To what extent is language or register decisive for the cognates' lexicogrammatical behaviour? – has been answered in the summary above, but in short: Both language and register have an impact. The former is reflected in the sense unique to Norwegian and the syntactic environments and senses unique to English, whereas the latter is reflected in the senses unique to the English match reports compared to the other English registers. Beyond these lexicogrammatical differences, the preferred uses of the two cognates also seem to depend on both language and register.

At a more general level, we can conclude that *see* and *se* in the fictional registers behave more similarly in English and Norwegian than they do in the match reports. It is therefore tempting to suggest that the meaning extensions and distribution of *see* in the English match reports arguably contribute to a more developed and established football match report register for English than for Norwegian, which is closer to fiction in every respect. To determine this with more certainty, more contrastive analyses of linguistic features in these and other registers are needed.

The study has demonstrated how a contrastive study can offer new insights into the languages (and registers) compared, both at a micro and macro level. At the micro level, the cognates *see* and *se* were analysed and compared in detail, uncovering preferred and unique uses within each language across registers. At the macro level, it was suggested that the uses of Norwegian *se* do not contribute the same register-specific flavour that *see* seems to do for English football match reports.

Acknowledgements

I would like to thank two anonymous reviewers for their insightful comments and suggestions.

Notes

1 See Hasselgård (2020) and the ENPC bibliography [https://www.hf.uio.no/ilos/tjenester/kunnskap/sprak/omc/enpc_omc_publications_2021update.pdf].

2 Hasselgård (2014), Rørvik and Monsen (2018), Johansen (2020), Ebeling (2021a).
3 For a more detailed discussion of what constitutes a register, see, for example, Neumann (2014).
4 For a more detailed description of the compilation process of the ENMaRC, see Ebeling (2019).
5 The ENPC also contains a nonfiction part which is not relevant here (see Johansson, Ebeling and Oksefjell 1999/2002 for a detailed description of the ENPC, including ENPC nonfiction).
6 The numbers for each sub-corpus differ slightly from Ebeling and Ebeling (2020a) due to different AntConc settings, for example the inclusion of numbers in the token counts.
7 See Johansson, Ebeling and Oksefjell (1999/2001) and Ebeling and Ebeling (2020a) for a more detailed account of the mark-up of dialogue in the ENPC.
8 Based on a t.test as implemented in R.
9 *Se* is used to represent both the *bokmål* form *se* and the *nynorsk* form *sjå* in the remainder of this chapter.
10 Based on a t.test as implemented in R.
11 According to a t.test, the frequency of SE in ENMaRC-NO differs significantly from that in both the narrative ($p < 0.0001$) and the dialogue ($p < 0.001$) parts of ENPC-NO.
12 In the English material, only one instance of *see* as a noun had to be removed from the material. In the Norwegian material, however, quite a lot of hits were removed: more than 3,100 of the form *så* (homograph of the adverb *så* 'so') and seventeen of the form *sett*, which is a homograph of the imperative form and the *nynorsk* past participle form of *sette* 'set'.
13 The Norwegian forms of the lemma SE include the *nynorsk* forms *sjå* (infinitive) and *såg* (past tense).
14 See also Usoniene (2003) and Øhman (2006).
15 Unlike the English modal auxiliaries, Norwegian modals have non-finite and tensed forms (Hasselgård, Lysvåg and Johansson 2012: 203). No non-finite forms were attested in the current material.
16 The number of imperative forms in the material is comparatively low, particularly in English: two occurrences in English narrative, two in English dialogue and none in the English match reports. In the Norwegian material, there are eight occurrences in the narrative sub-corpus, seven in dialogue and four in the match reports. The more frequent use of this form in Norwegian seems to be tied to one use in particular, albeit not exclusively, where imperative *se* means 'look' (i.e. the Behavioural use; see Section 2.4.2 and example (31)).
17 A note on dispersion across the texts: as can be gleaned from the medians, half of the data sets are normally distributed (ENMaRC-EN, ENMaRC-NO, ENPC-NO

narrative). The other half have several outliers and, in the case of Norwegian dialogue, sparse data.
18 'Adverbial' is used here as a cover term for adverbs and PPs functioning as Adverbials.
19 A note on dispersion: the few attestations in some of these patterns underlines the fact that even distribution across the texts cannot be achieved. Also, some of the texts are short and there is little opportunity for patterns to occur. Nevertheless, the most frequent patterns within each sub-corpus at least show a relatively sound distribution.
20 The NP is a reflexive pronoun in ten out of the eleven cases, e.g. *Molde måtte til slutt se seg slått av Sandefjord* (MFK) Lit.: Molde had in the end to see themselves beaten by Sandefjord.
21 These include adjective and NP + adjective.
22 But note that these patterns may not always overlap in meaning, as the verb followed by an NP+Vinf or NP+Ved 'expresses what is directly perceived' (Aijmer 2004: 256), whereas a *that* clause, according to Usoniene (2003: 20), is 'associated with indirect perception'. Although this difference may not always be evident (Aijmer 2004: 253), as is the case in (24) and (25), it is tempting to suggest that the Norwegian match reports may have a slight preference for more indirect perception compared to English.
23 This use was subsumed under the Mental cognition use in Ebeling and Ebeling (2020a) for narrative vs. fiction, and as can be seen in Table 2.5, it is not frequently attested in either, with four and three occurrences, respectively.
24 Note that their 'uniqueness' only refers to the current material; these uses are found elsewhere in English, cf. Halliday's (1994: 346) examples of lexical metaphor uses of *see*.
25 However, there is, arguably, one instance of *let's see* as a discourse marker (cf. Thompson 2002: 143–4), and one of *let me see* in the English dialogue material (e.g.: . . . *he said , "Oh, now, let me see, maybe I will try some at that"* . . . (ENPC/AT); these have, for the purpose of this study, been subsumed under the Mental cognition category. Thanks to one of the anonymous reviewers for drawing my attention to these uses.
26 'Although somewhat archaic', according to the OED (*see* §18a), there is an idiomatic imperative use of English *see* with the meaning of 'look', that is, the Behavioural sense.

References

Aijmer, K. (2004), 'The Interface between Perception, Evidentiality and Discourse Particle Use – USING a Translation Corpus to Study the Polysemy of See', *TradTerm*, 10: 246–77.

Alm-Arvius, C. (1993), *The English Verb See: A Study in Multiple Meaning*, Göteborg: Acta Universitas Gothoburgensis.

Altenberg, B. and S. Granger (2002), 'Recent Trends in Cross-linguistic Lexical Studies', in B. Altenberg and S. Granger (eds), *Lexis in Contrast. Corpus-based Approaches*, 3–48, Amsterdam and Philadelphia: John Benjamins.

Anthony, L. (2019), *AntConc* (version 3.5.8) [Computer Software], Waseda University. https://www.laurenceanthony.net/software

Dik, S. C. and K. Hengeveld (1991), 'The Hierarchical Structure of the Clause and the Typology of Perception-verb Complements', *Linguistics*, 29 (2): 231–59.

Ebeling, S. O. (2019), 'The Language of Football Match Reports in a Contrastive Perspective', in M. Callies and M. Levin (eds), *Corpus Approaches to the Language of Sports: Texts, Media, Modalities*, 37–62, London: Bloomsbury.

Ebeling, S. O. (2021a), 'Hope for the Future: An Analysis of HOPE/HÅP(E) across Genres and Languages', in A. Čermáková, S. O. Ebeling, M. Levin and J. Ström Herold (eds), *Crossing the Borders: Analysing Complex Contrastive Data*, Bergen Language and Linguistics Studies, 11 (1): 7–26.

Ebeling, S. O. (2021b), 'Minutes of Action! A Contrastive Analysis of Time Expressions in English and Norwegian Football Match Reports', in A. Čermáková, T. Egan, H. Hasselgård and S. Rørvik (eds), *Time in Languages, Languages in Time*, 229–54, Amsterdam: John Benjamins.

Ebeling, S. O. and J. Ebeling (2020a), 'Dialogue vs. Narrative in Fiction: A Cross-Linguistic Comparison', in S. Granger and M.-A. Lefer (eds), *The Complementary Contribution of Comparable and Parallel Corpora to Crosslinguistic Studies*, Special issue of *Languages in Contrast*, 20 (2): 288–313.

Ebeling, S. O. and J. Ebeling (2020b), 'Contrastive Analysis, *Tertium Comparationis* and Corpora', *Nordic Journal of English Studies*, 19 (1): 97–117.

Egbert, J. and M. Mahlberg (2020), 'Fiction – One Register or Two?', *Register Studies*, 2 (1): 72–101.

Falk, H. and A. Torp (1991), [first published 1903–06], *Etymologisk ordbog over det norske og det danske sprog* (Etymological Dictionary of the Norwegian and Danish Language), Oslo: Bjørn Ringstrøms antikvariat.

Gruber, J. S. (1967), 'Look and See', *Language*, 43 (4): 937–47.

Halliday, M. A. K. (1994), *An Introduction to Functional Grammar*, 2nd edn, London: Arnold.

Halliday, M. A. K. (2004), *An Introduction to Functional Grammar*, 3rd edn, revised by C. M. I. M. Matthiessen, London: Arnold.

Halliday, M. A. K. and C. M. I. M. Matthiessen (2014), *An Introduction to Functional Grammar*, 4th edn, London: Arnold.

Hasselgård, H. (2014), 'Discourse-Structuring Functions of Initial Adverbials in English and Norwegian News and Fiction', *Languages in Contrast*, 14 (1): 73–92.

Hasselgård, H. (2020), 'Corpus-based Contrastive Studies: Beginnings, Developments and Directions', in S. Granger and M.-A. Lefer (eds), *The Complementary Contribution of Comparable and Parallel Corpora to Crosslinguistic Studies*, Special issue of *Languages in Contrast*, 20 (2): 184–208.

Hasselgård, H., P. Lysvåg and S. Johansson (2012), *English Grammar: Theory and Use*, 2nd edn, Oslo: Universitetsforlaget.

Hunston, S. and G. Francis (2000), *Pattern Grammar: A Corpus-driven Approach to the Lexical Grammar of English*, Amsterdam and Philadelphia: John Benjamins.

Johansen, S. H. (2020), '"I Just Need to like See What I Can Do": A Contrastive Study of Hedging Strategies in English and Norwegian Informal Spoken Conversations', PhD diss., University of Oslo.

Johansson, S. (2011), 'A Multilingual Outlook of Corpora Studies', in V. Viana, S. Zyngier and G. Barnbrook (eds), *Perspectives on Corpus Linguistics*, 115–29, Amsterdam: John Benjamins.

Johansson, S., J. Ebeling and S. Oksefjell (1999/2002), 'The English-Norwegian Parallel Corpus: Manual', Department of British and American Studies, University of Oslo. https://www.hf.uio.no/ilos/english/services/knowledge-resources/omc/enpc/ENPCmanual.pdf

Johansson, S. and K. Hofland (1994), 'Towards an English-Norwegian Parallel Corpus', in U. Fries, G. Tottie and P. Schneider (eds), *Creating and Using English Language Corpora: Papers from the Fourteenth International Conference on English Language Research on Computerized Corpora, Zurich 1993*, 25–37, Amsterdam: Rodopi.

Miller, G. A. and P. N. Johnson-Laird (1976), *Language and Perception*, Cambridge: Cambridge University Press.

Neumann, S. (2014), *Contrastive Register Variation. A Quantitative Approach to the Comparison of English and German*, Berlin: De Gruyter Mouton.

Øhman, B. I. (2006), 'An SFG Perspective on the Polysemy of See: A Corpus-based Contrastive Study', MA diss., University of Oslo.

Oxford English Dictionary (OED) Online (2020), Oxford University Press. http://oed.com/

Quirk, R., S. Greenbaum, G. Leech and J. Svartvik (1985), *A Comprehensive Grammar of the English Language*, London: Longman.

R Core Team (2019), 'R: A Language and Environment for Statistical Computing', R Foundation for Statistical Computing, Vienna, Austria. https://www.R-project.org/

Rørvik, S. and M. Monsen (2018), 'Marked themes in English and Norwegian Academic Texts in the Field of Didactics', in S. O. Ebeling and H. Hasselgård (eds), *Corpora and Comparatio Linguarum: Textual and Contextual Perspectives*, Bergen Language and Linguistics Studies, 9 (1): 43–68.

Sinclair, J. (1991), *Corpus, Concordance, Collocation*, Oxford: Oxford University Press.

Thompson, S. A. (2002), '"Object Complements" and Conversation. Towards a Realistic Account', *Studies in Language*, 26 (1): 125–64.

Usoniene, A. (2003), 'Extension of Meaning: Verbs of Perception in English and Lithuanian', in K. M. Jaszczolt and K. Turner (eds), *Meaning Through Language Contrast: The Cambridge Papers*, vol. 1, 193–220, Amsterdam: John Benjamins.

Van Putten, S. (2020), 'Perception Verbs and the Conceptualization of the Senses: The Case of Avatime', *Linguistics*, 58 (2): 425–62.

Viberg, Å. (1984), 'The Verbs of Perception: A Typological Study', in B. Butterworth, B. Comrie and Ö. Dahl (eds), *Explanations for Language Universals*, 123–62, Berlin, New York and Amsterdam: Mouton.

Viberg, Å. (2001), 'The Verbs of Perception', in M. Haspelmath, E. König, W. Oesterreicher and W. Raible (eds), *Language Typology and Language Universals. An International Handbook*, 1294–309, Berlin: De Gruyter.

Viberg, Å. (2004/2005), 'The Lexical Typological Profile of Swedish Mental Verbs', *Languages in Contrast*, 5 (1): 121–57.

Warnock, G. J. ([1965] 1974), 'Seeing', in R. J. Swartz (ed.), *Perceiving, Sensing, and Knowing: A Book of Readings from Twentieth-Century Sources in the Philosophy of Perception*, 49–67, Berkeley: University of California Press.

Appendix. The content of the corpora used

Table 2.6 Overview of Premier League and *Eliteserie* clubs represented in the ENMaRC

English Premier League		Norwegian *Eliteserie*	
ID	Club	ID	Club
AFC	Arsenal	AaFK	Aalesund
AVFC	Aston Villa	BG	Bodø-Glimt
AFCB	Bournemouth	SKB	Brann
BHA	Brighton & Hove Albion	KBK	Kristiansund
BFC	Burnley	LSK	Lillestrøm
CCFC	Cardiff City	MIF	Mjøndalen
CFC	Chelsea	MFK	Molde
CPFC	Crystal Palace	OBK	Odd
EFC	Everton	RF	Ranheim
FFC	Fulham	RBK	Rosenborg
HT	Huddersfield Town	SaF	Sandefjord
HC	Hull City	S08	Sarpsborg 08
LC	Leicester City	SoF	Sogndal
LFC	Liverpool	STB	Stabæk
MC	Manchester City	IKS	Start
MU	Manchester United	SIF	Strømsgodset
MFC	Middlesbrough	TIL	Tromsø
NU	Newcastle United	VFK	Viking
NCFC	Norwich City	VIF	Vålerenga
SU	Sheffield United		
SFC	Southampton		
SC	Stoke City		
SAFC	Sunderland		
SCAFC	Swansea City		
TH	Tottenham Hotspur		
WFC	Watford		
WBA	West Bromwich Albion		
WHU	West Ham United		
WWFC	Wolverhampton		

Table 2.7 Overview of authors and texts in the ENPC used in this study

	English general fiction			Norwegian general fiction	
ID	Author	Title	ID	Author	Title
AB1	Brookner, Anita	*Latecomers*	BV1	Vik, Bjørg	*En handful lengsel*
ABR1	Brink, André	*The Wall of the Plague*	BV2	Vik, Bjørg	*Kvinneakvariet*
AH1	Hailey, Arthur	*Strong Medicine*	CL1	Loveid, Cecilie	*Sug*
AT1	Tyler, Anne	*The Accidental Tourist*	EFH1	Hansen, Erik Fosnes	*Salme ved reisens slutt*
BC1	Chatwin, Bruce	*Utz*	EH1	Hoem, Edvard	*Kjærleikens ferjereiser*
BO1	Okri, Ben	*The Famished Road*	EHA1	Haslund, Ebba	*Det hendte ingenting*
DL1	Lessing, Doris	*The Fifth Child*	HW1	Wassmo, Herbjørg	*Huset med den blinde glassveranda*
DL2	Lessing, Doris	*The Good Terrorist*	HW2	Wassmo, Herbjørg	*Dinas bok*
FW1	Weldon, Fay	*The Heart of the Country*	JM1	Michelet, Jon	*Orions belte*
GN1	Naylor, Gloria	*The Women of Brewster Place*	JW1	Wiese, Jan	*Kvinnen som kledte seg naken for sin elskede*
JB1	Barnes, Julian	*Talking It Over*	KA1	Askildsen, Kjell	*En plutselig frigjørende tanke*
JC1	Crace, Jim	*Arcadia*	KF1	Faldbakken, Knut	*Adams dagbok*
JH1	Heller, Joseph	*Picture This*	KF2	Faldbakken, Knut	*Insektsommer*
JSM1	Smiley, Jane	*A Thousand Acres*	KFL1	Fløgstad, Kjartan	*Dalen Portland*
MA1	Atwood, Margaret	*Cat's Eye*	KH1	Holt, Kåre	*Kapplopet*
MD1	Drabble, Margaret	*The Middle Ground*	LSC2	Christensen, Lars Saabye	*Jokeren*
NG1	Gordimer, Nadine	*My Son's Story*	OEL1	Lønn, Øystein	*Tom Rebers siste retrett*
RDA1	Davies, Robertson	*What's Bred in the Bone*	SL1	Lie, Sissel	*Løvens hjerte*
RDO1	Doyle, Roddy	*Paddy Clarke Ha, Ha, Ha*	TB1	Brekke, Toril	*Jakarandablomsten*
ST1	Townsend, Sue	*The Queen and I*			

3

Periphrastic Genitive Constructions in English and Norwegian

Hilde Hasselgård

3.1 Introduction

English and Norwegian both have an *s*-genitive and a periphrastic genitive in the form of a postmodifying prepositional phrase (PP) as in (1) and (2).[1] The English periphrastic genitive uses the preposition *of*, while Norwegian mostly uses *til* (to). The *s*-genitive differs only in that the Norwegian suffix -*s* is (normally) not accompanied by an apostrophe.[2] The periphrastic genitive may be translated congruently (*of* = *til*) between the languages, as shown in (1), by an *s*-genitive, as in (2) and (3), or by other means, as will be shown below.

(1) the voices *of* my spirit companions (BO1)
    stemmene *til* mine følgesvenner i åndeverdenen (BO1T)
    (the voices to my companions in the spirit-world)
(2) *Faren til Herman* er kranfører. (LSC1)
    (The father of Herman is crane-operator.)
    Herman's father is a crane operator. (LSC1T)
(3) he was asked what *the principal crop of Thailand* was (JB1)
    han ble spurt hva som var *Thailands viktigste jordbruksprodukt* (JB1T)
    (he was asked what which was Thailand's principal crop)

This chapter compares the formally similar periphrastic genitive constructions of English and Norwegian with regard to frequencies, distributions and meanings across fiction and nonfiction. It also examines the translations of the periphrastic genitives. The material comprises fiction and nonfiction, as the genitive alternation – visible in the current dataset through translation correspondences – is described as sensitive to register and formality (Biber et al. 1999: 302; Holmes and Enger 2018: 49). The translation alternatives are expected to also be sensitive to the meanings expressed by the periphrastic genitive in both directions of translation.

Considering previous (monolingual) descriptions of the genitive (see Section 3.3), *of*-genitives are expected to be more frequent than *til*-genitives because *of*-genitives seem to be less constrained than *til*-genitives, which in turn may express a more specialized range of meanings. For example, the periphrastic genitive may have alternative prepositions in Norwegian (Mac Donald 1985), whereas the preposition *of* expresses a wide range of meanings (Sinclair 1991). Since *s*-genitives are considered more formal in both languages (Biber et al. 1999: 302; Holmes and Enger 2018: 49), the periphrastic genitive may be preferred in fiction, considering that fiction in general tends 'towards simpler, more colloquial styles' (Biber and Conrad 2019: 245). Finally, the animacy of the possessor seems to favour *s*-genitives in English but not in Norwegian (Section 3.2), which may lead to differences in the frequency of the periphrastic genitive as well as a high number of noncongruent translations.

3.2 Identifying the construct: possessive expressions in English and Norwegian

Despite the present focus on the periphrastic genitive, it is useful to consider this construction in the context of its competitors in both English and Norwegian. As Table 3.1 shows, the means of expressing possessive relations in English and Norwegian are very similar, differing in only two types of expression: the English

Table 3.1 Expressions of possessive relations in English and Norwegian

	English	Norwegian
s-genitive	Apostrophe and suffix *-s*: *Tom's cat*, *the boys' cats*	Suffix *-s*: *Toms katt*, *guttenes katter*
periphrastic genitive	Preposition *of*: *the tail of the cat*	Preposition *til*: *halen til katten*
possessive determiner	Prenominal: *his cat*	Pre- or postnominal: *hans katt*, *katten hans*
possessive pronoun	*The cat is his.*	*Katten er hans.*
double genitive	*of* + *s*: *a cat of Tom's/his*	N.A.
garp genitive	N.A.	Possessor + determiner *sin* + possessum: *Tom sin katt* (Tom his cat)

double genitive and the Norwegian garp genitive, originally borrowed from Low German (Norde 2012).[3] The garp genitive has been described as a dialectal or colloquial alternative to the *s*-genitive (Holmes and Enger 2018: 49). Thus, the languages have the same number of translation alternatives for the periphrastic genitive. However, the typical conditions for choosing between the *s*-genitive and the periphrastic genitive, sometimes seen as (partially) interchangeable in studies of the so-called genitive alternation in English (e.g. Heller, Szmrecsanyi and Grafmiller 2017), appear rather different in the two languages, as detailed below. Notably, the animacy of the possessor favours the *s*-genitive in English (Biber et al. 1999: 302; Rosenbach 2003) but the periphrastic genitive (or the garp genitive) in Norwegian (Norde 2012).

PPs with prepositions other than *til/of* have not been included in Table 3.1. *Til* is generally regarded as the typical expression of the periphrastic genitive in Norwegian (Faarlund, Vannebo and Lie 1997: 263), though Mac Donald (1985: 5–8) describes several alternative prepositions that are found in genitive(-like) expressions, notably *av* (of), *på* (on) and *I* (in); see also Holmes and Enger (2018: 49). English *of* is more ubiquitous in periphrastic genitives. Rosenbach (2014: 221) mentions that *to* can have genitive meaning in expressions like *secretary to the Queen* but that this and other alternatives are marginal. The typical Norwegian preposition for partitive constructions is *av* (cognate with *of*) rather than *til*, and Lødrup (2009) discusses body part relations with *på* (on). See also Julien (2005: 144) for partitive constructions with *av* and *på*, which she regards as a type of possessive PP. While Faarlund, Vannebo and Lie (1997: 440) discuss these separately from possessives, English part-whole constructions tend to be analysed as a type of possessive (e.g. Heine 1997: 35; Keizer 2007: 30). However, like *s*-genitives, PPs with alternative prepositions will be discussed here only to the extent that they occur in translations of *til/of*-genitives (see Section 3.6.2),

3.3 Previous work

A large number of studies have discussed the genitive; in fact, 'genitive variation is arguably the best researched of all syntactic alternations in English' (Rosenbach 2014: 215). This literature review thus cannot hope to be exhaustive, but see Rosenbach (2014) for an excellent survey. The Norwegian genitive alternation has also been studied rather extensively, so the contribution of the present study will be to discover the differences and commonalities between the two systems. The following review will reflect this aim.

In the prototypical instance, possession implies a (human/animate) possessor and an inanimate possessum, with the relationship being a long-term one (Heine 1997: 5). However, not even all instances of so-called inalienable possession (Heine 1997: 10) are fully canonical, for example kinship (both possessor and possessum are human) and part-whole relationships (both possessor and possessum are often inanimate). Conversely, a genitive construction need not have possessive meaning (Lødrup 2012: 192), as in *en ukes ferie* (a week's holiday) (Faarlund, Vannebo and Lie 1997: 255). This is equally the case with the periphrastic genitive, especially in English, as demonstrated by Sinclair's (1991: 81 ff) discussion of the various uses of *of*.

Piotrowska and Skrzypek (2017: 27) observe that 'many languages exhibit possessive splits, that is, different classes of nouns require or favour different possessive constructions'. Such splits may be conditioned for example by the animacy of the possessor or the inalienability of the possessive relationship (Piotrowska and Skrzypek 2017: 27; see also Lødrup 2014). Furthermore, different types of inalienable relationships may allow or prefer different constructions, as seems to be the case with Norwegian kinship and body part relations, of which the former uses the preposition *til* while the latter allows – and often prefers – *på* (on) (Lødrup 2009, 2014).

The genitive alternation in English is known to be impacted by the animacy of the possessor, with human possessors favouring the *s*-genitive and inanimate possessors the *of*-genitive (Biber et al. 1999: 302). Johannessen, Julien and Lødrup (2014: 91) argue that humanness of the possessor is more important than animacy in Norwegian. However, the animacy constraint works differently across languages, even those that are closely related, such as English and Dutch (Rosenbach 2017). Other commonly identified constraints are definiteness and givenness of the possessor and the possessum, length of the NPs, final sibilancy (which may constrain the *s*-genitive), medium (speech vs. writing) and regional variety (Heller, Szmrecsanyi and Grafmiller 2017: 9; Rosenbach 2014: 252 ff). In addition, Mac Donald (1985: 13) observes that the Norwegian *til*-genitive tends to be read as a more literal case of ownership than the *s*-genitive, using the example of *Halleys komet* (Halley's comet). Both medium and style may influence the choice of genitive construction: the Norwegian *s*-genitive has been described as both more formal (Holmes and Enger 2018: 49) and potentially more poetic (Mac Donald 1985) than the periphrastic genitive, and Biber et al. (1999: 301) report that the proportion of *s*-genitives vs. *of*-genitives differ across registers (with academic prose favouring *of* more than the other registers).

Keizer (2007: 310) emphasizes that the constraints on the genitive are not absolute, and that for example an *of*-construction may be perfectly acceptable in a context that normally favours the *s*-genitive. Johannessen, Julien and Lødrup (2014) likewise show that different genitives can occur in similar contexts in Norwegian. Thus, while the existing literature makes it clear that the *s*-genitive and the periphrastic genitive prefer different contexts in English and Norwegian – in particular that inalienable possession favours the *s*-genitive in English and the *til*-genitive in Norwegian – it is also possible that the systems will show areas of overlap. The use of translations may indicate such areas, although Hasselgård (2021: 158) found that postnominal PPs with possessive meaning can be translated both congruently and (most often) noncongruently between English and Norwegian.

3.4 Material and method

This study is based on the English-Norwegian Parallel Corpus (ENPC). The ENPC consists of fifty text extracts in English and fifty in Norwegian, each of 12,000–15,000 words in length, plus translations into the other language.[4] Thirty represent fiction and twenty nonfiction (Johansson 2007: 13), and each text is accompanied by a published translation into the other language (Johansson 2007: 12). The corpus is bidirectional and balanced, thus having similar numbers of words in the two languages. Table 3.2 shows the size and structure of the source language parts of the corpus, which were the basis for the searches (see below). The word counts were performed in AntConc (Anthony 2019) and differ from Johansson's (2007: 14) figures. This was done to enable counts per corpus text.

The corpus was accessed through the search interface Glossa (Johannessen et al. 2008), in which the English texts are tagged with the TreeTagger[5] and the Norwegian texts with the Oslo Bergen Tagger (Johannessen et al. 2012). Searches

Table 3.2 The size and structure of the English-Norwegian Parallel Corpus (original texts only)

	Number of words	Number of texts	Mean text length	S.D.
English fiction	419,449	30	13,982	1,342
English nonfiction	250,937	20	12,547	2,095
Norwegian fiction	407,835	30	13,594	1,578
Norwegian nonfiction	221,681	20	11,084	3,314

were made for nouns directly followed by the prepositions *of* and *til*. This search string gave good recall, but poor precision, and it was necessary to clean up the concordances manually to exclude non-possessive meanings.

An important rule of thumb for inclusion was the possibility of paraphrasing the expression as 'N1 belongs to N2', 'N2 has N1', or an *s*-genitive. For example, *the collar of her shirt* can be paraphrased as *the collar belongs to her shirt, her blue shirt has a collar*, or *her shirt's collar* (although not all are equally idiomatic). It was not necessary for a phrase to be paraphraseable in all three ways in order to be included since the main object of study is the periphrastic genitive rather than the genitive alternation (Rosenbach 2003: 382). Thus, unlike, for example, Heller, Szmrecsanyi and Grafmiller (2017: 4) and other studies mentioned therein, the material for this study is not restricted to periphrastic genitives that are interchangeable with *s*-genitives. However, all non-possessive occurrences of N + *of*/*til* were omitted, that is, cases where the N2 cannot plausibly be interpreted as the possessor of the N1. This excludes most nominalizations, since the N2 cannot usually be interpreted as a possessor (as in for example *the restoration of the government, the hopelessness of his needs*). Similarly, most support noun constructions (Sinclair 1991: 89), such as *an act of vandalism*, cannot be understood in terms of possessum – possessor. Most combinations expressing a part-whole relationship were retained, but notably not those where the possessum can be said to mainly 'focus on a part' (Sinclair 1991: 87), as in *the beginning/middle/end of*; that is, the possessum is a less specific part of the whole than for instance in *the collar of her shirt*. The reason is that these often correspond to adverbial expressions in Norwegian (Hasselgård 2016) and are thus poor candidates for a cross-linguistic study of genitive expressions. The Norwegian preposition *til* often occurs postnominally with its directional meaning corresponding to English *to*. Such cases were excluded, except some cases where the preposition seemed ambiguous between a possessive and a directional reading, as in *inngangen til huset* (the entrance to/of the house).

The following types of expression were also excluded: double genitives (e.g. *a friend of hers*), quantifying expressions (e.g. *a couple of, a cup of, the rest of*), names and titles (e.g. *the king of England, University of Oxford*), cases where the N2 is a time expression (e.g. *the election of 1939*), cases where the prepositional complement is not an NP or where *of* denotes 'made of', and cases without a translation of the source sentence. Furthermore, lexicalized/grammaticalized expressions such as *kind of, sort of, in the course of, in front of, in the case of* and *in spite of* were excluded. The remaining concordances were annotated with the following information:

1. Animacy of N1 (possessum) and N2 (possessor)
2. Meaning relation between N1 and N2 (e.g. kinship, body part)
3. Congruence in translation (congruent – noncongruent – zero)
4. Correspondence in translation (e.g. s-genitive, PP with other prepositions…)

For example, the translation pair *the descendants of Abraham – Abrahams etterkommere* (Abraham's descendants) was classified as follows: N1 and N2 are +animate and +human. The meaning relation between them is one of kinship. The translation is noncongruent (*s*-genitive). Table 3.3 shows the meaning relations that were recognized between the N1 and the N2 in the material with examples from both languages. The list of meanings draws on Aikhenvald (2019), Sinclair (1991) and Hasselgård (2016).

Because of the great number of English examples (Table 3.4), random samples of 250 from each of English fiction and nonfiction were used for most of the qualitative analyses. The randomization was done in Excel.

Table 3.3 Possessive meaning relations

Relation	Explanation	Examples
Body / body parts	N1 is the body or a body part of N2	*the head of the woman*; *øynene til Tor* (the eyes of Tor)
Feature	N1 is feature or attribute of N2	*the weight of a child*; *navnet til foreldrene* (the name of the parents)
Kinship	N1 is related to N2	*son of the physician*; *faren til Eva* (the father of Eva)
Part of whole	N1 is a part of N2	*the roof of our truck*; *kronene til trærne* (the crowns of the trees)
People[6]	similar to kinship, but not family	*the neighbours of his pupils*; *vennen til prinsen* (the friend of the prince)
Place	N1 is located in/near N2	*the garden of no. 19*; *døren til kjøkkenet* (the door of the kitchen)
Property	N2 owns N1	*the farms of his neighbours*; *sykkelen til Johannes* (the bike of Johannes)
Sentiment	N1 is N2's feeling/reaction	*the anguish of his parents*; *latteren til Jo* (the laughter of Jo)
Other	Miscellaneous, often more abstract relationships	*the history of the city*; *the wages of sin*; *antitesen til det golde landet* (the antithesis of the barren land)

3.5 Contrastive analysis

3.5.1 Corpus frequencies

As expected, the *of*-genitive is much more frequent than the *til*-genitive in both fiction and nonfiction, as shown in Table 3.4. The periphrastic genitive is more frequent in nonfiction than in fiction in English, while in Norwegian, the reverse is the case.

While Table 3.4 shows the raw and normalized frequencies of periphrastic genitives and their mean frequencies per text, Figure 3.1 visualizes their dispersion across corpus texts. The 95 per cent confidence limits are non-overlapping between English and Norwegian and between English fiction and

Table 3.4 Frequencies of periphrastic genitives in English and Norwegian fiction and nonfiction

	N	Freq per 10k	Mean per text (per 10k)
English fiction	1,510	36.0	35.93
English nonfiction	1,851	73.8	75.91
Norwegian fiction	323	7.9	8.12
Norwegian nonfiction	111	5.0	4.45

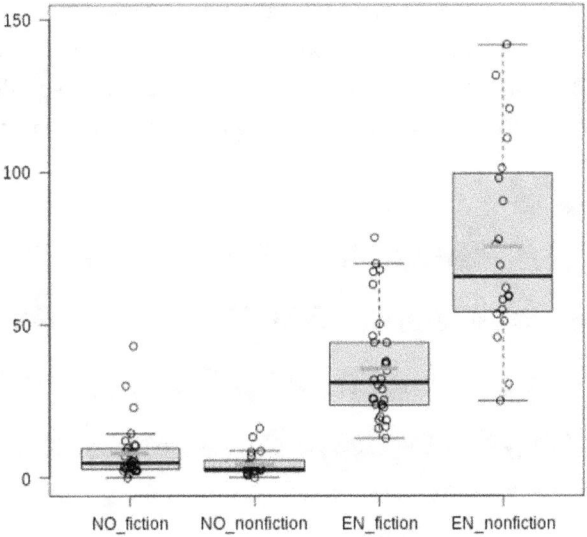

Figure 3.1 Dispersion of the Norwegian *til*-genitive and the English *of*-genitive (frequencies per 10,000 words per text).

nonfiction.[7] There is great intertextual variation as to the frequencies of the periphrastic genitive in all four sub-corpora.

The cross-linguistic difference is smaller in fiction than in nonfiction, and the outliers in Norwegian fiction are within the interquartile range of English fiction. The two texts with the highest frequencies of *til*-genitives are novels in which the topics of kinship, property and the human body are prominent. Similar topics are found in the two nonfiction texts with the highest frequencies of *til*-genitives. The English fiction text with the highest number of *of*-genitives (JH1) revolves around a painting of Aristotle by Rembrandt, which is reflected in many of the genitives, for example, *the wishes of the artist, the golden age of Athens*. Likewise, the uppermost outlier in English nonfiction (KA1) has a good number of genitives that reflect its topic of the 'History of God', for example, *the God of Israel*. While some of the textual variation within each sub-corpus can presumably be explained by topic, the cross-linguistic difference clearly cannot. The following sections will present a qualitative analysis of the meaning relations expressed by periphrastic genitives and the animacy of the possessor.

3.5.2 Possessive relations and periphrastic genitives

The entire Norwegian material and random samples of 250 concordance lines from each of English fiction and nonfiction were analysed in terms of the meaning relation between the nouns preceding and following the prepositions *til* and *of*. See Section 3.4 for explanations of the categories. The results are displayed in Figure 3.2, with a bar chart showing both raw frequencies and proportions.

Figure 3.2 shows that the Norwegian *til*-genitive most typically expresses kinship and ownership (property). Norwegian fiction also has a substantial

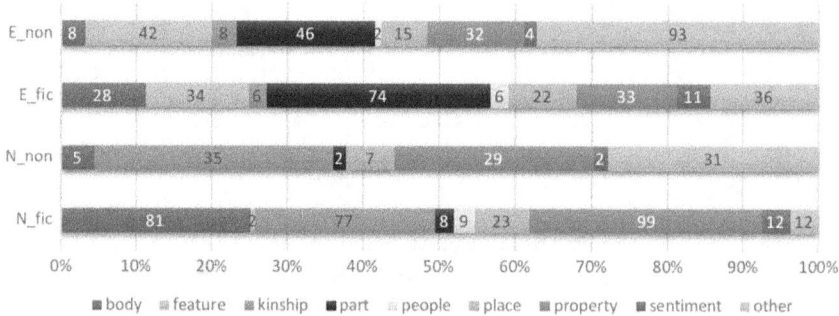

Figure 3.2 Possessive relations in periphrastic genitives (figures for English from random samples of 250).

proportion of body part relations. The part-whole relationship is more salient with *of*-genitives than with *til*-genitives. The feature relation is also more common in English, as is the category of 'other', which typically refers to some abstract relationship between N1 and N2 (often because at least one of the nouns is abstract). Some meanings are generally infrequent in the material, especially 'people' and 'sentiment'.

The kinship relation takes up similar proportions of Norwegian fiction and nonfiction. It should be noted, however, that nineteen of the thirty-five kinship expressions in nonfiction come from a text entitled *Children and parents – The relationship between children and parents according to Norwegian law*. Example (4) illustrates the style of this text. Yet, even without this text, the proportion of kinship expressions is greater in Norwegian nonfiction than in English fiction and nonfiction alike.

(4) Prinsippet om at morens ektemann blir *far til de barn hun føder*, er nå slått fast i B §3. Her heter det: 'Som *far til barnet* skal reknast den mannen som mora er gift med ved fødselen.' (LSPL1)
(... father of those children she bears ... father of the child ...)[8]
The principle stating that the mother's husband is the father of the children she bears is laid down in B sec. 3. This section states that: 'The man to whom the mother is married at the time of the birth will be considered to be the child's father.' (LSPL1T)

There are register differences in both languages, in particular body (part) relations are more frequent in fiction, while the 'other' category is more frequent in nonfiction.

3.5.3 Animacy of the possessor

This section presents findings concerning the animacy of the possessor. Human possessors have been distinguished from other types of animates. As Figure 3.3 shows, the languages differ in this respect.

As expected from the works cited in Sections 3.2 and 3.3, the possessor is most often inanimate in *of*-genitives, but most commonly animate and human in *til*-genitives. All three types of possessors are, however, found in both languages and both registers. Especially in Norwegian fiction, the proportion of inanimate possessors is very low (c. 13 per cent) with examples often denoting part-whole relationships or spatial relations, as illustrated by (5). The preposition *til* is

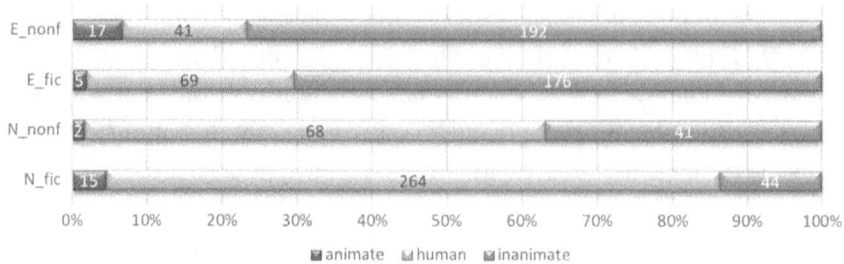

Figure 3.3 Animacy of possessor (N2). Random sample of 250 for English.

admittedly ambiguous here between a possessive and a directional reading, but the translator has opted for a possessive expression.

(5) På *inngangsdøren til huset* stod messingskiltet som ble pusset hver uke... (EFH1)
(On the entrance door of the house stood the brass plate...)
On the front door of the house hung the brass plate, which was polished every week... (EFH1T)

The proportion of non-human animate possessors is low in all four sub-corpora, which may be due simply to the scarce presence of such participants in most texts. An example from English nonfiction is given in (6), from a book called *Animalwatching – Field Guide to Animal Behaviour*, whose topic clearly promotes non-human animate possessors.

(6) *The main prey of predatory birds* are the hundreds of different rodent species (DM1)
Rovfuglenes viktigste byttedyr er de hundrevis av forskjellige gnagerarter (DM1T)
(The predatory birds' most important prey are ...)

Nonfiction has a greater share than fiction of inanimate possessors in both languages, although the heterogeneity of the nonfiction category of the ENPC makes it hard to say why this should be the case. It may, however, be instructive to explore the animacy of possessors in the context of their meaning relations with the possessum. Table 3.5 shows the three most frequent meaning relations in each sub-corpus with animate (including human) and inanimate possessors,

Table 3.5 The most frequent meaning relations with animate and inanimate possessors (raw frequencies)

		English fiction		English nonfiction		Norwegian fiction		Norwegian nonfiction	
Animate possessor		property	25	other	22	property	94	kinship	34
		body	22	property	12	body	80	property	25
		sentiment	11	body	7	kinship	76	other	5
Inanimate possessor		part	74	other	71	place	22	other	26
		other	33	part	46	part	8	place	7
		feature	31	feature	37	other	6	property	5

respectively. The frequencies are given in raw numbers because the main point is the ranked frequency of the meaning categories.

As Table 3.5 shows, animate and inanimate possessors favour different types of possessive relationships. For rather obvious reasons, the body part, kinship and sentiment relations figure more prominently with animate possessors in both languages (although the latter, illustrated in (7), reaches the top three only in English fiction). Kinship terms reach the top three only in Norwegian.[9] To the extent that body, sentiment and kinship occur at all with inanimate possessors it is in metaphorical or abstract expressions such as *ansiktet til månen* (the face of the moon) and *children of the Iliad*. The property relation is also most common with animate possessors, as in (8), from Norwegian fiction.

(7) that Dickens had had such an acute understanding of *the misery of boys*. (AB1)
at Dickens hadde en slik inngående forståelse for *gutters elendighet*.
(... understanding of boys' misery.)

(8) En av dem får tak i *øksa til tømmermannen*. (KH1)
(One of them gets hold of the axe of the carpenter.)
But then one of them got hold of an axe belonging to the carpenter. (KH1T)

On the other hand, part-whole relationships (other than body parts) are more common with inanimate possessors in both languages. Examples are given in (9) and (10), which are fairly typical of this category.

(9) On *the walls of the apartment* there were photographs of his family, his colleagues, his pupils, himself. (OS1)
På veggene i leiligheten var det fotografier av hans familie, kolleger, studenter og av ham selv. (OS1T)
(On the walls in the apartment...)

(10) Det er svalt og skyggefullt under *kronene til de høye trærne*. (TB1)
    (It is cool and shady under the crowns of the tall trees.)
    It's cool and shady under the tall tree crowns. (TB1T)

The feature relation figures prominently with inanimate possessors in English, as in (11), but not in Norwegian, where, by contrast, the place relation is more salient, as in (12). With place relations, the preposition *til* can be ambiguous between possessive and directional meaning, as indicated by the choice of *to* rather than *of* in the translation (but compare example (5)). The 'other' relation prefers inanimate possessors in both languages, especially in nonfiction. An example is given in (13).

(11) Then Big Ben spoke: BONG, *the thunderous boom of the first stroke of midnight*. (FF1)
    Så lød kvartslagene, og etter en ørliten pause kom Great Tom: BONG... det første tordnende midnattsslaget. (FF1T)
    (... the first thunderous midnightstroke.)
(12) *Inngangen til hovedhuset* hadde solide portaler... (HW2)
    (The entrance of/to the main house had solid portals...)
    The entrance to the main house was solid and imposing... (HW2)
(13) Fruktbarhetssymbolikken er *motstykket til forestillingen om det golde landet*, på samme måte som i T. S. Eliots The Waste Land. (JEEH1)
    The symbol of fertility is *the counterpart of the notion of the barren land*, just as it is in T. S. Eliot's The Waste Land. (JEEH1T)

3.6 Translation correspondences

3.6.1 Congruence in translation

The cross-linguistic differences described above would suggest that the two periphrastic genitive constructions are rarely each other's best translation option. An analysis of congruence in the translations confirms that this is indeed the case. The translations were classified as congruent (cf. Johansson 2007: 25) in the cases where the *of*-genitive was translated as a *til*-genitive and vice versa. All other overt translations were classified as noncongruent. Zero translations are those in which the translation did not contain a corresponding possessive construction. The results are shown in Figure 3.4.

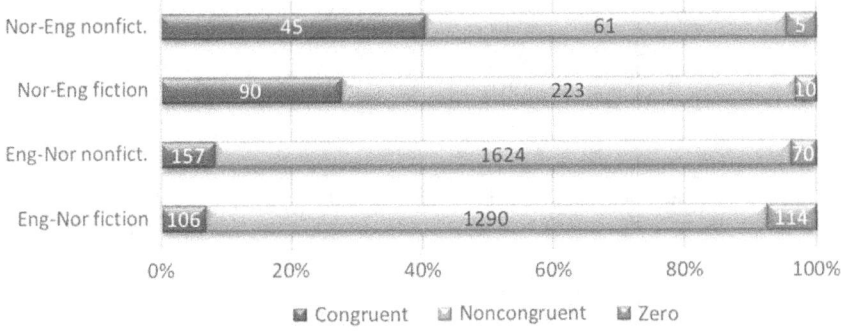

Figure 3.4 Congruent and noncongruent translation correspondences (complete dataset).

The high frequency of noncongruent translations gives a low degree of mutual correspondence (MC) between the *of*-genitive and the *til*-genitive. According to the formula for mutual correspondence in a bidirectional translation corpus, first presented in Altenberg (1999), the MC values for fiction and nonfiction are 10.7 and 10.3 per cent, respectively. Zero correspondences are relatively rare, and usually linked to the omission of *one* of the nouns in the periphrastic genitive construction in the source, as in (14).

(14) She *touched the soft material of the shawl* on both my shoulders. (TH1)
 Så rørte hun lett ved *det myke stoffet* [Ø].
 (Then she touched lightly at the soft material)

The degree of congruence varies considerably across corpus texts, as shown in Figure 3.5. The input for the figure was the percentage of periphrastic genitives per text that had a congruent translation. Figure 3.5 shows even more clearly than Figure 3.4 that the degree of congruence is not symmetrical between the two directions of translation: translations into English are congruent more often than translations into Norwegian.

The very different interquartile ranges shown in Figure 3.5 indicate that translations from English into Norwegian are more similar as regards congruence (0–16 per cent + outlier 33 per cent) than translations from Norwegian into English (0–100 per cent congruence). Note, however, that the percentages of congruent translation from Norwegian are based on very low numbers. For example, of the two texts with 100 per cent congruent English translations of Norwegian nonfiction, one has a single *til*-genitive, and the other has three.

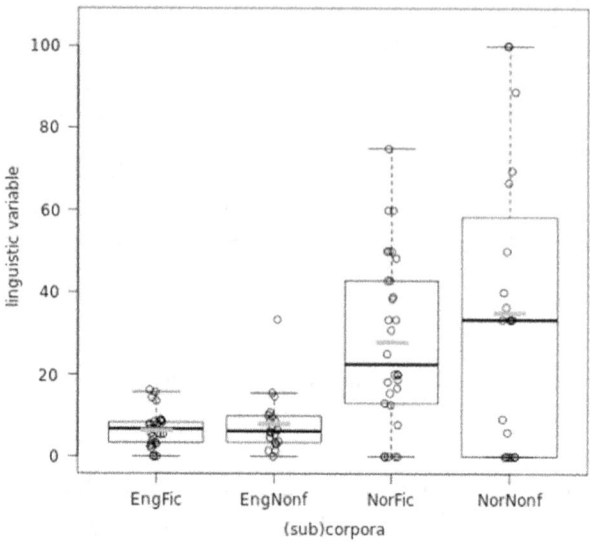

Figure 3.5 Distribution of congruent translations (*til* = *of*) across corpus texts (percentages)

Although the translations have all appeared in published texts, some of the congruent translations into English display 'shining through' of the original, that is, in contexts of possessor animacy and meaning relations where the two languages have been shown to differ in the use of periphrastic genitives. Examples (15) and (16) both have animate possessors; (15) expresses kinship and (16) property. The translations are not wrong, but are more typical of the ways the *til*-genitive is used than of the *of*-genitive in original texts.

(15) Det var hos Gerda tvers over veien, *kona til Johan Olsa*. (PEJ1)
 That was at Gerda's, right across the road, *the wife of Johan Olsa*. (PEJ1T)
(16) Huset ligger nå i tverrgata, men opprinnelig lå det i *bakgården til Bergseng*, med inngang fra Jernbanegaten. (AOH1)
 (... but originally it lay in the backyard of Bergseng...)
 It now stands in the crossroad, but originally stood in *the backyard of Bergseng*, with its entrance from Jernbanegata. (AOH1T)

3.6.1.1 *Meaning relations and congruence*

Not all meaning relations can easily be translated congruently. Table 3.6 shows the percentages of congruent translations among those meaning relations that

Table 3.6 Meaning relations and congruence (percentages, English samples)

%congr	N_fic > E	N_nonf > E	E_fic > N	E_nonf > N
body	30.86	20	25	37.5
kinship	22.07	48.57	33.33	25
other	36.36	40	6.06	7.5
place	39.13	28.57	27.27	6.67
property	20.2	41.38	21.21	21.88
sentiment	58.33	*100*	27.27	*50*

occur more than ten times in the source texts and that have at least one congruent translation. For the total frequencies of each meaning category, see Figure 3.2. The percentages printed in italics have been calculated from totals of less than ten, and should thus be interpreted with great caution.

The numbers underlying the percentages in Table 3.6 are very low (see Figures 3.2 and 3.4), so no firm conclusions can be drawn. The highest percentage in the non-shaded cells, sentiment in Norwegian fiction, reflects only seven out of twelve translations. However, the body part and property relations appear a bit more likely than the other meanings to be translated congruently in both directions of translation. They can therefore tentatively be said to be most similar between the languages, although at least two-thirds of them are translated noncongruently. Place and 'other' are more often translated congruently from Norwegian to English than vice versa. Likewise, many kinship expressions are translated congruently from Norwegian to English, while the figures in the other direction are too low for percentages to be reliable.

3.6.1.2 Animacy of possessor and congruence

As animacy of the possessor was one of the noted differences between the English and the Norwegian, it is interesting to see whether this factor makes a difference for congruence in translation. Figure 3.6 shows that the proportions of congruent and noncongruent translations are fairly similar with both types of possessors. In all cases, the vast majority of translations are noncongruent (as expected in view of Figure 3.4), though with a higher percentage of congruence in translations from Norwegian into English. However, there is a slightly higher percentage of congruent translations if the Norwegian source has an inanimate possessor (as is the main tendency for *of*-genitives), and conversely, if the English source has an animate possessor (as it the main tendency for *til*-genitives).

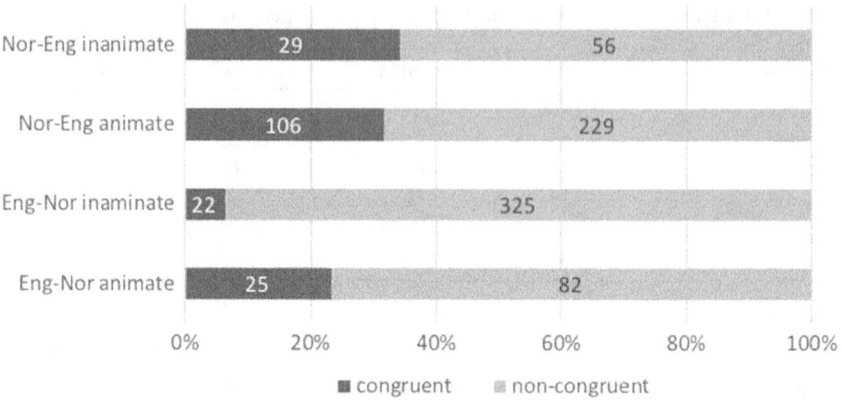

Figure 3.6 Percentages of animate and inanimate possessors in congruent and noncongruent translations between Norwegian and English (English samples).

3.6.2 Types of noncongruent correspondences

The formal types of noncongruent translation correspondences are displayed in Table 3.7. The *s*-genitive is a frequent choice across the board. Norwegian translators, however, turn to PPs with prepositions other than *til* even more often. Other types of possessive constructions are rare.

Only the most frequent noncongruent correspondence types will be discussed here, namely paraphrases, *s*-genitives and PPs with prepositions other than *of/til*. Paraphrases are extremely common in translations into Norwegian. They comprise a variety of expressions, some of which reflect the productivity of noun compounding in Norwegian (Holmes and Enger 2018: 458), for example, *the froth of the Guinness* → *Guinness-skummet* (the Guinness-froth). Other frequent types are NPs with premodifiers, for example, *the splendour of the meal* → *det praktfulle måltidet* (the splendid meal), or with a postmodifier which is not a PP, for example, *the railings of the medieval washing place* → *gjerdet som omga den*

Table 3.7 Noncongruent translation correspondences of the periphrastic genitive (complete dataset)

	Norwegian to English		English to Norwegian	
	Fiction	Nonfiction	Fiction	Nonfiction
s-genitive	169	26	285	614
other preposition	22	15	605	658
poss determiner	1	1	1	4
double genitive	1	0	0	0
garp genitive	0	0	0	1
paraphrase	31	19	398	346

middelalderske vaskeplassen (the fence that surrounded the medieval washing place). Compounds and postmodifying clauses are also found in translations into English, for example, *kontoret til selskapet* (the office of the company → the company office; *øksa til tømmermannen* (the axe of the carpenter) → *an axe belonging to the carpenter*.

Considering the differences in genitive alternation in the two languages (Section 3.3), it is no surprise that *s*-genitives are a frequent correspondence of periphrastic genitives in both directions of translation. Almost all the English *s*-genitives translated from Norwegian *til*-genitives have an animate, mostly human, possessor. Conversely, the majority of Norwegian *s*-genitives coming from English *of*-genitives have an inanimate possessor, although the tendency is less massive than in translations from Norwegian into English. As noted above (Section 3.2), the Norwegian *s*-genitive occurs with animate and inanimate possessors alike (Faarlund, Vannebo and Lie 1997: 258).

S-genitives occur as English translations of Norwegian *til*-genitives in between 50 and 60 per cent of the cases where the meaning relation between N1 and N2 is body, kinship or property as shown in (17), (18) and (19), respectively.

(17) Glenn holder *hodet til Herman* (LSC1)
(Glenn holds the head of Herman)
Glenn holds *Herman's head* (LSC1T)
(18) ... *moren til Hildegun* var i kirken. (BV1)
(the mother of Hildegun was in the church)
Hildegun's mother was in church. (BV1T)
(19) Han går forbi *hyttene til Rachel* (TB1)
(He walks past the huts of Rachel)
He walks past *Rachel's huts* (TB1T)

In translations from English into Norwegian, the most frequent meaning category among the *s*-genitives (48 per cent) is 'other', followed by property (45 per cent), as in (20) and (21). English body relations are translated as s-genitives in ten out of thirty-six cases (28 per cent), as in (22).

(20) ... the explosive social power of the word, written or spoken. (RF1)
... det talte og skrevne ords sosiale sprengkraft. (RF1T)
(the spoken and written word's social explosion-power)
(21) ... the territory of the EFTA States (AEEA1)
... EFTA-statenes territorium (AEEA1T)
(the EFTA-states' territory)

(22) At night *the eyes of the goddess* shone like moonstones. (BO1)
    Om natten skinte *gudinnens øyne* som månestein. (BO1T)
    (... the goddess's eyes ...)

It is interesting that periphrastic expressions of property and body relations can be translated as *s*-genitives into both languages. In translations into English this typically happens where the possessor is human, as in (17) and (19), as a reflection of the preference for the *s*-genitive with human possessors (Biber et al. 1999: 302) and a relation of inalienable possession such as body parts and kinship (Heine 1997: 10). *S*-genitives were found as Norwegian translations of *of*-genitives with both animate and inanimate possessors and may reflect the greater flexibility of the Norwegian *s*-genitive to occur with different types of possessors (Faarlund, Vannebo and Lie 1997: 258), as illustrated by (20)–(22).

Translations of the periphrastic genitive with a different type of PP than *of/til* occur very often in Norwegian translations from English, but are rare in the other direction of translation. This can be linked to the wider meaning of *of* compared to *til* (Section 3.2). Table 3.8 shows the prepositions that occur in the translations.

Many of the Norwegian prepositions have a locative meaning, as indicated by the glosses. This suggests that the relation between N1 and N2 may be interpreted as spatial rather than one of possession. Example (23) is a case in point, illustrating the most frequent preposition in the material, *i* (in).[10]

(23) *The door of* Number Eleven opened... (ST1)
    Døren *i* nr. 11 ble slått opp... (ST1T)
    (The door in No.11 was thrust open...)

Table 3.8 Prepositions corresponding to *of/til* in noncongruent translations of the periphrastic genitive (raw frequencies, complete dataset)

	English to Norwegian			Norwegian to English	
	fiction	nonfiction		fiction	nonfiction
av (of, off)	194	182	*at*	3	
etter (after)	3	6	*for*	5	6
for (for)	60	23	*from*	1	
fra (from)	36	29	*on*	2	
hos (by, with)	34	10	*to*	9	9
i (in)	220	203	*with*	2	
med (with)	13	4			
på (on)	57	120			
ved (at, by)	31	15			
other	10	13			

(24) the wrong *side of* the box (RDO1)
   den gale *siden av* esken (RDO1T)

As noted above, the idiomatic Norwegian preposition in most part-whole relationships is *av*, as shown in (24) and reflected by the frequency of this preposition in Table 3.8. Furthermore, *av* occurs regularly in kinship expressions when the first noun is indefinite, as in (25), as opposed to the use of *til* when the first noun is definite, as in (18) above.

(25) Rafael var, ifølge Vasari, *sønn av* en temmelig middelmådig maler. (ANR1)
   Vasari relates that Raphael was *the son of* a very mediocre painter. (ANR1T)

The English prepositions *to* and *for* are the most recurrent ones. They are believed to reflect the ambiguity of the Norwegian preposition *til* as a marker of possession, direction and beneficiary, as indicated by (26)–(27)

(26) Hun åpner *døren til* venteværelset... (LSC1)
   She opens *the door to* the waiting room... (LSC1)
(27) ...arbeidet hun med *støvlene til* veslebroren. (MN1)
   (worked she with *the boots of* the little brother)
   ...she had worked on *the boots for* Little Brother. (MN1T)

In some cases the change of preposition reflects idiomaticity, for example, the Norwegian *noten til Les Plaintes d'ùne Poupèe* being translated as *the music for Les Plaintes d'ùne Poupèe* and the English *the man of the house* becoming *mannen i huset* (the man in the house). In both cases, a different choice preposition would have looked odd.

3.7 Concluding remarks

Johansson (2012: 47) observes that 'formal similarity is no guarantee that there is identity of use'. The *s*-genitive and the periphrastic genitive in English and Norwegian are a prime example of this. It is puzzling that two languages with such similar resources for expressing possessive relationships have almost diametrically opposed rules for the use of the *s*-genitive and the periphrastic genitive. A striking cross-linguistic difference is that the periphrastic *of*-genitive is vastly more frequent than the *til*-genitive, to an even greater extent than expected. The two registers differed as to the frequency of periphrastic genitives in both languages, but the register differences showed opposite patterns with more *til*-genitives in fiction and more *of*-genitives in nonfiction. However, the frequency of periphrastic genitives also appears to be influenced by topic, so the register feature needs to be investigated further. As for semantic features of the possessive constructions, the *til*-genitive was found to be typical of animate possessors, whereas the *of*-genitive is typical of inanimate possessors. Furthermore, the *til*-genitive often refers to inalienable possession (Heine 1997; Johannessen, Julien and Lødrup 2014), except part-whole relationships that do not involve human possessors. This shows up clearly in kinship genitives and their translations. The English *of*-genitive generally expresses a wider range of meanings than the *til*-genitive. Again, part-whole relationships are a case in point, where Norwegian typically uses *av* not *til*. Another is when Norwegian uses a locative preposition in a possessive(-like) relation between an N1 and an N2.

The high degree of noncongruent translations was expected (Hasselgård 2021) but can now with more certainty be linked to the animacy of possessor and type of possessive relation. For example, the fact that the *til*-genitive and the English *s*-genitive are both typical of inalienable possession with animate possessors explains the frequent use of the English *s*-genitive for translating Norwegian *til*-genitives. The frequent use of prepositions other than *til* in Norwegian translations of the *of*-genitive reflects the variety of prepositions used in Norwegian constructions generally (Mac Donald 1985; Johannessen, Julien and Lødrup 2014; Holmes and Enger 2018) and suggests that the Norwegian *til*-genitive is less grammaticalized and stable than the English *of*-genitive. Moreover, it may indicate that possessive-like relations are seen in terms of location, considering the literal, directional meaning of *til* as well as the meanings of the prepositions used in translation.

Another frequent type of translation correspondence was the use of paraphrases such as compound nouns (especially Eng-Nor), premodifying adjectives and nouns, and postmodifying clauses. The relations most likely to receive a congruent translation were property relations (with human possessors) and body part relations, suggesting some degree of commonality in this area. However, even these are translated noncongruently most of the time. On the whole, translations into English showed a higher degree of congruence than translations into Norwegian, sometimes suggesting translation effects.

While the present study has uncovered some systematic differences between *til*-genitives and *of*-genitives, it has several limitations which may give rise to further studies. For example, the lack of focus on *s*-genitives in original texts gives only a partial insight into cross-linguistic differences in genitive alternations. Furthermore, the heterogeneity of the nonfiction part of the ENPC calls for closer inspection of nonfictional registers. It would be particularly interesting to look at those registers where one type of genitive is prevalent, such as academic writing for the *of*-genitive and news for the *s*-genitive (Biber et al. 1999: 301) to further explore the extent of variability. In addition, the variables of givenness and length of the NPs involved in a genitive expression have been discussed in the literature, especially on the English genitive, but have not been investigated here. In other words, this study has only taken some small steps into this rich area of research. Rosenbach (2014: 245) concedes that '[t]he more we learn about English genitive variation, the more new questions and directions emerge'. This is unquestionably true from a cross-linguistic perspective.

Notes

1 The examples are from the English-Norwegian Parallel Corpus (ENPC, see Section 3.4). In each case the original appears before its translation. Norwegian examples are followed by a literal translation in brackets except when the corpus translations are fairly literal. The tags after the examples refer to corpus texts; those ending in 'T' are from translations. Italics have been added for emphasis.
2 After proper nouns ending in -*s*, an apostrophe is used instead of the suffix (Holmes and Enger 2018: 47).
3 A similar construction existed in sixteenth- and seventeenth-century English according to Altenberg (1982: 44), who calls it the 'his'-genitive, exemplified by, for example, *Holmes his ship* and *my Lord's were disabled*.
4 One Norwegian nonfiction text has only 1,201 words.
5 See www.cis.uni-muenchen.de/~schmid/tools/TreeTagger/.
6 The kinship and people categories were kept apart in spite of their similarity of meaning in case there were cross-linguistic differences in the expression of them.
7 The plot was made with Lancaster Stats Tools Online: http://corpora.lancs.ac.uk/stats/toolbox.php (Brezina 2018).
8 Kinship expressions are exempt from the general requirement that the possessum NP should have definite form (Johannessen, Julien and Lødrup 2014: 72).
9 As noted above, many Norwegian kinship genitives occur in a single nonfiction text, but even disregarding this text, kinship would be at rank 2 with animate possessors (fifteen examples).
10 *Til* would have been an equally acceptable alternative here, but not *av* (unlike the next example).

Corpus

English-Norwegian Parallel Corpus (ENPC). http://www.hf.uio.no/ilos/english/services/omc/, accessed through Glossa at https://tekstlab.uio.no/glossa2/omc4

References

Aikhenvald, A. Y. (2019), 'Expressing "Possession": Motivations, Meanings, and Forms', in L. Johanson et al. (eds), *Possession in Languages of Europe and North and Central Asia*, 7–25, Amsterdam: John Benjamins.

Altenberg, B. (1982), *The Genitive v. the of-Construction. A Study of Syntactic Variation in 17th Century English*, Lund Studies in English 62, Lund: CWK Gleerup.

Altenberg, B. (1999), 'Adverbial Connectors in English and Swedish: Semantic and Lexical Correspondences', in H. Hasselgård and S. Oksefjell (eds), *Out of Corpora. Studies in Honour of Stig Johansson*, 249–68, Amsterdam: Rodopi.

Anthony, L. (2019), *AntConc* (Version 3.5.8) [Computer Software], Tokyo: Waseda University. https://www.laurenceanthony.net/software

Biber, D. and S. Conrad (2019), *Register, Genre and Style*, Second edn, Cambridge: Cambridge University Press.

Biber, D., S. Johansson, G. Leech, S. Conrad and E. Finegan (1999), *Longman Grammar of Spoken and Written English*, Harlow: Longman.

Brezina, V. (2018), *Statistics in Corpus Linguistics: A Practical Guide*, Cambridge: Cambridge University Press.

Faarlund, J. T., K. I. Vannebo and S. Lie (1997), *Norsk Referansegrammatikk*, Oslo: Universitetsforlaget.

Hasselgård, H. (2016), 'The Way of the World: The Colligational Framework "the N1 of the N2" and its Norwegian Correspondences', *Nordic Journal of English Studies*, 15 (3): 55–79.

Hasselgård, H. (2021), 'Lexicogrammar through Colligation: Noun + Preposition in English and Norwegian', in A. Čermáková, S. O. Ebeling, M. Levin and J. Ström Herold (eds), *Crossing the Borders: Complex Contrastive Data and the Next Generation. Bergen Language and Linguistics Studies (BeLLS)*, 11 (1): 145–61.

Heine, B. (1997), *Possession. Cognitive Sources, Forces and Grammaticalization*, Cambridge: Cambridge University Press.

Heller, B., B. Szmrecsanyi and J. Grafmiller (2017), 'Stability and Fluidity in Syntactic Variation World-wide: The Genitive Alternation across Varieties of English', *Journal of English Linguistics*, 45 (1): 3–27.

Holmes, P. and H.-O. Enger (2018), *Norwegian. A Comprehensive Grammar*, Abingdon: Routledge.

Johannessen, J. B., K. Hagen, A. Lynum and A. Nøklestad (2012), 'OBT+stat. A Combined Rule-based and Statistical Tagger', in G. Andersen (ed.), *Exploring Newspaper Language. Corpus Compilation and Research Based on the Norwegian Newspaper Corpus*, 51–65, Amsterdam: John Benjamins.

Johannessen, J. B., M. Julien and H. Lødrup (2014), 'Preposisjoner og Eierskapsrelasjoner: et Menneskesentrert Hierarki', in K. Hagen and J.B. Johannessen (eds), *Språk i Norge og nabolanda*, 65–97, Oslo: Novus forlag.

Johannessen, J. B., L. Nygaard, J. Priestley and A. Nøklestad (2008), 'Glossa: A Multilingual, Multimodal, Configurable User Interface', in *Proceedings of the 6th International Conference on Language Resources and Evaluation*, 617–22. http://urn.nb.no/URN:NBN:no-46163

Johansson, S. (2007), *Seeing through Multilingual Corpora*, Amsterdam: Benjamins.

Johansson, S. (2012), 'Cross-linguistic Perspectives', in M. Kytö (ed.), *English Corpus Linguistics: Crossing Paths*, 45–68, Amsterdam: Rodopi.

Julien, M. (2005), *Nominal Phrases from a Scandinavian Perspective*, Amsterdam: John Benjamins.

Keizer, E. (2007), *The English Noun Phrase. The Nature of Linguistic Categorization*, Cambridge: Cambridge University Press.

Lødrup, H. (2009), 'External and Internal Possessors with Body Part Nouns: The Case of Norwegian', *SKY Journal of Linguistics*, 22: 221–50.

Lødrup, H. (2012), 'Forholdet mellom prenominale og postnominale possessive uttrykk', in H.-O. Enger, J. T. Faarlund and K. I. Vannebo (eds), *Grammatikk, Bruk og Norm. Festskrift til Svein Lie på 70-årsdagen, 15. april 2012*, 189–203, Oslo: Novus Forlag.

Lødrup, H. (2014), 'Split Possession and the Syntax of Kinship Nouns in Norwegian', *The Journal of Comparative Germanic Linguistics*, 17 (1): 35–57.

Mac Donald, K. (1985), 'Verden Ligger for Føttene til Liv Ullmann. Om Preposisjoner som Alternativ til Genitiv', *NOA – Norsk som andrespråk*, 1: 1–15.

Norde, M. (2012), 'On the Origin(s) of the Possessor Doubling Construction in Norwegian', in H. Van der Liet and M. Norde (eds), *Language for its Own Sake. Essays on Language and Literature Offered to Harry Perridon*, 327–58, Amsterdam: Scandinavisch Instituut.

Piotrowska, A. and D. Skrzypek (2017), 'Inalienable Possession in Swedish and Danish – A Diachronic Perspective', *Folia Scandinavica Posnaniensia*, 23 (1): 25–45.

Rosenbach, A. (2003), 'Aspects of Iconicity and Economy in the Choice between the s-genitive and the of-genitive in English', in G. Rohdenburg and B. Mondorf (eds), *Determinants of Grammatical Variation in English*, 379–412, Berlin and New York: De Gruyter Mouton.

Rosenbach, A. (2014), 'English Genitive Variation – The State of the Art', *English Language and Linguistics*, 18 (2): 215–62.

Rosenbach, A. (2017), 'Constraints in Contact: Animacy in English and Afrikaans Genitive Variation – A Cross-linguistic Perspective', *Glossa: A Journal of General Linguistics*, 2 (1) (72): 1–21.

Sinclair, J. (1991), *Corpus – Concordance – Collocation*, Oxford: Oxford University Press.

4

Double Object Constructions in English and Norwegian

Verbs of SENDING, BRINGING, LENDING and SELLING

Thomas Egan

4.1 Introduction

This chapter presents the results of a study of double object constructions containing the cognate verbs English *send*, *bring*, *lend* and *sell* and Norwegian *sende*, *bringe*, *låne* and *selge*, all four of which code acts of transfer, unaccompanied distal transfer in the case of the SEND verbs, accompanied distal transfer in the case of the BRING verbs, temporary transfer in the case of the LEND verbs, and transfer of ownership in the case of the SELL verbs. The data for the study are taken from the English-Norwegian Parallel Corpus (ENPC: see Johansson 2007: 10). It is the third and final paper on cognate verbs in the two languages that partake of the dative alternation. The first two papers dealt with the two most common English ditransitive verbs, *give* and *tell*, labelled 'typical ditransitive verbs' by Mukherjee (2005), and their Norwegian cognates. Egan (2023) presents an analysis of English *give* and Norwegian *gi* constructions and shows that these are remarkably similar, both in their semantics and their distribution. Egan (2021) contains an analysis of English *tell* and Norwegian *fortelle* constructions and shows that these are very dissimilar indeed.

The four pairs of verbs in the present study resemble the GIVE verbs, rather than the TELL verbs, in that they tend to code acts of physical transfer. The THEME, encoded as the direct object, is most often a concrete entity encoded by an NP. The RECIPIENT, encoded as an indirect object or prepositional object, is almost always animate. In one of the four pairs of verbs, the SEND verbs, the English member, *send*, is labelled a 'habitual ditransitive verb' by Mukherjee (2005), signifying that it is regularly employed with two objects, though not nearly as often as *give* and *tell*. The other three English verbs are classed as 'peripheral ditransitive verbs', since they only occur occasionally with an indirect object. An examination of the occurrences of the four Norwegian verbs in the ENPC suggests that this distinction between the SEND verb and the other three verbs also applies to them.

Three research questions are posed for each of the four pairs of verbs in the study:

1. How similar to/different from one another are the distributions of the ditransitive and prepositional constructions containing the English and Norwegian verbs in the original texts in the two languages?
2. Are there some kinds of tokens that are usually, or seldom, translated by congruent constructions? What characterizes these?
3. What characterizes translations that are divergent in form?

The first of these research questions is answered by comparing the source texts in English and Norwegian, and the second and third by comparing the source texts in Norwegian and English with their targets in the translations. In Section 4.2, I introduce the corpus, some relevant theory and the methods employed to retrieve relevant tokens and analyse these. Section 4.3 presents the results of the corpus searches for double object constructions in the original texts in English and Norwegian together with the translations of these. Section 4.4 contains a discussion of the results presented in Section 4.3. Section 4.5 contains a summary and conclusion.

4.2 Theory, corpus and method

This study is concerned with the resemblances and differences between constructions in two languages. Although it is not a translation study as such, it does make use of translation data, and some words are therefore in order about the appropriateness of such data for this sort of contrastive study of constructions. The verbs in the study are cognates and, according to the neurolinguist Michel Paradis, a cognate automatically activates its counterpart in the mind of a bilingual. He writes: 'When a word in a known language is a cognate of a word in another known language, it is recognised by both language subsystems: directly in one, and by immediate "completion" in the other' (Paradis 2004: 218, see also Vandevoorde 2020: 205–209). While all translators may not be bilingual in the narrowest sense of the term, they necessarily master the subsystems of both languages. Of course, it is one thing to recognize a word, another to actively make use of it in the act of translating. It seems reasonable to hypothesize, however, that the probability of the cognate being chosen is increased if the verb occurs in a syntactic construction that is found in both languages. According to Ebeling (1998: 169), translators will tend to employ congruent constructions where these are available in the target language. One may further hypothesize that a neglect to employ the relevant cognate or corresponding construction on the part of a number of translators is likely to be due to differing lexicogrammatical or pragmatic properties of the languages being contrasted, rather than the idiosyncrasies of individual translators or individual registers or genres.

Both constructions in the study contain two objects, one encoding a THEME, the other a RECIPIENT. Numerous papers have been published on such double object constructions in English. Mukherjee (2005: 3–63) contains a comprehensive overview of studies of ditransitives, and recent years have seen the publication of multifactorial studies of the English dative alternation by Bresnan and Ford (2010), Szmrecsanyi et al. (2017), Röthlisberger, Grafmiller and Szmrecsanyi (2017), among others. Much less has been written about these constructions in Norwegian: among those who have tackled them are Anderssen et al. (2012: 24), who state that 'the DA [dative alternation] in Norwegian is very similar to that in English, at least in the most straightforward cases'.

The four pairs of verbs in the study all encode acts of transfer from a GIVER to a RECIPIENT. The most neutral transfer verbs in the two languages are *give* and *gi*. Newman (1996) contrasts predications of GIVING in a plethora of languages. Common to the most central, or core senses of the predications in these languages, which code physical transfer and which he calls 'literal *give*', are the following three semantic components.

GIVING: [a has x] -> [a transfers x to b] -> [b has x]

Dixon describes GIVING as involving 'three semantic roles – a Donor transfers possession of some Gift to a Recipient' (Dixon 2005: 119). These three semantic roles are represented by 'a', 'x' and 'b' respectively in the above schema. The four verb pairs in this chapter all add one or more features to this basic transfer schema. In the case of SENDING and BRINGING, one of the additions involves movement. In BRINGING predications it is the BRINGER herself who moves with the THEME, in SENDING predications it is an intermediary who assumes responsibility for the transfer.[1] It is the element of movement that prompts Levin (1993) to avoid grouping them with *give* in the class of basic transfer verbs. Instead she assigns *send* to a class of verbs of unaccompanied location changing, together with other verbs such as *forward* and *mail*, and *bring* to a small class comprising just itself and *take*, both of which code accompanied location changing. The verbs in these two classes are subsumed by the umbrella category 'Verbs of Sending and Carrying' (Levin 1993: 132). She classifies the verbs *sell* and *lend* as belonging to the same class as *give*, labelled 'Verbs of Change of Possession' (Levin 1993: 45). Dixon (2005: 120) also assigns *sell* and *lend* to the same class as *give*, a class he labels GIVING. He assigns *send* and *bring* to the same class as *take*, labelled 'MOTION-C, the TAKE subtype' (Dixon 2005: 105).

Since one of the aims of the present study is to compare the two types of double object constructions, the ditransitive and the prepositional dative, the data investigated are limited to active voice examples with an explicitly coded SENDER, SELLER, LOANER or BRINGER (except in the case of imperatives) and explicitly coded THEMES, coded syntactically as direct objects, and RECIPIENTS, coded syntactically as indirect or prepositional objects.

The comparison of the English and Norwegian double object constructions is based on data from the ENPC, which contains extracts from fifty English texts, both fictional and nonfictional, aligned with their translations into Norwegian, and extracts from fifty texts in Norwegian with their English translations. These extracts are between 10,000 and 15,000 words in length, yielding a total of about 650,000 words both of original texts in, and translations into, each language. All utterances containing forms of the English lemmas *send*, *bring*, *lend* and *sell* and Norwegian lemmas *sende*, *bringe*, *låne* and *selge* in the original texts were downloaded from the corpus, together with sufficient context to determine their meaning. The tokens retrieved were sorted manually to weed out nominals, such as *sell* in *hard sell*. From the remaining verbal uses were selected all instances with an explicit subject (except in the case of imperatives) and two explicit objects.

4.3 Results

Table 4.1 contains details of the total number of tokens in the original language texts in the ENPC of each of the eight verbs and the number of examples of these found in double object constructions.

The number of examples with two explicit objects found for the four verb types range from thirteen in the case of the LEND verbs to fifty-eight in the case of the SEND verbs. These numbers may be compared to those of the two typical ditransitive verbs, 846 for GIVE verbs and 569 in the case of the TELL verbs. The salience of the constructions for the pairs of verbs (i.e. the likelihood of the verb

Table 4.1 Number of double object examples in the ENPC original language texts

Verb type	Verb	Total instances of verbs	Tokens in double object constructions and percentage of total numbers of instances	
SEND verbs	send	146	20	(14%)
	sende	175	38	(22%)
BRING verbs	bring	308	26	(8%)
	bringe	89	5	(6%)
SELL verbs	sell	161	11	(12%)
	selge	76	12	(16%)
LEND verbs	lend	15	9	(60%)
	låne	49	4	(8%)

occurring in a double object construction) as indicated by the percentages in the fourth column of Table 4.1, is broadly similar, except for the LEND verbs. However, in this case the Norwegian verb is polysemous, occurring in another construction in which the RECIPIENT is encoded as subject and the LENDER, if at all, in an adverbial. In other words, it corresponds to the English BORROW construction. Section 4.3.1 contains an overview of the occurrences of the eight sets of examples in the two double object constructions, and of the extent to which these receive congruent and divergent translations. Sections 4.3.2 to 4.3.5 present the results for each of the four pairs in turn.

4.3.1 Overview of the eight transfer verbs

The first research question listed in Section 4.1 deals with the distribution of the ditransitive and prepositional constructions containing the English and Norwegian verbs in the original texts in the two languages. Percentages for the two types of double object construction with all eight verbs are given in Figure 4.1.

Figure 4.1 shows that the SEND verbs bear the closest resemblance to one another in their division between the two constructions, while the LEND verbs are most different. However, the latter are also the verbs represented by the fewest number of tokens in the corpus. Moreover, according to Fisher Exact tests, none of the four pairs display statistically significant differences at the level of $p = 0.05$.

The second research question asks about the extent to which the constructions containing the eight verbs receive syntactically congruent or divergent translations. Figure 4.2 contains percentages for the two translation types.

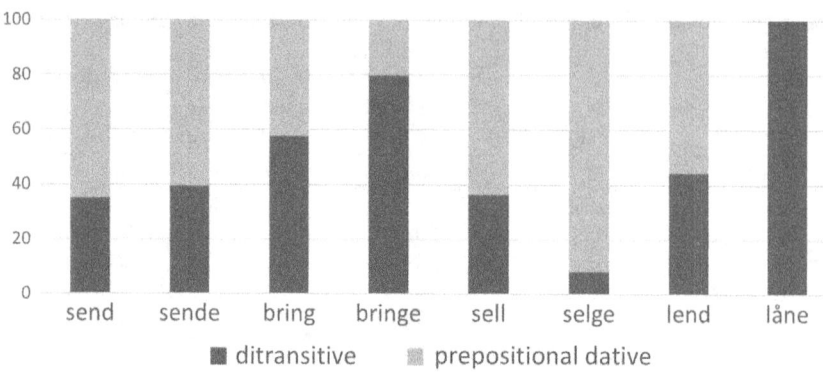

Figure 4.1 Percentages for the ditransitive and prepositional dative with the eight verbs in the original texts in the ENPC.

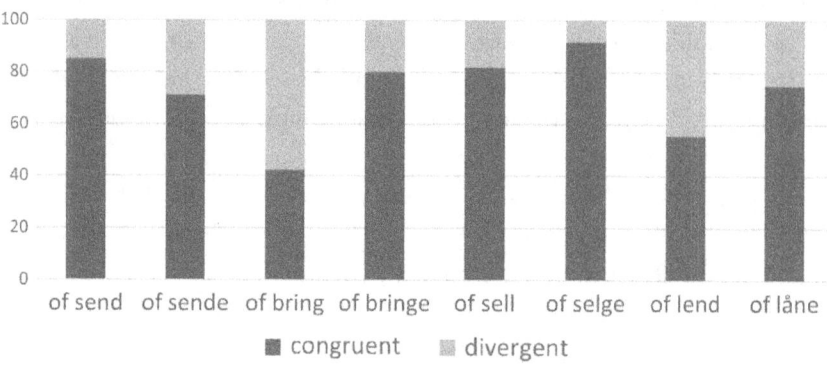

Figure 4.2 Percentages of syntactically congruent and divergent translations of the eight verbs.

According to Figure 4.2, six of the eight verbs are translated by a congruent construction in 70 per cent or more instances. The two exceptions are *lend* with 56 per cent congruent translations, and *bring* with just 42 per cent. There are only nine examples of *lend* according to Table 4.1, so it would take only a few translations to skew the results. There are as many as twenty-six tokens of *bring*, so clearly the fact that only a minority of these receive a congruent translation may be indicative of a real difference in the lexicogrammar or pragmatics of *bring* and its Norwegian cognate. The BRING verbs will be examined in Section 4.3.5. Prior to that I present the results for the SEND verbs in Section 4.3.2, the SELL verbs in Section 4.3.3 and the LEND verbs in Section 4.3.4.

4.3.2 The SEND verbs

There are almost twice as many examples of *sende* as *send*. One text is responsible for eight of the thirty-eight tokens of *sende*, the remainder being widely dispersed. Table 4.2 contains details of all the verbs used in both the congruent and divergent translations of constructions containing the two verbs.

Table 4.2 shows that the majority of translations in both directions are congruent (85 per cent of *send* and 71 per cent of *sende*). The majority of translations also contain the cognate verb (90 per cent of *send* and 74 per cent of *sende*). The percentage of congruent translations containing the cognate verb is 94 per cent for *send* and 74 per cent for *sende*. The English source expressions would seem to fit more seamlessly into the Norwegian language target texts than vice versa. The push and pull factors in the translation process, terms used by Halverson (2007) for the influence of the source and target language structures respectively on the translator, are working in parallel for the translators into Norwegian. There are only four exceptions to this pattern, two of which contain a verb other than *sende*. In one, the fixed phrase *gi beskjed* (give message) translates *send a message*. In the other, the phrase *se på* (look at) translates the light verb expression *send a glance*. The latter is one of only three divergent translations of *send*. In the other two, (1) and (2), the cognate verb is used.

(1) They printed the piece I *sent* to them (RDA1)[2]
    De trykket det stykket jeg *sendte* dem (RDA1T)
    (They printed the piece I sent them)
(2) It's the photo I *sent* the gallery. (MA1)
    Det er bildet jeg *sendte* til galleriet. (MA1T)
    (It is the picture I sent to the gallery.)

Table 4.2 Verbs used in congruent and divergent translations of *send* and *sende*

Verb	Congruent translations		Divergent translations		Total	
send	sende	16	sende	2	sende	18
	gi (give)	1	se på (look at)	1	other	2
sende	send	20	send	8	send	28
	give	3	pass	1		
	take	3	refer	1		
	deliver	1	Ø	1	other	10

In (1) the ditransitive replaces the prepositional dative and in (2) the prepositional dative replaces the ditransitive. In both instances, the verb and RECIPIENT are in a relative clause modifying the THEME. In such clauses the order of the constituents is the same in both constructions, the only difference between them being that the prepositional dative construction is slightly more explicit in marking the RECIPIENT with a preposition. The change from the source sentence to its target in these two examples must therefore be considered minimal, not least since it occurs both to and from the ditransitive/prepositional dative. To sum up, if one can use *send* in English one can almost certainly use *sende* in the corresponding construction in Norwegian.

Translations from Norwegian into English are more varied than translations in the other direction, as may be seen in Table 4.2. There are seven syntactically congruent translations containing verbs other than *send*. Three of these contain the more general transfer verb *give*, with two of them translating predications in which *send* functions as a light verb, as in (3).

(3) Her *sendte* hun Rulle et så sint blikk (EG1)
     (Here sent she Rulle a so angry look)
     Mrs Brandt *gave* Rudolf such a severe look (EG1T)

Give a look, with ten tokens, is one of the most common light verb expressions containing *give* in the original English texts in the ENPC (Egan 2023), where it is twice translated congruently by the Norwegian SEND verb. The replacement of *sende* by *give* as the light verb is clearly motivated by the pull factor, labelled 'magnetism' by Halvorsen (2017). More puzzling at first sight than the use of the GIVE verb for the SEND verb is the fact that three examples of *sende*, a verb coding unaccompanied transfer, are translated by *take*, a verb coding accompanied transfer. However, all three are from the same source text (LSPL1) and all three contain the phrase *sende saken til retten*, literally 'send the case to court', which is more idiomatically expressed in English by 'take the case to court'.

Turning to the divergent translations of *sende*, we note first that eight of these contain the cognate *send*. In two of these, the prepositional dative is rendered by the ditransitive. In another four, the translator passivizes the predication, as in (4). The other three passive translations containing *sende*, in addition to one containing *refer*, are from the same legal text as the congruent *take* translations (LSPL1), indicating that this usage is most likely restricted to the legal register.

(4) En slik person ville han neppe *sende* til paven (ANR1)
(Such a person would he hardly send to the Pope)
A person like this was not one to be *sent* to the Pope (ANR1T)

There remain two divergent translations of *sende*, (5) and (6).

(5) Kan du *sende* meg smøret? (JG1)
(Can you send me the butter?)
Would you *pass* the butter, please? (JG1T)

(6) Han *sendte* Magdas kylling diablo en vemodig tanke. (EG2)
(He sent Magda's chicken diablo a sad thought.)
He had a brief vision of his wife's steak and onions. (EG2T)

The replacement of the ditransitive *sende* construction in (5) by the monotransitive *pass* construction is easily explained since *pass* is the default English verb for transfer requests at table. As for (6), I have classified it as a zero translation. One could argue that it is a very loose translation, but for present purposes, the point is that the *sende* predication is not translated as such.

Let us round off this discussion of the SEND verbs by viewing them with respect to the research questions in Section 4.1.

1. The ratio of ditransitive to prepositional dative constructions in the original texts in the two languages is practically identical (40 to 60 per cent).
2. The majority of tokens in Norwegian (71 per cent) and the vast majority in English (85 per cent) receive a syntactically congruent translation.
3. The most prominent characteristic of translations that are divergent in form is that the majority of these employ the cognate verb.

4.3.3 The SELL verbs

There are eleven tokens of *sell* and twelve of *selge* in the original texts. There are four tokens of the ditransitive in English but just one in Norwegian. In the Norwegian example of the ditransitive and three of the English ones the BUYER is encoded by a personal pronoun (the other English example is *my great-grandfather*). Apart from one instance of zero translation, all tokens are translated by the cognate verb. Table 4.3 contains details of the translations.

Table 4.3 Verbs used in congruent and divergent translations of *sell* and *selge*

Verb	Congruent translations		Divergent translations		Total	
sell	*selge*	8	*selge*	2	*selge*	10
			Ø	1	other	1
selge	*sell*	11	*sell*	1	*sell*	12

Table 4.3 shows that the majority of translations in both directions are congruent (92 per cent of *sell* and 73 per cent of *selge*). The majority of translations also contain the cognate verb (91 per cent of *sell* and 100 per cent of *selge*). The percentage of congruent translations containing the cognate verb is 100 per cent in both directions. In other words, if translators decide to use retain the syntax of the original, they also make use of the cognate verb.

In the single divergent translation into English, (7), the indefinite THEME is omitted. In one of the divergent translations into Norwegian, (8), the generic RECIPIENT is omitted; in the other, the prepositional dative is preferred, for no obvious reason.

(7) Og man er nødt til det hvis man skal *selge* noe til dem. (EG2)
(And one needs to (do) it if one shall sell something to them.)
And you have to if you're going to *sell* to them. (EG2T)

(8) Butchers, for instance, are not content merely to *sell* you meat. (PM1)
Slakterne er for eksempel ikke fornøyd med bare å *selge* kjøtt. (PM1T)
(Butchers are for example not satisfied with just to sell meat.)

Finally, there is one instance of a zero translation, (9)

(9) He picks up additional income constructing crossword puzzles which he *sells* to a couple of those pint-sized 'magazines' you can purchase in a supermarket check-out line. (SG1)
Litt ekstrainntekter får han også ved å lage kryssord for slike knøttsmå 'blader' som man kan kjøpe ved kassa i supermarkedene. (SG1T)
(A little extra income gets he also by making crosswords for the sort of tiny 'magazines' one can buy at the checkout in the supermarkets.)

(9) is an example of 'implicitation' (Vinay and Darbelnet 1995: 344). Given the statement that the activity in question results in income for the SELLER and must therefore of necessity involve a sale, there is no need to mention the act of SELLING explicitly.

I round off this discussion of the SELL verbs by viewing them with respect to the research questions in Section 4.1.

1. There is a greater proportion of ditransitive constructions in English (4 of 11) than Norwegian (1 of 12). This may just be a reflex of a greater number of given RECIPIENTs in the English examples.
2. The majority of tokens (92 per cent of *sell* and 73 per cent of *selge*) receive a syntactically congruent translation.
3. Apart from one zero translation into Norwegian, the divergent translations all employ the cognate verb, although sometimes in a different construction.

4.3.4 The LEND verbs

There are nine tokens of *lend* and four of *låne* in the original texts. There are four tokens of the ditransitive in both languages and five of the prepositional dative in English. In two of the prepositional dative examples, the RECIPIENT is a pronoun. Ten tokens are translated by the cognate verb. Table 4.4 contains details of the translations.

Table 4.4 shows that the majority of translations in both directions are congruent (56 per cent of *lend* and 75 per cent of *låne*). The majority of translations also contain the cognate verb (78 per cent of *lend* and 75 per cent of *låne*). As was the case with the SELL verbs, the percentage of congruent translations containing the cognate verb is 100 per cent in both directions. Two of the divergent translations into Norwegian contain the cognate verb. In one of these, (10), the only syntactic difference between the source and target text is that the latter lacks pied-piping (both are prepositional dative). Pied-piping cannot occur with the relative pronoun *som* in Norwegian (see, for instance, Taraldsen 1978: 625). In the other divergent translation containing *lend*, the RECIPIENT is

Table 4.4 Verbs used in congruent and divergent translations of *lend* and *låne*

verb	Congruent translations		Divergent translations		total	
lend	*låne*	5	*låne*	2	*låne*	7
			sette (place)	1		
			støtte (support)	1	other	2
låne	*lend*	3			*lend*	3
			Ø	1	other	1

recoded as subject, as in cases where *give* predications are translated by *få* (get) (see Egan 2023).

(10) Banks are generally not opposed to imposing standards upon those to whom they *lend* money. (LT1)
Banker har som regel ingenting imot å trumfe igjennom sin standard overfor dem som de *låner* ut penger til. (LT1T)
(Banks have as a rule nothing against to force through their standard on those who they lend money to.)

There are two instances in which *lend* is translated by a divergent construction containing a verb other than *låne*. In both of these the THEME is an event rather than a concrete object. In one case, the translator has replaced the light verb form *lend support to* by the semantically equivalent single verb *støtte* (support). In the other, (11), the translator has retained the trivalent predicative structure of the original. In both cases, the use of *lend* deviates from the general LEND schema, insofar as there is no implication that the THEME is to be returned to the LENDER.

(11) But now Paul's wish to get married had suddenly *lent* the weight of finality to what had come about by itself. (ABR1)
Men Pauls ønske om å gifte seg hadde plutselig *satt* et endelig stempel på noe som hadde skjedd av seg selv. (ABR1T)
(But Paul's wish to marry had suddenly put a final stamp on something that had happened of itself.)

I round off this discussion of the LEND verbs by viewing them with respect to the research questions in Section 4.1.

1. There is a greater proportion of prepositional dative examples in English (5 of 9) than Norwegian (0 of 4).
2. The majority of tokens (75 per cent of *låne* and 56 per cent of *lend*) receive a syntactically congruent translation.
3. There are five divergent translations. One of these is a zero translation, two employ the cognate verb, and in the other two *lend* is used with a non-concrete THEME.

4.3.5 The BRING verbs

There are over five times as many tokens of *bring* as *bringe* in the original texts. Moreover, the twenty-six examples of *bring* are dispersed over 21 texts. The impression that the English verb is more common is reinforced by the fact that only 23 per cent of its tokens are translated by *bringe* as opposed to 100 per cent in the other direction. There are fifteen tokens of the ditransitive and eleven of the prepositional dative in English, while four of the five tokens of *bringe* are ditransitive. An overview of the translations in both directions is given in Table 4.5.

All five tokens of *bringe* are translated by *bring*. Four of the translations are congruent. In the fifth, (12), the RECIPIENT is recoded as a possessive pronoun.

(12) Yngre menn enn ham *brakte* ham nå maten. (KHI)
(Younger men than him brought him now the food.)
Men younger than he now *brought* his food. (KH1T)

Just five of the eleven congruent translations of *bring*, two of the ditransitive and three of the prepositional dative, contain *bringe*. One congruent ditransitive translation, (13), contains the verb *servere* (serve). There are five congruent translations of the prepositional dative containing another verb. Two of these contain the phrasal verb *ta med* (take with), as in (14).

(13) Harriet was [...] drinking the tea David had *brought* her. (DL1)
Harriet [...] drakk teen David hadde *servert* henne. (DL1T)
(Harriet [...] drank the tea David had served her.)

Table 4.5 Verbs used in congruent and divergent translations of *bring* and *bringe*

verb	Congruent translations		Divergent translations		total	
bringe	bring	4	bring	1	bring	5
bring	bringe	5	bringe	1	bringe	6
	ta med (take with)	2	komme med (come with)	5		
	føre (lead)	1	ta med (take with)	3		
	føye (add)	1	få (get)	1		
	kaste (throw)	1	gi (give)	1		
	servere (serve)	1	Ø	4	other	20

(14) When you have chosen the book you want, *bring* it to me. (RD1)
Når du har funnet den boka du vil låne, kan du bare *ta* den *med* bort til meg. (RD1T)
(When you have found the book you want to borrow, can you just take it with over to me.)

We also find *ta med* (take with) used to translate *bring* in three divergent translations, where the prepositional dative translates the ditransitive, as in (15). This use of a TAKE verb to translate a BRING verb will be discussed further in Section 4.4. Of all fifteen divergent translations of *bring*, only three are of the prepositional dative, and two of these are zero. One of the translations of the ditransitive retains the BRING verb, but in passivized form, while five translations omit the RECIPIENT and code the THEME as the object of the prepositional verb *komme med* (come with), as in (16).

(15) *Bring* me a taste Sunday. (GN1)
Ta med en smak til meg på søndag. (GN1T)
(Take with a taste to me on Sunday.)
(16) His wife *brought* him a large bottle of Guinness. (BO1)
Kona hans *kom med* en stor flaske Guinness. (BO1T)
(Wife his came with a big bottle Guinness.)

The BRING verbs may be summarized with respect to the research questions as follows:

1. There is a greater proportion of ditransitive examples in Norwegian (4 of 5) than English (15 of 26).
2. Four out of five tokens of *bringe* (80 per cent) receive a congruent translation, as opposed to just 11 of 26 tokens of *bring* (42 per cent).
3. The single divergent translation into English employs the cognate verb. Just one of fourteen divergent translations into Norwegian contains *bringe*.

4.4 Discussion of results

We have seen in Section 4.3 that the eight verbs differ, sometimes considerably, in the degree to which they are translated by their respective

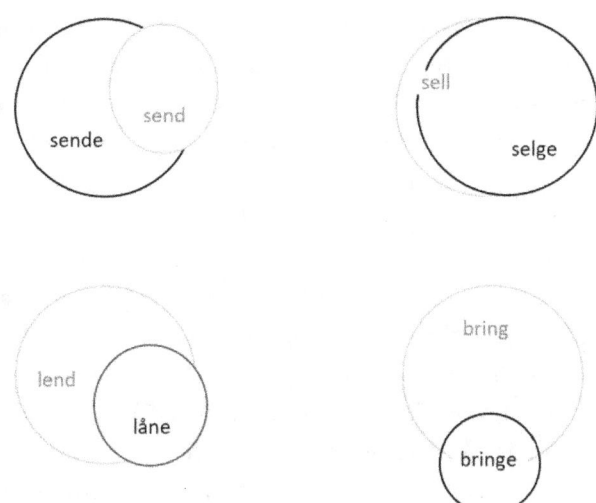

Figure 4.3 The extent of semantic overlap between the verbs of sending, selling, lending and bringing in double object constructions.

Table 4.6 Mutual correspondence of pairs of verbs in double object constructions

	Lexical mutual correspondence	Syntactically congruent translations	Lexical + syntactic mutual correspondence
SEND verbs	79%	76%	62%
SELL verbs	96%	87%	83%
LEND verbs	77%	62%	62%
BRING verbs	35%	48%	29%

cognates. Figure 4.3 illustrates the semantic overlap between the cognates, as revealed by their translations, with the size of the circles representing the number of the verbs in double object constructions in the original language texts.

The four images in Figure 4.3 only illustrate the lexical correspondence between the verbs and their translations when they occur in double object constructions. Percentages for the lexical mutual correspondence (Altenberg 1999; Ebeling and Ebeling 2013: 27) of each of the four pairs of verbs are given in Table 4.6, together with percentages for syntactically congruent translations, and syntactically congruent translations containing the cognate verb.

As shown by Figure 4.3 and Table 4.6, it is the SELL verbs that resemble one another most closely. Apart from a single instance of zero translation, the verb is always translated by its cognate, most often in a congruent construction. This is no doubt due to the fact that the semantic field covered by the action of SELLING is practically identical in the two languages, with comparatively few extensions from the central sense of transferring a concrete THEME to a RECIPIENT in exchange for money. In addition, neither language contains a commonly used synonym of its SELL verb. The SEND and LEND verbs resemble one another in that the verb that occurs most frequently in original texts is used to translate its cognate more often than the less frequent of the pair. In other words, the verbs *sende* and *lend*, when they occur in the double object constructions, cover more semantic space, at least in the texts in the ENPC, than do *send* and *låne*. Thus *sende* is used in some light verb constructions where it is translated by English *give*, and in legal formulations where it is translated by English *take* (see Section 4.3.2). As for *lend*, we saw in Section 4.3.4 that it is used with abstract THEMES (*the weight of finality, support*) that do not lend themselves easily to translation by *låne*. The verbs that differ most from one another are *bring* and *bringe*, with all tokens of the latter being translated by the former, but only 23 per cent of *bring* being translated by *bringe*. The remainder of this section is devoted to this pair of verbs.

At first sight, it seems puzzling that the verbs *bring* and *bringe* behave so differently. After all the verbs are cognates, and their first definitions in standard monolingual dictionaries are very similar.

> Norwegian definition: *føre, ha med sig, komme med (til et ell. Annet bestemmelsessted)* (Bokmålsordboka) ('move, have with oneself, come with (to Some destination or other)')
>
> English definition: *To cause to come along with oneself* (OED)

The definition of *bring* in the OED continues:

> it implies motion towards the place where the speaker or auditor is, or is supposed to be, being in sense the causative of *come*; motion in the opposite direction is expressed by *take*. (OED)

The semantic relationship between BRINGING and COMING is reflected in the fact that five of the Norwegian translations, including (16) and (17), contain the prepositional verb *komme med* (come with), used in the definition of *bringe* quoted above.

(17) Then tell somebody to *bring* me a bottle of champagne. (RDA1)
 Og få noen til å *komme med* en flaske champagne. (RDA1T)
 (And get someone to come with a bottle of champagne)

Komme med expresses the same deictic content as *bringe*. Ebeling (2017), in a study of the two BRING verbs in all syntactic constructions, shows that they differ in their degree of formality, with *bringe* being more formal than *bring*. This would help explain the use of the more informal *komme med* to translate *bring*, but not the use of *ta med* (take with), which if translated word for word into English would imply motion in the opposite direction (away from the speaker/auditor). However, unlike the English verb *take*, its Norwegian cognate *ta* does not imply movement in a particular direction: that is, it is not deictic. Rather it codes accompanied movement in any direction whatsoever, including towards the speaker/auditor. It is this absence of implied direction in the verb *ta* that facilitates the use of the phrasal verb *ta med* (take with) in the accompanied transfer construction, as in (15).

To sum up, the two verbs *bring* and *bringe* are not themselves that different in their semantics, at least in double object constructions. Nor are they very different in their semantics in Caused Motion constructions. There is however a pragmatic difference between them, insofar as they differ in their degree of formality (see Ebeling 2017). To fully explain the low extent of their mutual correspondence we also need to consider the semantic field of accompanied transfer as a whole, especially the difference between the semantics of TAKE verbs in the two languages. The English verb *take* is deictic, but its Norwegian cognate *ta* is not, making the latter a possible correspondent of English *bring*.

4.5 Summary and conclusion

This chapter presented the results of a study of double object constructions containing the cognate verbs English *send*, *bring*, *lend* and *sell* and Norwegian *sende*, *bringe*, *låne* and *selge*, all four of which code acts of transfer. Each of the four types of transfer adds one or more features to the basic GIVE schema, coded by the verbs *give* in English and *gi* in Norwegian. In the case of the SEND verbs, the GIVER transfers the THEME to a third party (which may be inanimate) for transport to the RECIPIENT. In the case of the SELL verbs, the RECIPIENT transfers money to the GIVER. In the case of the LEND verbs, the RECIPIENT is under an obligation to transfer the THEME back to the GIVER at some future time. And in the case of the BRING verbs, the GIVER moves towards the RECIPIENT to transfer the THEME to the latter.

The following three research questions were outlined in Section 4.1:

1. How similar to/different from one another are the distributions of the ditransitive and prepositional constructions containing the English and Norwegian verbs in the original texts in the two languages?
2. Are there some kinds of tokens that are usually, or seldom, translated by congruent constructions? What characterizes these?
3. What characterizes translations that are divergent in form?

The answer to the first question is that there are considerable differences in the extent to which the verbs in the four pairs resemble one another in their division between the two constructions, with the SEND verbs bearing the closest resemblance to one another and the LEND verbs being most different. However, none of the four pairs display statistically significant differences at the level of $p = 0.05$. As for the second question, six of the eight verbs are translated by a congruent construction in 70 per cent or more instances. The two exceptions are *lend* with 56 per cent congruent translations, and *bring* with 48 per cent. Since there are only nine examples of *lend*, one cannot draw any conclusions from the fact that four of these receive divergent translations, especially since two of them contain an abstract THEME, and thus instantiate a construction less likely to be found in Norwegian. The BRING verbs were discussed in more detail in Section 4.4, where the difference between them was ascribed to two main factors, firstly a difference in the degree of formality, with the Norwegian verb deemed to be more formal, and secondly the fact that the Norwegian TAKE verb is not deictic and thus can function as a natural correspondent for the English BRING verb.

Two hypotheses were mentioned in Section 4.2. The first asserted that the probability of the cognate verb being chosen in a translation is increased if the verb occurs in a syntactic construction that is found in both languages. The second hypothesis stated that a neglect to employ the relevant cognate or corresponding construction on the part of a number of translators is likely to be due to differing lexicogrammatical or pragmatic properties of the languages being contrasted, rather than the idiosyncrasies of individual translators or individual registers or genres. The analysis of the corpus material in Sections 4.3 and 4.4 was not designed to examine the first of these hypotheses, since all four pairs of verbs in the study were chosen because they occurred in both the ditransitive and the prepositional dative constructions. However, the hypothesis may be said to receive indirect support from the fact that in the case of three of the verb pairs, the exception being the BRING verbs, the measure of mutual lexical correspondence is over 70 per cent in total and over 60 per cent in congruent translations. Some data relevant to the second hypothesis are provided by translations of Norwegian *sende* and English *lend* and *bring*, although again one should be wary of drawing conclusions on the basis of small corpus samples. The first two verbs cover a broader expanse of semantic space than their cognates in the other language. Thus in English, but not in Norwegian, *lend* is used with abstract THEMEs and these are translated divergently by different (admittedly just two) translators. On the other hand, just one translator renders *sende* as *take*, a translation influenced, if not dictated, by the genre in question (legal documents) rather than the individual translator. As for *bring*, the fact that five translators render it as *ta med* (take with), points to there being a genuine difference between the two languages with respect to the coding of accompanied transfer.

It is now time to consider the full picture of the six cognate verbs that display the dative alternation in English and Norwegian. The GIVE, SEND, SELL and LEND verbs are all similar in their distribution in the two languages. The TELL and BRING verbs are different in that their correspondences are asymmetrical. In both cases, the English verb is the more frequent of the two in double object constructions and is used to translate the Norwegian verb much more than vice versa. In both cases, Norwegian often uses an alternative expression. In TELL predications, Norwegians often use the verb *si* (say), which can be used ditransitively, unlike its English cognate. In BRING predications, Norwegians often use the expressions *komme med* (come with) or *ta (med)* (take (with)), which differs from English *take* in not implying direction away from the speaker/auditor.

Two of the four pairs of verbs in this study, the SEND verbs and the BRING verbs, also occur in the Caused Motion construction in both languages. In future research, it might be worth looking into whether the differences between the distribution of these two types of verbs in English and Norwegian shown in the present study is replicated in the Caused Motion construction. Another possible fruitful area to explore consists of pairs of corresponding verbs that occur in both the ditransitive and the prepositional dative, but which are not cognates, such as the TEACH verbs English *teach* and Norwegian *lære*, in order to establish if these behave differently in their distribution that the pairs of cognates in the present study.

Acknowledgement

I wish to thank the editors for including this chapter in the present volume, and two anonymous reviewers for their detailed and helpful comments.

Notes

1 As pointed out by one reviewer, the intermediary may be a non-human conduit, such as an e-mail server.
2 The first part of the code 'RDA1' refers to the text in the English-Norwegian Parallel Corpus from which the example has been taken, with 'RDA' being the initials of the author. 'RDA1T' stands for the translation of the same text. The full titles of the original works and the translations are listed in Johansson (2007: 329–38). An English gloss is provided in italics for the relevant part of the predication in Norwegian whenever this is not faithfully rendered by the English translation in the corpus, or when it is not a faithful rendition of an English original.

References

Altenberg, B. (1999), 'Adverbial Connectors in English and Swedish: Semantic and Lexical Correspondences', in H. Hasselgård and S. Oksefjell (eds), *Out of Corpora: Studies in Honour of Stig Johansson*, 249–68, Amsterdam: Rodopi.

Anderssen, M., P. Fikkert, R. Mykhaylyk and Y. Rodina (2012), 'The Dative Alternation in Norwegian Child Language', *Nordlyd*, 39 (1): 24–43.

Bresnan, J. and M. Ford (2010), 'Predicting Syntax: Processing Dative Constructions in American and Australian Varieties of English', *Language*, 86 (1): 168–213.

Dixon, R. M. W. (2005), *A Semantic Approach to English Grammar*, Oxford: Oxford University Press.

Ebeling, J. (1998), 'Using Translations to Explore Construction Meaning in English and Norwegian', in S. Johansson and S. Oksefjell (eds), *Corpora and Cross-linguistic Research: Theory, Method and Case Studies*, 169–95, Amsterdam: Rodopi.

Ebeling, S. O. (2017), 'Bringing Home the Bacon! A Contrastive Study of the Cognates bring/bringe in English and Norwegian', *Kalbotyra*, 70: 104–26.

Ebeling, J. and S. O. Ebeling (2013), *Patterns in Contrast*, Amsterdam: John Benjamins.

Egan, T. (2023), 'Giving in English and Norwegian: A Contrastive Perspective', in M. Röthlisberger, E. Zehentner and T. Colleman (eds), *Ditransitive Constructions in Germanic Languages*, 365–403, Amsterdam: John Benjamins.

Egan, T. (2021), 'Telling in English, Norwegian and French: A Three-way Contrast', in A. Cermakova, S. O. Ebeling, M. Levin and J. Ström Herold (eds), *Crossing the Borders, Complex Contrastive Data and the Next Generation, Bergen Language and Linguistics Studies*, 11 (1): 47–68.

Halverson, S. L. (2007), 'Investigating Gravitational Pull in Translation: The Case of the English Progressive Construction', in R. Jääskeläinen, T. Puurtinen and H. Stotesbury (eds), *Text, Processes, and Corpora: Research Inspired by Sonja Tirkkonen-Condit*, 175–96, Joensuu: University of Eastern Finland.

Halverson, S. L. (2017), 'Gravitational Pull in Translation. Testing a Revised Model', in G. De Sutter, M.-A. Lefer and I. Delaere (eds), *Empirical Translation Studies. New Methodological and Theoretical Traditions*, 9–46, Berlin and New York: Mouton de Gruyter.

Johansson, S. (2007), *Seeing through Multilingual Corpora: On the Use of Corpora in Contrastive Studies*, Amsterdam: John Benjamins.

Levin, B. (1993), *English Verb Classes and Alternations: A Preliminary Investigation*, Chicago: University of Chicago Press.

Mukherjee, J. (2005), *English Ditransitive Verbs: Aspects of Theory, Description and a Usage-based Model*, Amsterdam: Rodopi.

Newman, J. (1996), *Give: A Cognitive Linguistic Study*, Berlin and New York: Mouton De Gruyter.

Paradis, M. (2004), *A Neurolinguistic Theory of Bilingualism*, Amsterdam: John Benjamins.

Röthlisberger, M., J. Grafmiller and B. Szmrecsanyi (2017), 'Cognitive Indigenization Effects in the English Dative Alternation', *Cognitive Linguistics*, 28 (4): 673–710.

Szmrecsanyi, B., J. Grafmiller, J. Bresnan, A. Rosenbach, S. Tagliamonte and S. Todd (2017), 'Spoken Syntax in a Comparative Perspective: The Dative and Genitive Alternation in Varieties of English', *Glossa*, 2 (1): 1–27.

Taraldsen, K. T. (1978), 'The Scope of Wh Movement in Norwegian', *Linguistic Inquiry*, 9 (4): 623–40.

Vandevoorde, L. (2020), *Semantic Differences in Translation: Exploring the Field of Inchoativity*, Berlin: Language Science Press.

Vinay, J.-P. and J. Darbelnet (1995), *Comparative Stylistics of French and English: A Methodology for Translation*, trans. and ed. J. C. Sager and M.-J. Hamel, Amsterdam: John Benjamins.

Corpora and dictionaries

English-Norwegian Parallel Corpus. https://www.hf.uio.no/ilos/english/services/knowledge-resources/omc/enpc/

Bokmålsordboka | Nynorskordboka. https://ordbok.uib.no/

OED (1994), *The Oxford English dictionary*, On compact disc, Oxford: Oxford University Press.

5

Prepositional Patterns in English and Czech Newspaper Discourse

Denisa Šebestová and Markéta Malá

5.1 Introduction

The study[1] aims to identify and describe the functional types of phraseological units employed in newspaper reporting. It focuses on patterns comprising frequent prepositions, which are expected to participate in building textual relations (Hunston 2008) as well as to manifest particular semantic prosodies (Partington 2004). Prepositional patterns are compared between English and Czech newspaper reports to ascertain how the communicative purposes of the register interact with the phraseology of typologically distinct languages. At the same time, the study tests the potential of the corpus-driven, n-gram-based methodology in contrastive research, focusing on a specific register.

5.2 Theoretical background

5.2.1 Newspaper register

The newspaper register is primarily intended to present information, reporting on current events. However, its function goes beyond a purely informational one: it also offers a particular interpretation of the reality, since 'newspaper editors make selections from what they could report, when deciding what they will report' (Scott and Tribble 2006: 162). Hence, in order to characterize newspaper discourse comprehensively, we also approach it from the perspective of semantic/evaluative prosody and semantic preference (e.g. Partington 2004; Sinclair 2004), that is, looking at the tendency of patterns to be involved in conveying positive or negative evaluative meanings (semantic prosody) and/or to co-occur with items from a particular semantic field (semantic preference).

5.2.2 Grammatical words in patterns

Using closed-class items such as prepositions as the starting point towards analysing the semantic features of a register may seem counter-intuitive since these words are typically perceived as having grammatical functions only. However, evidence from corpus phraseology suggests that meanings are conveyed through word combinations rather than isolated words (Ebeling and Ebeling 2013; Groom 2010: 61). Consequently, 'the supposedly meaningless closed-class words make just as important a contribution to the overall meaning of each phraseology as do the open-class items [...], and therefore constitute equally valid starting points for a semantically-oriented analysis' (Groom 2010: 62).

We presume grammatical words may in fact be a highly suitable basis for characterizing a particular register, because they are very frequent and evenly dispersed throughout discourse (cf. Sinclair 1991), occurring in a range of cotexts and uses:

> Given that closed-class words are the commonest words in virtually all corpora, it follows that an analysis based on even a small selection of them will account for a far greater proportion of the data as a whole than can be achieved through an analysis of even a large selection of open-class items [...]. (Groom 2010: 71)

Therefore, closed-class words in a phraseological analysis may even help identify 'a much wider range of phraseological phenomena than might otherwise be possible' (Groom 2010: 71), and point towards phraseological units of varying degrees of formulaicity.

The relevance of grammatical words is further highlighted by their involvement in discourse structuring, fulfilling a variety of textual functions and contributing to coherence; thus on a larger scale, these grammatical patterns can also help reveal pervasive discourse patterning (Hunston 2008).

To sum up, since the primary communicative function of conveying information is shared by newspapers across languages, we expect Czech and English newspapers to share similar function word patterns. However, the respective national newspapers may be shaped by culturally specific style conventions. Therefore, the study aims to find out what function word patterns can reveal about the phraseology of journalism in the two languages compared.

5.3 Data and method

5.3.1 Data

The present study explores the phraseology connected with the most frequent[2] Czech preposition *v/ve* (in) and its most frequent English translation counterpart[3] *in*. The phraseology of prepositions in Czech and English newspaper reporting was examined using comparable corpora of journalistic texts (cf. Table 5.1) and the same methodology.

5.3.2 Method

Lemmatized 3–5-grams comprising the prepositions v and IN were extracted from each corpus; all lengths were retrieved together; the cut-off frequency was set at 10,000. Before describing the annotation of the data, we will comment on the method and explain the motivations for the parameters of the search, mainly including punctuation, n-gram length and lemmatization.

Due to the large degree of their variability, all figures in the data were automatically replaced with the # placeholder in the Czech data to allow for n-grams containing a figure to be lumped together.[4] In Sketch Engine, 'non-words', that is, tokens which do not start with a letter of the alphabet, such as numbers and punctuation,[5] were included in the n-grams. In both languages, the n-grams were retrieved from lemmatized data, including punctuation, to subsume a variety of n-grams, while bearing in mind their potential informational value. Malá, Šebestová and Milička (2021) indicated that including punctuation in n-grams[6] – commas above all – may help reveal more realistically how patterns are involved in text structuring. In the study cited, including punctuation identified patterns containing subordinators and occurring around syntactic boundaries, introducing dependent clauses – for example, *chvíle*,

Table 5.1 The corpora and tools used in the present study

	Czech	English
Corpus used	SYN2009PUB[7]	SiBol (Siena-Bologna) corpus – a sub-corpus of texts from the UK and USA
Size	844 million tokens	630 million tokens
Type of newspaper	mostly broadsheets	mostly broadsheets
Year of publication	1995 – 2007	1993, 1995, 2010, 2013
Tools used	KonText	SketchEngine

kdy jsme ('moment when we'), where commas are obligatory in Czech (Malá, Šebestová and Milička 2021.). Combining multiple n-gram sizes is intended to retrieve a broad range of patterns. Admittedly, it results in a number of n-grams overlapping, for example, V SOBOTA OD # and V SOBOTA OD are represented as separate hits. These overlaps call for a cautious interpretation of the frequencies, bearing duplicities in mind.

Another caveat is posed by typological differences between the languages: in analytical English, shorter n-grams such as trigrams may be less informative since they are largely composed of function words. Hence the combination of 3–5-grams was employed as a compromise.

Finally, lemmatization was employed to subsume variant word forms under one n-gram, which is relevant especially in Czech, given its rich morphological paradigms. Lemmatization, however, may obscure usage differences between individual word forms and had to be complemented by the word form frequency analysis. For example, in the lemmatized 3-gram V TENTO DEN, it is the plural form *v těchto dnech* (in these days) that is vastly predominant in the newspaper data (93.3 per cent of the 3-gram tokens). It reports on events currently in progress (1) or serves as a vague time marker referring to recent events, presumably where the focus is on the event and precise timing is not considered essential (2). On the contrary, the less frequent singular form *v tento den* (lit. in this day) serves to pinpoint a particular date (3).

(1) 'Je prostě právě to období [. . .], kdy houby přilákají do hor více lidí,' uvedl Karel Palička z Horské služby Beskydy. Houbaři mohou *v těchto dnech* celkem snadno najít atraktivní druhy [. . .].
('Right now it's this time of year [. . .] when mushrooms attract more people to the mountains', said Karel Palička from the Beskydy Mountain Rescue. *In these days* mushroom pickers can fairly easily find attractive specimen [. . .])[8]

(2) Nový bronzový odlitek vysoký 3,5 metru odhalí 17. listopadu na Churchillově náměstí na Žižkově bývalá britská premiérka Margaret Thatcherová, která *v těchto dnech* potvrdila svou účast.
(A new bronze statue, 3.5 m in size, will be unveiled on 17 November in Churchillovo náměstí in Žižkov by former UK PM Margaret Thatcher, who has confirmed her attendance *in these days*.)

(3) Zajímalo nás, proč revoluce vypukla právě *v tento den*.
(We were interested in why the revolution started *on this day* in particular.)

In order to exclude n-grams which generally occur frequently across all registers (e.g. BE IN A, TEN BÝT V (THAT BE IN)), we compared the frequencies of the IN/V n-grams in the newspaper corpora and in large balanced national corpora – the Czech National Corpus SYN2010 (Křen et al. 2010a) and the British National Corpus 2014 (Brezina, Hawtin and McEnery 2021).[9] Only the n-grams overused significantly[10] in the newspapers in comparison with the general reference corpus were further analysed.

In the analysis, we distinguish between n-grams, that is, recurrent sequences of n words/lemmata extracted on the basis of their frequency in the corpus; and patterns, that is, meaningful sequences of words/lemmata identified on the basis of n-grams which were found to perform a particular function in newspaper reporting.

5.4 Prepositional n-grams and patterns

5.4.1 The structure of in/v n-grams

This section describes the formal properties of the IN/V n-grams, namely the position of the preposition within the n-gram and the structure of the n-grams. The numbers of prepositional n-grams analysed are given in Table 5.2.

In both languages, the preposition occupied the initial position in the n-gram most frequently (Table 5.3), indicating that prepositions tend to form recurrent chunks with their prepositional complements, for example, IN RECENT YEAR; V LOŇSKÝ ROK. In the English data, the medial position of IN (e.g. LIVE IN THE) was slightly more frequent than the final position (e.g. BE BEAR IN). In Czech, V occurred in the final position (e.g. KTERÝ SE V) more often than in the medial one (e.g. SE V SOBOTA). The two Czech n-gram types tagged as 'initial/final' start and end with the preposition V, for example, V SOBOTA V.

A comparison of the numbers of n-gram types and n-gram tokens reveals similar ratios for both initial and final patterns, suggesting a similar degree of lexical richness on either side of the prepositions.

Table 5.2 The frequencies of the prepositional n-grams analysed

	n-gram types	n-gram tokens	The most frequent pattern and its frequency (tokens)
V n-grams	137	4,021,277	V [NUMBER]. 314,254
IN n-grams	198	4,447,236	IN [NUMBER], 316,042

Table 5.3 The position of the prepositions IN and V in the n-grams

Position (example)	IN				V			
	Types		Tokens	Type/token ratio	Types		Tokens	Type/token ratio
Initial (IN RECENT YEAR)	125	63.1 %	3,071,592	0.004	78	56.9 %	2,395,095	0.003
Medial (LIVE IN THE)	42	21.2 %	798,482	0.005	27	19.7 %	533,872	0.005
Final (BE BEAR IN)	31	15.7 %	577,162	0.005	30	21.9 %	1,046,652	0.002
Initial/final (V SOBOTA V)	0	0 %	0	0	2	1.5 %	45,658	0.004

The structural classification of prepositional n-grams draws partly on Biber, Conrad and Cortes (2004) in distinguishing among phrase-based and clause-based n-grams. Apart from these, there are n-grams which do not contain any lexical word, that is, 'grammatical' n-grams (cf. Čermáková and Chlumská 2016). The structural types of n-grams are exemplified in Table 5.4. The n-grams with initial prepositions comprise a complement of the preposition realized by a noun phrase or its fragment (e.g. IN HIS FIRST) or by a numerical expression. The final preposition typically follows a verb or a noun. Two structural types are peculiar to the medial position, where the preposition often links a verb and the following noun phrase (verb * noun/number), or a noun phrase with another noun phrase fragment (noun * noun). The latter type was attested only in the English data, highlighting the role of prepositional phrases as postmodifiers of nouns. The rare clause-based n-grams comprise fragments of adjectival relative clauses (two types in English, and four in Czech[11]) and the n-gram THEY BE IN.

The number of n-grams comprising numerical expressions is striking. The class 'number' in Table 5.4 comprises only n-grams in which the numerical expression functions as an equivalent of a phrase. The numbers, however, are also used as determiners in numerous n-grams. In the English data, forty-seven n-gram types (23.7 per cent) comprise at least one numerical expression; in Czech the ratio is even higher, 37.2 per cent (fifty-one n-gram types).

Punctuation marks (full stops, commas, hyphens, quotation marks, and brackets), for example, , IN WHICH, , V KTERÝ occurred in forty-two English and forty-three Czech n-gram types (21.2 and 31.4 per cent, respectively).

Table 5.4 Structural classification of prepositional n-grams

		English (IN)		Czech (V)	
		% (types)	Example	% (types)	Example
Grammatical		4.5	IN WHICH HE	7.3	, ALE I V
Phrase-based	noun	57.6	IN APRIL [NUMBER]	60.6	V MINULÝ ROK
	number	12.1	IN [NUMBER] WHEN	9.5	V [NUMBER],
	verb	7.1	BE KILL IN	5.1	SE KONAT V
	adverb (* noun/number)	2.0	, ESPECIALLY IN	2.2	DNES V [NUMBER]
	verb * noun/number	10.1	BE IN CHARGE	12.4	BÝT V SOBOTA
	noun * noun	5.1	PEOPLE IN THE	0.0	-
Clause-based		1.5	WHO LIVE IN	2.9	, KTERÝ BÝT V
Total		100.0		100.0	

5.4.2 The functions of in/v n-grams

5.4.2.1 *The classification*

The n-grams were further analysed with regard to their semantics and/or the textual function they fulfilled, considering the collocates of the n-gram where necessary. The semantic/functional properties of the n-grams are more difficult to classify than the structural features. Some n-grams cannot be assigned a general function; this applies in particular to the n-grams comprising numerical expressions, whose function is highly context-dependent. For instance, in the most frequent IN n-gram IN [NUMBER], the numerical expression typically refers to a year (4a). There are, however, numerous instances where it is used to describe a game of golf (4b).

(4)   a. After a decline *in 2011,* the market had opened 2012 on negative note as investors maintained cautious approach.
     b. He raced to the turn *in 30,* made up of five birdies and four pars.

Some n-grams were assigned several functional labels at the same time. The n-grams V DRUHÝ POLOČAS, V DRUHÝ KOLO, V PRVNÍ KOLO, V PRVNÍ POLOVINA, V PRVNÍ PŮLE (IN THE SECOND HALF, IN THE SECOND ROUND, IN THE FIRST ROUND, the last two both translate as IN THE FIRST HALF) are associated with sports commentaries (the second/first half of a match), and can be considered 'aboutness' patterns. At the same time, the ordinal numbers DRUHÝ and PRVNÍ (SECOND, FIRST) allow for the association with other patterns describing order or rank, such as I V DALŠÍ or its equivalent IN THE NEXT, which refer to time. We will therefore aim at exploring general tendencies rather than providing a rigorous quantitative overview of the functions, bearing in mind the polyfunctionality of some n-grams and the fact that their function may be context-dependent.

Generally, the prepositional n-grams can be divided into three broad types. 'Aboutness' n-grams reflect the topic of the newspaper report. Their frequency and types therefore depend on the composition of the corpus. In both corpora used in the present study, patterns associated with sports reporting can be identified, for example, IN THE PREMIER LEAGUE, PLAYER IN THE, MISTROVSTVÍ SVĚT V (WORLD CHAMPIONSHIP IN), V [NUMBER]. KOLO (IN THE [NUMBER] ROUND). Other areas include, for instance, film and theatre, for example, IN THE FILM, V HLAVNÍ ROLE (starring), crime and justice, for example, BE KILLED IN, KRAJSKÝ SOUD V (REGIONAL COURT IN), or business, for example, IN THE MARKET. 'Aboutness' n-grams form approximately 8 per cent of n-gram types, overlapping to a large extent with other classes. A small proportion (1 per cent) of n-grams, viz. 'grammatical' ones, neither comprises any lexical word, nor expresses any specific textual function, for example, HAVE BE IN THE, SE V ON (SE-reflexive IN HE). In the following sections, we will explore the third group of n-grams, namely those which form register-specific patterns associated with a particular meaning or function, such as temporal patterns or multi-word prepositions.

5.4.2.2 Time and place patterns

In both languages, most IN/V patterns perform temporal and locative functions, highlighting the newsworthiness of the 'when' and 'where' in newspaper reporting. The patterns in which the temporal function is indicated by a lexical or grammatical word (e.g. IN JANUARY [NUMBER], example 5a) constitute 18 and 40 per cent of the IN and V pattern types, respectively. The inclusion of patterns where time is indicated only by a numeral, for example, IN [NUMBER] , THE, further increases the ratio (5b). This applies in particular to the English patterns comprising a [NUMBER] slot which typically refers to a year, for example, IN [NUMBER] , AND; IN [NUMBER] , HE; IN [NUMBER] -. The corresponding Czech patterns were classified as temporal due to the expression V ROK (IN YEAR), the standard way of referring to years in Czech (5c).

There are also differences between the two languages in the lexical words used in temporal patterns. The Czech frequent general pattern V [DAY OF THE WEEK] [NUMBER] (example 5d) suggests a higher proportion of regional newspapers focusing on local events in the Czech data. On the other hand, the frequent general English temporal pattern IN [MONTH] [NUMBER] (e.g. *in January 2012*) has no direct counterpart among the frequent Czech patterns.

(5) a. Keith Williams became British Airways' chief executive *in January 2011*, following the merger with Iberia.
 b. *In 2011, the* number of accidents was 271 (with 47 killed and 98 injured).
 c. V Sapporu Neumannová už závodila *v roce 1995 a* tehdy se jí nedařilo. (In Sapporo, Neumannová took part in a race already *in the year 1995 and* did not succeed then.)
 d. [. . .] *ve čtvrtek 6. 8.* se v Tučapech u Soběslavi ztratil pětiletý zlatý kokršpaněl slyšící na jméno Ben.
 (on Thursday 6 August, a five-year-old golden cocker-spaniel named Ben was lost in Tučapy near Soběslav)

The 'place' patterns form 19 and 14 per cent of the English and Czech n-gram types, respectively. In both languages, the prevalent form of the pattern consists of the initial preposition complemented by a noun phrase referring to a location (6 a, b).

(6) a. But *in the United States*, the outlook is less favourable.
   b. Průměrný věk osobních vozidel *v České republice* je neuvěřitelných 13 a půl roku.
   (The average age of cars *in the Czech Republic* is an incredible 13 and a half year.)

Apart from indicating the geographical scope of events covered by the newspapers in the two corpora, the results also suggest potential methodological caveats of the n-gram method. The English patterns referring to general locations (IN THE REGION, IN THE CITY, IN THE WEST) had no corresponding counterpart in the Czech data. This may be because the Czech translations (v regionu, ve městě, na západě) would be bigrams and hence too short to be revealed by our n-gram search. This points to the limitations of our method, as well as to typological differences between the languages – unlike English, Czech noun phrases do not contain determiners. The Czech place patterns are most often toponyms comprising several words, overrepresented in the data because they are more readily captured by the n-gram method than other, shorter expressions.

The temporal or local specification can also be expressed by patterns indicating an order or sequence (8 and 6 per cent of n-gram types in English and Czech, respectively), for example, IN THE NEXT, THE FIRST TIME IN, SE V POSLEDNÍ (SE-reflexive IN LAST), *I V DALŠÍ* (ALSO IN OTHER) (examples 4 a, b).

5.4.2.3 *Communication patterns*

What was termed 'communication patterns' here comprises n-grams which contain SAY/ŘÍCI, a noun describing the type of communication (INTERVIEW/ ROZHOVOR, STATEMENT), and/or quotation marks. From the content point of view, communication patterns underline the importance of quoting opinions and attitudes in newspaper reporting. From the methodological point of view, patterns with quotation marks, such as [QUOTE] *IN THE* (example 7), may justify the inclusion of punctuation in the n-gram definition, drawing our attention to this prominent feature of newspaper discourse.

(7) The statement said: '*In the first instance*, Chief Timipre Sylva is not having 48 properties anywhere in the world.'

5.4.2.4 Verbal patterns of occurrence, existence, and inclusion or relationship

Apart from the communication verbs SAY/ŘÍCI, the verbs attested in the n-grams can be classified as verbs and verbo-nominal expressions of occurrence, existence or relationship (cf. Biber et al. 1999: 360–6), for example, APPEAR IN THE, TAKE PLACE IN, BE HOLD IN, BE INVOLVE IN, SE STÁT V (HAPPEN IN), SE KONAT V (TAKE PLACE IN). This is an expected semantic class since writing about events held or happening at particular times or places, and including particular participants can be seen as the core of newspaper reporting.

5.4.2.5 Patterns at clausal boundaries and multi-word idiomatic expressions

These two types of patterns are perhaps more interesting to consider with respect to the method than to the register. Both display little variation. Idiomatic multi-word phrases, such as IN AN ATTEMPT TO, IN THE LONG TERM/RUN, V POŘÁDEK (IN ORDER), are by definition invariable. We have also observed relatively fixed patterning around clausal boundaries signalled by commas, conjunctions *(but/ale, že* (that)) and relative pronouns, for example, , IN WHICH, , JENŽ V (, WHICH IN). We may include in this group also the clausal patterns – in most cases fragments of dependent relative clauses, for example, WHO BE IN, , KTERÝ BÝT V (, WHO/WHICH BE IN). These recurrent patterns are easier to spot using the method adopted here due to the obligatory comma preceding a subordinative conjunction or relative pronoun in Czech.

5.4.2.6 Multi-word (complex) prepositions

In both languages, between 5 and 6 per cent of n-gram types function as secondary multi-word prepositions, most often with the structure IN/V (THE) [NOUN] [PREPOSITION], for example, *in connection with, in the face of, v souvislosti s, v rozporu s* (cf. Klégr 2002, Cvrček et al. 2015: 333–4).

To explore the textual functions of the multi-word prepositions, we examine their collocations (within a window of three positions on either side, ordered by LogDice to favour typical collocates). We first describe the results separately for Czech and English and then compare the functions of complex prepositions in newspapers cross-linguistically.

5.4.2.6.1 Complex prepositional patterns in Czech newspapers

Complex prepositions containing V were represented by six types of V patterns. Table 5.5 and the following discussion give the prepositions as word forms, which are the only manifestations of the lemmatized n-grams.[12]

Table 5.5 Complex prepositions containing *v* sorted by frequency

Preposition	Translation	Frequency
v souvislosti s	'in connection with', 'regarding', 'concerning'	49,197
ve spolupráci s	'in cooperation with', 'in collaboration with'	39,987
v případě, že	'in case that', 'in the event that'	33,382
v čele s	'led by'	20,770
v rozporu s	'in contradiction to', 'contrary to'	13,157
v době od	'in the time since/from'	10,257
Total		**166,750**

This section addresses each complex preposition, analysing its left- and right-hand collocates separately. We considered the top 50 collocates as ordered by LogDice. We focus on identifying potential semantic preferences or evaluative prosodies of each complex preposition.

- ***V souvislosti s*** (in connection with, regarding, concerning)

The left collocates of *v souvislosti s* include expressions related to criminal investigation: VYŠETŘOVAT, STÍHAT, ZATKNOUT, OBVINIT, POLICIE, PODVOD, TRESTNÍ OZNÁMENÍ, ÚPLATEK (INVESTIGATE, PROSECUTE, ARREST, CHARGE, POLICE, FRAUD, CRIMINAL COMPLAINT, BRIBE). These collocates suggest a semantic preference for crime-related contexts and a negative evaluative prosody. Other typical left collocates were verbs of speaking: HOVOŘIT, MLUVIT (both SPEAK), SKLOŇOVAT (lit. DECLINE but used in the sense of MENTION; example 8), ZMIŇOVAT (MENTION).

(8) Jméno plavkyně Yvetty Hlaváčové je v posledních letech skloňováno v souvislosti s legendární úžinou La Manche.

(The name of the swimmer Yvetta Hlaváčová has been mentioned in the recent years in connection with the legendary English Channel.)

On the right, the top-ranking collocates CHYSTANÝ, PŘIPRAVOVANÝ (under preparation), BLÍŽÍCÍ (approaching), VÝSTAVBA (construction) suggest an association with plans and future outlooks, as do further collocates referring to changes, viz. PRIVATIZACE, REFORMA, UKONČENÍ, NOVELA, REKONSTRUKCE (PRIVATIZATION, REFORM, TERMINATION, NOVELIZATION, RECONSTRUCTION). Apart from this, most right collocates of *v souvislosti s* again point towards a negative semantic prosody: AFÉRA, KAUZA, KRACH, ATENTÁT, ÚTOK, VRAŽDA, KRIZE, POVODEŇ, SKANDÁL, VYŠETŘOVÁNÍ (AFFAIR, CASE, BANKRUPTCY, ASSASSINATION, ATTACK, MURDER, CRISIS, FLOOD, SCANDAL, INVESTIGATION) and the adjectives KORUPČNÍ and TERORISTICKÝ (CORRUPTION, TERRORIST). While SOUVISLOST (CONNECTION) itself seems emotionally inexpressive,[13] the complex preposition *v souvislosti s* shows a negative semantic prosody and a preference for contexts related to crime and/or other undesirable phenomena. Other uses of the preposition were neutral in terms of evaluative prosody but were frequent in sports reporting. The findings confirm that a word's negative semantic prosody is often not identifiable solely on the basis of the word itself – it is only revealed through an analysis of its recurrent contexts (cf. Sinclair 1987, in Partington 2004: 132; or Sinclair 2004: 142–7).

- ***Ve spolupráci s*** (in cooperation with, in collaboration with)

The left collocates of *ve spolupráci s* include verbs referring to organizing: the synonyms POŘÁDAT, USPOŘÁDAT, ORGANIZOVAT (ORGANIZE), VZNIKAT, PŘIPRAVIT, REALIZOVAT (FORM, PREPARE, CARRY OUT). The collocates BELETRISTICKÝ, RUBRIKA, VÝSTAVA, DENÍK, MUSEUM, KNIHOVNA (FICTION, NEWSPAPER SECTION, EXHIBITION, DAILY NEWSPAPER, MUSEUM, LIBRARY) indicate a preference for the semantic areas of media and cultural events. Other left collocates, REDAKCE, SDRUŽENÍ, NAKLADATELSTVÍ, SPOLEK (EDITORIAL BOARD, ASSOCIATION, PUBLISHING HOUSE, CLUB), as well as frequent right-hand collocates, for example, NADACE, AGENTURA, INSTITUT, VELVYSLANECTVÍ, ÚSTAV, ÚŘAD, MUZEUM (FOUNDATION, AGENCY, INSTITUTE, EMBASSY, INSTITUTE, OFFICE, MUSEUM), reveal a clear semantic preference; they all refer to institutions. To sum up, *ve spolupráci s* shows a preference for contexts informing readers about (cultural) events and introducing their organizers.

- ***V případě, že*** (in case that, in the event that)

Apart from the synonymous focusing adverbs *jedině, pouze, jen* (only), most of the strongest left collocates of *v případě, že* are verbs, which together with the preposition delineate the conditions or rules of particular procedures: POSTUPOVAT, NASTAT, PLATIT, HROZIT, VYPLATIT, UHRADIT, POSKYTNOUT, ZASÁHNOUT, UPLATNIT (PROCEED, OCCUR, APPLY, THREATEN, IMBURSE, PAY, PROVIDE, INTERVENE, IMPLEMENT). Some of verbs, together with the nouns SANKCE (SANCTION) and POJIŠTĚNÍ (INSURANCE) point to a possible preference for financial contexts.[14]

The right collocates comprise the general verb DOJÍT K (OCCUR); and a number of further verbs referring to official interactions: PROKÁZAT, PORUŠIT, SPLNIT, UZNAT, SCHVÁLIT, PŘESÁHNOUT (PROVE, BREACH, FULFIL, APPROVE, AUTHORIZE, EXCEED). Nominal right-hand collocates refer to participants in such interactions: KLIENT, DLUŽNÍK, NÁJEMCE, ŽADATEL, POPLATNÍK, ZAMĚSTNAVATEL (CLIENT, DEBTOR, TENANT, APPLICANT, TAXPAYER, EMPLOYER).

Although the preposition *v případě, že* carries a very general meaning, the collocations indicate its semantic preference in Czech newspapers: it tends to refer to formal, official interactions which may also involve financial transactions.

- *V čele s* (led by)

The left collocates of *v čele s* comprise words referring to groups of people for example, DELEGACE, POROTA, PRŮVOD, KONSORCIUM (DELEGATION, JURY, PARADE, CONSORTIUM), whose leader is introduced by *v čele s*. There are several positively evaluative expressions: ŠPIČKA, ZRUČNÝ, ELITA, HVĚZDA (TOP, SKILLED, ELITE, STAR). The right-hand collocates of *v čele s* introduce an agent, referring to professions or other positions (FRONTMAN), and proper names (JÁGR). They reveal persons who are presented as holding a position of power. These can be grouped into the following clusters: artists (FRONTMAN, REŽISÉR – director, DIRIGENT – conductor), sportspeople (JÁGR, BRANKÁŘ, GÓLMAN – GOALKEEPER, KAPITÁN – CAPTAIN[15]), politicians (HEJTMAN – GOVERNOR, PRIMÁTOR – MAYOR, PREMIÉR – PM, ARAFAT), (marginally) military officers (GENERAL – GENERAL). As regards semantic preference, most collocates were descriptive agent and proper nouns, yet others point towards a positively evaluative prosody of *v čele s*: CHARISMATICKÝ, LEGENDÁRNÍ, VYNIKAJÍCÍ (CHARISMATIC, LEGENDARY, OUTSTANDING), in line with the left collocates.

- *V rozporu s* (in contradiction to, contrary to)

V rozporu s collocates with expressions from the legal field: PŘEDPISY, ÚSTAVA, LEGISLATIVA (REGULATIONS, CONSTITUTION, LEGISLATION). Further collocates were ETIKA, LOGIKA, PRINCIP, TVRZENÍ, ROZKAZ (ETHICS, LOGIC, PRINCIPLE, ASSERTION, ORDER) or DOBRÉ MRAVY (GOOD MANNERS). Here, *v rozporu s* manifests a negative semantic prosody, implied by the lexical meaning of ROZPOR.

- *V době od* (in the time since/from)

The left collocates of *v době od* revealed an unexpected negative evaluative prosody and a semantic preference for crime report contexts: VLOUPAT, VNIKNOUT, ODCIZIT / UKRÁST, KRÁDEŽ, VYPÁČIT, PACHATEL, ZLODĚJ / NENECHAVEC / POBERTA (BURGLE, INTRUDE, STEAL, THEFT, PRY OPEN, PERPETRATOR, THIEF). The collocates VÝLUKA (DISRUPTION, e.g. on the railway), PŘISTAVIT (MAKE AVAILABLE) present local residents with practical topical information.[16] Finally, several collocates, both left and right, are temporal expressions and numbers expressing time, in line with the meaning of the preposition: NĚKDY, PONDĚLÍ, VŠEDNÍ, PROSINEC (SOMETIME, MONDAY, WORKDAY, DECEMBER).

5.4.2.6.2 Complex prepositional patterns in English newspapers

In this part of the study, an analogous study to that on Czech newspapers is conducted. We focus on complex prepositions identified among *in* patterns. The complex *in* prepositions found in the English data are listed in Table 5.6. Overlaps between some 3-grams and 4-grams were found, indicating that the prepositions *in the face (of)* and *in the wake (of)* are often followed by *of*. During the collocation analysis, we bore this in mind but only looked for collocates using the shorter variant as our starting point (i.e. without *of*). The longer variants (containing *of*) are not included in the total count.

The complex prepositions were again examined through their collocations to reveal semantic preferences and/or evaluative prosodies, focusing on left and right collocates separately for each prepositional pattern. Collocations were ranked by LogDice in SketchEngine to prioritize typicality.

- ***In favour of***

The preposition *in favour of* shows a semantic preference for legal or political contexts: left collocates are related to decisions of political entities or courts (*VOTE*, *RULED*), as well as evaluative collocates pointing to an imbalance (*WEIGHTED*,

Table 5.6 Complex prepositions with *in* ordered by frequency

Preposition	Frequency
in favour of	24,971
in the face	21,693
in charge of	20,931
in the wake	19,697
in the wake (of)	19,628
in touch with	15,844
in the face (of)	15,781
in the event	12,112
in search of	11,794
in connection with	11,201
in the hope	10,242
Total (without overlaps)	**148,485**

BIASED, SKEWED): though *in favour of* itself expresses positive meaning, its evaluative prosody seems rather negative. Right collocates were varied: the subjects of the voting, ruling and so on. (MOTION, BAN, STRIKE, AMENDMENT), MARRIAGE,[17] and RETAINING, KEEPING as opposed to REFORM and ACTION.

- **In the face (of)**

In the face typically occurs as part of the idiomatic FLY *in the face of*. Apart from that, it is preceded by adjectives and nouns referring to strength (RESILIENCE, COURAGE, BRAVERY, DIGNITY) or the contrary (POWERLESS, HELPLESS). Right collocates refer to challenging (COMPETITION, ODDS) or unfavourable conditions (ADVERSITY, OPPOSITION, CRITICISM, HOSTILITY, ONSLAUGHT, PROVOCATION, THREATS), some are emphasizing modifiers (MOUNTING, OVERWHELMING, STIFF, FIERCE). The left and right collocates combine to portray an agent coping with a difficult situation.

- **In charge of**

Left collocates of *in charge of* are job titles, referring to public figures in positions of authority: OFFICER, COMMISSIONER, MINISTER, ASSISTANT, VICE-PRESIDENT, OFFICIAL, DETECTIVE, COMMANDER, SECRETARY. Few collocates can be considered to have a particular semantic prosody, the negative *drunk in charge of*, typically referring to drunk driving (9).

(9) 'A person can be arrested for being drunk in charge of a vehicle if they have their car keys and approach their vehicle.'

Right collocates of *in charge of* refer to activities: nouns (*affairs, operations, finances, investigation, project, security*), or -ing verb forms (*policing, overseeing, implementing, organizing*); less typically to people (*under-21s, team*), institutions or workplaces (*station, police, ward, department*) or geographical regions (*Pradesh, Iraq's*). In sum, *in charge of* typically identifies a person responsible for a particular activity, place or area which is the subject of newspaper reporting.

- **In the wake (of)**

In case of *in the wake*, some left collocates are neutral (COME, INTRODUCE, ASSUME, SIGNIFICANCE), others negative (GUN; RESIGN, QUIT). A negative prosody is fully revealed by the right collocates: the majority of the top 20 refer to negative phenomena (*scandal, crisis, bombings, hurricane, shootings, collapse, tragedy*, including the topical *Katrina, Sandy* and *LIBOR*).

- **In touch with**

On the left, *in touch with* collocates most strongly with frequent verbs: KEEP, STAY, PUT, GET, and reinforcing adverbs *constantly*, *closely*, *always*. The right-hand collocates provide more insight into various contexts of use: they refer to people (*ex*, *relatives*, *friends*, *specialists*, *therapist*) but also include more abstract entities such as *feminine* (part of the phrase *in touch with their feminine side*, referring to men's behaviours, example 10), *roots*, *emotions*, *realities*, *sensuality*, *feelings* or *nature*.

(10) Either they get in touch with their feminine side, use moisturizer and all that, or they reject it and become badly behaved lads.

The collocates suggest that *in touch with* describes people's relationships and/or interactions, either with other individuals or with some abstract entities.

- **In the event**

In the event was revealed by both its left and right collocates to have a negative evaluative prosody. On the left it collocates with *liability*, *compensation*, *compete*, *exposed*, *retaliate*, *evacuation*, *emergency*, *losses*, *damages*. The top right collocate is *hung*; it refers almost exclusively to *hung parliament*, reflecting topical issues represented in the media. The rest of the right collocates are even more clearly negative than the left ones: *accident*, *emergency*, *pandemic*, *insolvency*, *invasion*, *error*, *divorce*, *death*, *failure* and many more – virtually all of the top 50 strongest collocates point to negative referents.

- **In search of**

The left collocates are mostly verbs of motion: GO, TRAVEL, VENTURE, MIGRATE, ROAM, WANDER. On the right, *in search of* is followed by a variety of complements, all of which refer to something desirable: *treasure*, *adventure*, *prey*, *clues*, *answers*; adjectival collocates include *cooler*, *perfect*.

The strongest collocates according to LogDice on both the left (*clubgoing*) and right side (*diversion*) were due to an advertisement repeated verbatim in the data (11). This confirms the importance of examining the collocates in context to identify potentially skewed results.

(11) Fuerza Bruta: Look Up' A sensory bath aimed at *clubgoing* college kids *in search of* cultural *diversion* (1:05). Daryl Roth Theater, 20 Union Square East, at 15th Street, (212) 239-6200, telecharge.com.

- ***In connection with***

The left and right collocates of *in connection with* unanimously point to a strikingly negative semantic prosody: left collocates include verbs referring to legal proceedings (*arrested, charged, detained, question, suspect, jail, interrogation*). Right collocates predominantly refer to crimes or other acts of violence (*murder, scam, robbery, kidnapping, rape, assault, blasts, bombing*), or potential crimes (*alleged, case, investigation*).

In connection with is a translation equivalent of the Czech preposition *v souvislosti s*, which was likewise prominent in Czech newspaper data. Interestingly both these corresponding prepositions were found to have a negative evaluative prosody, which is only revealed through the collocates, the preposition itself being neutral at face value.

In summary, the findings identified through collocates of complex prepositions support the assumption that journalism is not a purely neutral informative register. In both languages, complex prepositions exhibit semantic preferences (e.g. *in favour of* and *v rozporu s* occurring in legal contexts, or *in connection with* and *v době od* in crime reporting) as well as evaluative, usually negative, prosodies. The evaluative prosody of some complex prepositions containing *v* is directly derived from the lexical meaning of the noun contained in the preposition, as in *v rozporu s*. Elsewhere, the negative semantic prosody is not derivable from the lexical meaning of the complex preposition itself, as in *v souvislosti s*, *in the wake of*, *in the event*, and may even be in contrast with the evaluation expected on the basis of the meaning of the preposition, viz. the negative prosody associated with *in favour of*.

Notably, the semantic prosody or preference may not apply to all occurrences of the complex prepositions, and some uses are neutral in this regard.

5.5 Conclusions

5.5.1 Newspaper phraseology: summary of results

This study examined the register of newspaper reporting through the lens of n-grams, contrasting English and Czech newspapers. The focus was on prepositional patterns since prepositions (due to their frequency and even dispersion) allow for the identification of a variety of frequent and pervasive recurrent patterns. The study focused on *v*, the top frequent preposition in Czech, and its English counterpart IN. The n-gram method was complemented by an analysis of left and right collocations of selected n-grams forming complex prepositions, aiming to reveal their semantic preferences and/or prosodies.

From the contrastive perspective, the Czech 3–5-grams with v (with a minimum frequency of 10,000 tokens) displayed a lower relative frequency and greater variability (type/token ratio) than the English n-grams comprising IN. There were no marked structural differences between the English and Czech n-grams, the only exception being the pattern with the preposition linking two noun phrases, for example, PEOPLE IN THE, not attested in the Czech data.

In both Czech and English, prepositional patterns convey a range of meanings corresponding to the informational function of the newspaper register: reference to events (using verbs of occurrence and existence), their times and locations, or quoting people as sources of information. The text-organizing function of prepositional patterns is manifested by recurrent patterns at clause boundaries, comprising conjunctions, pronouns and punctuation. Some prepositional patterns were found to display similar semantic preferences in both languages. For instance, the (near-)equivalent pair of complex prepositions *in charge of* and *v čele s* (led by) introduces public figures and people holding various positions of power, suggesting that this textual function occurs in journalism regardless of the language or cultural background.

The findings of the collocation analysis seem in line with the assumption that newspaper texts are not purely informational, as reflected in prepositional patterns manifesting evaluative semantic prosodies, for example, the negative evaluative prosody of *in connection with s* or its Czech equivalent *v souvislosti*. However, the analysis of evaluative prosody raises a more general question of the delineation of evaluativeness. Even though some prepositional patterns manifest evaluative prosodies when occurring in newspapers, this alone does not reveal whether (and how) such evaluation contributes to newspaper texts carrying specific biases. This question needs to be addressed with the help of a close reading of particular texts, perhaps using critical discourse analysis methodology. A further potential bias which should be considered is the tendency of newspaper reporting to generally focus more on negative or problematic events, as these are deemed newsworthy.

5.5.2 Methodological findings

The n-gram method was adapted through the inclusion of punctuation in n-grams, working with lemmatized data and combining n-grams with collocation. In this section, we will briefly evaluate the method and discuss some other areas which still remain to be explored.

Lemmatization was introduced to allow for collapsing n-grams which only differ in inflection (prototypically morphological suffixes). This was seen as advantageous especially in Czech, and the Czech patterns which include verb lemmata appear to prove the point. The n-gram BÝT V SOBOTA (BE IN SATURDAY), for instance, comprises twenty-three different forms of the verb BÝT, presenting future or past events. However, some of our results confirmed that lemmatization can be problematic, concealing relevant differences between patterns (Čermáková and Chlumská 2016; Granger 2014): for example, V TENTO DEN in its plural form *v těchto dnech* (in these days) refers to current issues in progress, while its singular variant *v tento den* (in this day) pinpoints a particular date. In complex preposition patterns, lemmatization posed no major advantage, as they occur in invariable forms. Hence, the overall contribution of lemmatization is questionable. Reliably assessing to what degree lemmatization is beneficial would require a focused comparison of lemmatized and non-lemmatized n-grams retrieved from the same dataset, which is beyond the scope and goals of the present study.

Frequent recurrent patterning was identified around clause boundaries also thanks to including punctuation in the n-gram search. Yet punctuation is contained at the expense of wordforms or lemmata, hence the resulting n-grams reflect less about the lexical meanings of patterns. Further, due to the frequency of punctuation and overlaps between n-grams, a number of patterns may be represented multiple times.

We have opted for combining several n-gram sizes in the n-gram search to address typological differences between analytical English and inflectional Czech; the downside is that it results in numerous overlaps between n-grams, and hence does not allow for precise quantification of the findings. Furthermore, the semantic classification of n-grams proved problematic due to the polyfunctionality of some n-grams, and their functions being context-dependent.

The study has pointed towards several aspects of the newspaper register that can be efficiently revealed by n-grams: complex prepositions (a fruitful starting point towards identifying semantic prosodies and preferences through collocations), or lexical style markers which proved typical of the newspaper register in comparison with a general reference corpus. Hence the n-gram method seems suitable for revealing register-specific phraseological patterns. However, complementing n-grams with another method is advisable since it provides a more comprehensive portrayal of the register phraseology. The study combined several corpus methods to this end: n-grams were combined with a predetermined grammatical word – preposition, in order to identify patterns evenly dispersed throughout the data. The n-grams were checked against a reference corpus to identify those typical of the newspaper data. Next, collocations of selected patterns were explored to reveal how the patterns are employed in context and contribute to textual meanings, including evaluative ones. Overall, n-grams containing a function word were found to be an efficient gateway towards patterns with text-organizing functions.

Notes

1 This study was adapted from the previously unpublished chapter 4 of the Ph.D. dissertation by Denisa Šebestová, supervised by Markéta Malá (Šebestová 2022).
2 The preposition *v/ve* is the most frequent preposition both in the SYN2009PUB corpus (25,434.97 items per million tokens) and in the general representative SYN2010 corpus (19,335.33 items per million tokens). It has two forms; the vocalized form *ve* is used where the following word starts with *v* or *f* (*ve vesmíru*) or a consonant cluster (*ve středu*) (Cvrček et al. 2015: 340–1). Where v is spelt in small capitals as a lemma here, it comprises both forms.
3 In the InterCorp corpus (Rosen, Vavřín and Zasina 2020), the Treq tool (Škrabal and Vavřín 2017; Vavřín and Rosen 2015) retrieves 910,451 instances of *in* as the translation equivalent of *v*, followed by *at* with only 66,221 hits.
  Treq version 2.1, available at https://treq.korpus.cz/index.php (accessed 1 September 2021). Settings used: lemma, *v* from Czech to English, restricted to Collections.
4 This pertains to n-grams containing a figure such as 2; the # placeholder did not subsume n-grams containing a numeral word such as *two*. Thanks to dr. Michal Křen and dr. Pavel Vondřička from the Institute of the Czech National Corpus for their kind assistance with retrieving the data.
5 https://www.sketchengine.eu/my_keywords/non-word/ (accessed 1 March 2023).
6 In their statistical analysis of n-grams in the Norwegian Newspaper Corpus, Lyse and Andersen (2012: 86–7) adopted a similar approach to the extraction of n-grams, recording 'all punctuation marks as separate tokens in a sequence'; prior to the application of statistical association measures, however, n-grams with non-alphanumeric characters were removed from the dataset.
7 Křen (2009), Křen et al. (2010b).
8 All English translations of Czech corpus examples are ours, unless stated otherwise.
9 The SYN2010 corpus was accessed via the KonText interface (Machálek 2014); the British National Corpus 2014 via LancsBox X (Brezina and Platt 2023).

10 Log-likelihood statistic was used, with $p < 0.01$ (critical value = 6.63). Log-likelihood was calculated using the online Log-likelihood and effect size calculator, available online at https://ucrel.lancs.ac.uk/llwizard.html (accessed 1 March 2023).
11 In Czech, we analysed the particle SE as a component of a reflexive verb, and hence the n-gram KTERÝ SE V as a clause fragment with the subject KTERÝ and predicate verb represented by SE.
12 The English translations in Table 5.5 are ours and were consulted with equivalents found through the Treq database (Vavřín and Rosen 2015). Available at treq.korpus.cz (accessed 5 March 2023).
13 To verify this, we considered the collocates of the lemma *souvislost* in the representative SYN8 corpus (Křen et al. 2019) (collocation span 3L – 3R, ordered by logDice to prioritize typical collocates). The strongest collocates were mostly neutral (*tento* – this, *široký* – broad, *příčinný* – causal, *historický* – historical, *hovořit* – speak and other speaking verbs); only few could be regarded as negatively charged: *kauza*, *aféra* – affair, *vyšetřování* – investigation, *krize* – crisis.
14 Another collocate in this group was DAŇOVÝ ODEČET (TAX DEDUCTION). However, the concordances also revealed that thirty-six out of the thirty-eight occurrences of the collocate were identical, occurring in a repeated advertisement. Some collocates may therefore be overrepresented due to their occurrence in a newspaper section which is frequently reprinted. Sadly, we were not able to check this for each collocate due to their large numbers.
15 Thanks to the reviewer for pointing out that *kapitán* could (likely more often) refer to sportsmen apart from army officers.
16 All the occurrences of *přistavit* occurred in notices about scheduled dumpster days (cf. *Ve stanovený den budou kontejnery přistaveny vždy v době od 14 do 18 hodin.* 'On the date given, dumpsters will be available from 14 to 18 o'clock.')
17 The sequence *in favour of marriage* was marked as a typical collocate through the LogDice metric; admittedly it only occurred sixteen times – it seems to typically refer to marriage generically, as a public institution or a political topic (cf. *the Church had previously argued strongly in favour of marriage*).

References and sources

Biber, D., S. Johansson, G. Leech, S. Conrad and E. Finegan (1999), *Longman Grammar of Spoken and Written English*, London: Longman.
Biber, D., S. Conrad and V. Cortes (2004), 'If You Look at. . .: Lexical Bundles in University Teaching and Textbooks', *Applied Linguistics*, 25 (3): 371–405.
Brezina, V., A. Hawtin and T. McEnery (2021), 'The Written British National Corpus 2014 – Design and Comparability', *Text and Talk*, 41 (5–6): 595–615.

Brezina, V. and W. Platt (2023), '#LancsBox X' [software], Lancaster University. http://lancsbox.lancs.ac.uk

Čermáková, A. and L. Chlumská (2016), 'Jazyk dětské literatury: Kontrastivní srovnání angličtiny a češtiny', in A. Čermáková, L. Chlumská and M. Malá (eds), *Jazykové paralely*, 162–87, Prague: Nakladatelství Lidové noviny.

Cvrček, V., et al. (2015), *Mluvnice současné češtiny 1: Jak se píše a jak se mluví* (2.), Prague, Charles University: Nakladatelství Karolinum.

Ebeling, J. and S. O. Ebeling (2013), *Patterns in Contrast*, Amsterdam and Philadelphia: John Benjamins.

Granger, S. (2014), 'A Lexical Bundle Approach to Comparing Languages: Stems in English and French', *Languages in Contrast*, 14 (1): 58–72. https://doi.org/10.1075/lic.14.1.04gra

Groom, N. (2010), 'Closed-class Keywords and Corpus-driven Discourse Analysis', in M. Bondi and M. Scott (eds), *Keyness in Texts*, 59–78, Amsterdam and Philadelphia: John Benjamins.

Hunston, S. (2008), 'Starting with the Small Words. Patterns, Meaningful Units and Specialized Discourses', *International Journal of Corpus Linguistics*, 13 (3): 271–95.

Klégr, A. (2002), *English Complex Prepositions of the Type in Spite of and Analogous sequences. A Study and Dictionary*, Prague, Charles University: Nakladatelství Karolinum.

Křen, M. (2009), 'The SYN Concept: Towards One-Billion Corpus of Czech', in M. Mahlberg, V. González-Díaz and C. Smith (eds), *Proceedings of the Corpus Linguistics Conference*, Liverpool: University of Liverpool.

Křen, M., T. Bartoň, V. Cvrček, M. Hnátková, T. Jelínek, J. Kocek, R. Novotná, V. Petkevič, P. Procházka, V. Schmiedtová and H. Skoumalová (2010a), 'SYN2010: žánrově vyvážený korpus psané češtiny', Institute of the Czech National Corpus, Faculty of Arts, Charles University.

Křen, M., T. Bartoň, M. Hnátková, T. Jelínek, V. Petkevič, P. Procházka and H. Skoumalová (2010b), 'SYN2009PUB: korpus psané publicistiky', Institute of the Czech National Corpus, Faculty of Arts, Charles University. http://www.korpus.cz

Křen, M., V. Cvrček, T. Čapka, A. Čermáková, M. Hnátková, L. Chlumská, T. Jelínek, D. Kováříková, V. Petkevič, P. Procházka, H. Skoumalová, M. Škrabal, P. Truneček, P. Vondřička and A. Zasina (2019), 'SYN, Version 8 Out of 12', Institute of the Czech National Corpus, Faculty of Arts, Charles University. http://www.korpus.cz

Lyse, G. I. and G. Andersen (2012), 'Collocations and Statistical Analysis of n-grams. Multiword Expressions in Newspaper Text', in G. Andersen (ed.), *Exploring Newspaper Language: Using the Web to Create and Investigate a Large Corpus of Modern Norwegian*, 79–110. Amsterdam and Philadelphia: John Benjamins.

Machálek, T. (2014), 'KonText – Corpus Query Interface', Institute of the Czech National Corpus, Faculty of Arts, Charles University. http://www.kontext.korpus.cz

Malá, M., D. Šebestová and J. Milička (2021), 'The Expression of Time in English and Czech Children's Literature', in A. Čermáková, T. Egan, H. Hasselgård and S. Rørvik (eds), *Time in Languages*, 283–304. Amsterdam and Philadelphia: John Benjamins..

Partington, A. (2004), '"Utterly Content in Each Other's Company": Semantic Prosody and Semantic Preference', *International Journal of Corpus Linguistics*, 9 (1): 131–56. https://doi.org/10.1075/ijcl.9.1.07par

Rosen, A., M. Vavřín and A. J. Zasina (2020), 'The InterCorp Corpus, version 13 of 1 November 2020'. Institute of the Czech National Corpus, Faculty of Arts, Charles University. https://kontext.korpus.cz/

Scott, M. and C. Tribble (2006), *Textual Patterns: Key Words and Corpus Analysis in Language Education*, Amsterdam and Philadelphia: John Benjamins.

Šebestová, D. (2022), 'A Contrastive Description of English and Czech using the Methodology of n-gram Extraction', PhD diss., Faculty of Arts, Charles University.

Sinclair, J. (1991), *Corpus, Concordance, Collocation*, Oxford: Oxford University Press.

Sinclair, J. (2004), *Trust the Text*, London and New York: Routledge.

Škrabal, M. and M. Vavřín (2017), 'The Translation Equivalents Database (Treq) as a Lexicographer's Aid', in I. Kosem et al. (eds), *Electronic Lexicography in the 21st Century. Proceedings of eLex 2017 Conference*, 124–37, Lexical Computing CZ.

Vavřín, M. and A. Rosen (2015), *Treq (v. 2.1)*, Institute of the Czech National Corpus, Faculty of Arts, Charles University.. https://treq.korpus.cz/

6

A Cross-Linguistic Study of Journalistic Phraseology

Jiajin Xu, Guying Zhou, Xinlu Liu, Yuanyuan Wei, Ruchen Yu and Suhua Zhang

6.1 Introduction

The identification of a common ground, that is, 'tertium comparationis' (TC), is at the outset of most, if not all, contrastive linguistic studies. Contrastive linguists agree that a functional, semantic or conceptual notion may serve as the preferred TC. However, corpus linguistics may be characterized as a form-before-function field of inquiry. Thus, to delineate a comparable unit of analysis for comparing five typologically different languages: English (en), Chinese (cn), Swahili (sw), Arabic (ar) and Malay (ms) (the largest languages in each of the five largest language families, that is, Indo-European, Sino-Tibetan, Niger-Congo, Afro-Asiatic and Austronesian, by number of speakers; Eberhard, Simons and Fennig 2022), is no easy task. When we examine different schools of corpus linguistics, we see that among Birmingham-influenced corpus scholars, the unit of meaning, represented by the phrase, has become a central research focus (Sinclair 1996, 2008). Hence, we take phrase-level units as the TC ad hoc for our current contrastive study. More specifically, we propose to retrieve phrase-frames (henceforth, p-frames) from the five languages as meaning-based TCs for our contrastive analysis. Unlike most previous studies, this study does not focus on one or a few specific linguistic units, but instead on the 100 most frequent phrasal units in our multilingual dataset. We regard phrasal meaning units as a cumulative TC; that is, the aggregate of retrieved chunks plus variable content words (i.e. words in slots) presents a cross-linguistically comparable common entity.

In this study, p-frames serve as a window through which to examine structural and functional characteristics across the five languages. It is hypothesized that the p-frames of the five languages share similar functional distributions, as per the generic nature of journalism, but different structural patterns, given the morpho-syntactic differences or distances among them. Specifically, these five languages may appear, at least newswise, with different degrees of formulaicity. Some languages may exhibit a higher degree of variability in slot fillers as evidenced by higher type-token ratio (TTR) values; others may exhibit a greater degree of predictability in their use of meaning units, as reflected by higher normalized entropy values. Another very tentative, if not overambitious, aim of this study is to determine whether phraseological formulaicity can serve as an alternative measure for the typological classification of world languages, which has heretofore been informed by, for example, morphology, namely, isolating, agglutinative and inflected languages, as discussed in Sapir (1921), or by word order, namely, the subject-verb-object (SVO) and subject-object-verb (SOV) canonical word orders, as proposed by Greenberg (1963).

6.2 Previous studies on phraseological units in contrast

6.2.1 Phraseological units in general

As a growing number of researchers have recognized the importance of multi-word units (e.g. Firth 1957; Palmer 1933; Pawley and Syder 1983; Sinclair, Jones and Daley 1970/2004), phraseology has gradually come to the forefront of corpus analysis. This implies that the grammar-lexicon dichotomy may not always hold. As Sinclair (2008: 409) put it, the normal primary carrier of meaning is the phrase, not the word; he considers the phrase 'quite central and pivotal' to the description of meaning (2008: 408). Indeed, the term 'phrase' is usually loosely used to refer to 'multi-word combinations' resulting in varied definitions (see Gray and Biber 2013; Hunston 2022). In this chapter, we take a corpus-driven approach, considering a phraseological unit to be a contiguous and non-contiguous combination of two or more words that has a comparatively high frequency in the corpus and constitutes a semantic unit (cf. Römer 2010: 96).

Corpus studies and phraseology are intimately related, since the prevalence of recurrent multi-word units can hardly be noticed unless one studies texts and corpora (Stubbs 2009: 15). Conceptually rooted in language pedagogy, phraseological units have frequently been studied in corpus-linguistic research on L2 language use. They are often analyzed as having a particular interest in learner corpus studies, given the significance of acquiring productive knowledge of phraseology for L2 learners. The most common topics addressed in these studies concern the use of phraseological units by non-native and native speakers (e.g. Ädel and Erman 2012; Chen and Baker 2010; De Cock 2004; Juknevičienė 2009; Ren 2022), learners at different proficiency levels (e.g. Garner 2016; Hyland 2008a; Leńko-Szymańska 2014; Römer 2009; Tan and Römer 2022) and learners with different L1 backgrounds (e.g. Juknevičienė and Grabowski 2018; Paquot 2013, 2014; Wang 2016). In addition, phraseological units have received considerable attention in ESP (more specifically, EAP) studies. In this area of research, considerable attention has been focused on extracting and providing lists of pedagogically relevant academic phraseological items (e.g. Ackermann and Chen 2013; Golparvar and Barabadi 2020; Hyland 2008b; Lu, Yoon and Kisselev 2018; Martinez and Schmitt 2012; Simpson-Vlach and Ellis 2010). This line of research also yields important insights into register or genre variation, as it suggests that different genres or registers are characteristic of their corresponding sets of formulaic expressions and vice versa. Thus, such research is mostly concerned with formulaicity across different disciplines (e.g. Cortes 2013; Durrant and Mathews-Aydınlı 2011; Omidian, Shahriari and Siyanova-Chanturia 2018), although a series of studies by Biber and colleagues have focused on formulaicity across speech and writing (e.g. Biber 2009; Biber and Barbieri 2007; Biber, Conrad and Cortes 2004; Gray and Biber 2013).

However, the existing literature appears to have given inadequate consideration to phraseology across different languages. A number of studies have been devoted to non-compositional multi-word sequences, such as idioms or metaphors, cross-linguistically; however, as revealed by corpus studies, these opaque units are fairly marginal from a purely quantitative point of view (Colson 2008: 197). Recently, the compositional type has also been the subject of phraseological interest and discussion, particularly among corpus linguists (Ebeling and Ebeling 2013: 2). A growing number of corpus studies have begun to investigate multi-word combinations from a cross-linguistic perspective (e.g. Čermáková and Chlumská 2017; Granger 2014; Tognini-Bonelli 2002; Xiao 2011; Xiao and McEnery 2006). In this chapter, we assume that phraseology should be recognized as a fundamental aspect of language, with different languages encoding it in distinct formulaicities. Specifically, here we take phrase-frames (i.e. p-frames), which have thus far received only limited attention, as our point of departure.

6.2.2 P-frames

The corpus-based studies on phraseology mentioned above predominantly focus on continuous multi-word sequences, whereas relatively few investigations have focused on non-continuous phraseological units. Continuous phraseological units, such as lexical bundles, are uninterrupted multi-word strings, as exemplified by *the end of*; by contrast, discontinuous phraseological units such as p-frames feature a variable slot that distinguishes them from lexical bundles. One instance of such phraseological units is *the * of*, where * represents a variable slot that can be filled with words such as *rest* or *number*.

An increasing number of studies have focused on discontinuous multi-word sequences. Among others, p-frames allow researchers to account for not only the frequency of recurrent sequences of words but also their fixedness and pattern variability (cf. Forsyth and Grabowski 2015: 540). It has been demonstrated that p-frames can provide valuable insights into the formulaicity of a particular text type (Römer 2010), genre (Vincent 2013), register (Römer 2009) or language (Juknevičienė and Grabowski 2018). In our view, a contrastive analysis of p-frames across different languages allows for a more comprehensive understanding of the formulaic properties of a language.

In the initial stages, Renouf and Sinclair (1991: 128) referred to recurrent discontinuous multi-word expressions as 'collocational frameworks', identifying them in a top-down corpus-based way. While this shares similarities with the present-day understanding of p-frames, it differs in that p-frames are derived through a bottom-up, corpus-driven methodology, as exemplified by Fletcher (2002–2007). The predominant trend in this research area is the adoption of frequency-based approaches that utilize automatic identification techniques based on a frequency threshold. In contrast, the present study used a mixed method, combining a corpus-driven approach based on frequency with a manual filtering process that considers semantic completeness when the asterisk-marked slots are filled.

The most commonly examined aspects of p-frames in existing research are their variability, predictability and functions. Variability, also called 'variant/p-frame ratio' (VPR), is assessed by computing the TTR of the slot fillers within each p-frame (Römer 2010: 105). The TTR values range from 0 to 1, with values closer to 1 indicating higher variability. A p-frame is considered to exhibit high variability if the ratio of variant types in the slot per p-frame token is high. Predictability, which is used to evaluate the difficulty of determining which variant types will appear in the * slot of a p-frame, is usually calculated using normalized entropy (Tan and Römer 2022: 4). It is a measure of the uncertainty of a probability distribution and is computed by dividing the entropy by the logarithm of the number of possible outcomes, thus ranging from 0 to 1. A value closer to 1 indicates an even distribution (i.e. uncertainty), and all variants have an equal likelihood of occurrence. Broadly speaking, these two measures serve as indications of the co-selection between a given p-frame and its filler. In related studies, these measures have been primarily employed to examine whether native and non-native speakers (e.g. Ren 2022), as well as learners at varying levels of proficiency (e.g. Garner 2016; Tan and Römer 2022), demonstrate differential levels of sensitivity with respect to the typical fillers of particular p-frames. Furthermore, p-frames are often analyzed to investigate the relationship between linguistic forms and their rhetorical (e.g. Lu, Yoon and Kisselev 2021) or discourse functions (e.g. Golparvar and Barabadi 2020; Lu, Yoon and Kisselev 2018). Among the various categorization systems, the most commonly used is based on Biber, Conrad and Cortes's (2004) functional taxonomy, originally developed for lexical bundles.

Previous research on p-frames has primarily focused on examining the varying degrees of formulaicity within learner corpora, text types, genres and registers. By utilizing measures such as variability, predictability and functional analysis, these studies shed light on phraseological competence within or across learner groups as well as on formulaic characteristics within or across specific genres of language. Given this background, we assume that p-frames can also reflect varying degrees of formulaicity across languages, which has received limited attention in prior research. In the current study, p-frames are extracted based on frequency thresholds and semantic completeness across the five languages. The variability, predictability and discourse functions of phraseological units are examined to determine the extent to which meaning patterns were shared or distinct across these languages, thus reflecting the elasticity of the basic meaning units of a language.

6.3 Corpora and methods

6.3.1 Corpora

The data used in this study were newswire texts in Arabic, Chinese, English, Malay and Swahili. The data consists of approximately 176,000 words of diversely sampled news texts in each language. To maximize data comparability, the Brown corpus sampling frame (Francis and Kučera 1964, 1967) was followed: forty-four reports, twenty-seven editorials and seventeen reviews in five languages were collected.[1] Each language is represented by eighty-eight composite 2000-plus-word news texts, in which short texts were pieced together to form one 2000-word text but saved separately and marked with A, B, C and so on in the filenames. Since the running Chinese texts do not have spaces between words, the Jieba tokenization Python package was used to insert spaces between Chinese words. The genre subtypes were the same across the five languages: politics, sports, finance, society, culture and others. The newspapers in the five languages are broadsheets, mostly national newspapers with some local newspapers. The untagged raw texts were utilized for this study. All articles were published between 2019 and 2022. Hence, news texts in the five languages are highly comparable in terms of genre type, publication date and corpus size.

6.3.2 P-frame retrieval and analysis

Automatic retrieval and manual filtering were performed to collect legitimate three- to five-word discontinuous p-frames with one inner variable slot using AntGram (Anthony 2021). Unlike the morphological and word order approaches to classifying world languages, p-frames can serve as basic meaning units performing basic discourse functions, and they therefore constitute a worthwhile unit of analysis for cross-linguistic and typological generalization. N-grams with initial and final slots were disqualified in line with Garner (2016: 39). P-frames were automatically extracted based on frequency thresholds across the five languages. The length of the p-frames was determined on an incremental, trial basis. In all five languages, two-word phrases do not contain internal slots, and most of them are semantically incomplete. At the other extreme, there were too few instances of p-frames with more than five words in our dataset. Therefore, the top 150 three- to five-word p-frames were used for subsequent manual filtering (see the Appendix for the top 50 p-frames).

Four exclusion criteria were used to manually filter the p-frames: (1) semantically incomplete units; (2) units that cross clausal boundaries; (3) units that only consist of proper nouns, symbols, year or date, or punctuation; and

(4) units that belong to larger p-frames. For example, في * في ('in * in'), 月 * 日 ('month * day'), to * the, yang * dan ('where * and') and ya * ya ('of * of') were excluded. Manual filtering was performed by at least three people on average. Each analyst had to have full professional proficiency in the target language. The second or third analyst double-checked the annotations by the first analyst, as per the exclusion criteria.

Table 6.1 presents examples of frequent p-frames in the five languages. The top 100 p-frames were selected for follow-up analyses. If the 100th p-frame had immediate adjacent p-frames with the same frequency counts, then p-frames with the same frequency were also selected for further analysis. In our dataset, 100 plus 1–5 p-frames were analyzed from the p-frame lists of the five languages.

The variability, predictability and function of p-frames were of central concern in our study. The first two parameters were analyzed quantitatively, and the functional categories were manually annotated and quantified. All three aspects were compared across the five languages.

Table 6.1 Top 5 p-frames in the five languages

	Top 1	Top 2	Top 3	Top 4	Top 5
Arabic	في * من 110 'in many of'	من * في 96 'of its kind in'	من * أن 83 'without that'	من * إلى 80 'access to'	على * من 76 'in spite of'
Chinese	在 * 的 148 'with the new'	是 * 的 122 'is ours'	为 * 的 105 'centred/oriented'	有 * 的 91 'to some extent'	最 * 的 90 'most important'
English	the * of 1152 the end of	a * of 410 a lot of	the * to 192 the right to	the * that 187 the fact that	the * in 183 the most in
Malay	dan * yang 169 'and those who'	yang * di 131 'which takes place in'	memberi * kepada 102 'give effect to'	yang * dalam 95 'involved in'	yang * dengan 92 'related to'
Swahili	na * wa 692 'and the Minister of'	na * ya 628 'and some of'	kwa * ya 490 'for the sake of'	katika * ya 412 'in the case of'	kwa * wa 404 'in accordance with'

Note: For non-English p-frames, English translations of the units with the most frequent internal slot words and overall p-frame frequency are provided alongside the original script.

Variability was computed based on the TTR, and predictability was computed based on the normed entropy value of the probability distribution, provided by AntGram. The parameters of variability and predictability are concerned with the extent to which phraseological meaning units in news texts across the five languages adhere to conventionalized meaning patterns, thus reflecting the flexibility or creativity of a language.

The identification of the discourse-pragmatic functions of p-frames was performed qualitatively and independently by at least three people for each of the languages. The functional analysis employed in this study is based on Biber, Conrad and Cortes's (2004) functional taxonomy, which proposes four primary discourse functions: referential, stance, discourse organizer and special conversational expressions. Considering that the language data in the five languages are written text, only the first three categories were identified and assigned to p-frames in the current study. Furthermore, we adhered to the 'variant-based approach' (Lu, Yoon and Kisselev 2018: 79), in which the function of a p-frame was assigned according to the most frequent slot filler. See Table 6.2 for examples of multilingual p-frames with various functions.

Disagreements regarding the inclusion or exclusion of certain p-frames and functional identification were resolved through discussion. Subsequently, we utilized statistical methods based on R (R Core Team 2022) to investigate the structural and functional characteristics of p-frames across the five languages.

Table 6.2 Examples of discourse-pragmatic functions of p-frames in the five languages

	Referential	Stance-marking	Discourse-organizing
Arabic	من * إلى 'access to'	لا * أن 'it must be'	من * أخرى 'on the other hand'
Chinese	在 * 中 'in the speech of *'	最 * 的 'the most important'	等 * 的 'aspects such as'
English	a * of *a lot of*	was * to *was supposed to*	as * as *as well as*
Malay	di * negara 'all over the country'	yang * menjadi 'which will become'	pada * sama 'at the same time'
Swahili	katika * ya 'in the case of'	ni * wa 'it's time to'	ili * na 'in order to have'

Note: English translations of meaning units with most frequent slot filler are provided.

To analyze the variability and predictability of the p-frames provided by AntGram, we first created density plots and calculated median values. To determine whether there were statistically significant differences between the languages, a Wilcoxon test was used for pairwise comparisons. To explore the potential association between languages and discourse functions, we employed the chi-squared test and Cramer's V; additionally, a mosaic plot was used to visualize the strength and direction of the associations between the variables.

6.4 Results and discussion

Table 6.3 summarizes the distribution of identified p-frames across the five languages. For each language, three- to five-word p-frames were selected based on frequency threshold and semantic completeness. When the 100th p-frame had a few immediate adjacent p-frames with the same frequency count, additional p-frames were also included. Therefore, we identified 100(+) p-frames for further analysis for each language.

Based on the identified p-frames, the following discussion examines variability, predictability and discourse functions more closely to shed light on formulaic features across the five languages.

6.4.1 Variability and predictability

To attain a holistic understanding of the variability and predictability of p-frames across the five languages, we first used density plots to visualize the distribution of data and provide insights into the underlying data patterns. In Figure 6.1, the density plot on the left reflects the variability of p-frames across

Table 6.3 Summary of the 100 top 3–5-word p-frames of the five languages

	Arabic	Chinese	English	Malay	Swahili
3-word p-frames	100	96	97	103	90
4-word p-frames	0	6	7	2	9
5-word p-frames	0	0	0	0	1
Total	100	102	104	105	100
Freq. threshold	14	16	39	21	32

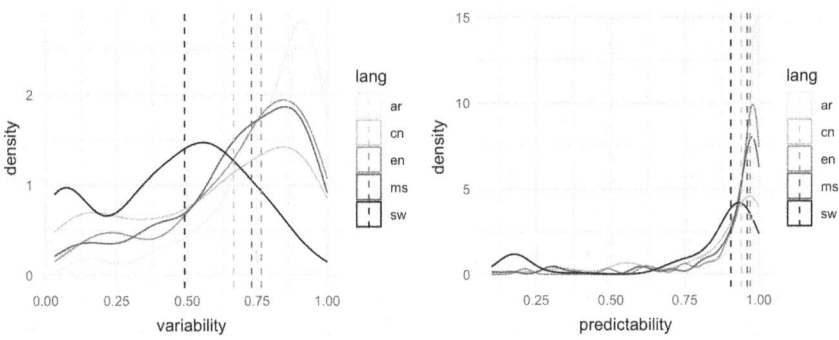

Figure 6.1 Density plots of variability and predictability across five languages, two parts.

Table 6.4 Median variability and median absolute deviation of the 100 top p-frames across the five languages

	Arabic	Chinese	English	Malay	Swahili
Median	0.8600	0.6650	0.7650	0.7300	0.4900
Median Absolute Deviation	0.1483	0.3262	0.2298	0.2372	0.2743

the five languages, with the median variability of each language indicated by dashed lines. Similarly, the density plot on the right shows the distribution of predictability and the median value for each language.

In each plot, the *x*-axis represents the values of variability (TTR) and predictability (normalized entropy), both ranging from 0 to 1, where a value closer to 1 indicates higher variability or uncertainty (i.e. lower predictability). The *y*-axis represents the density, that is, the relative frequency of the data points. Roughly, the distributions of variability and predictability take on similar patterns across the five languages; both plots are left-skewed, with a long tail extending to the left of the peak. The five language groups (ar, cn, en, ms and sw) exhibited a distinct central tendency in their variability. Arabic has the highest peak, at around 0.90, English (en) and Malay (ms) shared a similar peak at around 0.87, and Swahili (sw) and Chinese (cn) showed relatively low peaks at around 0.56 and 0.87. The median variability values of the five languages, indicated by the dashed lines in the plot, can be ranked in the following order: $0 < sw < cn < ms < en < ar < 1$. Table 6.4 lists the actual median values and median absolute deviations. Regarding predictability, Arabic (ar) exhibited the highest peak at approximately 1.0, indicating the highest degree of uncertainty among the five groups; Swahili (sw) demonstrated the lowest peak at around 0.9, reflecting a

Table 6.5 Median predictability and median absolute deviation of the 100 top p-frames across the five languages

	Arabic	Chinese	English	Malay	Swahili
Median	0.9800	0.9400	0.9700	0.9600	0.9050
Median Absolute Deviation	0.0297	0.0741	0.0297	0.0445	0.0815

comparatively lower level of uncertainty. The peaks for the intermediate groups – English (en), Malay (ms) and Chinese (cn) – exhibited gradually decreasing intermediate values, indicating correspondingly decreasing levels of uncertainty. The median entropy values of the five languages were ranked as follows: 0 < sw < cn < ms < en < ar < 1; these are also presented in Table 6.5.

Overall, the descriptive statistics suggest differentiated variability and predictability across the five languages. The median values for TTR and normalized entropy indicate the existence of a flexibility or creativity continuum across the five languages, with Arabic occupying the highest end of the spectrum, followed by English, Malay, Chinese and Swahili, in decreasing order of variability and increasing order of predictability.

However, the statistical significance of these findings requires further investigation. To this end, we employed the Wilcoxon test and applied a multiple-comparison procedure that computes all pairwise comparisons while controlling for the type-I error rate (see Kabacoff 2015: 162). With regard to variability, both Arabic (ar) and Swahili (sw) are statistically different from the other three languages: ar and cn ($W = 3187.5$, $p < 0.001$), ar and en ($W = 3990.0$, $p < 0.01$), ar and ms ($W = 3725.5$, $p < 0.01$), ar and sw ($W = 1396.5$, $p < 0.001$), sw and cn ($W = 3399.5$, $p < 0.001$), sw and en ($W = 2431.5$, $p < 0.001$), and sw and ms ($W = 2613.0$, $p < 0.001$). In contrast, there were no significant differences between Chinese (cn), English (en) and Malay (ms): cn and en ($W = 2613.0$, $p = 0.107$); cn and ms ($W = 4674.0$, $p = 0.228$); and en and ms ($W = 5180.0$, $p = 0.522$).

The situation was very similar in terms of predictability. Significant, pairwise, differences were found for Arabic (ar) and Swahili (SW). The distribution of the predictability values of Arabic (ar) was significantly different from that of the other languages studied here except English: ar and cn ($W = 3415.0$, $p < 0.001$), ar and ms ($W = 4156.5$, $p < 0.05$), ar and sw ($W = 1904.0$, $p < 0.01$), and ar and en ($W = 4403.0$, $p = 0.171$). Swahili (sw) was found to exhibit statistically significant differences from all the other languages: sw and ar ($W = 1904.0$, $p < 0.01$), sw and cn ($W = 3803.0$, $p < 0.05$), sw and en ($W = 2663.0$,

$p < 0.01$), and sw and ms (W = 3084.0, $p < 0.01$). There were no significant differences between Chinese (cn), English (en), and Malay (ms): cn and en (W = 4283.0, $p = 0.066$), cn and ms (W = 4645.5, $p = 0.197$), and en and ms (W = 5107.5, $p = 0.419$).

In summary, it is statistically supported that Arabic (ar) is the most variable and least predictable, while Swahili (sw) is the least variable and most predictable of the five languages. We thus consider these two languages to occupy opposite ends of the creativity and flexibility continuum. The remaining three languages, English (en), Malay (ms) and Chinese (cn), displayed gradually decreasing levels of variability and increasing levels of predictability; however, this ordering is only supported by the density plots and median values and is not statistically significant. Thus, based on both descriptive and analytical statistics, the flexibility or creativity continuum of the five languages can be roughly summarized as sw < (cn < ms < en) < ar, where brackets indicate statistically non-significant differences.

6.4.2 Functions

Having examined the variability and predictability of p-frames across the five languages, we now focus on the discourse functions of the identified p-frames. All of the top 100 p-frames were manually classified as either referential, stance-marking or discourse-organizing, following Biber, Conrad and Cortes (2004). The initial round of discourse function labelling of each of the five languages was completed by the author proficient in that language, and all uncertain instances, accounting for about 10 per cent of the data for the five languages, were discussed among the authors and other language experts based on the original p-frames and their English translations until unanimous agreement was reached. By analyzing the functions of these phraseological units, we can gain insights into how they are used cross-linguistically.

Table 6.6 summarizes the functional distributions of p-frames across the five languages. In all languages, referential expressions constitute the largest proportion, followed by stance-marking and discourse-organizing expressions. However, there were statistically significant differences in the functional distribution of p-frames across the five languages, with a small but almost medium effect size ($\chi^2 = 25.112$, $df = 8$, $p < 0.001$, Cramer's $V = 0.157$). These results suggest a weak-to-moderate relationship between language and the functional distribution of p-frames.

Table 6.6 Mean predictability of the 100 top p-frames across five languages

	Arabic	Chinese	English	Malay	Swahili
Referential	91	89	75	92	89
Stance-marking	6	11	25	9	6
Discourse-organizing	3	2	4	4	5
Total	100	102	104	105	100

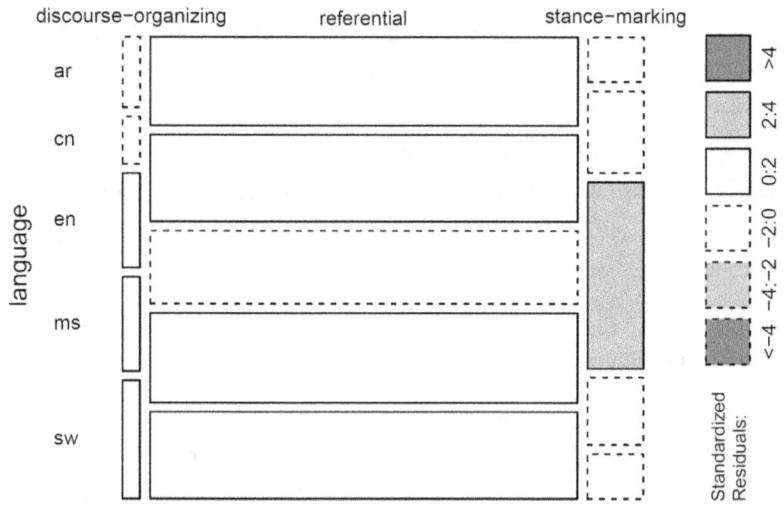

Figure 6.2 Mosaic plot of functional characteristics across five languages.

Furthermore, a mosaic plot was used to provide a visual representation of the chi-squared and Cramer's *V* statistics. In particular, a mosaic plot can help visually represent the structure of a contingency table, as well as the strength and direction of associations between the variables. In our case, this will help to identify and illustrate the relationship between discourse functions and different languages.

As shown in Figure 6.2, each rectangle in the mosaic plot represents a cell in the contingency table (see Table 6.6), with its area proportional to the observed frequency. Shading indicates the standardized residual, which reflects the degree to which a cell in a contingency table deviates from what would be expected if the row and column variables are independent. A positive standardized residual value indicates that the observed value in a cell is greater than expected, whereas a negative standard residual value indicates that the observed value is less than expected, based conventionally on a value of ±2 standard deviations. In our case, the mosaic plot demonstrates that the most notable difference between the five languages is the significantly more frequent usage of stance-marking expressions in English than in the other four languages.

Based on our findings, we can draw general conclusions about the distribution of the discourse-pragmatic functions of p-frames in newswire texts across the five languages. First, referential expressions comprise the largest proportion of p-frames in all five languages, followed by stance-marking and discourse-organizing expressions. This trend in the functional distribution of p-frames suggests that referring is a communicative or functionally dominant concept in newswire texts across languages.

Second, our analysis revealed that English employs a significantly higher proportion of stance-marking expressions, which may convey attitudes or assessments of certainty that frame other propositions (Biber, Conrad and Cortes 2004: 384). This difference in language use may be due to different media types and their attributes in the respective countries. For instance, English-language news media are often characterized by commerciality as opposed to state affiliation, which may influence language use in newswire texts. Additionally, the extent to which the English language per se typologically contains more stance-marking expressions than other languages remains in need of further exploration.

The structural variability/predictability and functional categorization of p-frames connect languages on a structural and functional continuum rather than dividing them into discrete islands. Morphological and word-order-motivated language classifications are either too local or syntactic. Phraseological units are the middle ground of unit of language analysis and, most importantly, they are meaning units for which a TC can be better identified for contrastive analysis. Alternatively, the automatically extracted p-frames can be examined using other functional frameworks.

6.5 Conclusion

This study demonstrates how a p-frame approach to phraseology can contribute to cross-linguistic comparisons among languages representing the five largest language families. The contrastive analysis sheds light on the structural and functional characteristics of p-frames in newswire texts across five languages: Arabic, Chinese, English, Malay and Swahili. Overall, we summarized a cross-linguistic variability cline, sw < (cn < ms < en) < ar, and a cross-linguistic predictability cline, sw > (cn > ms > en) > ar; the former represents an increasing degree of creativity, whereas the latter reflects descending idiomaticity across the five languages. Thus, through the window of p-frames, we have attained valuable insights into the complex and dynamic nature of language use, which is in line with how Sinclair (1991: 109–12) described the nature of language: the 'open-choice principle' and the 'idiom principle'. Moreover, regarding discourse functions, we found that the functional distribution of these phraseological units demonstrated a similar pattern across all languages. Specifically, referential expressions constitute the largest proportion of p-frames, followed by stance-marking and discourse-organizing expressions. This indicates the existence of communicative or functional universality in newswire texts across different languages. Our analysis also revealed statistically significant differences in the use of stance-marking expressions, with English employing a significantly higher proportion than other languages.

However, the current study has a major drawback in its generalizability: its reliance on single-genre news-text data. Therefore, the findings must be interpreted with caution, as they may not be representative of the entire language. The extent to which these findings can be generalized as typological features of the five languages, or others, remains to be explored and confirmed. A four-genre corpus project for these five languages is currently underway. The balanced corpora-based p-frame comparison will shed more light on the shared and individualistic phraseological behaviours of the five languages. A methodological limitation should also be noted, as the same frequency thresholds for all p-frame lengths appear to be arbitrary and require better justification in future research.

Acknowledgements

The work reported in this chapter was supported by the National Social Science Fund of China (Ref. No. 21BYY021) and the support of the National Research for Foreign Language Education, Beijing Foreign Studies University. We would like to thank Yingying Su, Professor of Malay, and Junyu Mao, graduate student in Arabic at Beijing Foreign Studies University, for their assistance in data collection and analysis. We are also grateful to the reviewers and editors for their constructive comments on the manuscript.

Note

1. The news corpora for the five languages (i.e. arBrown Press, ToRCH2019, CROWN2021, msBrown Press and swBrown Press) are accessible online at BFSU CQPweb Multilingual Corpus Portal (http:// 114.251.154.212/cqp/, user ID: test; password: test).

Appendix. The top 50 phrase-frames across the five languages

The top 50 phrase-frames in Arabic

Rank	P-frame	Frequency	Variability	Predictability	Function
1	في * من	110	0.66	0.93	referential
2	من * في	96	0.94	0.99	referential
3	من * أن	83	0.52	0.91	referential
4	من * إلى	80	0.89	0.98	referential
5	على * من	76	0.66	0.88	discourse-organizing
6	التي * في	67	0.93	0.99	referential
7	على * في	63	0.87	0.99	referential
8	من * التي	59	0.9	0.98	referential
9	أن * في	58	0.93	0.99	referential
10	في * على	53	0.81	0.97	referential
11	إلى * في	52	0.96	1	referential
12	التي * بها	51	0.75	0.96	referential
13	إلى * من	50	0.8	0.98	referential
14	في * التي	45	0.8	0.93	referential
15	في * إلى	42	0.79	0.97	referential
16	الذي * في	41	0.93	0.99	referential
17	من * من	41	0.98	1	referential
18	في * مع	40	0.68	0.89	referential
19	عن * في	36	0.97	1	referential
20	في * ما	36	0.86	0.99	referential
21	لا * أن	36	0.69	0.94	stance-marking

The top 50 phrase-frames in Arabic (Continued)

Rank	P-frame	Frequency	Variability	Predictability	Function
22	ما * من	36	0.86	0.98	referential
23	التي * فيها	34	0.88	0.98	referential
24	أن * من	33	0.73	0.94	referential
25	التي * على	33	0.94	0.99	referential
26	في * أن	29	0.69	0.93	referential
27	في * الأخيرة	29	0.41	0.86	referential
28	في * العربية	29	0.59	0.96	referential
29	لا * في	29	0.76	0.92	referential
30	أن * إلى	27	0.89	0.99	referential
31	بعد * من	27	0.7	0.94	referential
32	قطاع * بنسبة	27	0.44	0.94	referential
33	التي * عليها	26	0.96	1	referential
34	لا * من	26	0.69	0.89	stance-marking
35	ما * في	26	0.88	0.98	referential
36	لا * على	25	0.72	0.91	referential
37	أو * في	24	0.96	1	referential
38	الذي * به	24	0.83	0.98	referential
39	الذي * على	24	0.88	0.99	referential
40	أن * لم	23	0.96	0.99	referential
41	على * أن	23	0.87	0.98	referential
42	في * عن	23	0.78	0.94	referential
43	في * هذا	23	0.87	0.99	referential
44	لم * في	23	0.87	0.99	referential
45	ومن * أن	23	0.57	0.9	stance-marking
46	التي * من	22	0.91	0.99	referential
47	في * الذي	22	0.77	0.94	referential
48	في * لا	22	0.95	0.99	stance-marking
49	قد * في	22	0.91	0.99	referential
50	مع * من	22	0.73	0.95	referential

The top 50 phrase-frames in Chinese

Rank	P-frame	Frequency	Variability	Predictability	Function
1	在 * 的	148	0.78	0.95	referential
2	是 * 的	122	0.86	0.98	stance-marking
3	为 * 的	105	0.42	0.79	stance-marking
4	有 * 的	91	0.87	0.98	stance-marking
5	最 * 的	90	0.71	0.94	stance-marking
6	对 * 的	89	0.87	0.99	referential
7	在 * 中	75	0.68	0.95	referential
8	更 * 的	73	0.55	0.91	stance-marking
9	中国 * 的	70	0.73	0.97	referential
10	中国 * 社会主义	66	0.05	0.14	referential
11	又 * 了	61	1	1	referential
12	初心 * 使命	60	0.05	0.76	referential
13	所 * 的	58	0.78	0.97	referential
14	文化 * 的	55	0.6	0.93	referential
15	一个 * 的	54	0.8	0.97	referential
16	以 * 为	51	0.65	0.87	referential
17	不 * 的	49	0.71	0.94	stance-marking
18	在 * 上	48	0.76	0.97	referential
19	新 * 中国	47	0.04	0.15	referential
20	一 * 的	47	0.66	0.95	referential
21	与 * 的	47	0.94	0.99	referential
22	以 * 的	46	0.87	0.99	referential
23	发展 * 的	41	0.76	0.95	referential
24	中华民族 * 复兴	38	0.07	0.52	referential
25	把 * 的	37	0.63	0.9	referential
26	也 * 了	37	0.84	0.98	referential
27	习近平 * 在	37	0.05	0.99	referential
28	新 * 的	36	0.43	0.8	referential
29	经济 * 的	34	0.47	0.89	referential
30	就 * 了	34	0.91	0.99	stance-marking
31	社会 * 的	32	0.88	0.98	referential
32	从 * 到	32	0.94	0.99	referential
33	伟大 * 的	32	0.19	0.54	referential
34	而 * 的	32	0.88	0.98	referential
35	都 * 了	31	0.88	0.98	stance-marking
36	到 * 的	28	0.9	0.99	referential
37	更加 * 的	28	0.75	0.96	stance-marking
38	还 * 了	27	0.82	0.98	discourse-organizing
39	很 * 的	27	0.56	0.91	stance-marking
40	总书记 * 讲话	27	0.11	0.52	referential
41	被 * 的	26	0.93	0.99	referential
42	中国 * 地	26	0.08	0.24	referential
43	时代 * 的	25	0.62	0.81	referential
44	大 * 的	24	0.64	0.94	referential
45	世界 * 的	24	0.67	0.93	referential
46	国家 * 的	24	0.88	0.99	referential
47	对 * 进行	23	0.67	0.95	referential
48	中国 * 在	23	0.52	0.86	referential
49	主席 * 访	23	0.13	0.32	referential
50	人民 * 的	23	0.65	0.92	referential

The top 50 phrase-frames in English

Rank	P-frame	Frequency	Variability	Predictability	Function
1	the * of	1152	0.57	0.95	referential
2	a * of	410	0.55	0.91	referential
3	the * to	192	0.73	0.95	referential
4	the * that	187	0.78	0.96	referential
5	the * in	183	0.89	0.99	referential
6	the * is	177	0.77	0.98	referential
7	a * to	137	0.73	0.95	referential
8	the * for	135	0.78	0.96	referential
9	and * to	120	0.95	1	referential
10	is * to	120	0.56	0.93	stance-marking
11	a * that	115	0.82	0.97	referential
12	as * as	115	0.35	0.73	discourse-organizing
13	s * to	113	0.71	0.95	referential
14	a * in	107	0.84	0.99	referential
15	the * was	103	0.86	0.99	referential
16	to * in	98	0.76	0.97	referential
17	and * of	97	0.8	0.98	referential
18	in the * of	97	0.68	0.96	referential
19	to * to	85	0.68	0.95	stance-marking
20	of * in	84	0.92	0.99	referential
21	are * to	83	0.7	0.94	stance-marking
22	to * that	78	0.76	0.97	discourse-organizing
23	and * in	77	0.92	0.99	referential
24	at the * of	76	0.47	0.9	referential
25	the * has	75	0.75	0.97	referential
26	and * s	74	0.46	0.82	referential
27	to * it	74	0.78	0.95	stance-marking
28	was * to	74	0.77	0.97	stance-marking
29	the * as	73	0.85	0.98	referential
30	in * of	72	0.53	0.88	referential
31	in * to	70	0.54	0.85	referential
32	s * of	69	0.83	0.98	referential
33	be * to	68	0.71	0.94	stance-marking
34	a * for	67	0.75	0.95	referential
35	to * on	63	0.68	0.96	referential
36	the * states	62	0.08	0.2	referential
37	it * to	61	0.69	0.92	discourse-organizing
38	the * on	61	0.89	0.98	referential
39	for * to	60	0.72	0.97	stance-marking
40	the * said	60	0.63	0.93	referential
41	that * is	59	0.63	0.92	referential
42	to * with	59	0.59	0.94	referential
43	to the * of	56	0.96	1	referential
44	was * in	55	0.84	0.98	referential
45	the * are	54	0.93	0.99	referential
46	on the * of	51	0.88	0.99	referential
47	a * on	50	0.84	0.98	referential
48	i * to	50	0.56	0.9	stance-marking
49	it * not	49	0.24	0.62	stance-marking
50	and * it	48	0.98	1	discourse-organizing

The top 50 phrase-frames in Malay

Rank	P-frame	Frequency	Variability	Predictability	Function
1	dan * yang	169	0.91	0.99	referential
2	yang * di	131	0.57	0.88	referential
3	memberi * kepada	102	0.43	0.88	referential
4	yang * dalam	95	0.63	0.93	referential
5	yang * dengan	92	0.64	0.96	referential
6	yang * oleh	91	0.68	0.96	referential
7	yang * untuk	88	0.67	0.96	referential
8	di * ini	83	0.24	0.59	referential
9	dengan * yang	74	0.84	0.97	referential
10	baru * ini	73	0.03	0.1	referential
11	dan * di	72	0.94	1	referential
12	dan * untuk	70	0.94	1	referential
13	di * negara	67	0.27	0.7	referential
14	dan * dalam	63	0.95	1	referential
15	yang * pada	59	0.73	0.95	referential
16	dan * dengan	57	0.89	0.99	referential
17	adalah * yang	56	0.71	0.96	referential
18	tidak * dengan	53	0.77	0.97	referential
19	dalam * itu	51	0.37	0.61	referential
20	pada * ini	50	0.34	0.85	referential
21	di * yang	49	0.65	0.94	referential
22	kepada * yang	49	0.65	0.91	referential
23	dalam * yang	48	0.69	0.93	referential
24	berusia * tahun	46	0.57	0.9	referential
25	dalam * ini	45	0.47	0.78	discourse-organizing
26	dan * tidak	45	0.87	0.99	referential
27	yang * kepada	45	0.73	0.97	referential
28	yang * tidak	44	0.77	0.98	stance-marking
29	pada * sama	41	0.05	0.17	discourse-organizing
30	pada * lalu	40	0.42	0.93	referential
31	ada * yang	39	0.9	0.99	referential
32	dan * negara	38	0.58	0.88	referential
33	di * hari	37	0.19	0.38	referential
34	pada * yang	37	0.57	0.82	referential
35	yang * sebagai	37	0.76	0.96	referential
36	atau * yang	36	0.94	0.99	referential
37	di * itu	36	0.42	0.81	discourse-organizing
38	tidak * untuk	36	0.69	0.97	referential
39	yang * ini	36	0.61	0.89	referential
40	negara * yang	35	0.66	0.94	referential
41	satu * yang	35	0.86	0.98	referential
42	sini * ini	35	0.14	0.32	referential
43	di sini * ini	35	0.14	0.32	referential
44	di * hari ini	34	0.12	0.29	referential
45	dan * akan	33	0.76	0.96	stance-marking
46	dan * serta	32	1	1	referential
47	lebih * berbanding	32	0.44	0.89	referential
48	dalam * politik	31	0.55	0.93	referential
49	yang * kita	31	0.74	0.96	stance-marking
50	yang * menjadi	31	0.81	0.98	stance-marking

The top 50 phrase-frames in Swahili

Rank	P-frame	Frequency	Variability	Predictability	Function
1	na * wa	692	0.42	0.92	referential
2	na * ya	628	0.42	0.93	referential
3	kwa * ya	490	0.22	0.7	referential
4	katika * ya	412	0.31	0.86	referential
5	kwa * wa	404	0.3	0.72	referential
6	na * kwa	323	0.69	0.96	referential
7	kwa * na	280	0.53	0.91	referential
8	ni * wa	193	0.55	0.94	stance-marking
9	katika * wa	190	0.44	0.89	referential
10	katika * za	169	0.28	0.81	referential
11	na * katika	158	0.84	0.98	referential
12	na * la	114	0.38	0.86	referential
13	za * wa	107	0.71	0.96	referential
14	kwenye * ya	104	0.7	0.96	referential
15	katika * la	96	0.32	0.83	referential
16	kuwa * wa	96	0.56	0.89	referential
17	na * kuwa	92	0.59	0.91	stance-marking
18	na * yake	91	0.52	0.91	referential
19	kuwa * ya	88	0.55	0.95	referential
20	na * ni	86	0.79	0.98	referential
21	katika * cha	82	0.21	0.73	referential
22	kuwa * na	82	0.77	0.97	referential
23	kwa * la	81	0.36	0.79	stance-marking
24	kwa * kwa	80	0.78	0.97	stance-marking
25	katika * hiyo	79	0.53	0.95	referential
26	na * mbalimbali	76	0.59	0.91	referential
27	kwenye * wa	73	0.51	0.85	referential
28	na * wake	71	0.66	0.94	referential
29	kwa * wake	70	0.36	0.73	referential
30	kwa * ni	66	0.53	0.86	referential
31	katika * mbalimbali	64	0.48	0.87	referential
32	ni * kwa	64	0.7	0.94	referential
33	kwa * za	63	0.49	0.89	referential
34	kwa * katika	62	0.73	0.96	referential
35	na * vya	62	0.39	0.89	referential
36	kwa * hiyo	61	0.57	0.94	referential
37	na * ili	61	0.95	0.99	discourse-organizing
38	na * cha	53	0.45	0.93	referential
39	rais * magufuli	52	0.08	0.29	referential
40	rais * tanzania	51	0.08	0.21	referential
41	chama * katika	49	0.06	0.18	referential
42	kuwa * nafasi	49	0.06	0.18	referential
43	na * watatu	49	0.06	0.18	referential
44	naibu * dk	49	0.06	0.18	referential
45	saba * ya	49	0.06	0.18	referential
46	siku * tatu	49	0.06	0.18	referential
47	ili * na	48	0.71	0.96	discourse-organizing
48	kupitia * hicho	48	0.04	0.15	referential
49	kutoka * ya	48	0.54	0.92	referential
50	na * hiyo	48	0.62	0.95	referential

References

Ackermann, K. and Y. H. Chen (2013), 'Developing the Academic Collocation List (ACL): A Corpus-driven and Expert-judged Approach', *Journal of English for Academic Purpose*, 12 (4): 235–47.

Ädel, A. and B. Erman (2012), 'Recurrent Word Combinations in Academic Writing by Native and Non-native Speakers of English: A Lexical Bundles Approach', *English for Specific Purposes*, 31 (2): 81–92.

Anthony, L. (2021), *AntGram* (Version 1.3.0) [Computer Software], Tokyo: Waseda University. https://www.laurenceanthony.net/software

Biber, D. (2009), 'A Corpus-driven Approach to Formulaic Language in English: Multi-word Patterns in Speech and Writing', *International Journal of Corpus Linguistics*, 14 (3): 275–311.

Biber, D. and F. Barbieri (2007), 'Lexical Bundles in University Spoken and Written Registers', *English for Specific Purposes*, 26 (3): 263–86.

Biber, D., S. Conrad and V. Cortes (2004), 'If you look at . . . : Lexical Bundles in University Teaching and Textbooks', *Applied Linguistics*, 25 (3): 371–405.

Čermáková, A. and L. Chlumská (2017), 'Expressing Place in Children's Literature', in T. Egan and H. Dirdal (eds), *Cross-linguistic Correspondences: From Lexis to Genre*, 75–96, Amsterdam: John Benjamins.

Chen, Y. H. and P. Baker (2010), 'Lexical Bundles in L1 and L2 Academic Writing', *Language Learning and Technology*, 14 (2): 30–49.

Colson, J. P. (2008), 'Cross-linguistic Phraseological Studies: An Overview', in S. Granger and F. Meunier (eds), *Phraseology: An Interdisciplinary Perspective*, 191–206, Amsterdam: John Benjamins.

Cortes, V. (2013), 'The Purpose of this Study is to: Connecting Lexical Bundles and Moves in Research Article Introductions', *Journal of English for Academic Purposes*, 12 (1): 33–43.

De Cock, S. (2004), 'Preferred Sequences of Words in NS and NNS Speech', *Belgian Journal of English Language and Literatures (BELL)*, 2 (1): 225–46.

Durrant, P. and J. Mathews-Aydınlı (2011), 'A Function-First Approach to Identifying Formulaic Language in Academic Writing', *English for Specific Purposes*, 30 (1): 58–72.

Ebeling, S. and J. Ebeling (2013), *Patterns in Contrast*, Amsterdam: John Benjamins.

Eberhard, D. M., G. F. Simons and C. D. Fennig, eds (2022), *Ethnologue: Languages of the World*, 25th edn, SIL International. http://www.ethnologue.com

Firth, J. R. (1957), 'A Synopsis of Linguistic Theory, 1930–1955', in *Studies in Linguistic Analysis*, 1–32, London: Blackwell.

Fletcher, W. H. (2002–2007), *KfNgram* [Computer Software], United States Naval Academy. http://www.kwicfinder.com/kfNgram/kfNgramHelp.html

Forsyth, R. S. and Ł. Grabowski (2015), 'Is there a Formula for Formulaic Language?', *Poznan Studies in Contemporary Linguistics*, 51 (4): 511–49.

Francis, W. N. and H. Kučera (1964), *Manual of Information to Accompany a Standard Corpus of Present-Day Edited American English*, Providence: Brown University Press. http://icame.uib.no/brown/bcm.html

Francis, W. N. and H. Kučera (1967), *Computational Analysis of Present-Day American English*, Providence: Brown University Press.

Garner, J. R. (2016), 'A Phrase-Frame Approach to Investigating Phraseology in Learner Writing across Proficiency Levels', *International Journal of Learner Corpus Research*, 2 (1): 31–67.

Golparvar, S. E. and E. Barabadi (2020), 'Key Phrase Frames in the Discussion Section of Research Articles of Higher Education', *Lingua*, 236: 1–15.

Granger, S. (2014), 'A Lexical Bundle Approach to Comparing Languages: Stems in English and French', *Languages in Contrast*, 14 (1): 58–72.

Gray, B. and D. Biber (2013), 'Lexical Frames in Academic Prose and Conversation', *International Journal of Corpus Linguistics*, 18 (1): 109–36.

Greenberg, J. (1963), 'Some Universals of Grammar with Particular Reference to the Order of Meaningful Elements', in J. Greenberg (ed.), *Universals of Language*, 73–113, Cambridge, MA: The MIT Press.

Hunston, S. (2022), *Corpora in Applied Linguistics*, Cambridge: Cambridge University Press.

Hyland, K. (2008a), 'Academic Clusters: Text Patterning in Published and Postgraduate Writing', *International Journal of Applied Linguistics*, 18 (1): 41–62.

Hyland, K. (2008b), 'As Can Be Seen: Lexical Bundles and Disciplinary Variation', *English for Specific Purposes*, 27 (1): 4–21.

Juknevičienė, R. (2009), 'Lexical Bundles in Learner Language: Lithuanian Learners vs. Native Speakers', *Kalbotyra*, 61: 61–72.

Juknevičienė, R. and Ł. Grabowski (2018), 'Comparing Formulaicity of Learner Writing through Phrase-frames: A Corpus-driven Study of Lithuanian and Polish EFL Student Writing', *Research in Language*, 16 (3): 303–23.

Kabacoff, R. I. (2015), *R in Action: Data Analysis and Graphics with R*. Shelter Island, New York: Manning.

Leńko-Szymańska, A. (2014), 'The Acquisition of Formulaic Language by EFL Learners: A Cross-sectional and Cross-linguistic Perspective', *International Journal of Corpus Linguistics*, 19 (2): 225–51.

Lu, X., J. Yoon and O. Kisselev (2018), 'A Phrase-frame List for Social Science Research Article Introductions', *Journal of English for Academic Purposes*, 36: 76–85.

Lu, X., J. Yoon and O. Kisselev (2021), 'Matching Phrase-frames to Rhetorical Moves in Social Science Research Article Introductions', *English for Specific Purposes*, 61: 63–83.

Martinez, R. and N. Schmitt (2012), 'A Phrasal Expressions List', *Applied Linguistics*, 33 (3): 299–320.

Omidian, T., H. Shahriari and A. Siyanova-Chanturia (2018), 'A Cross-disciplinary Investigation of Multi-word Expressions in the Moves of Research Article Abstracts', *Journal of English for Academic Purposes*, 36: 1–14.

Palmer, H. E. (1933), *Second Interim Report on English Collocations*, Tokyo: Kaitakusha.

Paquot, M. (2013), 'Lexical Bundles and L1 Transfer Effects', *International Journal of Corpus Linguistics*, 18 (3): 391–417.

Paquot, M. (2014), 'Cross-linguistic Influence and Formulaic Language: Recurrent Word Sequences in French Learner Writing', *EUROSLA Yearbook*, 14 (1): 240–61.

Pawley, A. and F. H. Syder (1983), 'Two Puzzles for Linguistic Theory: Nativelike Selection and Nativelike Fluency', in J. C. Richards and R. W. Schmidt (eds), *Language and Communication*, 191–226, London: Routledge.

R Core Team (2022), 'R: A Language and Environment for Statistical Computing'. R Foundation for Statistical Computing. https://www.R-project.org

Ren, J. (2022), 'A Comparative Study of the Phrase Frames Used in the Essays of Native and Non-native English Students', *Lingua*, 274: 1–22.

Renouf, A. and J. Sinclair (1991), 'Collocational Frameworks in English', in K. Aijmer and B. Altenberg (eds), *English Corpus Linguistics*, 128–43, London: Longman.

Römer, U. (2009), 'English in Academia: Does Nativeness Matter?', *Anglistik: International Journal of English Studies*, 20 (2): 89–100.

Römer, U. (2010), 'Establishing the Phraseological Profile of a Text Type: The Construction of Meaning in Academic Book Reviews', *English Text Construction*, 3 (1): 95–119.

Sapir, E. (1921), *Language: An Introduction to the Study of Speech*, New York: Harvest.

Simpson-Vlach, R. and N. C. Ellis (2010), 'An Academic Formulas List: New Methods in Phraseology Research', *Applied Linguistics*, 31 (4): 487–512.

Sinclair, J. M. (1991), *Corpus, Concordance, Collocation*, Oxford: Oxford University Press.

Sinclair, J. M. (1996), 'The Search for Units of Meaning', *Textus*, 9 (1): 75–106.

Sinclair, J. M. (2008), 'The Phrase, the Whole Phrase, and Nothing but the Phrase', in S. Granger and F. Meunier (eds), *Phraseology: An Interdisciplinary Perspective*, 407–10, Amsterdam: John Benjamins.

Sinclair, J. M., S. Jones and R. Daley (1970/2004), *English Collocation Studies: The OSTI Report*, ed. R. Krishnamurthy, London: Continuum.

Stubbs, M. (2009), 'Technology and Phraseology: With Notes on the History of Corpus Linguistics', in U. Römer and R. Schulze (eds), *Exploring the Lexis-Grammar Interface*, 15–32, Amsterdam: John Benjamins.

Tan, Y. and U. Römer (2022), 'Using Phrase-frames to Trace the Language Development of L1 Chinese Learners of English', *System*, 108: 1–10.

Tognini-Bonelli, E. (2002), 'Functionally Complete Units of Meaning across English and Italian', in B. Altenberg and S. Granger (eds), *Lexis in Contrast*, 73–95, Amsterdam: John Benjamins.

Vincent, B. (2013), 'Investigating Academic Phraseology through Combinations of Very Frequent Words: A Methodological Exploration', *Journal of English for Academic Purposes*, 12 (1): 44–56.

Wang, Y. (2016), *The Idiom Principle and L1 Influence: A Contrastive Learner-corpus Study of Delexical Verb+ Noun Collocations*, Amsterdam: John Benjamins.

Xiao, R. (2011), 'Word Clusters and Reformulation Markers in Chinese and English: Implications for Translation Universal Hypotheses', *Languages in Contrast*, 11 (2): 145–71.

Xiao, R. and T. McEnery (2006), 'Collocation, Semantic Prosody, and Near Synonymy: A Cross-linguistic Perspective', *Applied Linguistics*, 27 (1): 103–29.

7

Corpus-Based Contrast in Audiovisual Customization

A Pilot Study on *Can/Could* and Subject Pronouns in Spanish Dubbing

Camino Gutiérrez-Lanza and Rosa Rabadán

7.1 Introduction

The audiovisual industry needs technical, cultural and linguistic expertise to glocalize its products, drawing on many disciplines, including contrastive linguistics. In dubbing, cross-linguistic contrast is traditionally identified with visual phonetics and lip-syncing. However, creating fake spontaneous conversation among characters presents additional language-related difficulties, such as the transfer of interjections and discourse markers, which are often formally dissimilar across languages. Thus, linguistic customization is far from obvious. Word-for-word translation tends to be overused to favour isochrony. However, it is detrimental to the recreation of prefabricated orality, creating ineffective communication patterns and affecting acceptability, tenor and audience engagement. These practices are typical of cartoon dubbing and video and game localization, and Spanish audiences have developed a high tolerance from childhood. As a result, dubbese has moved into children's speech, turning into a peer-group language often used by Spanish teenagers, becoming a vacuous Spanish dialect.

This chapter reports on problem-triggers in the recreation of prefabricated orality. Uses of English modals *can* and *could*, which in the translations are devoid of the meaning functions they had in the original, becoming useless – and noisy – words (*puedo*, *podemos*, *podría* etc.) or overmarking inflected verbal meanings in Spanish, and uncalled for subject pronouns have become the mark of dubbed

Spanish. Our working hypothesis is that some of these 'dubbing lect' features have become the acceptable norm for native Spanish texts in the audiovisual industry. We aim to identify some of the elements that define this mode-bound variety and the consequences of their use, given the need for isochrony and lip-syncing.

7.2 Audiovisual customization

From the point of view of the target audience, 'an authentic and accurate reflection of the original dialogue becomes a matter of credibility' (Smith 1998: 141). Together with isochrony, that is, the perfect match between dubbed utterances and the beginning and end of actors' mouth movement (Whitman-Linsen 1992), prefabricated orality significantly contributes to ensuring dialogue credibility, translation equivalence and translation quality in dubbing, triggering the willing suspension of disbelief on the part of film audiences (Gutiérrez-Lanza 2000; Romero-Fresco 2009; Rabadán 2022). Referring to the features that make a film look like a credible copy of reality and, therefore, a piece of reality itself, Metz (1974: 6–7) states:

> The impression of reality [. . .] is always a two-sided phenomenon. One may seek to explain it by examining either the object perceived or the perception of that object. On the one hand, the reproduction resembles the original more or less closely; it contains a number, more or less great, of clues to reality. On the other hand, the vital, organizing faculty of perception can more or less realize (to make real) the object it grasps. Between the two factors, there is a constant interaction. A reasonably convincing reproduction causes affective and perceptual participation phenomena to be awakened in the spectator, giving reality to the copy.

Prefabricated orality is a peculiar type of discourse 'written to be spoken as if not written' (Gregory and Carroll 1978: 42), creating fake spontaneous conversation written to be delivered orally by fictional characters (Chaume 2001). Apart from its informative function, prefabricated orality fulfils an interactional function among characters, usually indicating the position adopted by the speaker and clarifying whether the listener's reception and understanding of the message are satisfactory. In this respect, 'the challenge does not lie so much in trying to imitate spontaneous conversation, but in selecting specific features of this mode of discourse that are widely accepted and recognized as such by the audience'

(Baños-Piñero and Chaume 2009). Lip-syncing and visual phonetics (Fodor 1976) also play a relevant role, especially when mirroring open vowels and bilabial and labio-dental sounds in close shots. These, together with coherence between images and words, convincing dramatization on the part of voice talents and clear sound quality, are what the viewers expect from a dubbed audiovisual product (Chaume 2007, 2012). However, the need for isochrony may cause translated prefabricated orality to be affected by 'third code' dubbese, a particular kind of interference defined as certain source language features which are transferred to dubbed products and differ from non-translated target language usage (for Spanish, Chaume 2004; Romero-Fresco 2006; Pérez-González 2007; for Italian, Pavesi 2016, 2018). It affects dubbing and video and game localization, becoming a lect readily associated with audiovisual texts (Gómez-Capuz 2001) and turning into a peer-group language that Spanish teenagers often use in real-life situations. In this pilot study, dubbese is understood as the statistically significant differences in using certain features of translated as compared to non-translated film dialogue in the target language. This practice creates ineffective communication patterns (Rabadán 2008, 2010), negatively affecting acceptability, tenor and audience engagement (Rabadán and Gutiérrez-Lanza 2023).

When dealing with language transfer subordinated to syncing, one of the most frequently cited characteristics is the accommodation of dubbed utterances to the limitations imposed by the image. Among the elements affected by this procedure are adverbial intensifiers (Baños-Piñero 2013), discourse markers (Chaume 2004; Romero-Fresco 2009) and conversational markers (Gutiérrez-Lanza 2021). The following section analyses the case of modal forms and subject pronouns.

7.3 Problem-triggers: *Can/could > poder* and subject pronouns

The English modal verbs often constitute a problem trigger in the English>Spanish recreation of prefabricated orality. While they are a separate verb class in English, Spanish has no clear formal resources to convey their meanings and encode their functions. We will study two of the most problematic modals: *can* and *could*. In order to describe their meanings and their most likely counterparts in Spanish, we capitalize on previous work by Coates (1983/2015) and Rabadán (2006), who, from a translationally relevant point of view, provide an efficient classification of modal meanings and resources in both languages.

Can shows a great diversity of semantic functions: possibility, ability, permission and aspectual, when it appears with verbs of perception, prediction and obligation/advisability. For our purposes, since it affects the translation of this modal into Spanish, the semantic function 'ability' will cover those cases in which *can* means 'to know how to do something', and the semantic function 'capability' will account for those cases in which it means 'to be capable of doing something'. Since these two functions are very much related, they will be analysed together under the label '(cap)ability'. In addition, our list is enlarged with three other meanings of *can* represented in our parallel corpus: request, offer and prohibition. *Could* conveys a more restricted variety of semantic functions: possibility, capability, permission, aspectual and request, permission not being represented in our parallel corpus. Although some linguists, for example, Biber et al. (1999: 485) claim that *could* can express ability, our data do not corroborate the existence of this particular function.

A perfectly acceptable translation option for *can* and *could* when they express possibility, capability, permission, prediction and prohibition is the modal periphrasis *poder* + infinitive (Rabadán 2006). However, in the case of the remaining functions, *poder* tends to be lexically redundant, as the grammatical marking is done in Spanish by other means, for example, tenses and mood. So, obligation/advisability needs to be expressed by resources such as *deber* + infinitive, *deber de* + infinitive or *tener que* + infinitive, while offer and request require the use of the corresponding lexical verb. The aspectual use needs to be transferred by using other means, for example, the present tense of the lexical verb accompanying the modal. Finally, ability (i.e. know-how) is usually conveyed by *saber* + infinitive in Spanish.

Subject pronouns constitute another grammatical area that may be relevant for our study. Both languages feature a complete (for their needs) subject pronoun set, but there are fundamental cross-linguistic differences in this area of grammar that require additional information and some explanation. We draw on classic works such as Enríquez (1984), Fernández-Soriano (1999), Luján (1999) as well as De Cock (2014) and Sampedro-Mella (2021). Findings in pronoun acquisition and learning are valuable here as evidence of mediated language (Lubbers-Quesada and Blackwell 2009; Moreno 2011; Cautín-Epifani 2015).

English pronouns are required in the text to mark person, number and gender agreement (in the case of 3rd p. sing.), whereas Spanish marks them through verbal inflections. Spanish subject pronouns are frequently disposed of if their function in the text is reduced to this neutral grammatical marking. While English makes an exception of gender marking only on third-person singular pronouns, Spanish marks it formally in all persons but for, obviously, the first-person singular (*I-yo*).

English *you* may translate as *tú* (sing.) – *vosotros* (pl.) and *usted* (sing.) – *ustedes* (pl.) in Spanish, mark person, number and gender agreement (*vosotras*, fem 2nd p. pl.). Additionally, these two sets of subject pronouns convey information about the interpersonal tenor between the participants: *usted(es)* mark a more distant, respectful relationship or simply politeness on the part of the speaker, in the same way that *vous* does in French, *Lei* in Italian or *você* in Portuguese (Sampedro-Mella 2021). *Tú–vosotros* signals a relationship between peers based on previous knowledge or, simply, on age similarity. The choice of pronoun may vary according to circumstances, according to cultural conventions, for example, at work, on a social occasion, or be stable if the hearer's status is perceived invariable, for example, service encounters between hotel receptionist and clients, interaction between different ranks in the military (Serrano 2012). Grammatically, the use of the informal (*tú–vosotros*) or the formal markers (*usted–es*) conditions verbal usage: whereas the informal pronouns are conjugated as second persons, the formal ones require a third-person verbal form.

Concerning their usage, Spanish subject pronouns may adopt different roles. The primary, unmarked function of pronouns is *deixis* and, according to Enríquez (1984: 106–7), marking the subject as 'human' (1). Together with *emphasis* (see below), this is one of the functions where it is perfectly acceptable to omit the subject pronoun; that is, if it appears, there is usually an additional reason, such as emphasis, and, in the case of the third-person singular, example (1), the loss of gender marking, which is absent from the verbal inflection and left to the context.

(1) *Ella* nos enseñó a leer y a escribir/ Nos enseñó a leer y a escribir.[1]
    (*She* taught us to read and write/ Ø 3rd p. *sing*. taught us to read and write.)

Another is *contrast or individuation*, marking the distinction between participants within the same sentence, as in example (2), where the third-person pronoun is necessary to convey the information clearly.

(2) Como *yo* salgo para Madrid, *él* se encargará de recogerte.
    (As *I* am leaving for Madrid, *he* will pick you up.)

Emphasis applies to an excess function of the pronoun, which may be considered optional, as in example (3), where *usted* delivers an additional hint of welcoming and cordiality. It is not omitted if required syntactically, as in example (4).

(3) *Usted*, don U., venga cuando quiera.
 (*You*, Mr. U., come whenever you want.)
(4) (Tú) deberías saberlo, porque fuiste *tú* quien me hizo roja.
 (You should know because it was *you* who turned me a communist.)

Pronouns, particularly second-person *tú*, are not optional when they adopt a *formulaic role* in fixed expressions (5).

(5) Muy bien. *Tú mismo*. Pero luego no me llores.
 (OK. *It is up to you*. But then don't come to me if it goes wrong.)

As in English, Spanish pronouns also function as a *marker of (personal) co-reference* in the text (endophoric) or the communicative situation (exophoric) (Halliday and Hasan 1976: 44–52). Pronouns in this role give instructions to retrieve information from somewhere else in the text or the context. Semantically (and very generally), pronouns are defined by their roles in speech, with the first and second persons, that is, speaker and addressee, being considered 'speech roles' and third persons being classified as 'other roles' (Halliday and Hasan 1976: 31–56). In written registers, only endophoric uses signalled by 'other roles' are considered cohesive, as in example (6), where *ellos/ they* signals backwards to *mis hermanos/ my siblings*. However, in fictional or real dialogue, the identity of the hearer and speaker, signalled by speech roles (first and second persons), is exophoric, as in example (7), and must be retrieved from the context of the situation.

(6) A mis hermanos casi no los veo. *Ellos* tienen sus vidas.
 (I hardly see my siblings. *They* have their lives.)
(7) ¿*Tú* crees? *Yo* lo dudo.
 (Do *you* think so? *I* doubt it.)

In this chapter, these functions provide the *tertium comparationis* used in Section 7.5.2, dealing with the results and discussion.

7.4 Data and method

The script data come from parallel corpus TRACEci (Gutiérrez-Lanza 1999) and include the source texts in English (STs), the intermediate, draft translations (TT1s) and the 'synchronized' customized translations (TT2s). The section of TRACEci used here is an addition of contemporary materials to the general TRACEci sub-corpus, which features texts dated 1950s–1985 and contains 62,689 words, distributed as follows: STs (En) contains 35,066 words, while TT1s (Es) include 12,799 and TT2s (Es) feature 14,824 words. The Spanish versions add up to 27,623 words.

The STs amount to 35,066 words and contain three differentiated types of text: technical information on reels and timing, setting and acting directions, and the dialogue and notes for translators and adaptors. The setting directions include information about actors' kinetics and positioning, which may become vital for dubbing decisions, for example, if the actor's lips are in full view or his/her face is obscured, as in example (8). The ST intended for translation for dubbing also includes clarification and explanations for those in charge of the versions into different languages, for example, the italicized text between square brackets in example (8).

(8) BONES: [face obscured] [sighing] Ohhh, damn it, man! [on] That was our ride! You just stunned our. . .

   [*damn it: note that this phrase of complaint is often used by the character of Bones in the 'Star Trek' television series and feature*]
   [*That: referring to the fallen creature*]
   [*That was our ride: meaning that they had intended to ride the creature to safety*]
   [*stunned: rendered unconscious – note that in the 'Star Trek' universe, phasers [phase-modulated particle weapons] can be used to kill or can be placed on the non-lethal 'stun' setting to temporarily render a target unconscious*]

TT1s amount to 12,799 words and contain reel information, translated dialogue and some dubbing symbols, that is, valuable indications for voice talents, example (9).

(9) KIRK: (G) Es... ¿por qué el archivo? Ehm... toda esa información e-es. .. es de dominio público. S-si de verdad quería perjudicar a la Flota Estelar... (ASP.) esto puede ser sólo el principio.
(ST: KIRK: (GESTURES) I ju-, why the archive? Eh... all that information i-, is... [off]... is public record. I-if he really wanted to damage Starfleet... [takes a breath and pauses]... this could just be the beginning.)

TT2s amount to 14,824 words and contain reel information including timing, take segmentation, a comprehensive account of dubbing symbols to facilitate the task of voice talents, any changes needed to adapt dialogue to actors' mouth movement in favour of isochrony, any other changes that the ST may have suffered during the film making process (marked in bold) and the addition of background voices (also marked in bold), example (10).

(10) TAKE #127 01:07:59 **TRIPUL. PUENTE: (8.43) (AMBIENTE GRAL.) (¿M/E?) (DE FONDO) (AD LIBS) ¿Has comprobado esas variables?/ Sí, son las habituales./ Bien, si hubiera alguna variación, avísame. (ETC.)**

TAKE #127 01:07:59 KIRK: (8.46) (P) (JADEA)
TAKE #128 01:09:07 SPOCK: (ESCAF.) (RESPIRACS.)
TAKE #128 01:09:07 KIRK: ¡Spock! / (JADEA) ¿Está bien? (ON/DE) (JADEA)
(**BRIDGE CREW: (BACKGROUND CHATTER) (¿MUSIC/EFFECTS?) (BACKGROUND) (IMPROVISED DIALOGUE**[2]**) Have you checked those variables?/Yes, they are the usual ones./OK, if there is any change, let me know. (ETC.)** KIRK: (PARALANGUAGE) (PANTING) SPOCK: (IN SPACE SUIT) (BREATHING) KIRK: Spock! / (PANTING) Are you OK? (ON SCREEN/BACK TO CAMERA) (PANTING))

Since dubbing scripts are generally marketed by linguistic regions, this sociolinguistic situation is essential for gauging the consequences of translated uses. The TRACEci target texts used as a basis for this pilot study are marked as standard European Spanish.[3] In addition, only dialogue has been analysed since the fictional orality is considered the main component of this written-to-be-spoken textual mode. The customized TT2s have been aligned with the intermediate, uncustomized translations, TT1s and ST scripts, using TAligner 3.0 (Gutiérrez-Lanza and Alonso 2011).[4] Data yield essential information about the origin(s) of the Spanish renderings and their meanings in the English text's prefabricated orality.

The corpus queries yield the frequencies of our chosen anchors in translated TT1s and TT2s (TRACEci). TT1 and TT2 materials are measured against contemporary original Spanish data from the equivalent script sub-corpus (*guiones*) of the reference corpus of 21st century Spanish, CORPES XXI (Real Academia Española 2021), which contains 1,501,683 words in the 0.94 version used for this research.

The *tertia comparationes* discriminate the function(s) of *poder* and the Spanish subject pronouns in prefabricated orality. The English-Spanish parallel materials require a target-based double search, as TT1s are the intermediate texts and TT2s are the final, usable, dubbing scripts offered to audiences. Results for both stages are contrasted with those of CORPES XXI and, given the disparity in the size of the sub-corpora, computed for statistical significance using the Z test for two proportions. Testing clarifies whether the null hypothesis holds, that is, that translated (TT1s and TT2s) and non-translated usage (CORPES XXI) are equal or if it is rejected; that is, translations and non-translations are different in terms of the frequency distribution of the functions of the modals. The test has been calculated for a 95 per cent degree of confidence and shows no results when there are zero occurrences of a particular resource in any of the corpora. Z results falling between +1.96 and −1.96 and a p-value above 0.05 are in the non-reject region, meaning that the difference is not significant, whereas figures outside these limits would confirm that the null hypothesis is rejected and that translated script usage is different, either overused or underused.

The analysis (Sections 7.5.1 and 7.5.2) focuses on those forms and functions that show translation differences with the standard usage in non-translated Spanish scripts. Our input list includes modal *can* and *could* > *poder* and subject pronouns. Both features have already been analysed for other fictional genres (Rabadán 2006 for modals; Ramón and Gutiérrez-Lanza 2018 for pronouns), providing insight into potential differences between varieties.

7.5 Results and discussion

This section presents the results and discussion of the analysis of the chosen problem-triggers: *can/could* and subject pronouns.

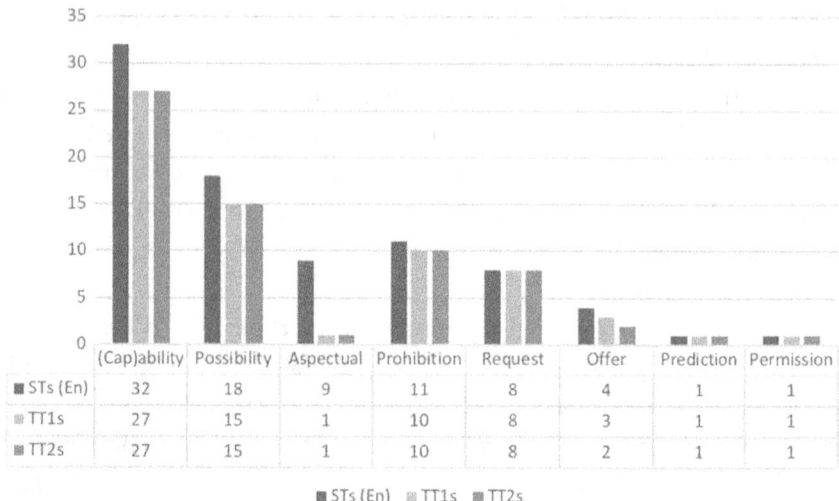

Figure 7.1 *Can* (STs) > *poder* (TT1s and TT2s).

7.5.1 *Can/could > poder*

Our first step in the corpus-based procedure is to identify *can* and *poder* in the TRACEci English-Spanish parallel corpus. Figure 7.1 shows the number of *can* cases in the STs, classified by function, which has been translated as *poder* in the TT1s, and how many remain in the TT2s after synchronization.

Acceptable uses of *poder < can* (those of non-translated Spanish) include capability, that is, being capable of doing something (11), possibility (12), prohibition (13), prediction (14) and permission (15).

(11) (ST) MRS. SAWYER: [overlapping] [low] I just *can't* do it by myself!
(TT1) SRA. SAWYER: [P] [BAJO] ¡No *puedo* hacerlo yo sola!
(TT2) SRA. SAWYER: [P] [DE FONDO] ¡Yo no *puedo* hacerlo todo sola!
(12) (ST) HELEN: [face obscured] You . . . . . . *can't* prove that.
(TT1) HELEN: Eso no lo *puedes* demostrar.
(TT2) HELEN: [DE] No lo *puedes* [ON] demostrar.
(13) (ST) SPOCK: [over comm] The. . . [over comm] [breaking up]. . . rule *cannot* be broken under any circumstances.
(TT1 and TT2) SPOCK: [OFF] [COMLINK] [ENTRECORTADO] No se *puede* infringir bajo ninguna circunstancia.
(14) (ST) HELEN: I have to believe the money you're making *can't* possibly be enough to justi-.

(TT1 and TT2) HELEN: . . . me hace pensar que el dinero que gana no *puede* ser suficiente para justi-. . .
(15) (ST) SAKHARINE: You *can* kill the boy.
(TT1 and TT2) SAKHARINE: *Podéis* matar al chico.

However, when *can* expresses ability, that is, know-how, modal periphrasis *poder* + infinitive has been conveniently substituted for *saber* (to know) + infinitive (16), which is the acceptable choice in Spanish.

(16) (ST) UNICORN SOLDIER #2: [face obscured] [overlapping] [low] I *can't* swim!
(TT2) MARINERO UNICORNIO 2: [P] ¡No *sé* nadar!

Out of the nine instances of aspectual *can* in the STs, only one has been translated by *poder*, which proves that the translator/adaptor is aware that other options, usually the present tense, are preferred in non-translated Spanish (17).

(17) (ST) CHEKOV: [over intercom] Engineering to bridge. Eh, hello! Captain, *can* you hear me?
(TT2) CHEKOV: [OFF] [COMLINK] ¡Ingeniería a puente!/ Ehm, ¡hola!/ Capitán, ¿me *oye*?

However, redundant *poder* is the most common solution both in the TT1s and the TT2s to express request and offer, as in examples (18) and (19), respectively:

(18) (ST) SPOCK: *Can* we stop?
(TT1) SPOCK: ¿*Podemos* frenar?
(TT2) SPOCK: [OFF/ON] ¿*Podemos* parar?
(19) (ST) CASH: What *can* I do you for, Mister Ward?
(TT1) CASH: ¿Qué *puedo* hacer por usted, señor Ward?
(TT2) CASH: ¿En qué *puedo* ayudarle, señor Ward?

Figure 7.1 also shows that, except for the omission of one instance of *poder* when expressing offer, no changes have been practised during the transition from the TT1s to the TT2s. This means that *poder* < *can* tends not to be targeted by the adaptor during synchronization.

Next, to determine whether dubbese exists in any of the functions, we compare translated and non-translated *poder* in TRACEci (TT1s and TT2s) and the corresponding CORPES XXI *guiones* sub-corpus. The Z test shows the following results (Table 7.1).

Table 7.1 *Poder* < *Can*: Verification of dubbese (TRACEci-CORPES XXI)

Poder	z	p	TT1	z	p	TT2
(Cap)ability	−2.848	0.0044	overused	−2.932	0.0034	overused
Possibility	3.419	0.0006	underused	3.344	0.0008	underused
Aspectual	0.525	0.5993	not rejected	0.51	0.6099	not rejected
Prohibition	−1.913	0.0557	not rejected	−1.959	0.0501	not rejected
Request	−1.442	0.1492	not rejected	−1.483	0.1381	not rejected
Offer	−1.673	0.0944	not rejected	−0.933	0.3509	not rejected
Prediction			no data			
Permission	2.315	0.0206	underused	2.291	0.0219	underused

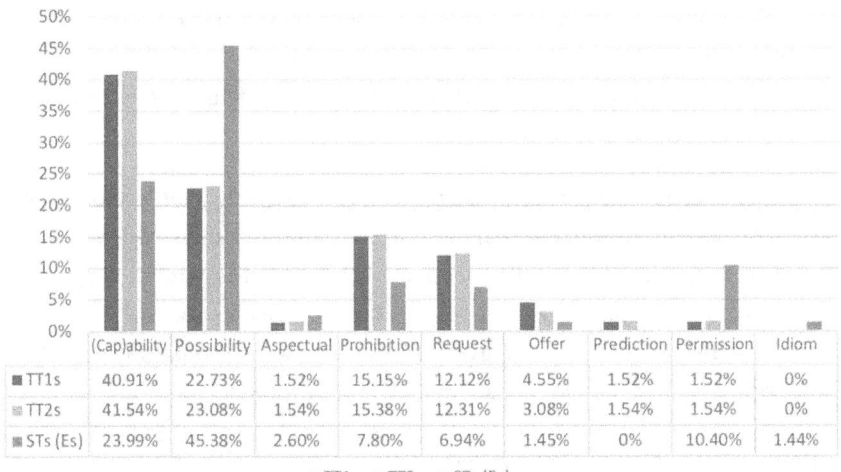

Figure 7.2 *Poder < can*: TT1s, TT2s and STs (Es).

Quantitative results would have been expected to show more functions of *poder < can* as being affected by dubbese, especially by overuse, compared to non-translated Spanish. However, Table 7.1 proves that *poder* is overused only when expressing capability and underused when expressing possibility and permission, the difference not being statistically significant for any other function. Figure 7.2 illustrates that translated (TT1s and TT2s) and non-translated (Spanish STs) usage is not statistically different and may help to understand the reasons why dubbese does not affect any of the remaining functions, especially the most problematic ones: ability, aspectual, request and offer.

Ability and the aspectual function of *poder* show no overuse or underuse, and they are very scarcely used in translated and non-translated language. However, although neither overused nor underused when expressing request and offer, *poder < can* is used more often than expected in translated and non-translated language. This expectation is based on empirical results for other genres, that is, fiction and nonfiction (Rabadán 2006; Rabadán, Labrador and Ramón 2009). So, request and offer are affected by unnecessary qualitative redundancy. This indicates that they may have been transferred from translated to non-translated Spanish (CORPES XXI), as in examples (20) and (21), respectively.

(20) (ST) ¿*Podemos* hablar a solas?
('Can we talk alone?')

(21) (ST) Recuerdo los viejos tiempos cuando estabas en una discoteca, se te acercaba un tío y te decía: '¿*Puedo* invitarte a algo?'
('I remember the old days when you were in a nightclub, a guy would come up to you and say, "Can I buy you a drink?"')

Our second step in the corpus-based procedure is to identify *could* and *poder* in the TRACEci English-Spanish parallel corpus. Figure 7.3 shows the number of cases of *could* in the STs, classified by function, translated as conditional *poder* in the TT1s, and how many remain in the TT2s after synchronization.

Acceptable (non-translated) uses of *could* and conditional *poder* both in English and Spanish include capability (22) and possibility (23).

(22) (ST) EMERSON: Someone who *could* kill that girl with one punch.
(TT1 and TT2) EMERSON: A alguien que *podría* matar a esa chica de un puñetazo.
(23) (ST) HELEN: [off] He *could* be goin' anywhere.
(TT1 and TT2) HELEN: *Podría* ir a cualquier parte.

The two aspectual cases of *could* in the STs have been translated with the corresponding verb of perception in the present perfect (24), which demonstrates that the translator/adaptor is aware that other options are preferred in non-translated Spanish.

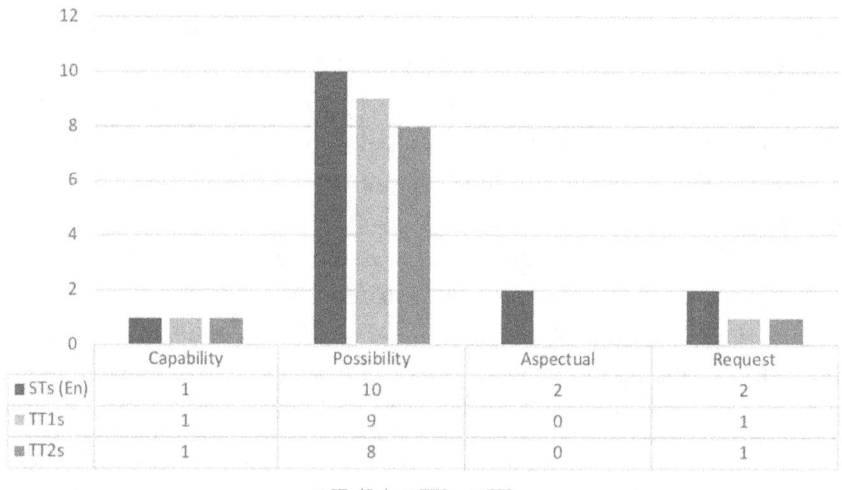

Figure 7.3 *Could* (STs) > *poder* (TT1s and TT2s).

(24) (ST) BARR: No. But I *could* hear the nurses talk-. . . . . . .-in' to those cops out there.
(TT1) BARR: No. Pero *he oído* a las enfermeras hablando con esos polis de ahí.
(TT2) BARR: No. Pero *he oído* a las enfermeras hablando con esos policías.

On the other hand, the two examples of *could* meaning request have been translated differently: while example (25) avoids redundant *poder*, example (26) uses it both in TT1 and TT2.

(25) (ST) REACHER: Any chance I *could* look at the evidence?
(TT1) REACHER: ¿*Sería posible* ver las pruebas?
(TT2) REACHER: ¿*Me dejarían* ver las pruebas?
(26) (ST) SPOCK: DOCTOR McCoy. . . you inadvertently activated a torpedo. *Could* you. . . [face obscured]. . . replicate the process?
(TT1) SPOCK: (RESP.) Doctor McCoy. . . usted inadvertidamente activó un torpedo. ¿*Podría* reproducir el proceso?
(TT2) SPOCK: Doctor McCoy, / usted activó involuntariamente un torpedo. ¿*Podría* [DE] repetir el proceso?

Figure 7.3 also shows that, except for the omission of one instance of *poder* when expressing possibility, no changes have been practised during the transition from the TT1s to the TT2s. This means that *poder* < *could* tends not to be targeted by the adaptor during synchronization.

Next, to determine whether dubbese exists in any of the functions, we compare translated and non-translated *poder* in TRACEci (TT1s and TT2s) and the corresponding CORPES XXI *guiones* sub-corpus. The Z test shows the following results (Table 7.2):

Table 7.2 *Poder* < *Could*: Verification of dubbese (TRACEci-CORPES XXI)

Poder	z	p	TT1	z	p	TT2
(Cap)ability	0.559	0.5761	not rejected	0.454	0.6496	not rejected
Possibility	−1.75	0.0801	not rejected	−1.558	0.1193	not rejected
Aspectual			no data			
Request	0.37	0.7113	not rejected	0.269	0.7883	not rejected

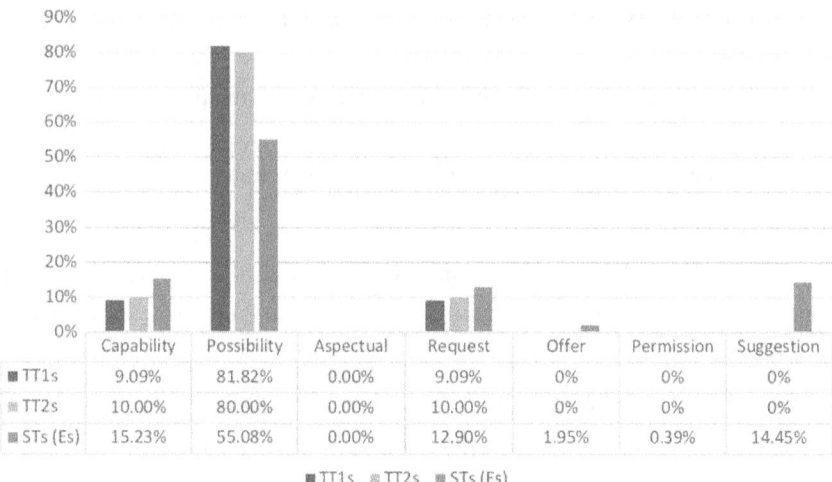

Figure 7.4 *Poder* < *could*: TT1s, TT2s and STs (Es).

Quantitative results show that none of the functions of *poder* < *could* are affected by dubbese, that is, overuse or underuse in translated as compared to non-translated Spanish. Figure 7.4 shows no statistically significant differences between translated (TT1s and TT2s) and non-translated (Spanish STs) usage. This explains why dubbese is absent from the translations.

Regarding the acceptable uses of *poder* < *could*, Figure 7.4 shows that it is widely used in the translations when conveying possibility and less frequently used when expressing capability. The aspectual use of *poder*, non-existent in non-translated Spanish, is conveniently changed in the translations by other options available, demonstrating that the translator/adaptor is aware that the aspectual use is problematic in Spanish. In addition, although redundant *poder* can be found expressing request in the translations, there is no statistical dubbese because this use can also be found in non-translated Spanish. This indicates that this redundant use of *poder*, request, may have been transferred from translated to non-translated Spanish (CORPES XXI), as in example (27).

(27) (ST) Disculpe, ¿*puede* traducirlo?
 ('Sorry, can you translate it?')

On the other hand, Figure 7.4 also shows that three functions of conditional *poder* in non-translated Spanish (offer, permission and suggestion) are not represented in the translations.

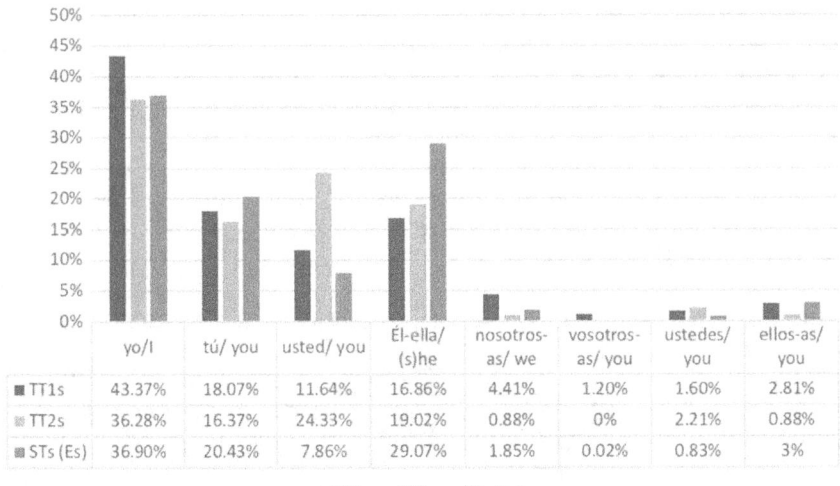

Figure 7.5 Subject pronouns in Spanish: TT1s, TT2s and STs (Es).

7.5.2 Subject pronouns

Our first results identify subject pronouns in the TRACEci and the corresponding CORPES XXI sub-corpora (Figure 7.5).

Data show that singular pronouns are far more frequent in original and translated Spanish. Since the plural pronouns do not offer enough evidence to carry out the analysis, for example, for *ustedes* (2nd plural you, formality), there are just four and five raw cases for TT1 and TT2, respectively; we focus on the singular forms.

While in original Spanish *yo/I* and *él-ella/(s)he* are the commonest, translated scripts favour the speech roles, particularly *usted*. Results also disclose that there are adjustments in pronoun usage when going from TT1s to TT2s. Whereas the speech roles show a reduction of pronominal subject forms in the TT2, *usted* and *él-ella* increase their presence in the final, customized TT2 sub-corpus. In the case of *usted*, subject pronoun use is about three times what it is in original Spanish. Although it is underused in both TT1s and TT2s, *él-ella* shows an increment in TT2s, which may be associated with the co-reference function (Figure 7.5).

Table 7.3 shows that the statistical tests confirm that singular subject pronouns present significant differences in usage. Overall, they are overused both in the TT1s and TT2s. The speech roles (first and second persons), particularly the formal *usted*, tend to be overused, while third-person singular usage is underused.

Table 7.3 Subject pronouns: Verification of dubbese (TRACEci-CORPES XXI)

Pronouns	z	p	TT1	z	p	TT2
All	−16.031	0	overused	−11.302	0	overused
Yo	−2.091	0	overused	0.1911	0.8485	not rejected
Tú	0.916	0.3596	not rejected	1.503	0.1329	not rejected
Vd	−2.183	0.029	overused	−8.937	0	overused
Él-ella	4.207	0	underused	3.3	0.001	underused

Table 7.4 *Yo*: Verification of dubbese by function (TRACEci-CORPES XXI)

Yo/ I	z	p	TT1	z	p	TT2
Deixis	−4.929	0	overused	−2.8009	0.005	overused
Contrast	1.851	0.0642	not rejected	0.9022	0.367	not rejected
Emphasis	1.761	0.0782	not rejected	1.578	0.1144	not rejected
Formulaic	1.633	0.1024	not rejected	0.6508	0.5152	not rejected
Co-reference			no data			

To find the possible reasons underlying this behaviour, our next step is to determine which functions are affected in these cases of overuse or underuse. Our *tertium comparationis* contemplates the following functions: deixis, contrast, emphasis, formulaic uses and co-reference marker. The aim is to verify where the overuse or underuse applies in the translations and whether they are corrected in the TT2s, as shown in Tables 7.4 to 7.6.

According to data, the most frequent function in both TT1s and TT2s is deixis, which tends to appear in contexts where it is expendable as the marking of agreement and reference is already signalled by the verbal inflections. As shown by the corrections in TT2, these pronouns tend to be omitted in example (28).

(28) (ST) MR. CRABTREE: Oh, *I'm* sorry, *I* just sold it to this young gent.
 (TT2) CRABTREE: Oh, Ø lo siento, Ø acabo de vendérselo a este joven.

The contrast cases are generally kept in the TT2 customized script to ensure intelligibility, as in example (29).

(29) (ST) THOMPSON: (overlapping) *I* am not your sidekick! *You* are mine!
 (TT1) FERNÁNDEZ: \¡*Yo* no soy tu segundo! ¡*Tú* eres el mío!
 (TT2) FERNÁNDEZ: \¡*Yo* no soy tu segundo! ¡*Tú* eres el mío!

Table 7.5 *Usted*: Verification of dubbese by function (TRACEci-CORPES XXI)

Usted/ you	z	p	TT1	z	p	TT2
Deixis	−2.5237	0.0116	Overused	−2.4187	0.0156	overused
Contrast	−0.883	0.3772	not rejected	0.3677	0.7132	not rejected
Emphasis	1.698	0.0894	not rejected	1.851	0.064	not rejected
Formulaic	−1.1588	0.2466	not rejected	0.4686	0.6394	not rejected
Co-reference	0.8064	0.42	not rejected	1.109	0.2672	not rejected

Table 7.6 *Él-ella(s)*: Verification of dubbese by function (TRACEci-CORPES XXI)

Él-ella(s)	z	p	TT1	z	p	TT2
Deixis	−1.648	0.1086	not rejected	−0.3358	0.737	not rejected
Contrast	2.845	0.0044	underused	2.908	0.0036	underused
Emphasis	0.4951	0.6206	not rejected	−1.1598	0.2462	not rejected
Formulaic	0.691	0.4894	not rejected	−0.666	0.505	not rejected
Co-reference	−1.7876	0.0738	not rejected	−1.6282	0.1034	not rejected

Results for *usted* suggest that adaptors have added subject pronouns when syncing as a customization resource, as there is evidence of additional pronoun redundancy in the TT2, as in example (30).

(30) (ST) HELEN: This is classified information. [classified- designated as officially secret and to which only authorized people may have access] face obscured] [realizing] And that's why......the privilege. [soft breath] But *you* were ready to tell this to the D.A. [the privilege – i.e. 'I'm considering this conversation privileged [Reel 1AB]'] [D.A. – see Reel 1AB]
(TT1) HELEN: Esto es información clasificada. De ahí la confidencialidad. Pero estaba Ø dispuesto a contarle esto al fiscal.
(TT2) HELEN: Esto es información clasificada. [DL] De ahí la [DLON] confidencialidad. Pero *usted* pensaba contárselo al fiscal.

The non-speech role works as a marker of co-reference in dialogue, as in example (31), although deixis is still the most frequent function. While *él* is kept in TT1 to create cohesion and differentiate Harrison from Admiral Marcus, the solution in TT2 (*Ø Sabe que si nos acercamos al espacio klingon, sería la guerra total*) is unclear. The subject of the verb *sabe* may be the fugitive (*he/él*) or the admiral (*he/usted*), as the latter is being addressed as *you/usted*.

(31) (ST) ADMIRAL MARCUS: [overlapping] So *Harrison's* gone to the Klingon home world. Is *he* defecting?
KIRK: Uh... we're not sure, sir. [pants]
SPOCK: [overlapping] *He* has taken refuge in the Ketha Province, a region uninhabited for decades.
KIRK: [overlapping] Eh, well, *he's* gotta be hiding there, sir! [quick breath] *He* knows if we even go near Klingon space, it'd be all-out war. Starfleet can't go after him, but I can. [pants] Please, sir. [panting ebbs]
(TT1) ALMIRANTE MARCUS: Así que *Harrison* se ha ido al hogar de los klingons. ¿Ha desertado?
KIRK: Ehm... no estamos seguros. (JADEA)
SPOCK: (P) Se ha refugiado en la provincia de Ketha, una región deshabitada desde hace décadas.
KIRK: (P) ¡Ehm, tiene que estar escondido allí, señor! *Él sabe que si nos acercamos siquiera al espacio klingon, sería la guerra total.* La Flota Estelar no puede ir tras él, pero yo sí. (JADEA) Por favor, señor. (JADEA)
(TT2) ALMIRANTE MARCUS: Así que *Harrison* se ha ido al mundo de los klingons. ¿Estará desertando?
KIRK: Ehm, no estamos seguros./ (JADEA)
SPOCK: (P) Se ha refugiado en la provincia de Ketha, deshabitada desde hace décadas.
KIRK: (P) ¡Tiene que estar escondido allí! Ø *Sabe que si nos acercamos al espacio klingon, sería la guerra total.* (S) La Flota no puede ir tras él, pero yo sí. (JADEA)/ Por favor. (JADEA)

7.6 Conclusions

Results indicate that in the case of *poder* < *can/could*, no changes have been practised during the transition from the TT1s to the TT2s, suggesting that *poder* tends not to be targeted by the adaptor during synchronization. Concerning functions, the use of *poder* is acceptable for the following: capability, possibility, prohibition, prediction and permission. However, capability is overused, and possibility and permission are underused. Ability and aspectual *poder* are conveyed by alternative means. *Poder* expressing request and offer is consistently mistransferred into prefabricated orality in non-translated Spanish, creating an additional meaning that seems restricted to audiovisual genres, as opposed to written genres (Rabadán 2006; Rabadán, Labrador and Ramón 2009).

In the case of subject pronouns, results suggest that they may be used as an adjusting tool, as shown by the modifications from TT1s to TT2s, especially with *usted* and *él-ella*, which display a greater occurrence of unnecessary, redundant pronouns in the TT2s than in the TT1s. Concerning functions, deixis is overused in the case of the speech roles, while the third-person singular (other roles) presents underuse when expressing contrast, creating situations of referential ambiguity in the Spanish dialogue. In the case of *yo*, marks of deixis are generally expendable. However, the translations present an unnecessary redundancy in marking grammatical agreement, which may add unwanted emphasis, thus slightly modifying the final result.

This pilot study indicates that certain grammatical items seem to undertake the role of syncing tools. While TT2 synchronization is non-negotiable in dubbing, which linguistic parts are affected can be negotiated. Despite first-class work on the part of translators and adaptors, film dialogue constitutes a separate genre/medium-bound dialect which often runs on unnecessary transfer and redundancy. More data and further analysis are needed to identify other 'negotiable' linguistic phenomena.

Notes

1 Examples (1) to (7) come from CORPES XXI.
2 From 'ad libitum', here meaning extra dialogue in the target language added by the adapter at his own will.
3 This excludes usage in the Canary Islands, where the regional variety applies *usted(es)* as an informal form of address but follows third-person verbal agreement.
4 All texts have been provided by professional translator/adaptor Quico Rovira-Beleta.

References

Baños-Piñero, R. (2013), '"That is so Cool": Investigating the Translation of Adverbial Intensifiers in English-Spanish Dubbing through a Parallel Corpus of Sitcoms', *Perspectives Studies in Translatology*, 21 (4): 526–42.

Baños-Piñero, R. and F. Chaume (2009), 'Prefabricated Orality. A Challenge in Audiovisual Translation', *TRAlinea*. Special Issue: *The Translation of Dialects in Multimedia*. http://www.intralinea.org/archive/article/1714

Biber, D., S. Johansson, G. N. Leech, S. Conrad and E. Finegan (1999), *Grammar of Spoken and Written English*, London: Longman.

Cautín-Epifani, V. (2015), 'Uso de pronombres de primera persona singular omitidos y expresos en producciones de aprendices de español' (Use of Null and Overt First Person Pronouns in Oral Production of Learners of Spanish), *Literatura y lingüística*, 31: 205–20.

Chaume, F. (2001), 'La pretendida oralidad de los textos audiovisuales y sus implicaciones en traducción' (The alleged orality of audiovisual texts and its implications in translation), in F. Chaume and R. Agost (eds), *La traducción en los medios audiovisuales (Translation in the audiovisual media)*, 77–88, Castelló: Universitat Jaume I.

Chaume, F. (2004), 'Discourse Markers in Audiovisual Translation', *Meta*, 49 (4): 843–55.

Chaume, F. (2007), 'Quality Standards in Dubbing: A Proposal', *Tradterm*, 13: 71–89.

Chaume, F. (2012), *Audiovisual Translation: Dubbing*, London: Routledge.

Coates, J. ([1983] 2015), *The Semantics of the Modal Auxiliaries*, London: Routledge.

De Cock, B. (2014), *Profiling Discourse Participants: Forms and Functions in Spanish Conversation and Debates*, Amsterdam and Philadelphia: John Benjamins.

Enríquez, E. V. (1984), *El pronombre personal sujeto en la lengua española hablada en Madrid (The subject pronoun in the Spanish spoken in Madrid)*, Madrid: CSIC.

Fernández-Soriano, O. (1999), 'El pronombre personal. Formas y distribuciones. Pronombres átonos y tónicos' (The personal pronoun. Forms and distribution. Atonic and tonic pronouns), in I. Bosque and V. Demonte (eds), *Gramática descriptiva de la lengua española (Descriptive Grammar of the Spanish Language)*, 1209–74, Barcelona: Espasa.

Fodor, I. (1976), *Film Dubbing*, Hamburg: Buske.

Gómez-Capuz, J. (2001), 'La interferencia pragmática del inglés sobre el español en doblajes, telecomedias y lenguaje coloquial: una aportación al estudio del cambio lingüístico en curso' (The pragmatic interference of English with Spanish in dubbing, telecommunication and colloquial language: A contribution to the study of ongoing linguistic change), *Tonos Digital, Revista Electrónica de Estudios Filológicos*, 2. http://www.um.es/tonosdigital/znum2/estudios/Doblaje1.htm

Gregory, M. and S. Carroll (1978), *Language and Situation: Language Varieties and the Social Contexts*, London: Routledge.

Gutiérrez-Lanza, C. (1999), *TRACEci Corpus* (version 2, TRACEci XML ed.). https://trace.unileon.es/es/fondos-trace/catalogos/textos-audiovisuales-cine-y-tv/

Gutiérrez-Lanza, C. (2000), *Traducción y censura de textos cinematográficos en la España de Franco: Doblaje y subtitulado inglés-español (1951–1975) (Translation and censorship of films in Franco's Spain: English-Spanish dubbing and subtitling (1951–1975))*, León: Universidad de León.

Gutiérrez-Lanza, C. (2023), 'Film Dialogue Synchronization and Statistical Dubesse: A Corpus-based Pilot Study of English-Spanish Conversational Markers', in M. Izquierdo and Z. Sanz-Villar (eds), *Corpus Use in Cross-Linguistic Research. Paving the Way for Teaching, Translation and Professional Communication*, 124–41, Amsterdam and Philadelphia: John Benjamins.

Gutiérrez-Lanza, C. and J. Alonso (2011, April 7–9), 'The TRACE Corpus Aligner: Developing a New Electronic Tool for Language Researchers', Paper presentation, III Congreso Internacional de Lingüística de Corpus. CILC 2011. Las tecnologías de la información y las comunicaciones: Presente y futuro en el análisis de corpora, Valencia, Spain.

Halliday, M. A. K. and R. Hasan (1976), *Cohesion in English*, London: Routledge.

Lubbers-Quesada, M. and S. E. Blackwell (2009), 'The L2 Acquisition of Null and Overt Spanish Subject Pronouns: A PragmaticApproach', in J. Collentine, M. García, B. Lafford and F. Marcos (eds), *Selected Proceedings of the 11th Hispanic Linguistic Symposium*, 117–30, Somerville: Cascadilla Press.

Luján, M. (1999), 'Expresión y omisión del pronombre personal' (Null and overt personal pronouns), in I. Bosque and V. Demonte (eds), *Gramática descriptiva de la lengua española [Descriptive Grammar of the Spanish Language]*, 1275–315, Barcelona: Espasa.

Metz, C. (1974), *Film Language. A Semiotics of the Cinema*, Oxford: Oxford University Press.

Moreno, A. (2011), 'Sujetos explícitos e implícitos en la adquisición bilingüe y monolingüe del español' (Overt and null subjects in bilingual and monolingual Spanish acquisition), *Lengua y Habla*, 15: 73–85.

Pavesi, M. (2016), 'Formulaicity In and Across Film Dialogue: Clefts as Translational Routines', *Across Languages and Cultures*, 17 (1): 99–121.

Pavesi, M. (2018), 'Reappraising Verbal Language in Audiovisual Translation. From Description to Application', *Journal of Audiovisual Translation*, 1 (1): 101–21.

Pérez-González, L. (2007), 'Appraising Dubbed Conversation. Systemic Functional Insights into the Construal of Naturalness in Translated Film Dialogue', *The Translator: Studies in Intercultural Communication*, 13 (1): 1–38.

Rabadán, R. (2006), 'Modality and Modal Verbs in Contrast. Mapping out a Translation(ally) Relevant Approach English-Spanish', *Languages in Contrast*, 6 (2): 261–306.

Rabadán, R. (2008), 'Refining the Idea of Applied Extensions', in A. Pym, M. Shlesinger and D. Simeoni (eds), *Beyond Descriptive Translation Studies: Investigations in Homage to Gideon Toury*, 103–17, Amsterdam and Philadelphia: John Benjamins.

Rabadán, R. (2010), 'Linguistic Preferences in Translation English-Spanish: A Case of "Missing Identity"?', in M. Muñoz-Calvo and C. Buesa-Gómez (eds), *Translation and Cultural Identity. Selected Essays on Translation and Cross-cultural Communication*, 61–81, Newcastle: Cambridge Scholars Publishing.

Rabadán, R. (2022), 'Equivalence', in *ENTI (Encyclopedia of Translation and Interpreting)*, AIETI. https://doi.org/10.5281/zenodo.6366939

Rabadán, R. and C. Gutiérrez-Lanza (2020), 'Developing Awareness of Interference Errors in Translation: An English-Spanish Pilot Study in Popular Science and Audiovisual Transcripts', *Lingue e Linguaggi*, 40: 379–404.

Rabadán, R., B. Labrador and N. Ramón (2009), 'Corpus-based Contrastive Analysis and Translation Universals: A Tool for Translation Quality Assessment English-Spanish', *Babel*, 55 (4): 303–28.

Ramón, N. and C. Gutiérrez-Lanza (2018), 'Translation Description for Assessment and Post-editing: The Case of Personal Pronouns in Translated Spanish', *Target – International Journal of Translation Studies*, 30 (1): 112–36.

Real Academia Española (2021), *CORPES XXI. Corpus del Español del Siglo XXI [Corpus of 21st Century Spanish]* (version 0,94, CORPES XXI XML ed.). https://www.rae.es/banco-de-datos/corpes-xxi

Romero-Fresco, P. (2006), 'The Spanish Dubbese: A Case of (un)Idiomatic Friends', *The Journal of Specialised Translation*, 6: 134–51.

Romero-Fresco, P. (2009), 'A Corpus-based Study on the Naturalness of the Spanish Dubbing Language: The Analysis of Discourse Markers in the Dubbed Translation of Friends', PhD diss., Heriot-Watt University. http://www.ros.hw.ac.uk/handle/10399/2237

Sampedro-Mella, M. (2021), 'Las formas de tratamiento en la tradición académica del español' (Forms of address in the Spanish academic tradition), *Anuario de Letras. Lingüística y Filología*, 9 (1): 105–32.

Serrano, M. (2012), 'El sujeto pronominal usted/ustedes y su posición: variación y creación de estilos comunicativos' (The pronominal subject usted/ustedes and its position: variation and creation of communicative styles), *Spanish in Context*, 9 (1): 109–31.

Smith, S. (1998), 'The Language of Subtitling', in I. Gambier (ed.), *Translating for the Media*, 139–49, Turku: University of Turku.

Whitman-Linsen, C. (1992), *Through the Dubbing Glass: The Synchronization of American Motion Pictures into German, French and Spanish*, Bern: Peter Lang.

Part II

Discourse in Contrast

8

The Social Functions and Linguistic Patterns of *Please* and Its Norwegian Correspondences

Stine Hulleberg Johansen and Kristin Rygg

8.1 Introduction

The word *please* in English has many functions ranging from expressing politeness (Watts 2003; Wichmann 2004; Sato 2008), intensifying the directive force of a request (House 1989; Murphy and De Felice 2019) to simply being an indicator of ritualistic discourse (Kádár and House 2019). *Please* has even been associated with impoliteness (Aijmer 2015; Fedriani 2019). Whereas *please* has been extensively studied, its Norwegian correspondences have not. *Please* does not have a straightforward counterpart in Norwegian, and previous research on the Norwegian translations of *please* shows that various expressions are used to carry the meanings of *please* (Fretheim 2005; Johansson 2007); however, little is known about the social functions these expressions perform and the linguistic patterns in which they occur.

This study aims to address this gap by investigating the functions and patterns of *please* and its Norwegian correspondences. The study utilizes data from The English-Norwegian Parallel Corpus (ENPC) (Johansson 2007; Johansson, Ebeling and Oksefjell 2002) with aid from other more recently compiled Norwegian and English monolingual corpora in its pursuit to discover how the various functions of *please* are expressed in Norwegian; which social and linguistic factors condition the use of *please* and its Norwegian correspondences; and whether there are any potential sociopragmatic and pragmalinguistic differences in the use of *please* and its Norwegian correspondences. The analysis of the linguistic patterns largely follows the format of Aijmer (2009), who conducted a study of *please* and its correspondences in Swedish, using data from the English-Swedish Parallel Corpus (ESPC). The analysis of the social functions builds on the Ritual Frame Analysis Model developed by House and Kádár (2021) with the additions made by Rygg and Johansen (2022).

8.2 Theoretical background

In English, the adverb *please* does not only accompany requests but carries the illocutionary force of a request alone (Fraser 1996) and is therefore often called a request marker. In addition, Watts (2003: 183) calls *please* '[t]he most obvious example of a politeness marker in English', where politeness markers may be defined as expressions that 'show deference to the addressee and bid for cooperative behaviour' (House and Kasper 1981: 166). Thus, Wichmann (2004: 1521) finds that the omission of *please* in some contexts 'makes a request less courteous rather than less like a request, so its function must be, at least to some extent, to convey interpersonal, "attitudinal" meaning'. However, Sato (2008: 1250) argues that *please* comes 'with a varying degree of politeness and directive force'. By comparing American and New Zealand English texts, she finds that when *please* appears in a unit-initial position, the speaker strongly asserts compliance, resulting in the directive acts of either a demand or a plea. In a unit-final position, however, when the request is transactional or formulaic, and the recipient is subject to comply, *please* carries limited politeness effect. This formulaic quality of *please* is what House and Kádár (2021) call an 'RFIE' (ritual frame indicating expression) where a ritual frame is understood as the participants' awareness of the rights and obligations that a particular standard situation holds. When, for instance, *please* is used by a judge in a courtroom, it is not necessarily used to intensify or mitigate the request but rather to remind the audience about the ritual frame associated with the institution (Kádár and House 2020a). The more conventional the meaning of a particular RFIE becomes, the less directly related it is to individualistic politeness (Kádár and House 2020b). This idea that *please*, especially in British English, often primarily is part of a conventional requesting routine rather than a mitigator of a face-treat has also been advocated by others (Wichmann 2004; Terkourafi 2015). From an American-English perspective, however, Murphy and De Felice (2019) argue that *please* is interpreted less like a routine and more as a marker of upward (an order) or downward (a plea) relational power differences. When *please* occurs in non-standard situations, that is, where the requestee's right to utter the request is unclear, House (1989) finds that it seldom accompanies requests because of its requestive force. Instead, House discovers that using other linguistic means is much more common to mitigate the face-treat, such as hedges and supportive moves. Based on several studies on British English requests, Stewart (2005) concludes that indirect (negative politeness/deference) strategies are favoured even when the face threat is low.

In Norwegian, according to Fretheim (2005: 158), 'conventionalised indirectness in the performance of requests exists, but too much linguistic embroidery for the sake of mitigating requests is normally counter-productive'. For instance, Savić (2018) finds that when Norwegian students write e-mail requests in English, their tutors deem them impolite because of the level of directness, lack of hedging and an overly informal tone. However, this does not mean that politeness markers are completely absent in Norwegian. Fretheim (2005) mentions the verb *vær* (imperative form of 'to be') combined with the adjectives *snill* ('kind') and *vennlig* ('friendly') as expressions that come closest in corresponding to *please*: Vær så snill å ikke døm Oliver så hardt ('be so nice not to judge Oliver so severely') or Vær vennlig å ikke bruke den slags språk her ('be kind to not use that sort of language here'). Other Norwegian expressions mentioned as corresponding to *please* are *er du snill* ('are you kind') (Urbanik 2017) and *vennligst* ('kindly') (Rygg and Johansen 2022). In a study of Norwegian and Polish politeness markers, Urbanik (2017) finds that neither *vær så snill* ('be so kind') nor *er du snill* ('are you kind') are regular modifiers in Norwegian and that if they are used, it is typically to emphasize a strong desire for compliance, rather than for politeness purposes. According to Rygg and Johansen (2022), *vennligst* ('kindly') may be the lexical item that mostly resembles *please* in form as it is a sentence-adverbial consisting of one lexeme followed by an imperative verb. By examining the use of *vennligst* in two different corpora, they find that most instances are indicators of a ritual frame (RFIE) used in public notifications and on signposts. When *vennligst* is used in private communication between individuals, however, it is in danger of being interpreted as an impolite command rather than a polite request. Andersen (2022) uses four spoken corpora to explore the distribution of the borrowed form *please* versus its domestic forms *vær så snill* ('be so kind') and *vennligst* ('kindly') in Norwegian requests. He argues that both *vær så snill* and *please* have insistent and begging qualities, but the illocutionary force of *please* is stronger than that of *vær så snill*. Andersen (2022: 257) claims that *vær så snill* and *vennligst* both serve as an 'explicit marking that adds to politeness by mitigating the face threat induced by the request'. However, Rygg and Johansen (2022) find that this is often not true in non-standard situations where the social roles of the interlocutors are unclear.

There are also some indications that request markers are not required in Norwegian to the same extent as in English. Thus, Awedyk (2003) finds that Norwegian learners of English use *please* more frequently in English (34.5 per cent) than they use request markers in Norwegian (7.5 per cent). Further, Johansson (2007: 32) maintains that *please* is underused in translations from Norwegian to English. From a similar Swedish context, Aijmer (2009) uncovers that *please* is frequently added to English translations where the source text had no such marker. She hypothesizes that the reason may be that formulaic politeness markers are needed in certain situations in English where there is no such need in Swedish. When asking for permission in Norwegian, a typical construction is an interrogative containing the auxiliary verb *kan/kunne* ('can/could') + infinitive/past participle of the main verb (*Kan/Kunne jeg få en kaffi takk?* 'can/could I get a coffee, thank you?') (Fretheim 2005), often with a negation (*kan ikke jeg få en kaffi?* 'can't I get a coffee?') (Urbanik and Svennevig 2019). According to Urbanik (2020), the *Can I*-interrogative is the default format used to mitigate a request in Norwegian. Thus, Norwegian learners of English tend to use *can I* more than *could I* in English requests (Brubæk 2012; Savić 2018), something that frequently upsets English natives when communicating with Norwegians (Røkaas 2000).

The discussion above fosters several research questions. First, because there is no direct equivalent to *please* in Norwegian, various Norwegian expressions are used to signal the functions of *please*, but what social and linguistic factors condition their use and do any sociopragmatic and pragmalinguistic differences arise? Second, if no marker is used in Norwegian translations of *please* or in Norwegian source texts where the English translation has introduced a *please*, how are the functions of *please* expressed in Norwegian and what conditions the use of Ø (no marker)?

To answer these questions, we will look at the social functions and linguistic patterns of *please* and its correspondences in the ENPC, with additional evidence from more recently compiled monolingual corpora. To describe and distinguish different types of social functions, the study takes inspiration from the work of Kádár and House (2020a) who distinguish between the functions of *please* in 'standard situations', where the social roles are clear to the participants and the functions of *please* in 'non-standard situations', where the social roles are less clear. To describe the linguistic patterns of *please* and its Norwegian correspondences, the study largely follows the procedure of Aijmer (2009).

8.3 Material and method

To investigate how the different functions of *please* are signalled in Norwegian, an analysis of data from the English-Norwegian Parallel Corpus (ENPC) was performed. The results from the ENPC were further checked in monolingual English and Norwegian corpora as a means of verification and elaboration. The study is qualitative in its aim to describe the functions and patterns of *please* and its correspondences, but will refer to quantitative features, that is, frequencies from the corpus searches, where appropriate.

8.3.1 Corpora and search procedures

First, a search was made for *please* in the English original and translated texts in the ENPC. The ENPC is a bidirectional corpus of English and Norwegian original texts, both fiction and nonfiction, and their translations. The corpus was compiled in 1997 and consists of thirty fiction and twenty nonfiction text extracts from each language and their translations. Each text is about 10,000–15,000 words, amounting to some 2.6 million words in total (Johansson 2007; Johansson, Ebeling and Oksefjell 2002).

Second, as most of the instances of *please* in the ENPC appeared in fictional dialogue, the Spoken British National Corpus 2014 (The Spoken BNC2014) (Love et al. 2017) was consulted to confirm the various uses of *please* in authentic dialogue. The Spoken BNC2014 is an 11.5-million-word corpus of informal spoken English recorded between 2010 and 2016. It consists of conversations between 668 speakers of British English in a total of 1,251 recordings.

Third, the translations and the sources of *please* in Norwegian in the ENPC were studied. To ensure that the Norwegian translations of *please* did not include instances of pragmatic failure or translationese (Johansson 2001) and to check the extent of their use, some of the expressions were further investigated in monolingual Norwegian corpora. The monolingual data was gathered from The Corpus for Bokmål Lexicography (LBK) (Fjeld, Nøklestad and Hagen 2020). LBK is a corpus of written text compiled between 2008 and 2013 consisting of fictional and nonfictional texts, newspapers and periodicals, subtitles and leaflets and other unpublished texts. Thus, the text types were largely similar to those in the ENPC. LBK also includes translated texts, mainly from English into Norwegian, so to avoid source language influence in LBK, only Norwegian original texts were part of the search.

Since most of the results from the ENPC were from dialogues in fictional texts, monolingual spoken corpora with authentic dialogue were also consulted. The corpora consulted were The Norwegian Speech Corpus (NoTa) (Johannessen and Hagen 2008), The BigBrother corpus (BB) and the Norwegian part of The Nordic Dialect Corpus (NDC) (Johannessen et al. 2009); however, as there were few occurrences of the expressions in the spoken corpora and the occurrences mainly corroborated the results from LBK, the results from the spoken corpora will remain in the background in this study.

8.3.2 Classification

The instances of *please* and their Norwegian correspondences were analysed according to their social function and their linguistic pattern. The analysis of the linguistic patterns largely follows the format of Aijmer (2009) who identified twelve different linguistic patterns in the English original texts in the ESPC. In addition to describing the linguistic patterns, the present analysis also considers the position of the marker in the text unit in which it occurs, that is, whether it occurs in initial, medial, final or (semi-)freestanding position. The terms 'freestanding' and 'semi-freestanding' are borrowed from Sato (2008) and refer to markers used alone in a turn and to simple constructions such as *yes/no, please* and *NP + please*.

The social analysis builds on the Ritual Frame Analysis Model developed by House and Kádár (2021) and the additions made by Rygg and Johansen (2022). Kádár and House (2019) hypothesized that so-called 'politeness markers', such as *please*, function as indicators of a ritual frame, that is, clusters of standard situations in which the rights and obligations of the interlocutors are clear, and developed a model for analysing and comparing such ritual frames indicating expressions (RFIEs) across languages. In a monolingual study of the Norwegian politeness marker *vennligst* ('kindly'), Rygg and Johansen applied elements from the Ritual Frame Analysis Model to data from Norwegian corpora and looked at *vennligst* in both standard and non-standard situations. In the current study, the use of *please* and its correspondences are analysed according to whether they are indicators of a ritualistic situation that is, RFIEs (1), markers of politeness used to soften the illocutionary force (2) or request markers used to strengthen the requestive force (3). The analysis was performed and crosschecked by two researchers and ambiguous instances were discussed.

(1) The property is approached by pathway with garden and path to side entrance, together with garden to rear. *PLEASE* NOTE: We can give no

warranty as to whether or not any boiler or heating / water system to the property is operational

Ø MERK: Utleieren kan ikke garantere, og har heller intet ansvar for, at varmtvannsbereder og evt. sentralfyr virker.
(ENPC_ST1E.1.2.s197)

(2) 'Now, Sir, if you *please*, look at this one!'

'Og nu, Sir, *om De behager*, se på denne!'
(ENPC_BC1E.13.s41)

(3) [...] 'I have told you that story a hundred times already.' [...] 'But it's really my super favorite. Tell me again, okay? *Please*? [...]'

'Fortell den en gang til, *vær så snill*.'
(ENPC_TH1E.1.s376)

Example (1) illustrates the use of *please* in a *standard situation* (Kádár and House 2019). In a standard situation rights and obligations prevail and *please* functions as a reminder of such rights and obligations. Kádár and House distinguish between three categories of standard situations depending on the type of interpersonal scenario: 'dyadic', which are private interactions; 'multiparty', which are interactions with overhearers or interactions taking place in a communal setting, for example, in a classroom; and 'public', which are interactions designed to be accessible to both ratified participants and any audience (Kádár and House 2019: 9; House and Kádár 2021: 88). Example (1) illustrates the latter. Such 'public displays' are characterized by a total lack of personal involvement, and 'there is little pragmatic incentive for the creators of these messages to mitigate the requests being made, as there is no clearly identifiable addressee who requires mitigation in order to comply with the request' (Kádár and House 2019: 16–17). In the Norwegian version, the marker is left out altogether.

Example (2) illustrates *please* used in a non-standard situation, that is, situations in which the rights and obligations of the speakers are less clear and there may be a need to mitigate potential face threats (Rygg and Johansen 2022). The *please* in (2) signals deference, which is also reflected in the somewhat archaic expression *om De behager*, ('if You please'), in Norwegian.

Similar to example (2), the situation in example (3) is a non-standard situation; however, in (3) *please* functions more as a means to intensify the request rather than to mitigate it. The intensification is so powerful that the request becomes a plea. The speaker may expect compliance and feel that she is entitled to it (because it is her super favourite), even if the social roles of the interactants do not make this entitlement clear. In the Norwegian translation, the expression *vær så snill* ('be so good/kind'), which may have a begging quality, strengthens the request.

8.4 Results and discussion

The following sections present the social functions and the linguistic patterns of *please* in the ENPC. Following the presentation, the way the functions and patterns of *please* are represented in Norwegian in standard and non-standard situations are discussed.

8.4.1 Social functions of *please*

The search for *please* in the English original and translated texts in the ENPC gave a total of 109 instances, of which seventeen were instances of the verb *to please* and thus excluded from the analysis. The remaining ninety-two were analysed according to their social function and their linguistic pattern. Most of the uses of *please* in the data were in interactions between ratified persons, that is, either dyadic or multiparty (93.5 per cent). Only 6.5 per cent were public display uses. The situations in which *please* was used were distributed close to equally between standard and non-standard situations. *Please* was used in non-standard situations in 58 per cent of the instances and in standard situations 42 per cent. When *please* was used in non-standard situations between ratified persons, it typically functioned as a request marker strengthening the requestive force. There were only a few examples of *please* as a politeness marker, softening the illocutionary force. In standard situations, *please* functioned as an RFIE with limited illocutionary force simply reminding the speakers of the ritualistic aspects of the situation. A summary of situation types and interaction types can be found in Table 8.1.

An analysis of thirty random instances of *please* in the Spoken BNC2014 supported the impression from the ENPC, but there was a slight majority of *please* used in standard situations (56 per cent), while 43 per cent of the instances of *please* were in non-standard situations. Most of the situations were conversations between persons, which is natural since the Spoken BNC2014 is a conversational corpus, but there was one instance of a public display use of *please*, where a speaker is reading from a set of instructions. In non-standard

Table 8.1 Summary of types of situations and interaction types in the ENPC

Type of situation/Interaction type	Standard	Non-standard	SUM
Dyadic	27	40	67
Multiparty	6	13	19
Public	6	0	6
Sum	39	53	92

situations, there were examples of *please* used both as a request marker and as a politeness marker.

The analysis corroborates what previous studies have said about *please*, that is, that *please* comes 'with a varying degree of politeness and directive force' (Sato 2008: 1250) and that *please* also has a formulaic quality and functions as a reminder of social rights and obligations (Aijmer 1996; Kádár and House 2019, 2020a, 2020b).

8.4.2 Linguistic patterns of *please*

In line with results from previous studies (Sato 2008; Wichmann 2004), *please* was found in various positions within a unit. The analysis of the linguistic patterns of *please* in the ENPC gave a total of eighteen patterns, several of which corresponded to the patterns discovered by Aijmer (2009) in the ESPC. Table 8.2 gives an overview of the patterns of *please* and their positions in the English texts.

Most of the instances of *please* were found in initial position in the linguistic pattern of *please* followed by a verb in the imperative. In line with Aijmer's findings from the ESPC (2009: 67),[1] the pattern *please* + imperative was dominant, with thirty-eight of ninety-two occurrences. This is also supported by previous studies which have shown that *please* + imperative is a frequent pattern in both American English and New Zealand English (Sato 2008) and that *please* occurs more frequently with imperatives than with indirect questions in British English (Aijmer 1996).

To check whether the patterns discovered in the ENPC also occurred in authentic conversations, the patterns of thirty random instances of *please* in the Spoken BNC2014 were analysed. Several of the same patterns appeared; however, among the instances analysed, *please* used in final position (seventeen of thirty) in the pattern *can/could I have* [. . .] *please* was the most frequent. This pattern was often used in standard situations, for example, placing an order in a restaurant. This reflects Sato's (2008) findings that *please* used in final position tends to be formulaic and Kádár and House's (2019) findings that markers such as *please* are used as RFIEs in standard situations where the roles of the

Table 8.2 Patterns of *please* in English original and translated texts in the ENPC

	Unit position/ Linguistic pattern	Initial	Medial	Final	(Semi-)/ Freestanding	SUM
1	*Please* + imperative	38				38
2	Freestanding *please*				11	11
3	*Please* + [name, honorific, etc.]				8	8
4	Oh + *please*				7	7
5	Yes / no + *please*				5	5
6	Imperative + *please*			5		5
7	Will / would /won't you + *please* [...]		4			4
8	Would NP VP *please*			2		2
9	[Name] + *please*				2	2
10	If you *please*		1	1		2
11	*Please* will / would NP VP	1				1
12	*Please* + wh-question	1				1
13	Wh-question + *please*			1		1
14	Could I [...] *please*			1		1
15	Could you *please* VP		1			1
16	ADV + *please*			1		1
17	NP + *please*				1	1
18	If I would *please* VP		1			1
	Sum	40	7	11	34	92

participants are clear and predetermined and the degree of imposition is low. When *please* was used in initial position (5 of 30) in the Spoken BNC2014, the pattern *please* + imperative was the most frequent construction.

Even though *please* in medial position seems to have the widest functional variability, that is, it can express both commands and polite requests in this position (Sato 2008), it rarely occurred in this position in the data from the ENPC (8 per cent) and the Spoken BNC2014 (3 per cent). Wichmann (2004) found that the medial *please* typically occurred in public speech situations, for example, courtrooms, which may to some extent overlap with multiparty situations in Kádár and House's (2020a, 2020b) framework, of which there were few in our data.

8.4.3 Norwegian correspondences of *please*

The Norwegian correspondences of *please* in the ENPC are presented in Table 8.3. The most frequent correspondences were *vær så snill* and Ø (no marker).

Table 8.3 Correspondences of *please* in ENPC

Translations of *please*	Glossing	No. of instances
vær (så) snill	be (so) good/kind	44
Ø		23
er du/de snill	are you/You kind	5
vennligst	kindly/kindest	4
vær så god	be so good	4
takk	thanks	3
vær (så) vennlig	be (so) friendly	3
please		2
snille	kind	1
gode	good	1
(om De) behager	(if You) please	1
kjære	dear	1
Sum		92

Vær så snill appeared in both non-standard and standard situations and is discussed in Section 8.4.4 together with Ø (no translation) and *er du snill*. *Vennligst* and *vær (så) vennlig* were mainly used in standard situations and will be dealt with in Section 8.4.5.

The less common correspondences (listed with one or two occurrences in Table 8.3) will not be dealt with further in this study, for example, *snille* ('kind'), *gode* ('good') and *kjære* ('dear'). These expressions were used as positive politeness markers in pleas. An example is *kjære Gud* (a translation from 'please, God'), which is also a set phrase in Norwegian prayers. The English loanword *please* was used twice in sentence parts that had not been translated into Norwegian. Although the loanword *please* is used in Norwegian, it will not be discussed here. For an extensive overview of the use of *please* in Norwegian, see Andersen (2022). *Om De behager* ('if You please') is a Norwegian archaic expression mimicking a similar mode in the English source text. There were no instances of this expression in the Norwegian monolingual corpora consulted.

8.4.4 Norwegian correspondences of *please* in non-standard situations

When *please* was used in interactions between ratified persons in situations where the rights and obligations were unclear, it was mainly used to strengthen the request, in correspondence with Murphy and De Felice's (2019) observations. In fact, the majority, 44 of 53 instances of *please* in non-standard situations, were categorized as a plea, as illustrated in example (4). Of these, thirty corresponded to *vær så snill*, which made it the most frequent correspondence of *please* in non-standard situations.

(4) 'Can you give me a lift? Anywhere Cobb's Marsh direction. I've missed the bus. *Please.*'

'Kan jeg få sitte på? Jeg skal utover mot Cobb's March. Bussen gikk fra meg. Å, *vær så snill!*'
(ENPC_PDJ3E.1.1.s32)

In such pleas, *please* was often (semi-)/freestanding (20 of 30), as in example (4), or occurred in initial position as in the pattern *please* + imperative (9 of 30). The freestanding *please* often corresponded to a freestanding *vær så snill* and the pattern *please* + imperative corresponded to *vær så snill* + imperative or infinitive or a freestanding *vær så snill*. Thus, the linguistic patterns for *please* and *vær så snill* largely overlapped. The freestanding *please* may function as a means of influencing other people's behaviour or to express desperation (Aijmer 2009: 74); however, its function strongly depends on the adjacent utterances and the social context in which it occurs (Sato 2008). Our findings support Urbanik (2017) and Andersen (2022) in that *vær så snill* has insistent and begging qualities. *Vær så snill*, particularly in freestanding position, was the most frequent translation of *please* used to express a plea. In some cases, the intensity seemed to be even stronger in the Norwegian translation than in the English original, as in (5).

(5) My head in her lap, my arms around her: *please, oh please* . . .

Hodet mitt i fanget hennes, armene om livet hennes: *Vær så snill, åh, vær så snill. . .!*
(ENPC_KF2TE.1.2.s195)

Andersen (2022) argues that when *please* is used as a loanword in Norwegian, its illocutionary force is stronger than that of *vær så snill*. However, when comparing *please* in English to *vær så snill*, it seems as if the illocutionary force for *vær så snill* is stronger than *please,* at least when it occurs in a freestanding position with rising intonation.

The second-most frequent translation of *please* in non-standard situations was Ø. In total, fourteen of the instances of *please* did not have a corresponding Norwegian marker, as in example (6). Most of these instances were also pleas or demands.

(6) 'Talk to her, *please!*' he prayed earnestly.

Snakk til henne du Ø! ba han inntrengende.
(ENPC_HW2TES.1.2.s258)

Whereas the English original text has a verb in the imperative followed by *please*, the Norwegian translation has only a verb in the imperative. Thus, if the English *please* is used to strengthen the request in this example, the Norwegian request may not be perceived as equally strong.

There was no clear linguistic pattern in the occurrences of *please* corresponding to Ø in Norwegian. Among the fourteen occurrences, there were examples of *please* in initial, medial, final and (semi-)/ freestanding position and in a variety of linguistic patterns. The most frequent pattern was *please* in initial position followed by a verb in imperative (6 of 14).

In some instances where *please* in initial position was translated into a unit-final *er du snill* ('are you kind'), it was challenging to determine whether the use of *please* was a plea or a kind encouragement.

(7) She knew better than to insist, but she came over and kissed him on the cheek. '*Please* don't drink too much at the Blakes' tonight.'

'ikke drikk for meget hos Blakes i kveld, *er du snill*'.
(ENPC_FF1E.1.1.s230)

The expression *er du snill* was rare in the ENPC and was therefore investigated further in the monolingual Norwegian corpora. Fifty random instances of *er du snill* were analysed from LBK. Most of the instances in LBK were used in non-standard situations and functioned as request markers (34 of 50) that strengthen the requestive force, as in example (8).

(8) Ikke kall henne den amerikanske dama, *er du snill*, sa Cato Isaksen irritert – Hun er norsk statsborger

('Don't call her the American woman, *are you kind*, said Cato Isaksen annoyed – She is a Norwegian citizen')
(LBK_SK01LiUn01.2639)

Sato (2008) argues that *please* in a unit-final position has less intensity than in a unit-initial position. The Norwegian translation *er du snill*, however, occurs almost exclusively in final position (also noticed by Urbanik 2017) and mostly strengthens the illocutionary force of the request. Thus, this illustrates that the linguistic pattern or position indicating a social function in one language, is not necessarily the same across languages.

8.4.5 Norwegian correspondences of *please* in standard situations

In the thirty-three standard situations, *please* functioned as an RFIE with limited illocutionary force, reminding the interlocutors of the ritualistic aspects of the situations. As an RFIE, *please* occurred in various linguistic patterns, the most frequent being *please* + imperative and the semi-freestanding *yes/no* + *please*. In standard situations too *vær så snill* (14 of 33) was the most common Norwegian correspondence of *please*. In standard situations, the intensifying and begging quality of *vær så snill* becomes even more evident as illustrated in example (9) where *please* in the source text functioned as a marker of a ritual frame (RFIE) but the translation into *vær så snill* seemed to increase the illocutionary force into a plea.

(9)   *Please*, what will it cost?

   Vær så snill, hva vil det koste?
   (ENPC_GN1E.1.3.s259)

A corresponding Norwegian RFIE suitable to this situation would be *unnskyld* ('excuse me'), what will it cost. We consulted the LBK corpus in order to find other examples of *vær så snill* and although most of them were in non-standard situations expressing pleas, there were examples of *vær så snill* as an RFIE, as illustrated by example (10).

(10)   'Du kan ikke sitte her lenger. *Vær så snill* og kom tilbake i morgen tidlig.'

   ('You can't sit here anymore. *Be so kind* and come back tomorrow morning')
   (ENPC_SK01FrNi01.2392)

The few examples of *vær så snill* in standard situations among the fifty random instances investigated from LBK frequently were in the pattern *vær så snill og* + VP, as in (10).

Table 8.3 above showed a rather high occurrence of *please* not being translated into any corresponding marker (Ø). This was also frequently the case for *please* in standard situations (9 of 39). Furthermore, this was especially true when *please* is used by persons in authority (cf. example (11)) or is a part of a formulaic expression. In (11), the power relationship between the speakers is clear to all participants, and the children are obliged to comply with the professor's request.

(11) 'Good morning, children', the Professor said quietly. 'This is a commercial for cereal. Listen to me carefully, *please*. [...]'

'God_morgen, barn', sa Professoren stillferdig. 'Dette er et reklameinnslag for frokostkorn. Følg nå godt med Ø.'
(ENPC_SK1E.1.s616)

In example (11), there is no direct correspondence of *please* in the Norwegian translation. Similarly, in (12), the person making the statement is superior to the recipients.

(12) Then he made a direct appeal to the warring factions: '*Please* stop the fighting, *please* stop killing, drop your guns; *please!*'

Deretter kommer han med en direkte oppfordring til de stridende: 'Ø Stopp skytingen, Ø stopp drepingen, legg fra dere våpnene Ø.'
(ENPC_KB1TE.2.5.s16)

A Norwegian request marker such as *vær så snill* may make it sound like the superior was pleading and thus is often left out. The use of an RFIE may be considered redundant particularly if it is employed by the more powerful party, as in the Norwegian translation, but if used, it may be considered 'as a reminder to the participants of the validity of the ritual frame' (Kádár and House 2019: 14).

When *please* was used as part of a formulaic expression in English, it was typically not translated into a Norwegian RFIE if the equivalent formulaic expression in Norwegian does not normally contain an RFIE marker. Instead, the most common choices were imperatives (12 tokens) and various modal verbs. The typical patterns are illustrated in Table 8.4.

Two of the instances of *please* in standard situations were translated into *vær(e) (så) vennlig(e)* ('be (so) friendly'), typically in unit-initial or -medial positions. Aijmer (2009: 70) argues that the corresponding Swedish expression *var vänlig* is volitional or intentional and may be used for both strategic politeness purposes and to avoid conflicts. In the Norwegian translations *vær(e) (så) vennlig(e)* was used for *please* in both standard and non-standard

Table 8.4 Typical translations from *please* to Ø in the ENPC

Grammatical form	English source text	Norwegian translation
Imperative	Please do not disturb.	Ikke *forstyrr*. ('not disturb')
Kan, kunne 'can, could'	So, could I have him back please?	Så *kan* jeg få ham med meg nå? ('so, can I have him with me now')
Vil 'will'	Won't you please sit down?	*Vil* du ikke sette deg? ('will you not sit you')
Må 'must'	Please sit still.	Nå *må* du sitte stille. ('now must you sit still')

situations. In non-standard situations, it often signalled resignation or anger on behalf of the speaker. In standard situations, as exemplified in (13), *please* has a formulaic function, whereas *være så vennlige* seems a bit archaic and overtly polite.

(13) Above the noise he shouted, 'Would the ex-Royal Family join me, *please*?'

Han måtte rope høyt for å overdøve gnyet fra mengden. 'Vil medlemmene av den forhenværende kongelige familie *være så vennlige* å komme ut hit?'
(ENPC_ST1E.1.2.s107)

A search for *vær(e) så vennlig* and *vær vennlig* in the LBK indicated that there is a difference between the two. Whereas of *vær(e) så vennlig* was used for multiple purposes, including both intensifying and mitigating requests, the majority of *vær vennlig* were RFIEs with limited or little illocutionary force, as in (14).

(14) [...] – *Vær vennlig* å signere her, svarer funksjonæren og lar henne fylle ut alle steder, der det finnes en antydning til stiplet linje.

('[...] – Be kind and sign here, the clerk replies and lets her fill in all places where there is a hint of a dotted line.')
(LBK_SK01SeAd01.5435)

Please followed by an imperative or an ellipted imperative in offers or invitations corresponded to *vær så god* or Ø. *Vær så god* serves as a ritual frame indicating function, in the same way as *var så god* in Swedish (Aijmer 2009: 75). Similarly, *takk* ('thanks') in Norwegian is a ritualistic response in an exchange. The expression *yes, please* as a response to an offer was translated into *takk* in Norwegian (see also Fretheim 2005). Aijmer (2009: 73) states that *yes please* 'occurs in the response to an offer with a softening function'; however, *takk* is used to the extent that it has become bleached and more formulaic than softening in such exchanges.

(15) 'More champagne?' 'Yes, *please*'

'Mer champagne?' 'Ja *takk*.'
(ENPC_AH1E.1.s30)

In the few examples of *please* used in public displays, *please* was translated into *vennligst* or Ø.

(16) Welcome, *please* open your bags for the guard's security inspection.
Velkommen, *vennligst* åpne vesken for vakten av sikkerhetsgrunner.
(ENPC_CL1TE.3.1.7.s7)
(17) but there was one of those *Please* do not disturb signs on the door, so she left it at that.
men da hun så at Ø Ikke forstyrr-skiltet hang på døren, gikk hun ned igjen.
(ENPC_EG1TE.4.s56)

Rygg and Johansen (2022) found that *vennligst* ('kindly') was often used in online public communication from companies and organizations where neither the text producer nor the readers are ratified. In these 'public displays', *vennligst* represents a typical RFIE that carries very little directive force, which is why companies and organizations can use it extensively without offending. When *please* corresponded to *vennligst*, both expressions carried little directive or mitigating force, a total lack of personal involvement and function as reminders of the public's rights and obligations (Kádár and House 2019). This lack of personal involvement and need for mitigation may explain the lack of a Norwegian marker in the Ø-translations.

8.5 Conclusion

The results show that although *please* does not have a direct equivalent in Norwegian, the functions of *please* may be expressed in a variety of ways in Norwegian. In the ENPC, which is a relatively small corpus, ten different expressions corresponding to *please* were found in addition to several constructions without a marker. Our results from the ENPC indicate that *vær så snill* and no marker (Ø) are the most common correspondences of *please* irrespective of its function and across situations.

Nevertheless, the choice of Norwegian expression is not without consequences. The most common correspondence, *vær så snill*, was only used in interactions between ratified persons and, in some instances, intensified the pleading force of the request more than *please* did. This was especially true in standard situations where *please*, as an indicator of a ritual frame (RFIE), was intensified into a plea when translated into *vær så snill*.

Similarly, no marker (Ø) was found in both interactions between people and in public displays and in standard situations the lack of an explicit marker in Norwegian could be explained by the lack of personal involvement or need for mitigation in such situations; however in non-standard situations, where *please* typically functions as a politeness marker or a request marker, the lack of a marker in Norwegian may cause the Norwegian request not to be perceived as equally soft or strong unless it is performed with some other kind of hedging or boosting device.

Regarding the linguistic patterns, the results from this study indicate that *please*, when used to express a plea in non-standard situations, typically occurred in initial or (semi-)/freestanding position, often followed by an imperative, and corresponded to *vær så snill* in the same position and pattern. However, there does not seem to be any clear system to which any particular Norwegian marker, if any, is chosen to express the various functions of *please*.

Furthermore, previous studies have pointed out that the functions of *please* depend on its position in the unit (e.g. Sato 2008); however, the present study shows that the patterns established for the English *please* may not be directly transferable to Norwegian. *Er du snill*, which almost exclusively occurs in final position, is not necessarily formulaic or with low intensity, as *please* typically is in the same position. It is our hope that such differences may inspire future investigations into this topic.

Corpora
The BigBrother Corpus http://www.tekstlab.uio.no/nota/bigbrother/
The Corpus for Bokmål Lexicography https://www.hf.uio.no/iln/om/organisasjon/tekstlab/prosjekter/lbk/
The English-Norwegian Parallel Corpus http://www.hf.uio.no/ilos/english/services/omc/enpc/

The Nordic Dialect Corpus http://tekstlab.uio.no/nota/scandiasyn/
The Norwegian Speech Corpus http://www.tekstlab.uio.no/nota/oslo/index.html
The Spoken BNC2014 http://corpora.lancs.ac.uk/bnc2014/

Note

1 Some of the same English original texts are found in the ENPC and the ESPC (Johansson 2007: 12).

References

Aijmer, K. (1996), *Conversational Routines in English: Convention and Creativity*, London: Longman.

Aijmer, K. (2009), 'Please: A Politeness Formula Viewed in a Translation Perspective', *Brno Studies in English*, 35 (2): 63–77.

Aijmer, K. (2015), '"Will You Fuck Off Please". The Use of *Please* by London Teenagers', *Pragmática Sociocultural / Sociocultural Pragmatics*, 3 (2): 127–49. https://doi.org/10.1515/soprag-2014-0028

Andersen, G. (2022), 'What Governs Speakers' Choices of Borrowed vs. Domestic Forms of Discourse-Pragmatic Variables?', in E. Peterson, T. Hiltunen and J. Kern (eds), *Discourse-Pragmatic Variation and Change: Theory, Innovations, Contact*, 251–71, Cambridge: Cambridge University Press.

Awedyk, W. (2003), 'Request Strategies in Norwegian and English', *Folia Scandinavia*, 7: 287–300.

BigBrother-korpuset, Tekstlaboratoriet, ILN, Universitetet i Oslo. http://www.tekstlab.uio.no/nota/bigbrother/

Brubæk, S. (2012), 'Pragmatic Competence in English at the VG1 level: To What Extent Are Norwegian EFL Students able to Adapt to Contextual Demands When Making Requests in English?' *Acta Didactica Norge*, 6 (1): Art. 20.

Fedriani, C. (2019), 'A Pragmatic Reversal: Italian per Favore "Please" and Its Variants between Politeness and Impoliteness', *Journal of Pragmatics*, 142: 233–44.

Fjeld, R. V., A. Nøklestad and K. Hagen (2020), 'Leksikografisk bokmålskorpus (LBK) – bakgrunn og bruk', in J. B. Johannessen and K. Hagen (eds), *Leksikografi og korpus. En hyllest til Ruth Vatvedt Fjeld*, [Lexicography and Corpora. A Tribute to Ruth Vatvedt Fjeld]. *Oslo Studies in Language*, 11 (1): 47–59.

Fraser, B. (1996), 'Pragmatic Markers', *Pragmatics*, 6 (2): 167–90.

Fretheim, T. (2005), 'Politeness in Norway: How can you be Polite and Sincere?', in L. Hickey and M. Stewart (eds), *Politeness in Europe*, 145–58, Clevedon: Multilingual Matters Ltd.

House, J. (1989), 'Politeness in English and German: The Functions of Please and Bitte', in S. Blum-Kulka, J. House and G. Kasper (eds), *Cross-Cultural Pragmatics: Requests and Apologies*, 96–119, Norwood: Ablex.

House, J. and D. Z. Kádár (2021), *Cross-cultural Pragmatics*, Cambridge: Cambridge University Press.

House, J. and G. Kasper (1981), 'Politeness Markers in English and German', in F. Coulmas (ed.), *Conversational Routine. Explorations in Standardized Communication Situations and Prepatterned Speech*, 157–85, The Hague: Mouton Publishers.

Johannessen, J. B. and K. Hagen (2008), 'Om NoTa-korpuset og artiklene i denne boka' [About the NoTa Corpus and the Articles in this Book], in J. B. Johannessen and K. Hagen (eds), *Språk i Oslo. Ny forskning omkring talespråk* [Language in Oslo. New Research on Spoken Language], 7–14, Oslo: Novus forlag.

Johannessen, J. B., J. Priestley, K. Hagen, T. A. Åfarli and Ø. A. Vangsnes (2009), 'The Nordic Dialect Corpus – An Advanced Research Tool', in K. Jokinen and E. Bick (eds), *Proceedings of the 17th Nordic Conference of Computational Linguistics NODALIDA 2009. NEALT Proceedings Series Volume 4*, Reykjavik: Linköping University Electronic Press, Sweden.

Johansson, S. (2001), 'Translationese: Evidence from the English-Norwegian Parallel Corpus', in S. Allén, S. Berg, S. G. R. Malmgren, K. Norén and B. Ralph (eds), *Gäller stam, suffix och ord. Festskrift till Martin Gellerstam den 15 oktober 2001* [About base, suffix and word. Essays in honour of Martin Gellerstam 15 October 2001], 162–76, Gothenburg: Elanders Novum.

Johansson, S. (2007), *Seeing through Multilingual Corpora. On the use of Corpora in Contrastive Studies*, Amsterdam: John Benjamins.

Johansson, S., J. Ebeling and S. Oksefjell (2002), 'English-Norwegian Parallel Corpus: Manual'. https://www.hf.uio.no/ilos/english/services/knowledge-resources/omc/enpc/ENPCmanual.pdf

Kádár, D. Z. and J. House (2019), 'Ritual Frame and "Politeness Markers"', *Pragmatics and Society*, 10 (4): 639–47. https://doi.org/10.1075/ps.18079.kad

Kádár, D. Z. and J. House (2020a), 'Ritual Frames: A Contrastive Pragmatic Approach', *Pragmatics*, 30 (1): 142–68. https://doi.org/10.1075/prag.19018.kad

Kádár, D. Z. and J. House (2020b), '"Politeness Markers" Revisited-A Contrastive Pragmatic Perspective', *Journal of Politeness Research*, 17 (1): 79–109. https://doi.org/10.1515/pr-2020-0029

Love, R., C. Dembry, A. Hardie, V. Brezina and T. McEnery (2017), 'The Spoken BNC2014', *International Journal of Corpus Linguistics*, 22 (3): 319–44. https://doi.org/10.1075/ijcl.22.3.02lov

Murphy, L. M. and R. De Felice (2019), 'Routine Politeness in American and British English Requests: Use and Non-use of Please', *Journal of Politeness Research*, 15 (1): 77–100. https://doi.org/10.1515/pr-2016-0027

Røkaas, F. A. (2000), 'Potential for Misunderstandings: Social Interaction between Norwegians and Americans', in M. Isaksson and F. A. Røkaas (eds), *Conflicting Values: An Intercultural Challenge*, 111–29, Sandvika: Norwegian School of Management BI.

Rygg, K. and S. H. Johansen (2022, May 12–13), 'The Impolite Norwegian "Politeness Marker" Vennligst', Paper presentation, Subjectivity and Intersubjectivity in Language and Culture Conference, Tartu, Estonia.

Sato, S. (2008), 'Use of "Please" in American and New Zealand English', *Journal of Pragmatics*, 40 (7): 1249–8. https://doi.org/10.1016/j.pragma.2007.09.001

Savić, M. (2018), 'Lecturer Perceptions of Im/politeness and In/appropriateness in Student e-mail Requests: A Norwegian Perspective', *Journal of Pragmatics*, 124: 52–72. https://doi.org/10.1016/j.pragma.2017.12.005

Stewart, M. (2005), 'Politeness in Britain: It's only a Suggestion', in L. Hickey and M. Stewart (eds), *Politeness in Europe*, 116–29, Clevedon: Multilingual Matters Ltd.

Terkourafi, M. (2015), 'Conventionalisation: A New Agenda for Politeness Research', *Journal of Pragmatics*, 86: 11–18. https://doi.org/10.1016/j.pragma.2015.06.004

Urbanik, P. (2020), 'Getting Others to Share Goods in Polish and Norwegian: Material and Moral Anchors for Request Conventions', *Intercultural Pragmatics*, 17 (2): 177–220. https://doi.org/10.1515/ip-2020-0009

Urbanik, P. and J. Svennevig (2019), 'Managing Contingencies in Requests: The Role of Negation in Norwegian Interrogative Directives', *Journal of Pragmatics*, 139: 109–25.

Urbanik, P. K. (2017), 'Requests in Polish and Norwegian Informal Conversation: A Comparative Study of Grammatical and Pragmatic Patterns', Unpublished doctoral diss., University of Oslo.

Watts, R. J. (2003), *Politeness*, Cambridge: Cambridge University Press.

Wichmann, A. (2004), 'The Intonation of Please-Requests: A Corpus-based Study', *Journal of Pragmatics*, 36 (9): 1521–49. https://doi.org/10.1016/j.pragma.2004.03.003

9

Discourse Connectives in English and French

A Contrastive Study on Political Discourse

Diana Lewis

9.1 Introduction

Contrastive linguistics involves making links across multiple boundaries: not only linguistic boundaries between languages but equally importantly between different social communities and different cultural practices. This chapter reports on a study of the use of connectives in French and in English in interviews of politicians by journalists. Previous work on coherence marking in general has predominantly focused on written text in formal genres and on a single language. Scholman, Demberg and Sanders point out 'the insufficient treatment of spoken language in the area of discourse coherence' (2022: 8). Contrastive studies have tended to focus on particular expressions, often cognates. And previous contrastive studies of the usage in French and English of connectives have appeared to reach contradictory conclusions regarding their frequency. Some have claimed that connectives are more frequent in French, while others have claimed the opposite.

The present study investigates the usage of connectives across French and English in a specific genre of spoken language, using a comparable corpus. The aim is first to get an overview of connective usage in the two languages. In this genre, does one language show more frequent connective use than the other? Previous research has suggested that, independently of language, some relation types need to be signalled more than others. To what extent does this hold for both languages in this data? Second, the usage is examined of three lexemes (*alors, puis, then*) that all originate in temporal adverbs and have evolved similar polysemies, to test the extent to which the similar polysemies across the two languages correspond to similar distributions.

The next section presents the small comparable corpus on which the study is based. Section 9.3 then outlines the domain of coherence and coherence relations. Section 9.4 discusses the use of connectives in the corpus. The findings for the target lexemes are presented in Section 9.5, and Section 9.6 concludes the chapter.

9.2 A comparable corpus

9.2.1 Comparable genres, comparable corpora

Corpus-based contrastive analysis uses either parallel corpora or comparable corpora (Aijmer 2020: 29–32). The former contain sets of translated texts, usually bidirectional, that is, native texts in each language with their translations into the other language(s). The latter contains genre-matched texts in each language. An advantage of parallel corpora is that they enable equivalences across the different languages to be quickly identified, as each translated text contains the 'same' meanings as the original. The 'tertium comparationis' is the interpretation of the source text by the translator. The use of parallel texts 'provides a revealing picture of the main paradigms, or sets of expressions, that are used to express a certain "meaning" in the languages compared and the degree of correspondence between the expressions involved' (Altenberg 2007). Parallel corpora thus 'allow the researcher to make specific and fine-grained comparisons on the basis of texts which are interlingually comparable' (Aijmer 2020: 30). A disadvantage for discourse studies is that translation choice is less constrained at discourse level, where the distinctions between languages tend to be less grammatical and more rhetorical than at the level of clause or lexis. Mauranen (2002, §8) finds that 'translations appear to retain source cultural pragmatic features distinguishable from those of the target culture, while at the same time exhibiting fewer target-specific features'.

Comparable corpora also have many drawbacks. As Aijmer (2008: 278) explains, 'comparable corpora are not ideal for contrastive analysis . . . a comparable corpus gives a less clear picture of the correspondences of a lexical item or construction than does a parallel corpus'. It is thus not always obvious what features to compare for the contrastive analysis, as it becomes necessary to base their selection on general semantic notions as well as form (König and Gast 2018: 6; Hasselgård 2021). Because the 'tertium comparationis' is the social situations, it is harder to establish text comparability. What look like similar cultural practices in two linguistic communities can be expressed through what look like dissimilar linguistic registers. Nevertheless, 'a genre belongs to the (often highly specialized) discourse community that uses it and . . . such communities can cross linguistic boundaries' (Aijmer and Lewis 2017: 4). Comparable corpora have the advantage that, all the texts being native, they instantiate the particular discourse conventions of a linguistic community. And for spontaneous spoken language, it is not easy to find appropriate parallel texts.

9.2.2 The comparable corpus of political interviews

The present study is based on a small comparable corpus of transcripts of broadcast political interviews and discussions (Table 9.1).

Political interviews as a genre involve spontaneous, relatively formal speech. The corpus contains Metropolitan French and British English and is designed on the assumption that political discussion programmes in France and the UK are comparable. Each interview takes the basic form of question-answer: it is thus an asymmetric dialogue, with some discussion, over a short time-span, broadcast within a programme at a scheduled time of the day or week. Politicians and other personalities involved in politics are interviewed one-to-one, occasionally one-to-two or one-to-three.

The French data are mostly from broadcast programmes: forty-one radio interviews, twenty television interviews, five press conferences and five print media interviews. The English data are mostly from *The Politics Show* (BBC 2003–2011), broadcast on BBC One on Sundays from 2003 to 2011. The English discussion programme, *Any Questions* (BBC 2005), involves a four-person panel,

Table 9.1 The comparable corpus

Political interviews and discussions (unscripted dialogue)	
French part: 207,429 words	**English part: 195,113 words**
period 2000–2022	period 2004–2011
71 interviews	100 interviews (96% of corpus, 186,827 words)
54 politicians (interviewees)	66 politicians (interviewees)
12 journalists (interviewers)	5 journalists (interviewers)
2975 average no. of words per interview	1,776 average no. of words per interview
	1 discussion programme (4% of corpus, 8,286 words)
	3 politicians, 1 activist
	1 journalist (moderator)

under the direction of a moderator, answering in turn questions from audience members. The participants in each corpus element are therefore one or more politicians, one journalist and a silent programme audience. The topics range over wide areas of governmental responsibility. French and British political interviews share these features as well as the typical functions of challenging on the part of the journalists and defending and persuading on the part of the politicians. The speaking participants design their discourse as much or more for the wider, silent audience as for their journalist interlocutors.

The socio-cultural situation types that underpin the comparability of the comparable corpus are pre-theoretical notions: they are recognized by their participants as identifiable types, with predictable form, participant types and range of subject matter. They are generalizations over repeated occurrences of similar socio-cultural events. The structure of government, the nature of political parties, the conventions of public discourse and the design of broadcast programmes all vary across the two countries. Even allowing for the linguistic differences that make French 'wordier' than English, it is clear that the French interviews are longer on average than the comparable English ones.

The corpus is based on transcripts made available by the media that broadcast the programmes in the case of the English discourse and by government departments in the case of the French. The transcripts contain punctuation, show no prosodic features and non-linguistic material is edited out; otherwise, they appear to be relatively reliable records of the interactions (the audio was not available). A few erroneous spellings have been corrected.

9.3 Coherence, coherence relations and connectives

9.3.1 Coherence

Discourse coherence refers to the cumulative effect of a network of (marked or unmarked) relationships among discourse elements. The literature on discourse coherence suggests that it can be viewed from two perspectives. From one perspective it is a creation of the speaker/hearer/writer/reader. The mental representation that the hearer creates of a stretch of discourse includes an interpretation of how the incoming discourse segments or information units[1] relate to each other, to the wider discourse and to the situation of discourse. Coherence is thus an integral part of processing. Hellman (1995: 190) notes that "'coherence" is not something that the reader normally actively searches for, it is taken for granted'. Coherence also of course concerns speakers, who construct their discourse to reflect the relations between ideas as they perceive or wish to convey them. Coherence in this perspective can be thought of as the speaker's or hearer's representations of the relations between the discourse elements, such that the role of each element in the overall message is clear. These representations therefore make an essential contribution to the understanding of a stretch of discourse, which conveys more than the sum of its parts. Ideally, there is a close fit between the speaker's representations (intentions) and the hearer's representations (interpretations), as a mismatch can result in incoherence, that is, in the hearer misinterpreting or being unable to make sense of the discourse. In constructing coherence, hearers 'engage in inferencing processes to create connections between the individual elements and assign meaning to the text. [...] This meaning is not an inherent property of the text; rather, it is assigned by the comprehenders' (Scholman 2019: 12–13).

From the second perspective, coherence is a property of the discourse. For Taboada (2019: 205), for instance, coherence is 'a property of discourse that makes each instance of discourse felicitous in context. [. . .] discourse coherence, or text coherence, is the result of weaving together entity relations and propositional relations'. At first glance this definition seems incompatible with the first, but in fact it is better seen as the other side of the same coin. A stretch of discourse appears more or less coherent to the hearer if he is able to construct an interpretation of it that is acceptable to himself, and more or less incoherent if he is not.[2] It is of course possible for one hearer to construct a coherent interpretation of a given discourse while another can not, as much depends on common ground. Nonetheless, it is convenient to refer to coherence as pertaining to a discourse or text, to describe it as being coherent (or not), in much the same way as other meaning is commonly described as if it pertained to independent linguistic forms rather than to speakers' and hearers' mental representations.

9.3.2 Coherence relations

Models of coherence rely heavily on the identification of coherence relations,[3] where 'relation' refers to the relationship between two or more discourse units, and relation name is used for both tokens and types of relation. Most models treat relations as semantic links (Scholman, Demberg and Sanders 2022: §2). A causal relation is shown in (1): the hearer is to understand that situation [ ]$_1$ is caused by situation [ ]$_2$ and this relationship is expressed by the causative connective *because*. (In the examples, speaker J is an interviewer (journalist) and speaker P is an interviewee (politician); the name of the interviewee follows each example; where the example involves the interviewer's speech, both names are given, where known, in the form Interviewer : Interviewee. The relevant discourse units are separated by | (which also marks occasional disfluencies), and no punctuation is shown other than question marks.)

(1) P: [Mr Cameron can't bear to talk about Europe]$_1$ | because [half his party won't let him]$_2$ [Campbell 2006]

However, if *because* were omitted from (1) most hearers would infer a causal relationship.

Attempts have been made to set up taxonomies of coherence relations, but so far no stable map of the domain has emerged. Problems include whether and how to constrain the number of relations, their cross-linguistic validity, dealing with the different discourse levels at which relations can simultaneously hold, the gradient and potentially hierarchical nature of relations, and the degree to which coherence includes or interacts with turn management, topic progression and discourse prominence. In particular, 'there is disagreement about how many distinct coherence relations language users actually infer and how specific these relations are' (Hoek, Evers-Vermeul and Sanders 2019: 1). There is nevertheless a wide consensus on the less specific types of relation. Across different models of coherence, four coarse-grained relation types recur over and again. They are Temporal, Causative, Contrastive/Adversative and Additive. Demberg, Asr and Scholman refer to 'the major discourse relation classes (temporals, causals, contrastives, additives)' (2019: 113). Scholman et al. note that 'most proposals agree on four main types: causal, additive, temporal, and adversative relations' (2022: 4). For English, this division of the coherence space dates back at least to early work by Halliday and Hasan (1976), who wrote: 'There is no single, uniquely correct inventory of the types of conjunctive relation. . . . We shall adopt a scheme of just four categories: additive, adversative, causal and temporal' (1976: 238). The present study follows this tradition. On a cline of more objective to more subjective relations, temporal relations are at the objective end, with causal, contrastive and additive relations increasingly interpretable as subjective (see below and in Section 9.5). The focus here is on connectives in the three relational areas involving speaker stance: cause (including cause, reason, result, inference, etc.), contrast (including adversative, antithetical, concessive and counter-expectational relations), and addition/elaboration. The approach also draws on Murray's (1997) model for narrative text of continuous vs discontinuous relations. A cline is posited whereby the more two linked ideas appear compatible, the more continuous the relation, and the more they appear incompatible, the more discontinuous the relation. Continuous relations such as addition or elaboration thus reflect congruity, and are often assumed to require little or no marking; discontinuous relations such as contrast, concession or antithesis, reflect incongruity and are often assumed to require more marking to avert incoherence. This is the background to the hypothesis that relation type may affect frequency of marking.

9.3.3 Connectives

Connectives express coherence relations and may link ideas at different levels (Sweetser 1990). A connective such as *because* can express a perceived real-world cause, a speaker inference (modal level) or the reason for the utterance rather than for its content (illocutionary level). Almost all models of coherence distinguish between objective and subjective relations,[4] but there is arguably more of a cline than a clear distinction. Traugott (2022), for instance, puts 'discourse structuring markers' 'on a cline of pragmaticality from largely contentful, truth-conditional to largely pragmatic, non-truth-conditional' (2022: 63). In real discourse it is hard to find wholly objective relations, even of cause and result. For example, in (1) the causal relationship will be interpreted as more of a judgement by the speaker than a truly objective real-world causation (after all, Mr. Cameron would no doubt deny the claim). The cline results from the gradual diachronic development of more abstract and subjective coherence-marking functions in lexemes previously marking more contentful, objective relations (cf. Section 9.5). This is relevant to contrastive studies insofar as languages differ, for particular relations and connectives, as to the distinctions they make.

Coherence relations may be ranked on a cline of 'strength' from objective causal relations (necessity, where one event is the inevitable result of the other) to simple co-occurrence (Pagin 2014). Equally, connectives may be characterized by their 'strength' (Asr and Demberg 2012; Crible 2020; Crible and Demberg 2020), on a cline from 'strong' or relation-specific (having a narrow range of usage) to 'weak' or highly ambiguous (are applied to a wide spectrum of coherence, like *but* and *mais*). Again, this is linked to diachrony (through degree of abstraction or semantic expansion and bleaching), to frequency and to the semantic-pragmatic cline. But 'translation-equivalent' connectives across languages – those occurring in comparable discourse contexts – may be of different strengths.

9.3.4 Cross-linguistic comparison

As seen in Section 9.3.2, building models of coherence relies on linguistic clues, especially connectives, to identify relations, and models based on data from one language cannot necessarily be extrapolated to others. Scholman, Demberg and Sanders (2022) argue that 'a crosslinguistic, universal theory of discourse coherence is not desirable given the research that is currently available' and point to 'connectives that make fine-grained distinctions in only some languages' (2022: 22). A frequent connective in one language may suggest a major relational division, whereas its non-lexicalization in another language may suggest a fine distinction only (an example is the distinction in Spanish between contrast (*pero*) and correction (*sino*), both covered by *but* in English, *mais* in French). Nevertheless, the assumption in most of the literature (at this early stage of cross-linguistic and typological investigation) is that there is a universal conceptual space of coherence which can act as 'tertium comparationis' for comparisons across languages. It is further assumed that, despite variability at the level of fine distinctions, coarse-grained relation types will be cognitively salient and similar across languages.

As mentioned in Section 9.1, findings on the relative frequency of coherence relation marking in English and French have been inconclusive. Guillemin-Flescher (1981), for instance, finds that English translations from French need to make explicit relations that are left implicit in French (in particular, adversative relations). With reference mainly to adversative discourse relations, Mason (2001) cites a number of studies which purport to show that 'whereas there is a trend to junction-less juxtaposition in French, explicit coordination is preferred in English' (2001: 65). By contrast, Dupont (2019) finds from a literature survey that 'the dominant claim . . . has been that French tends to be more explicitly cohesive than English' (2019: 87) while she also documents several claims to the contrary (2019: 88ff, 131ff). Dupont concludes that 'the research currently available provides us with contradictory claims on the frequency of use of C[onjunctive] M[arker]s in English and French' (2019: 89). Dupont's own research deals with the relation of Contrast in a large comparable corpus of written language, where she finds that English marks contrast one and a half times more frequently than French, a result she describes as 'very surprising' (2019: 192).

Several methodological issues are likely to contribute to the inconclusive results of previous studies. They include the use of translations as data, unwarranted extrapolation from particular genres to the wider language, failure to distinguish among types of coherence relation and differences in how relations are delimited and categorized. Much of the previous research cited in Mason (2001) and Dupont (2019) and others was carried out on translated literary texts, a fairly stable finding being that adversative connectives were inserted in the English translations where there were none in the French originals. Mason shows why translations might be unreliable data, concluding that 'it would seem more logical to contrast spontaneously sourced texts in each language' (Mason 2001: 68). Genre has been found to correlate with very different patterns of connective usage. Across culturally similar linguistic communities, comparable genres may display similar discourse features, including coherence marking, especially where there is language contact. Taboada and Gómez González, for instance, found, for a contrastive study of concessive marking in English and Spanish, that 'differences in usage are more pronounced across genres than across languages' (2012: 35). Spoken genres have received much less attention than written ones (exceptions include Crible and Cuenca 2017; Crible 2018). Studies such as Degand et al. (2014) reveal differences in the same speaker across different genres. Lastly, certain relation types may tend to be more or less marked, again depending on not only the language but also the genre.

Overall, it has not yet been demonstrated that, for contrastive analysis of coherence features, it makes sense to try to generalize at the level of a language-as-a-whole. The question of whether French or English displays more relation marking by connectives may not be the right one to ask. A bottom-up approach to contrastive analysis, focusing on specific comparable genres and sub-genres and distinguishing between relation types, may be a more useful way to build up a wider picture of patterns of marking. Findings can in turn help refine a model of coherence as a 'tertium comparationis' for further studies.

9.4 Connectives in the comparable corpus

9.4.1 Method

Lists of French and English connectives of addition, contrast and cause were drawn up on the basis of reference works and previous research. The focus is on what Taboada (2019) calls 'propositional coherence', that is, relations between propositions or states of affairs. A unit of discourse is taken to be a proposition typically expressed by a clausal syntactic unit.[5] Included, therefore, are connectives that can scope over (finite or non-finite) clauses, and excluded are (complex) prepositions such as *because of*, *in addition to* or *en raison de*.

The connective forms were searched for in the corpus and extracted into concordances with the help of WordSmith Tools (Scott 2020). These were imported into spreadsheets and for each form, the KWICs containing occurrences expressing propositional relations were retained and were classified, according to function in context, by relation type. The connectives that occurred with a frequency of at least five per 100,000 words were retained for further analysis. Level was not coded, given how often more than one level was plausible (cf. Hasselgård 2014: 72). It is particularly difficult to distinguish between additive subject-matter relations and additive discoursal relations; between meaning that an additional state of affairs occurs and meaning that the speaker is presenting an additional idea or argument. Often it is both together (consistent with connectives marking more objective relations turning over time into markers of speaker stance or discourse organization). In (2), for instance, *in fact* can be interpreted as an elaboration (further information on the topic of the previous proposition), as an additional speaker argument, and as signalling that the upcoming proposition is rhetorically stronger than the idea that it links back to.

(2) J: they've got a pretty dim view of your crime policies | *in fact* the latest polls suggest that only 6 per cent of voters think you're best-placed to tackle crime [Vine – Oaten 2005]

The fact that additives appear vaguer and more difficult to analyse may be due to their greater abstraction and subjectivity. The more recent meaning of a connective was attributed where it clearly made more sense, as in (3), where *ensuite* makes much more sense as an additive than as a temporal adverb, even though any sanctions must come later than the evaluation.

(3) P: Il y a donc la règle d'or dont la conformité sera appréciée par la Cour de justice de l'Union européenne [. . .]. Il y a *ensuite* les sanctions lorsqu'on ne respecte pas la discipline budgétaire. Mais il y a aussi [. . .] [Juppé 2011]

['So there's the golden rule, adherence to which will be evaluated by the EU's Court of Justice . . . There are *ensuite* the sanctions when one doesn't adhere to budgetary discipline. But there is also . . .']

Given the gradient nature of connectivity and the different levels on which it can obtain, there is no clear-cut boundary to coherence marking. For instance, expressions occurring turn-initially in interaction (e.g. *well, alors*) can usually be interpreted as simultaneously backward-linking (indicating at speech-act level that what follows takes account of, answers or is otherwise a coherent reaction to the interlocutor's turn) and forward-linking (presenting the following utterance). Such expressions were taken to mark an additive coherence relation, pushing the conversation along. *Well* is notoriously vague and/or polysemous.[6] It is often characterized as a hedge, and it may seem counter-intuitive to include it among the additive connectives. Those counted were those that clearly contributed to coherence (connectives can simultaneously be hedges), their presence being conditioned by the previous utterance. They were in left-peripheral (pre-clausal) position and also acted as focus particles analogous to left-peripheral *alors* as described in Section 9.5. Temporal adverbials and agreement/disagreement particles (*okay, d'accord*, etc.) were omitted, along with *yes/oui, no/non* and *and/ et*.[7] First- and second-person expressions (*I mean, look, écoutez, vous savez*, etc.) were omitted, though they are arguably often coherence marking.[8] Where a relation was signalled redundantly by two markers (such as *even if* and *still* in the concessive construction *even if p, still q*), both were included in the count. Search results were manually sorted for the coherence-marking occurrences of polysemous items. The resulting collection of connectives is not exhaustive but is intended to uncover usage in the corpus.

9.4.2 Distribution

Figure 9.1 shows the distribution of expressions (tokens) that occurred in the corpus.

The following expressions occurred between one and five per 100,000 words. Many expressions that figure regularly in inventories of connectives did not occur in the data (for example, *tandis que, toutefois* in French and *besides, nonetheless* in English).

French: Contrastive: *de l'autre [côté] / d'un autre côté, maintenant, par contre, à l'inverse, cela dit, certes, cependant, malgré tout, contrairement à ce que, de toute[s] [les] manière[s], encore que, quand bien même, au lieu de +V, inversement*; Causal: *pour autant, c'est pourquoi, après tout, par conséquent, étant donné que, voilà pourquoi*; Additive/discourse-organizational: *de même, pour terminer, bref, autrement dit, pour commencer, pour résumer, du moins*.

English: Contrastive: *even though, on the other hand, whereas, anyway, while, otherwise, even then, nevertheless, on the contrary, in fact* (contrastive), *all the*

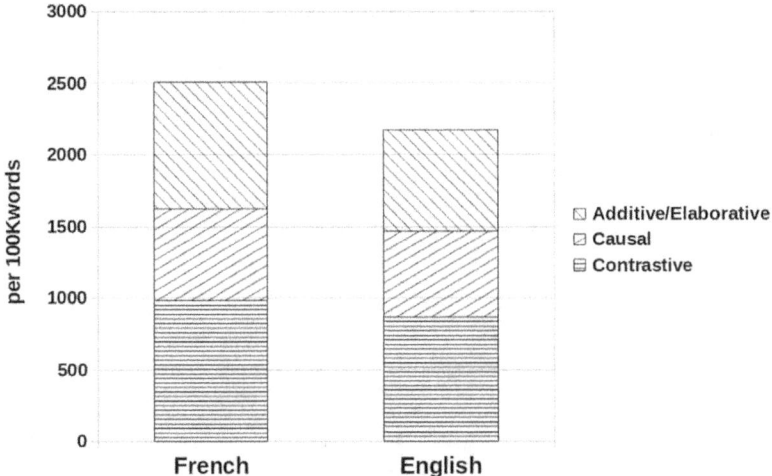

Figure 9.1 Token frequency of connectives that occurred at least once in the comparable corpus.

same, anyhow, even so, having said that, in any case, on the one hand; Causal: *after all, given that, as a result, thereby*; Additive/discourse-organizational: *first/ firstly, in other words, finally, above all, first and foremost, in addition, what's more, lastly, similarly, thus.*

Table 9.2 shows the expressions with frequencies above five per 100,000 words. Taking, for each language, all the listed expressions together, the English data shows a frequency per 100,000 words of 2,173 connectives, while for the French data, the figure is 2,507, that is, a token frequency about 15 per cent higher than for the English. The figures of course reflect not only the range of connectives but also the fact that individual speakers can show predilections for certain expressions. Overall, then, the figures suggest slightly more marking in the French genre.

Three related observations can be made, which together point to differences between the French and English political interview genres. First, in both languages, very few expressions account for a large proportion of the tokens. This is consistent with previous findings, such as those of Altenberg (2007), who found that the four most frequent English and Swedish resultative connectives in his corpus accounted for over 90 per cent of the marking. In our data, preponderance is greater for the English, where the three most frequent types (*but, well* and *because*) make up 64 per cent of total tokens. For the French (*mais, donc* and *aussi*[9]), the proportion is only 49 per cent. This finding differs slightly from that of Crible (2017), who reports for her comparable, French-English

Table 9.2 Normalized frequencies of coherence-marking expressions occurring more than five times per 100,000 words (*que* = *que/qu'*)

English		French	
Contrastive			
but	729.8	*mais*	681.2
though	22.6	*quand même*	69.4
rather	14.9	*en tout cas*	28.0
still	13.8	*alors [même] que*	25.1
although	11.8	*en même temps [que]*	23.6
yet	10.3	*même si*	16.4
at the same time	9.2	*or*	14.0
even if	8.7	*en revanche*	12.5
instead	8.2	*bien que*	9.6
however	6.7	*quoique*	9.2
		plutôt	8.7
		sinon	8.2
		au contraire	8.2
		pourtant	7.2
		d'une part . . . d'autre part	6.3
		néanmoins	6.3
		tout de même	6.3
		de toute façon	5.8
Causal			
because	261.4	*donc*	390.5
so	184.5	*parce que*	96.4
then (resultative)	102.5	*puisque*	71.3
that's why	28.7	*alors* (resultative)	28.9
therefore	11.3	*car*	26.0
		c'est pour ça / cela que	12.1
Additive / Discourse-organizational			
well	399.3	*aussi*	148.0
also	103.5	*alors* (discourse-organizational)	95.5
now	74.8	*d'ailleurs*	88.2
as well	34.9	*c'est à dire [que]*	80.0
first of all	16.4	*d'abord*	75.2
in fact	16.4	*[et] puis*	47.7
[and] then (additive)	14.4	*eh bien*	41.9
again	11.3	*enfin*	39.0
indeed	10.8	*effectivement*	37.6
too	10.8	*surtout*	33.7
		en fait	27.0
		finalement	21.7
		là aussi	19.8
		en effet	17.8
		également	17.8
		ainsi	17.8
		par ailleurs	13.5
		bon	12.5
		en plus	11.6
		là encore	8.7
		ensuite	7.7
		après	6.7

register-diverse oral corpus that (after *and*) the three most frequent connectives were *but/mais*, *so/donc* and *well/alors* in that order; that is, quasi translation equivalents. The overall distribution in the political interviews corpus suggests the hypothesis that French political interviewees adopt a more cumulative strategy than their English-speaking counterparts, who seem to favour a more justificatory strategy, but testing this remains for further research.

Second, for contrastive and additive/elaborative relations, the French data shows around twice as many types having a frequency of over five per 100,000 words. This greater variety of forms suggests greater attention to those relations by the French speakers. It could be that French political discourse is characterized by more fine-grained coherence distinctions, or by an aesthetic preference for formal variation, or by greater reinforcement of very bleached expressions by less bleached ones.

The third difference concerns the types of relation expressed. The largest divergence is in the continuous relations category, in which the French marks 22 per cent more often than the English, compared with 14 per cent more for contrastive marking and only 7 per cent more for causal marking. This goes along with the use of a larger array of French additive, elaborative and organizational connectives: twenty-one different types occur more than five per 100,000 words, compared with only ten for English. By contrast, there is little difference for causal marking (six for French, five for English). It was seen in Section 9.3.4 that Dupont (2019), in her comparable corpus of formal written genres, found that English showed a much greater frequency of contrastive connectives than French. Furthermore, beyond the hyper-frequent *but* and *mais*, the most frequent connective types are different, particularly so in the French data. For instance, the second-most frequent contrastive connective in Dupont's main written data was *pourtant*, which is 14th most frequent in the political interviews; the second-most frequent in the interviews (*quand même*) is 25th in Dupont's data. These findings point to considerable genre differences in frequency and distribution.

Continuous relations, being more predictable or default, are expected to need less and weaker marking than dissonant relations, which involve incongruence or counter-expectation that need acknowledgement for coherence to be maintained (cf. Taboada 2009). As Patterson and Kehler point out, 'the more difficult recovering the correct relation would be without a connective, the more necessary it is to include one' (2013: 915). According to the uniformity of information density (UID) hypothesis (Levy and Jaeger 2007), reduction correlates with predictability: the more predictable an upcoming item is, the more likely it is to be reduced or phonetically, syntactically or discoursally weak. Asr and Demberg (2015) apply this hypothesis to coherence marking, observing that (in written English) easily inferable relations are on average marked less or more ambiguously than relations which are less expected, thus achieving information density smoothing at the discourse level. The differences observed in the interviews corpus seem to correlate with the 'necessity' of the marking: the lower the necessity, the greater the difference between the two languages.

9.5 A comparison of *then, alors* and *puis*

9.5.1 The choice of expressions and their usage in the corpus

English *then* and French *alors* and *puis* have been chosen because they exemplify the cline of subjectivity mentioned in Section 9.3.2 and the multifunctionality that results from usage. They are all temporal expressions with the sense of 'at that time' (*then, alors*) or 'next' (*then, puis, alors*). English *then* and French *alors* have evolved very similar resultative[10] and inferential senses, in line with a well-attested tendency for semantic shift temporal > resultative. Kuteva et al. (2019: 427) refer to 'a widespread process whereby spatial and temporal markers are grammaticalized in specific contexts to markers of "logical" grammatical relations, such as adversative, causal, concessive, and conditional relations'.[11] The three expressions have also come to be used as discourse-organizational devices. Aijmer (2004: 251) notes that highly polysemous expressions are 'a fruitful topic for cross-linguistic study', because the ways in which their polysemies have developed, in parallel or not, can suggest hypotheses about the extent to which meaning extensions are driven by cognitive, social and/or cultural factors. Usage-based semantic shift in lexical items often results in 'complex patterns of partially overlapping polysemy' (Altenberg and Granger 2002: 14) across languages.

While *alors* and *then* have, to a great extent, developed similar meaning extensions, they display divergent polysemy in their discoursal and interactional usage and they differ in their frequencies and distribution. Figure 9.2, showing the relationships among *alors, puis* and *then*, is based on the semantic map concept, which provides 'a way to visualize regular relationships between two or more meanings or grammatical functions of one and the same linguistic form' (Narrog and van der Auwera 2011: 318), especially in cross-linguistic comparisons (Haspelmath 2003).

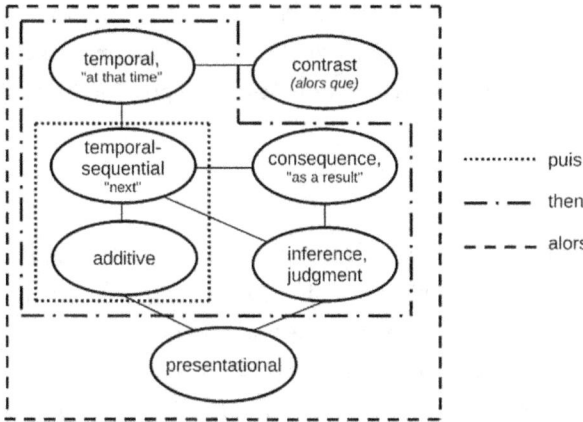

Figure 9.2 Main functions of *alors*, *then* and *puis* in the interviews data.

For many occurrences, the interpretation can be vague across two or more of the meanings identified in Figure 9.2 (those linked by black lines). In the analysis of multifunctional expressions, vagueness (a broad meaning) is often opposed to ambiguity (one meaning OR the other) (Haspelmath 2003: 211–14; Hasselgård 2014: 72). Only very rarely did the occurrences in the interview data lend themselves, in their contexts, to an ambiguity analysis in the sense of alternative, one-or-the-other readings. For example, the 'result' notion expressed in *alors* or *then* may be due to a real-world result (event q results from event p) or an inference (speaker reasons that if/given p, q must obtain) or a justification (congruent addition: given the current discourse context, speaker's utterance is justified). This spectrum is directional: *alors* or *then* can be used to assert that a situation was both later than another and resulted from it, whereas the use of *alors* or *then* to indicate that one situation is inferred from the existence of another does not entail a temporal sequence. And while temporal *puis* (meaning the following event occurred after some already mentioned event) may in a given case also be interpreted as the speaker introducing an additional idea, its use to introduce an additional idea does not entail any temporal order of events. When a broad interpretation made sense, the coding was conservative (temporal occurrences that might also be additive were coded 'temporal'). Figure 9.2 reflects an ongoing diachronic development from temporal to connective to discourse-structural.

The rest of Section 9.5 focuses on the uses that are comparable across the French and English data. It does not address the complex expression *alors que* ('whereas'), nor does it fully address the correlations between position and meaning within each language (on position, for *then* see Haselow 2011; Aijmer 2019; for *alors* see Degand and Fagard 2011). Initial or pre-clausal position will be termed 'left peripheral' and final or post-clausal position 'right-peripheral'.

9.5.2 Time

In the data, both *alors* and *then* are found encoding the temporal notion 'at that time', as illustrated in examples (4) and (5), where both *alors* and *then* refer back anaphorically to a time mentioned in the preceding discourse and still activated. In (5), for example, *then* is to be interpreted as 'in October' (*puis* does not occur in this usage, *alors* has been found to occur only rarely as a temporal anaphor in spoken French (Degand and Fagard 2011)).

(4) P: la banque a été considérée *alors* comme victime | et puis depuis la Cour d'appel a dit que la banque était partiellement responsable [Sapin 2016]
['the bank was seen *alors* ('at that time') as a victim | and then since then the Court of Appeal has said that the bank was partly responsible']

(5) P: now let's rewind to October and remember the situation we were in *then* [Cameron 2009]

A different temporal use is found in examples (6) to (8), where two situations are ordered temporally such that the second one expressed is marked by *alors* or *then* or *puis* as being the later. The time of the second situation is expressed relative to that of the first.

(6) P: il ne faut pas mettre la charrue avant les boeufs | lorsque nous aurons fait cette union | *alors* effectivement il y aura possibilité de mutualiser la dette [Juppé 2011]
['one mustn't put the cart before the horse | when we've achieved that union | *alors* it will be possible to mutualize the debt']

(7) P: first of all we've got to raise their awareness of the problem | *then* we've got to get them frankly taking more exercise [Richard 2009]

(8) P: dans un premier temps les observateurs internationaux ont donné plutôt un avis favorable | *puis* il y a eu des doutes sur la régularité des élections [Juppé 2011]
['at first the international observers gave rather a positive assessment | *puis* ('after that/later') doubts arose over whether the election had been conducted fairly']

Overlapping with these relative-time uses are the resultative senses. As can be appreciated for *alors* and *then* in examples (6) and (7) above, the temporally first situation can often be seen as facilitating the temporally second situation. It is easy to infer from (6) that achieving the union will make possible the mutualization of the debt or that the mutualization is conditional upon the union. It is thus that resultative senses can develop from temporal ones and this is the case for both English and French.

9.5.3 Result

Resultative *then* and *alors* occur in causal, conditional and inferential constructions. The commonest interpretation for both is 'in that case', referring back to the previous proposition, especially in the hypothetical-conditional constructions *if/ si p, then/alors q*, where *then* or *alors* are redundant, or to mark the outcome of an implied condition ('if it is as you say'). A continuum of 'result' is found, from more objective consequences to more subjective inferences: epistemic (inference) and deontic (stance). More objective uses are illustrated in (9) and (10).

(9) P: chacun est venu dire voilà | moi j'ai mon parlement | *alors* je ne peux pas faire ça [Moscovici 2000]
 ['each one came and said look | I've got my parliament | *alors* I can't do that']
(10) P: if a majority of the workforce want it | *then* they can get union recognition [Hewitt 2004]

Realis situations such as (9), where the consequence signalled by *alors* results from a real state of affairs, are not found for *then*. The most objective contexts of resultative *then* are generic conditionals like (10). And all *then*-introduced consequences are in contexts that combine temporal sequentiality with causation.

Inferential *alors* and *then* involve a speaker judgement ('it follows that'): a previous idea in the discourse leads the speaker to draw some conclusion (epistemic) or adopt some stance (deontic). The speaker reasons that, given *p*, *q* may be inferred or desired, as in examples (11) and (12). *Alors* and *then* therefore express modal meanings here (cf. Sweetser 1990: 116–17 on epistemic conditionals; Palmer 2001: 24; Haselow 2011; Traugott 2022: 68). In (11) and (12), for example, the speakers infer (reason) that an increase in spending would mean an increase in taxes.

(11) J: mais comment faire pour augmenter les dépenses ? | on augmente les impôts *alors* ? [Bourdin : Philippe, 2017]

['but how could we increase spending? | (would we) increase taxes *alors*?']
(12) J: if you're going to increase borrowing now | *then* there would have to be tax increases at a future date to pay for it [Brown, 2008]

Many occurrences of inferential *then* or *alors* can be seen as linking at the illocutionary level, signalling that the host utterance (rather than its content) follows from what has just been said; that is, that it is connected to the previous discourse by its being a coherent next move. This occurs in the question-answer interaction, particularly where a question arises as a result of, and is thus justified by, the previous discourse (13) and (14).

(13) J: is the cabinet united on it?
P: yes
J: why were there all those leaks *then*? [Sopel – Beckett, 2005]
(14) P: ils voient bien qu'il y a bien un problème entre eux les citoyens et la représentation politique
J: pourquoi sa cote est-elle bonne à lui *alors* ? [(Journalist) – Hue, 2000]
['P: they can see that there is a problem between them as citizens and their political representation
J: why is he [the president] so popular *alors*?']

While *alors* and *then* in (11) and (12) can be glossed respectively as 'does that imply that' and 'that implies that', this is not the case for (13) or (14). Aijmer (2019: 26) finds that '[t]hen in *wh*-questions generally emphasizes the speaker's argumentational aim'; this is borne out in the interviews data. The *then* in (13) and the *alors* in (14) both express a challenge on account of a perceived discontinuity in the content, that is, a violation of expectations. In (13) the expectation violated is that the cabinet being united should result in few leaks; in (14) it is that citizens seeing political representation problems should result in the president being less popular. The journalists' questions refer directly to the previous claim by the interviewee (with an implied 'if that is so'), asking for the apparent incongruity to be explained, and the role of *then* or *alors* is to justify the question.

About a quarter of inferential *then* (26/98) are at the right periphery (as in (13)); this compares with Haselow's (2011: 3608) finding of 24 per cent in his conversation data and Aijmer's (2019: 20–1) finding of almost half in her fiction data. Right-peripheral *then* is associated in the interview data with asking for a response: all but five are in questions or pseudo-questions (such as *tell me x then*).

However, unlike the findings Aijmer reports for her data, no obvious meaning difference between left-peripheral and right-peripheral usage in questions was apparent when comparing occurrences such as (13) and (15); likewise for *alors*, comparing (14) and (16).

(15) P: I think the Job Centre staff are absolutely fantastic | they are coping with a much higher . . . [interrupted]
J: *then* why bring in the private sector involvement? [Sopel – Purnell, 2009]

(16) P: sur ce sujet il n'y a aucune faille dans ce qui a été fait | au contraire | nous avons renforcé [. . .] . . .
J: *alors* pourquoi vous revenez sur ce que vous aviez fait si tout marche bien ? [De Malherbe – Blanquer, 2022]
['P: on this issue there's nothing wrong with what was done | on the contrary | we've improved [. . .] . . .
J: *alors* why are you revising what you did if everything's working well?']

The contexts and functions of resultative *then* and *alors*, at both modal and illocutionary levels, are thus very similar, but it will be seen in the next two sections that they differ in their more abstract uses and in their distributions.

9.5.4 Diverging polysemy

Beyond the temporal and resultative uses, *then* and *alors* appear to diverge. Along with [*et*] *puis*, they can serve as additives, extending the discourse by adding the congruent upcoming idea to the previous idea(s) (17), (18), (19). However, *alors* is very rare in the data in this context: in (17) addition is more obviously expressed by *aussi*. The sense of *then* illustrated in (18) is much closer to that of *et puis* (19).

(17) P: il y a moins d'activités physiques | *alors* il y a aussi l'habitude plus importante des écrans [Véran, 2022]
['there are fewer physical activities | *alors* there is also more screen use']
(18) P: you've got work permits | which you're talking about | and *then* you've got the whole business of bogus asylum seekers [Davis, 2004]
(19) P: il y a des problèmes de légitimité sur le réferendum | *et puis* il y a des problèmes dus au fait que c'est un traité extrêmement complexe [Moscovici, 2000]

['there are problems over the legitimacy of the referendum | *et puis* there are problems due to its being an extremely complex treaty']

In 90 per cent of its occurrences in the data, *puis* reinforces *et* to create an additive particle *et puis*, while its temporal sense has bleached to the point where it often needs to be reinforced by *ensuite* or *après* (20).

(20) P: le Panama est un peu | très habitué a faire des aller-retours | à faire le gentil | et *puis ensuite* à faire le méchant [Sapin, 2016]

['Panama is a bit | tends very much to see-saw | to play the good guy | *et puis ensuite* ('and then') to play the bad guy']

The major use of *alors* is at left periphery to present a new idea or a new topic (cf. Hansen 1996: 141–2 on the foregrounding role of *alors*). This 'presentational' use typically occurs at the start of a turn, both of an interviewee's answer to a question (21) and an interviewer's 'next question' (22).

(21) J: ça ça y est ? toutes les associations sont d'accord sur le texte ?
P: *alors* on est encore en train de faire les consultations avec les associations [Schiappa, 2021]
['J: is that it? are all the associations in agreement on the text?
P: *alors* we're still consulting the associations']
(22) P: . . . vous avez un certain nombre de montants à payer au fur et à mesure des années
J: *alors* prenons la situation à l'envers | qu'est-ce qui coince ?
P: *alors* pour le moment en dehors de la reconnaissance d'engagement juridique . . . [Teillard – Loiseau, 2017]
['P: you have a certain number of regular payments to make over the years
J: *alors* let's look at the situation the other way round | what's the sticking point?
P: *alors* for the moment apart from recognizing their legal commitments . . .']

This use might be regarded as an extension of the resultative use ('since you ask, . . .'). It is often the case, for left-peripheral *alors*, that the illocutionary use and the presentational or topic-shifting use seem simultaneously appropriate. But in all cases, *alors* focuses on what follows (as an introductory 'drum roll', akin to English *so*) and it occurs discourse-initially, to start a conversation by introducing a first topic (23).

(23) J: merci d'être avec nous ce matin | *alors* tout d'abord cette question | hier soir . . . [Campredon – Borne, 2021]

['J: thank you for being with us this morning | *alors* first of all this question | yesterday evening . . .']

Alors has thus acquired a presentational discourse-focusing function with no causal connectivity (other than perhaps a vague assumption, 'since we are here . . .'). By contrast, *then* remains connective, as a temporal and/or a resultative. Table 9.3, for reference, summarizes the overlap between the English and French expressions, with reference to the examples.

To summarize, *then* and *alors* in the data express very similar relations, temporal and resultative, at content, modal and illocutionary levels. But they diverge in their more abstract or 'weaker' meanings. While [*and*] *then* and [*et*] *puis* remain connective as additives, *alors* occurs as a dedicated focus particle and topic marker that can introduce virtually any utterance.

9.5.5 Distribution in the data

Figure 9.3 shows the distribution of uses in the interview data, where *then* has clearly advanced much less from its temporal roots towards discoursal usage than *alors* and *puis*.

Temporal *alors* is rare in spoken French, as is *alors* in the conditional construction. Only eleven conditionals were found with *alors* in the French data. Blanche-Benveniste (2010) reports that the pattern '*si* p *alors* q' was not found at all in the spontaneous spoken language corpora that she studied (it is a feature of written and formal spoken discourse only), whereas '*if* p *then* q' accounted for almost a third of the occurrences of *then* and is clearly a regular discourse template of the genre. These observations are in line with the greater degree of abstraction of *alors* compared with *then*, and with the relatively formal context of interviews for the broadcast media.

The cross-linguistic regularities whereby many types of semantic shift involving more concrete to more abstract meanings, such as temporal > causal in the case of *then* and *alors* (and *puisque*), are generally considered to be due to cognitive factors, such as inferential and analogical reasoning. The question then arises why further abstraction to discourse-organizing and interaction

Table 9.3 Usage of *then*, *alors* and *puis* in the interview data (excluding contrastive *alors que*)

Function			Expression			Examples
Connective	Temporal	temporal 'at that time'	*then*	*alors*		(4) (5)
		temporal-sequential 'next, after that'	*then*	*alors*	*puis*	(6) (7) (8)
	Causal (resultative)	consequence 'as a result'	*then*	*alors*		(9) (10)
		inference 'it follows that'	*then*	*alors*		(11) (12)
		inference at illocutionary level	*then*	*alors*		(13) (14) (15) (16)
	Continuous	additive	[*and*] *then*	[*et*] *alors*	[*et*] *puis*	(17) (18) (19)
Non-connective	Discourse prominence	presentational		*alors*		(21) (22) (23)

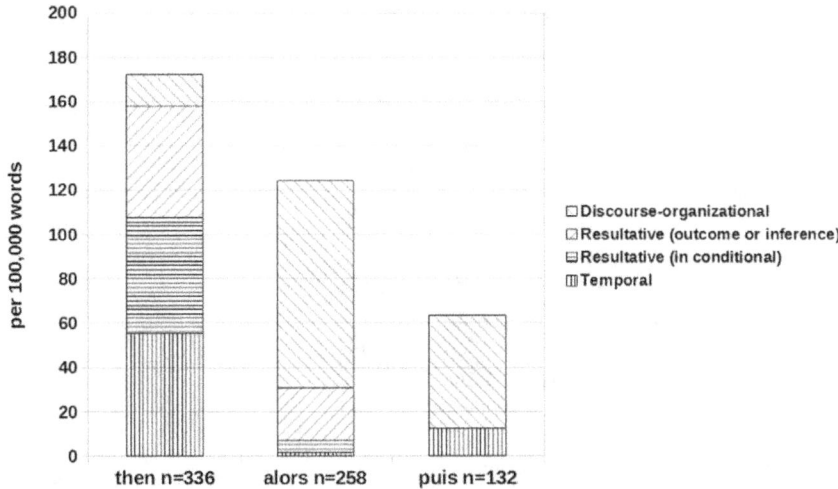

Figure 9.3 Distribution of *then*, *alors* and *puis* in the data (excluding *alors que*).

management uses appears to show less regularity. Altenberg and Granger note that '[t]he divergent meaning extensions that have evolved in different languages are especially striking in high-frequency words expressing certain basic meanings' (2002: 13), as is the case for the temporal adverbs. What could be the reason for more divergent polysemy at the discourse-organizational level? One hypothesis is that these uses are less motivated by cognitive factors than by sociocultural (rhetorical and aesthetic) ones. In other words, the discoursal uses may be regarded as what Aijmer (2004: 269) calls 'culture-dependent extensions', as the speaking styles of prestigious individuals within a speech community come to have an aesthetic value for which they are imitated. This kind of imitation may result in increased frequency within the community (within the political class, for example) of certain patterns of speech that, through their frequency, become schematic connective constructions into which propositions can be slotted.

Figure 9.4, finally, compares the findings on the distribution of *alors* and *then* in the political interview corpus with that in a study based on conversational data (Herment et al. 2022). The conversational data is spontaneous spoken interaction in semi-formal meetings, from the British National Corpus for English (BNC 2007; Coleman et al. 2012) and the CLAPI corpus for French (Baldauf-Quilliatre et al. 2016). As the frequencies are not directly comparable (the conversational study being based on a smaller corpus), percentages are shown. The distributions turn out to be very similar, suggesting that both data samples reflect semi-formal spontaneous spoken usage of these expressions.

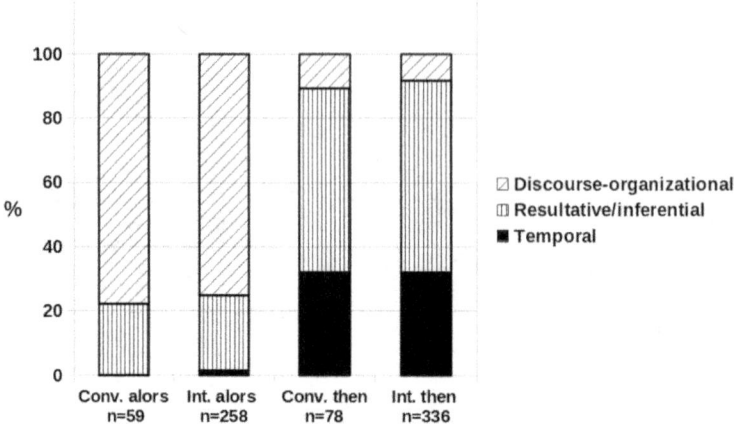

Figure 9.4 Comparison of distribution of *alors* and *then* in a conversational comparable corpus and in the political interviews comparable corpus.

9.6 Conclusion

Two main findings from the comparison of three broad types of connective in French and English political interviews reveal differences in usage across the two languages. One finding was that a greater number of connective types is found in the French data, reflecting perhaps an aesthetic preference for rhetorical variation, or for a more fine-grained articulation of coherence than is the case for English. The English relies more on a few very common connectives: three accounted for 64 per cent of all tokens, compared with just under half for French. The second, related finding was that the French data also shows a greater density of connective tokens than English, but that the difference is largely accounted for by the additive relations that are expected to be the least necessary to mark for communicative purposes. The most common French additive connectives are quite bleached compared with the causal and contrastive connectives, and often functionally, if not rhetorically, interchangeable. The effect of the optional markers is both of a cumulatively-built discourse – the piling up, in rhetorical parallelism, of points that contribute equally to the speaker's purpose – and of a more emphatic discourse, as many points are explicitly presented as being 'also the case'. Cross-genre comparisons are needed to test the extent to which this finding is genre-bound and whether genre differences are greater in French or English.

A closer look at the usage in the interviews of *alors*, *then* and *puis* revealed, first, that although they have very similar polysemies expressing temporal, resultative and additive meanings, these are very differently distributed. *Then* has grammaticalized considerably less than *alors*. Temporal uses are common and in its additive function – an extension from temporal posteriority to textual posteriority – it more closely resembles [*et*] *puis* than *alors*. But its major usage is as a resultative. By contrast, by far the most frequent use of *alors* is to focus on the upcoming idea and/or to open a new topic, in a split from its resultative meaning. Its use discourse-initially reveals how little connectivity it now signals. Whether resultative *then* eventually follows the same path as *alors* remains to be seen. All the expressions show signs of ongoing change. The finer-grained examination of these three expressions suggests the hypothesis that expressions with similar meanings on an objective plane in two languages may diverge more as they shift in usage towards more abstract and discourse-structuring meanings (Figure 9.2).

The examination of connectives gives us only one perspective on the marking of relations; prosody and syntactic structures should be investigated too. It remains to be shown (a) whether there is in fact a universal conceptual space of coherence or whether coherence varies across speech communities, (b) whether there are universal 'basic level' relation types and (c) how exactly coherence meanings interact, diachronically and synchronically, with other semantic fields. Contrastive linguistics can contribute via fine-grained comparisons to building a semantic map of coherence that may help answer such questions.

Relatively little research in coherence relations has focused on cross-linguistic differences and similarities across comparable (sub-)genres, and relatively little has focused on spoken language. The aim of this study was to contribute to filling gaps in our knowledge of coherence relation marking in English and French by focusing on one particular genre of spoken language. Given the inconclusive results obtained so far in contrastive studies of French and English (Section 9.3.3), further research might focus on specific comparable genres, both spoken and written, to improve our understanding of how coherence marking varies with genre and sub-genre across these two languages. And for a fuller picture, studies of connectives need to be complemented by studies of the distributions of syntactic, prosodic and other means of coherence marking. Overall, with a great deal of the research so far having focused on written genres in one language, there is a need for more contrastive linguistic research on spoken language in comparable socio-cultural contexts.

Acknowledgements

Many thanks to the editors of this volume and to two anonymous reviewers for their helpful comments on an earlier version of this chapter.

Notes

1. There is a considerable literature on the identification of discourse units; see Chafe (1994) on information units, Hoek, Evers-Vermeul and Sanders (2018) and Degand and Crible (2021) on segmentation for coherence analysis, among others.
2. See Das and Taboada (2018) on the cognitive status of coherence.
3. Overviews of two influential models, Rhetorical Structure Theory (RST) and Penn Discourse Tree Bank (PDTB) can be found in Jurafsky and Martin (2020: 444–7); comparisons of RST, PDTB and the Cognitive approach to Coherence Relations (CCR) in Sanders et al. (2021); see also Demberg, Asr and Scholman (2019) for an overview of differing models of coherence relations.
4. Level has been characterized in terms of objective vs. subjective marking (e.g. Pander Maat and Degand 2001), content marking vs. presentational marking (e.g. Mann and Thompson 1988), text-external vs. text-internal marking (e.g. Halliday and Hasan 1976), semantic vs. pragmatic (Sanders, Spooren and Noordman 1992).
5. Even relatively formal spoken discourse is not easily segmented into clauses. There was no rigid requirement for a verb to be present: connectives that typically signal propositional relations sometimes occur before NPs and these are included where an ellipted proposition makes sense.
6. On *well*, see Jucker (1997), Schourup (1999), Kirk (2018).
7. On *and*, see Crible and Demberg (2020).
8. For a contrastive English/French study of expressions such as *I think*, *je crois*, and so on, in political interviews, see Fetzer and Johansson (2010).
9. Excluding *là aussi* on the grounds that it has coalesced into a distinct lexeme with distinct usage.
10. No distinction is made here between 'resultative' and 'resultive' as used in Quirk et al. (1985: 634) and Altenberg (2007).
11. Historically *puis* has also given rise to a causal in the formation *puisque*, which marks a reason ('since', 'given that').

References

Aijmer, K. (2004), 'The Interface between Perception, Evidentiality and Discourse Particle Use - Using a Translation Corpus to Study the Polysemy of See', *TradTerm*, 10: 249–77.

Aijmer, K. (2008), 'Parallel and Comparable Corpora', in A. Lüdeling and M. Kytö (eds), *Corpus Linguistics. An International Handbook*, vol. 1, 275–92, Berlin: Walter de Gruyter.

Aijmer, K. (2019), 'Challenges in the Contrastive Study of Discourse Markers: The Case of Then', in O. Loureda, I. Recio Fernández, L. Nadal and A. Cruz (eds), *Empirical Studies of the Construction of Discourse*, 17–42, Amsterdam: John Benjamins.

Aijmer, K. (2020), 'Contrastive Pragmatics and Corpora', *Contrastive Pragmatics*, 1: 28–57.

Aijmer, K. and D. M. Lewis (2017), 'Introduction', in K. Aijmer and D. M. Lewis (eds), *Contrastive Analysis of Discourse-pragmatic Aspects of Linguistic Genres. Yearbook of Corpus Linguistics and Pragmatics*, 5: 1–9, Cham: Springer.

Altenberg, B. (2007), 'The Correspondence of Resultive Connectors in English and Swedish', *Nordic Journal of English Studies*, 6 (1): 1–26.

Altenberg, B. and S. Granger (2002), 'Recent Trends in Cross-linguistic Lexical Studies', in B. Altenberg and S. Granger (eds), *Lexis in Contrast. Corpus-based Approaches*, 3–48, Amsterdam: John Benjamins.

Asr, F. T. and V. Demberg (2012), 'Measuring the Strength of Linguistic Cues for Discourse Relations', in *Proceedings of the Workshop on Advances in Discourse Analysis and its Computational Aspects*, 33–42, The COLING 2012 Organizing Committee.

Asr, F. T. and V. Demberg (2015), 'Uniform Information Density at the Level of Discourse Relations: Negation Markers and Discourse Connective Omission', in *Proceedings of the 11th International Conference on Computational Semantics* (IWCS2015), London, 118–28.

Baldauf-Quilliatre, H., I. Colón de Carvajal, C. Etienne, E. Jouin-Chardon, S. Teston-Bonnard and V. Traverso (2016), 'CLAPI, une base de données multimodale pour la parole en interaction: Apports et dilemmes' [CLAPI, a multimodal database for interactive speech: Contributions and dilemmas], *Corpus*, 15. https://doi.org/10.4000/corpus.2991

BBC (2003–2011), *The Politics Show*, London: BBC.

BBC (2005), *Any Questions*, 8 July 2005, London: BBC.

Blanche Benveniste, C. (2010), *Approches de la langue parlée en français.* [Approaches to the spoken language in French], Paris: Ophrys.

BNC (2007), *British National Corpus*, version 3 (BNC XML Edition). Distributed by Bodleian Libraries, University of Oxford for the BNC Consortium. http://www.natcorp.ox.ac.uk/

Chafe, W. L. (1994), *Discourse, Consciousness, and Time: The Flow and Displacement of Conscious Experience in Speaking and Writing*, Chicago: University of Chicago Press.

Coleman, J., L. Baghai-Ravary, J. Pybus and S. Grau (2012), 'Audio BNC. The Audio Edition of the Spoken British National Corpus'. Phonetics Laboratory, University of Oxford. http://www.phon.ox.ac.uk/AudioBNC

Crible, L. (2017), 'Discourse Markers and (dis)fluencies in English and French: Variation and Combination in the DisFrEn Corpus', *International Journal of Corpus Linguistics*, 22 (2): 242–69.

Crible, L. (2018), *Markers and (Dis)fluency: Forms and Functions across Languages and Registers*, Amsterdam: John Benjamins.

Crible, L. (2020), 'Weak and Strong Discourse Markers in Speech, Chat and Writing: Do Signals Compensate for Ambiguity in Explicit Relations?', *Discourse Processes*, 57: 793–807.

Crible, L. and M.-J. Cuenca (2017), 'Discourse Markers in Speech: Characteristics and Challenges for Corpus Annotation', *Dialogue and Discourse*, 8 (2): 149–66.

Crible, L. and V. Demberg (2020), 'When do We Leave Discourse Relations Underspecified? The Effect of Formality and Relation Type', *Discours*, 26. https://doi.org/10.4000/discours.10848

Das, D. and M. Taboada (2018), 'Signalling of Coherence Relations in Discourse, Beyond Discourse Markers', *Discourse Processes*, 55 (8): 743–70.

Degand, L. and L. Crible (2021), 'Discourse Markers at the Peripheries of Syntax, Intonation and Turns. Towards a Cognitive-Functional Unit of Segmentation', in D. Van Olmen and J. Šinkūnienė (eds), *Pragmatic Markers and Peripheries*, 19–48, Amsterdam: John Benjamins.

Degand, L. and B. Fagard (2011), '*Alors* between Discourse and Grammar: The Role of Syntactic Position', *Functions of Language*, 18 (1): 29–56.

Degand, L., A. C. Simon, N. Tanguy and T. Van Damme (2014), 'Initiating a Discourse Unit in Spoken French: Prosodic and Syntactic Featuers of the Left Periphery', in S. Pons Bordería (ed.), *Discourse Segmentation in Romance Languages*, 243–73, Amsterdam: John Benjamins.

Demberg, V., F. T. Asr and M. Scholman (2019), 'How Compatible Are Our Discourse Annotation Frameworks? Insights from Mapping RST-DT and PDTB Annotations', *Dialogue and Discourse*, 10 (1): 87–135.

Dupont, M. (2019), 'Conjunctive Markers of Contrast in English and French: From Syntax to Lexis and Discourse', PhD diss., University of Louvain la Neuve.

Fetzer, A. and M. Johansson (2010), 'Cognitive Verbs in Context: A Contrastive Analysis of English and French Argumentative Discourse', in S. Marzo, K. Heylen and G. De Sutter (eds), *Corpus Studies in Contrastive Linguistics, International Journal of Corpus Linguistics*, 15 (2): 240–66.

Guillemin-Flescher, J. (1981), *Syntaxe comparée du français et de l'anglais: Problèmes de traduction*. [Comparative syntax of French and English: Problems for translation], Paris: Ophrys.

Halliday, M. A. K. and R. Hasan (1976), *Cohesion in English*, Oxford: Longman.

Hansen, M.-B. M. (1996), 'Some Common Discourse Particles in Spoken French', in M.-B. M. Hansen and G. Skytte (eds), *Le discours: cohérence et connexion. Actes du colloque international Copenhague le 7 avril 1995* [Discourse: Coherence and Connexion. Proceedings of the International Conference, Copenhagen 7th April 1995.], *Etudes Romanes*, 35: 105–49.

Haselow, A. (2011), 'Discourse Marker and Modal Particle: The Functions of Utterance-Final "Then" in Spoken English', *Journal of Pragmatics*, 43: 3603-23.
Haspelmath, M. (2003), 'The Geometry of Grammatical Meaning: Semantic Maps and Cross-linguistic Comparison', in M. Tomasello (ed.), *The New Psychology of Language*, vol. 2, 211-43, Mahwah: Erlbaum.
Hasselgård, H. (2014), 'Additive Conjunction across Languages: *Dessuten* and its Correspondences in English and French', in S. O. Ebeling, A. Grønn, K. Rå Hauge and D. Santos (eds), *Corpus-based Studies in Contrastive Linguistics. Oslo Studies in Language*, 6 (1): 69-89.
Hasselgård, H. (2021), 'Corpus-based Contrastive Studies: Beginnings, Developments and Directions', *Languages in Contrast*, 20 (2): 184-208.
Hellman, C. (1995), 'The Notion of Coherence in Discourse', in G. Rickheit and C. Habel (eds), *Focus and Coherence in Discourse Processing*, 190-202, Berlin: Walter de Gruyter.
Herment, S., L. Leonarduzzi, D. Lewis, C. Portes, L. Prévot, F. Sabio and G. Turcsan (2022), 'Périphéries gauche et droite' [Left and right peripheries], *TIPA (Travaux interdisciplinaires sur la parole et le langage)*, 38. https://doi.org/10.4000/tipa.5104
Hoek, J., J. Evers-Vermeul and T. J. M. Sanders (2018), 'Segmenting Discourse: Incorporating Interpretation into Segmentation?', *Corpus Linguistics and Linguistic Theory*, 14 (2): 357-86.
Hoek, J., J. Evers-Vermeul and T. J. M. Sanders (2019), 'Using the Cognitive Approach to Coherence Relations for Discourse Annotation', *Dialogue and Discourse*, 10 (2): 1-33. https://doi.org/10.5087/dad.2019.201
Jucker, A. (1997), 'The Discourse Marker Well in the History of English', *English Language and Linguistics*, 1 (1): 91-110.
Jurafsky, D. and J. H. Martin (2020), *Speech and Language Processing*, 3rd edn, Prentice Hall.
Kirk, J. M. (2018), 'The Pragmatics of Well as a Discourse Marker in Broadcast Discussions', in S. Hoffmann, A. Sand, S. Arndt-Lappe and L. M. Dillmann (eds), *Corpora and Lexis*, 140-72, Leiden: Brill.
König, E. and V. Gast (2018), *Understanding English German Contrasts*, 4th edn, Berlin: Erich Schmidt Verlag.
Kuteva, T., B. Heine, B. Hong, H. Long, H. Narrog and S. Rhee (2019), *World Lexicon of Grammaticalization*, 2nd edn, Cambridge: Cambridge University Press.
Levy, R. and F. T. Jaeger (2007), 'Speakers Optimize Information Density through Syntactic Reduction', in B. Schölkopf, J. Platt and T. Hofmann (eds), *Advances in Neural Information Processing Systems 19: Proceedings of the 2006 Conference*, 849-56, Cambridge: MIT Press.
Mann, W. C. and S. A. Thompson (1988), 'Rhetorical Structure Theory: Toward a Functional Theory of Text Organization', *Text*, 8 (3): 243-81.
Mason, I. (2001), 'Translator Behaviour and Language Usage: Some Constraints on Contrastive Studies', *Hermes*, 26: 65-80.

Mauranen, A. (2002), 'Where's Cultural Adaptation? A Corpus-based Study on Translation Strategies', *TRAlinea*, special issue CULT2K. https://www.intralinea.org/specials/article/1677

Murray, J. D. (1997), 'Connectives and Narrative Text: The Role of Continuity', *Memory and Cognition*, 25 (2): 227–36.

Narrog, H. and J. van der Auwera (2011), 'Grammaticalization and Semantic Maps', in H. Narrog and B. Heine (eds), *The Oxford Handbook of Grammaticalization*, 318–27, Oxford: Oxford University Press.

Pagin, P. (2014), 'Pragmatic Enrichment as Coherence Raising', *Philosophical Studies*, 168: 59–100.

Palmer, F. (2001), *Mood and Modality*, Cambridge: Cambridge University Press.

Pander Maat, H. and L. Degand (2001), 'Scaling Causal Relations and Connectives in Terms of Speaker Involvement', *Cognitive Linguistics*, 12: 211–45.

Patterson, G. and A. Kehler (2013), 'Predicting the Presence of Discourse Connectives', in *Proceedings of the Conference on Empirical Methods in Natural Language Processing EMNLP*, 914–23, Seattle: Association for Computational Linguistics.

Quirk, R., S. Greenbaum, G. Leech and J. Svartvik (1985), *A Comprehensive Grammar of the English Language*, Oxford: Longman.

Sanders, T. J. M., V. Demberg, J. Hoek, M. C. J. Scholman, F. T. Asr, S. Zufferey and J. Evers-Vermeul (2021), 'Unifying Dimensions in Discourse Relations: How Various Annotation Frameworks Are Related', *Corpus Linguistics and Linguistic Theory*, 17 (1): 1–71.

Sanders, T. J. M., W. P. M. S. Spooren and L. G. M. Noordman (1992), 'Toward a Taxonomy of Coherence Relations', *Discourse Processes*, 15 (1): 1–35.

Scholman, M. C. J. (2019), 'Coherence Relations in Discourse and Cognition: Comparing Approaches, Annotations, and Interpretations', Doctoral diss., Universität des Saarlandes.

Scholman, M. C. J., V. Demberg and T. J. M. Sanders (2022), 'Descriptively Adequate and Cognitively Plausible? Validating Distinctions between Types of Coherence Relations', *Discours*, 30. https://doi.org/10.4000/discours.12075

Schourup, L. (1999), 'Discourse Markers', *Lingua*, 107: 227–65.

Scott, M. (2020), *WordSmith Tools v. 8*. [Computer Software], Lexical Analysis Software. https://lexically.net/wordsmith

Sweetser, E. E. (1990), *From Etymology to Pragmatics. Metaphorical and Cultural Aspects of Semantic Structure*, Cambridge: Cambridge University Press.

Taboada, M. (2009), 'Implicit and Explicit Coherence Relations', in J. Renkema (ed.), *Discourse, of Course: An Overview of Research in Discourse Studies*, 127–40, Amsterdam: John Benjamins.

Taboada, M. (2019), 'The Space of Coherence Relations and their Signalling in Discourse', *Language, Context and Text*, 1 (2): 205–33.

Taboada, M. and M. de los A. Gómez González (2012), 'Discourse Markers and Coherence Relations: Comparison across Markers, Languages and Modalities', *Linguistics and the Human Sciences*, 6: 17–41.

Traugott, E. C. (2022), *Discourse Structuring Markers in English*, Amsterdam: John Benjamins.

10

Reporting Verbs in English, Czech and Finnish

Anna Cermakova and Lenka Fárová

10.1 Introduction

Reporting verbs introduce or report someone's direct or indirect speech; in English, the most frequent reporting verb is *say*. *Say* is perceived as a semantically neutral reporting verb, unlike other reporting verbs such as *ask*, *exclaim* or *whisper*. Recent research on reporting verbs has shown that their function often goes beyond mere speech reporting: it has been argued that they may substantially contribute to a characterization process (Ruano San Segundo 2016), or be gender-specific (Eberhardt 2017; Ruano San Segundo 2018; Cermakova and Mahlberg 2018; Mastropierro 2024). Reporting verbs have also received attention within translation and contrastive studies (e.g. Corness 2010; Fárová 2016; Ruano San Segundo 2017; Mastropierro 2020; Nádvorníková 2020) pointing to various translation shifts which may potentially influence the reader effect. The shifts in translations from English are largely due to the fact that English heavily relies on *say*, most frequently occurring in its past tense form *said*, which may create repetition that translators feel the need to address (Cermakova 2015); the translations thus often show a much higher degree of variation in reporting verbs than their English source texts.

In this chapter, we wish to argue that *said* frequently co-occurs with further modifications as in 'Good,' she **said firmly**, and the reporting phrase is thus no longer semantically neutral; the modifications that occur with *said* show a tendency to form distinct lexicogrammatical patterns. They not only add semantic nuance to the verb but also create a powerful stylistic variation. With this as our starting point, we wish to explore the nature of the lexicogrammatical patterning around *said* in contemporary English fiction. Our preliminary pilot study suggested that the patterning, though showing regularities, may, in fact, be, to a degree, author-specific. In this chapter, we will focus in detail on five novels by five different authors. We further wish to explore whether these patterns are also perceived by the translators as patterns and how/whether this is manifested in their translation. In order to make our research claims valid beyond one language pair, we explore translations of these five novels into two, typologically different, languages: Czech and Finnish. We ask the following research questions:

1. What lexicogrammatical patterns accompany the reporting verb *said* in English fiction?
2. How are these patterns manifested in translation to Czech and Finnish?

Our second research question is operationalized into two sub-questions:

2a. Is the stylistically neutral English *said*, when accompanied by further modification, translated by similarly neutral *řekl/ řekla* (he/she said) in Czech and *sanoi* in Finnish?
2b. What (if any) lexicogrammatical patterns can be observed in the translated texts?

The question (2b) will be explored through a case study focusing on the patterns '*said* + *with/without*'. Section 10.2 provides an overview of research on reporting verbs and their translations; Section 10.3 explains our data and methodology choices; Section 10.4 aims to answer our first research question, that is, provides an overview of the lexicogrammatical patterns we have identified; Section 10.5 aims to answer our second research question and focuses on the translations; and Section 10.6 offers some tentative conclusions arising from our analysis.

10.2 Reporting verbs and their translation

Fiction, as a register, is intriguing; it is linguistically very heterogenous, up to the point that it seems to consist of two distinct registers: the narrative and character speech (Egbert and Mahlberg 2020). Character speech in many ways resembles spoken language (Mahlberg et al. 2019) and displays different linguistic characteristics than narrative. Reporting verbs bridge the narrative and character speech and constitute an important part of fictional language. Reporting verbs are textually hard-working: in addition to speech reporting, they may mediate prosodic features and other extralinguistic contexts of character speech, they may convey the narrator's stance, and contribute to the overall discourse organization, plot development and discourse evaluation. Being linked to characters' speech, reporting verbs also have a powerful characterizing potential (Ruano San Segundo 2017, 2018; Cermakova and Mahlberg 2018; Mastropierro 2020, 2024) – they not only mediate how something is said but also contribute to the reader's character perception.

Reporting verbs have been explored in the field of stylistics (Semino and Short 2004). Carmen Caldas-Coulthard (1987) groups reporting verbs into five categories:

(i) Neutral reporting verb *said*
(ii) Structuring verbs, for example, *ask* or *reply*
(iii) Illocutionary verbs, such as *agree*
(iv) Discourse signalling such as *add* or *repeat*
(v) Descriptive verbs, such as *shout*, which add information on how things are being said and the person who is speaking

While *said* is classified as neutral, Ruano San Segundo (2016: 117) notes that when glossed with additional information *said* provides 'the accuracy and range of details supplied by more specific choices of verbs'. As far as we are aware, the semantic or lexicogrammatical typology of typical modification patterns of *said* has not been studied in detail.

Research on the translation of reporting verbs seems to have identified a trend common across several languages: translations from English generally show a greater variety of reporting verbs, see, for example, Mastropierro (2020) for Italian, Rojo and Valenzuela (2001) and Bourne (2002) for Spanish, Corness (2010) for Czech, and Winters (2007) for German. We may hypothesize that this is linked to the explicitation translation universal (Baker 1993; Blum-Kulka 2004), that is, translators tend to replace the frequently occurring *said* with a more explicit solution. We may, therefore, expect the modification patterns of *said* to influence the translation. The greater variation may also be simply linked to the fact that translators respect stylistic and rhetoric conventions of the target language, in which repetition may be less well tolerated, which certainly is a case in point for Czech (see Levý (2011: 113), who specifically discusses *said*). Translation strategies are complex, translation is never neutral: it is always a form of rewriting, interpreting and retelling (Lefevere 1992); literary translation in particular, with its focus on the aesthetic function, is to a degree governed by the rhetoric norms of the target culture. In this chapter, we aim to contribute to the body of research on reporting verbs and stylistic repetition by focusing on the core reporting verb *said*, as the most frequently occurring verb form in the reporting function, and its translations into Czech and Finnish.

10.3 Data and method

As argued above, the English reporting verb *said* frequently occurs with other accompanying information on how, when and where something is being said. To answer our first research question and to explore the lexicogrammatical patterning that makes up the 'accompanying information', we use a small corpus of broadly contemporary English fiction. Our second research question focuses on the translation of these patterns into Czech and Finnish – for this purpose, we use a parallel corpus of the English source texts aligned to their Czech and Finnish translations. We use a limited dataset for several reasons; in our pilot study, we have observed that while the same lexicogrammatical patterns tend to occur across many books, there seem to be nuanced but clear differences among both authors and translators. To control for these differences, we use a small corpus, in which we can fully inspect the whole dataset. Suitable large datasets to confront our results with are not readily available. We therefore cannot make any claims on larger trends across English fiction or translation in general as this is outside the scope of this study. However, to make our findings valid beyond one specific language pair, we analyse two, typologically different, language pairs.

Our English fiction corpus (about 680,000 words) consists of five well-known and widely read novels published between 1986 to 2018 and representing several genres; see Table 10.1. Kazuo Ishiguro is a British Nobel Prize author (2017) with Japanese roots, John Grisham is an extremely popular American novelist,[1] Tracy Chevalier is an American-British novelist, whose novel *Girl with a Pearl Earring* rose to popularity, particularly after its film adaptation (2003), Zadie Smith is a widely read English novelist with a Jamaican background, and Robert Galbraith is J. K. Rowling's[2] pseudonym in the detective genre. The corpus is selected from the resources available in the *InterCorp* corpus (Čermák and Rosen 2012). *InterCorp* is a freely accessible multilingual parallel corpus developed by the Czech National Corpus project (available at https://www.korpus.cz/), which contains a variety of different text genres with an extensive fiction component. Each text is aligned to its translation. We have chosen texts in English that all have aligned with both Czech and Finnish translations. In order to avoid bias due to multiple translations by one translator, each of the source texts has been translated by a different translator, see Table 10.2.

Table 10.1 The English fiction corpus

Author	Born	Title	Genre	Year of publ.	No. of words (incl. punctuation)
Ishiguro Kazuo (Br)	1954	*An Artist of the Floating World*	novel	1986	79,332
Grisham John (Am)	1955	*The Partner*	thriller	1997	137,675
Chevalier Tracy (Am)	1962	*Girl with a Pearl Earring*	novel	1999	83,367
Smith Zadie (Br)	1975	*On Beauty*	novel	2006	194,691
Galbraith Robert (Br)	1965	*The Silkworm*	detective novel	2014	185,621
Total					680,686

Table 10.2 Translation corpus

English source text	Czech translator, title, year of publ.	Finnish translator, title, year of publ.
Ishiguro Kazuo, *An Artist of the Floating World*	Hanuš Jiří, *Malíř pomíjivého světa*, 1999	Bützow Helene, *Menneen maailman maalari*, 2017
Grisham John, *The Partner*	Kříž Pavel, *Partner*, 1998	Sappinen, Jorma-Veikko, *Partneri*, 1998
Chevalier Tracy, *Girl with Pearl Earring*	Breznenová Ivana, *Dívka s perlou*, 2004	Gothoni Arja, *Tyttö ja helmikorvakoru*, 2001
Smith Zadie, *On Beauty*	Diestlerová Petra, *O kráse*, 2006	Ruuska Irmeli, *Kauneudesta*, 2013
Galbraith Robert, *The Silkworm*	Šenkyřík Ladislav, *Hedvábník*, 2015	Rekiaro Ilkka, *Silkkiäistoukka*, 2014

Our research design consists of three consecutive steps. In the first step, we analyse all instances of *said* in the English source texts to distinguish between occurrences where reporting *said* occurs without any further modification as in example (1) and when it occurs with further information on how things are being said, as in example (2).

(1) 'Oh, Lord, Howard,' **said** Kiki. (Smith)
(2) 'Prince William,' **said** Robin, **amused**, 'and Kate Middleton'. (Galbraith)

Fabricius-Hansen and Haug (2012) refer to these as 'small clauses' or, more technically, '(non-finite) co-eventive adjuncts' (CEA). They are characterized as being 'adverbal' rather than adnominal, they are 'clause-like' but 'non-finite' and '[t]hey introduce eventualities that are "co-located" with and "participant-connected" to the eventuality described by the main clause [...] the adjunct event is understood as spatio-temporally overlapping its host' (Fabricius-Hansen and Haug 2012: 2), as in example (2), where Robin is speaking and is amused at the same time. These modifiers are linked through the subject of the main clause, the person speaking in our case. This linking can be manifested syntactically; that is, the main clause and the CEA have the same subject as in (2) above (Robin) and/or semantically, the CEA has a different overt 'subject', which is however clearly linked to the main clause subject as in 3 below – *she* is the main clause subject and *her voice* is the 'subject' of the CEA (cf. Fabricius-Hansen and Haug 2012: 424). The other feature that these modifiers share is temporal, they either express simultaneity (as in 2 and 3) or immediate time sequence (in 4 below).[3]

(3) 'You know what, Levi?' she **said, her voice breaking**. (Smith)
(4) 'All right, then,' she **said after a short pause**. (Galbraith)

In addition to CEAs, we are also interested in other types of modification that frequently co-occur with *said*, these may be one-word modifications, typically *-ly* adverbs, as in (5).

(5) 'They weren't the same thing at all,' **said** Fancourt **flatly**. (Galbraith)

We also include time and place adverbs and adverbials, as we consider the spatio-temporal aspect of the speech reporting one of its key characteristics. In our data, we identify all instances of modified *said* (we consider both postmodification, which seems to be the default option, but also premodification). Based on lexicogrammatical characteristics, the identified patterns are classified and quantified, for details see Section 10.4.

10.4 Reporting *said* in English fiction

The classification of *said* into modified and unmodified instances was, perhaps surprisingly, not always clear-cut. While instances as in examples (2) and (3) above are unproblematic, other occurrences were more difficult to interpret, particularly when semantic and stylistic effects were considered. We adopted a fairly broad definition of modification, including all cases where the verb modification directly following, occasionally preceding, the verb *said* semantically relates to how (including where and when) things are being said: to use Fabricius-Hansen and Haug's (2012: 423) words – instances where there is an 'increase in the descriptive granularity' of the verb *said*. In line with Fabricius-Hansen and Haug (2012: 2), we did not include finite clauses (examples 6 and 7), though semantically and stylistically, many of these are alternatives to some of the non-finite constructions, particularly *and*- and *as*-clauses, which express simultaneity and have the same subject as in (7) and some of the *wh* clauses that seem to be particularly favoured by Galbraith (cf. (6) and (3)). We excluded these based on formal syntactic criteria.

(6) 'They say he's got a lot better,' **said** Nina, **who was still gazing** towards Fancourt. (Galbraith)

(7) 'Ah . . . ' **said** Kiki, **and folded her arms**. (Smith)

Table 10.3 gives an overview of the distribution of the verb *said* in our data. In most of its occurrences, *said* occurs in a reporting function (column 3), but, for example, Chevalier has a high proportion of non-reporting *said* (41 per cent) which suggests a different narrative style. The amount of reported speech, approximated through the relative frequency of reporting *said*, also differs among the authors: Galbraith has the highest frequency of the reporting *said* (89.9 instances per 10,000 words) and Chevalier the lowest (20.6). The reporting *said* is, on average, slightly more frequent when modified (52 per cent), rather than unmodified

Table 10.3 Distribution of *said* in the English fiction corpus. The percentages in brackets in columns 2 and 3 indicate percentage of the total of reporting *said* (column 4). The relative frequencies (column 4 in square brackets) are calculated in relation to the overall word count of each book.

Author	*said* only	*said* with modification	Reporting *said* total [rel. freq. per 10,000 words]	Not reporting direct speech	Total *said*
Ishiguro	174 (48%)	187 (52%)	361 [45.5]	44	405
Grisham	269 (60%)	177 (40%)	446 [32.4]	146	592
Chevalier	79 (49%)	83 (51%)	162 [20.6]	111	273
Smith	330 (36%)	578 (64%)	908 [46.6]	100	1,008
Galbraith	846 (51%)	825 (49%)	1671 [89.9]	144	1,815
Total	1,698 (48%)	1,850 (52%)	3548 [52.1]	545	4,093

(48 per cent), which confirms our hypothesis that a substantial proportion of reporting *said* occurs not as semantically neutral but further modified.[4] There are differences between the individual authors: while, for example, Grisham prefers to use unmodified *said* (60 per cent) and Smith prefers modified *said* (64 per cent), the other authors seem to have the ratio more or less balanced.

We have classified the occurrences of modified *said* (in Table 10.3, column 3 '*said* with modification') into patterns based on formal, lexicogrammatical, criteria, see Table 10.4 for overview. We have found several instances of multiple modifications, as in (8), where the NP (*his anger newly virulent*) is followed by *-ing*-PART (*still holding the door*). In Table 10.4, these are counted as two instances. These multiple modifications are most frequent in Chevalier (11 per cent of reporting *said*) and least in Grisham (6 per cent).

(8)   . . .he said, **his anger newly virulent, still holding the door** but leaning in towards Levi. (Smith)

Table 10.4 Distribution of the lexicogrammatical patterns modifying reporting *said*. The last column gives two figures: total number of sentences where modification occurred plus, in brackets, the number of instances, where the modification was complex (i.e. more than one modification pattern occurred), the remaining cells contain overall counts.

Author	ADJP	ADV	NP	PART	PP	Total
Ishiguro	0	87 (43.2%) *-ly* (27)	3 (1.5%)	46 (22.9%) *-ing* (45) *-ed* (1)	65 (32.4%) *to*-PP (23) *with*-PP (20)	187(+14)
Grisham	4 (2%)	56 (30%) *-ly* (38)	10 (5.2%)	65 (34.6%) *-ing* (60) *-ed* (5)	53 (28.2%) *with*-PP (20) *to*-PP (11)	177(+11)
Chevalier	0	39 (42.4%) *-ly* (27)	7 (7.6%)	12 (13%) *-ing* (11) *-ed* (1)	34 (37%) *in*-PP (12) *to*-PP (12)	83(+9)
Smith	5 (0.8%)	222 (34.8%) *-ly* (208)	20 (3.2%)	301 (47.2%) *-ing* (285) *-ed* (16)	88 (14%) *with*-PP (26) *in*-PP (24)	578(+58)
Galbraith	25 (2.8%)	270 (30.6%) *-ly* (254)	32 (3.6%)	362 (41%) *-ing* (325) *-ed* (37)	194 (22%) *with*-PP (95) *to*-PP (17)	825(+58)
Total	**34 (1.7%)**	**674 (33.7%)**	**72 (3.6%)**	**786 (39.3%)**	**434 (21.7%)**	**2,000**

Majority of the modifications follow *said* (postmodification), but we include in our counts also those that precede *said* because all the authors occasionally use them in the preceding positions; the preceding position is particularly characteristic of Ishiguro, see below for further discussion.

We have identified five major patterns, which we discuss below in the order of their frequency of occurrence (see also Table 10.4). The most frequent modification is a participle (PART) (39.3 per cent of all modifications). Both *-ing* and *-ed* participles are used, *-ing* is substantially more frequent (92 per cent of the participles), see examples (2), (3) and (8) above. As discussed above, these may have the same subject as the main clause (example 2) or the modification has a different 'subject' (example 3), which is however semantically clearly related to the main subject, for example, *she* and *her voice*; we do not further distinguish between the two.

The second-most frequent pattern (33.7 per cent) is an adverbial phrase (ADV), which is most frequently simply realized by a *-ly* adverb, as in (5) and (9).

(9) 'There are some, Mrs Saito,' I **said**, perhaps a little **loudly**, . . . (Ishiguro)

The third most frequent (21.7 per cent) is a prepositional phrase (PP), with a range of prepositions taking part in the pattern,[5] see example (10):

(10) 'Have you been in the master's things?' she **said in an accusing tone**. (Chevalier)

Noun phrases (NP), as in (11) are relatively infrequent (3.6 per cent)

(11) 'So?' **said** Fancourt, **hands in his pockets**. (Galbraith)

Even less frequent (1.7 per cent), and not used by all authors, are adjective phrases (ADJ), as in (12).

(12) 'Blasphemer,' **said** Jerome, not entirely **unserious**. (Smith)

As Table 10.4 shows, there are some differences in the stylistic preferences of the individual authors (the most frequent patterns for each author are shaded). While adverbs/adverbials (ADV) are one of the most preferred patterns in all the authors, PART is preferred by Grisham (34.6 per cent of all modifications), Smith (47.2 per cent) and Galbraith (41 per cent). Ishiguro and Chevalier are stylistically different in several respects. Neither of them uses adjectives, Chevalier uses relatively frequently NPs (7.6 per cent – which is double, the average use across the corpus) and they both frequently use PPs: *to*-PPs (35 per cent of all PPs both in Ishiguro and Chevalier), which signal the direction of the speech, see (13):

(13) 'I don't know what I should do,' she had **said to** me. (Ishiguro)

The second-most preferred PP in Ishiguro is *with*-PP (30 per cent of all PPs) and in Chevalier, it is *in*-PP which is used with the same frequency (twelve instances) as *to*-PP; all the instances of *in*-PP in Chevalier refer to the tone of the voice, the word *voice* is used eleven times and *tone* once, see example (14).

(14) 'It's punishment,' he **said in a low voice**. (Chevalier)

Ishiguro stylistically differs from the other authors also in other respects – in addition to his clear preference to contextualize the character's speech in space (*to*-PP), he also emphasizes the timing of the speech, this is particularly striking with his frequent use of the time adverb *then* (46 times), often placed in the preceding position, as in (15):

(15) But **then** he **said, without turning from the window**: 'Perhaps if he has not returned soon, you should not detain yourself further from your other business.' (Ishiguro)

Another clearly noticeable feature present in Ishiguro's text is his attention to laughter and smiling, which he highlights through the use of *-ing*-PART (13 out of 45 *-ing*-PARTs contain *laughing* or *smiling*) and *with*-PP (fifteen out of twenty contain *laugh* or *smile*), see example (16).

(16) 'She probably will,' I **said, laughing** again myself. (Ishiguro)

Detailed semantic classification is outside the scope of this chapter; however, let us note that the lexicogrammatical patterns point to several trends – in addition to the spatio-temporal modifications discussed above, which is typical for Ishiguro, the speech can be modified, for example, in terms of its acoustic qualities (e.g. the *in*-PP pattern as in (14) and many of the *-ly* adverbs), see also, for example, *over*-PP in (17), which conveys both spatial and acoustic sense of how the speech is delivered.

(17) 'He's a detective,' said Leonora loudly, **over her daughter**. (Galbraith)

Despite the importance of spatio-temporal qualities and specifically, the simultaneity conveyed both explicitly, for example, '*said + at once*', and, implicitly, through using, for example, *-ing*-PART or *with*-PP, the manner how things are said and the descriptions of accompanying circumstances are perhaps the most frequent. These range from descriptions of body language (see above 'laughter' in Ishiguro, example (16)) to conveying complex emotions (example 8). Body language descriptions are extremely frequent, ranging from descriptions of conventionalized gestures (*pointing*) and verbs of 'looking' (*staring*) (cf. Cermakova and Malá 2021) to very specific descriptions such as *taking a sip from his mug of tea, lighting a cigarette* to more unusual ones, such as *polishing off the last of the chocolate*. No doubt there are clear author-specific differences in choices of these descriptions, which would deserve more attention; there is no scope in this chapter to dig deeper into individual authors' styles, as the main aim is to identify recurring lexicogrammatical patterns accompanying the reporting *said* and explore whether these patterns are perceived as such also by the translators. We will aim to do so in a case study of two related PPs: *with* and *without*.

10.5 *Said with* and *said without* in translation to Czech and Finnish

Literary translation is a creative process focusing not only on rendering the semantic content but also on aesthetic qualities and an emphasis on elegant stylistic variation may be expected. The translation solutions aim to capture the content, style and aesthetics of the source text while adapting it to target cultural, stylistic and other textual norms. The individual style of a translator will influence the final product in a significant way as well. In addition to stylistic considerations, translation solutions will be influenced by numerous factors depending on the availability of corresponding, or partly corresponding, lexical items in the target language, corresponding grammatical structures but also functional sentence perspective.

In this section, we present a case study of two related patterns – '*said with*' and '*said without*' and their translations into Czech and Finnish. We are interested in whether *said* is perceived by the translators as a neutral – and repetitive – reporting verb, in which case perhaps more creativity can be expected to compensate for the repetitiveness as discussed in Section 10.2; or, whether *said with/without* is, thanks to its frequency, perceived as a pattern, in which case, we could expect a dominant translation strategy, including a lexical blend[6] if a suitable one exists (see Section 10.5.3). The translations were examined in two steps. First, we map to what degree the translators preserve the nearest equivalent of the English *said* – that is, do the translators use similarly neutral

Czech verb *řekl* (for masculine subjects) or *řekla* (for feminine subjects) and *sanoi* in Finnish? In the next step, we examine the translations with the aim of identifying the corresponding lexicogrammatical patterns of the English *with*-PP and *without*-PP in Czech and Finnish respectively. *With*-PPs were among the dominant PP patterns across our corpus; though, interestingly, it occurs only once in Chevalier. The negative variant, *without*-PP is considerably less frequent, see Table 10.5 for an overview.

As Table 10.5 shows, *with*-PP is one of the dominant PP patterns – 38 per cent of all PPs contain the preposition *with*. Again, there are some clear differences among the authors – Chevalier uses *with*-PP modification only once and this is in combination with a time adverbial, which precedes the PP (*he said at last with a sigh*), while in Galbraith this is the most frequent PP modification. *Without*-PP is much less frequent and though the overall number of instances we identified is low (31) and we cannot therefore make any generalization, it is interesting to note it is relatively more frequent as part of multiple modifications. Semantically, *with*-PPs and *without*-PPs express the 'opposite' meanings and, as we are in the following looking at two typologically different languages, we will examine the translation solutions separately.

English and Czech, both belong to Indo-European languages but represent two different subgroups: English is a Germanic language and Czech is one of

Table 10.5 Frequency distribution of *with*- and *without*-PP. The percentages in brackets indicate the proportion in relation to the overall frequency of PP modifications. 'Premodif.' indicates how many times the PP occurred before the reporting verb; 'multiple mod.' indicates how many times the PP was part of a complex pattern.

Author	PP (all)	*with*-PP	*without*-PP
Ishiguro	65	21 (32%) Premodif. 0 Multiple mod. 1	6 (9.2%) Premodif. 1 Mulitple mod. 3
Grisham	53	20 (38%) Premodif. 2 Multiple mod. 1	6 (11.3%)
Chevalier	34	1 (0.3%) Multiple mod. 1	0
Smith	88	26 (30%) Premodif. 1 Multiple mod. 3	5 (5.6%) Multiple mod. 1
Galbraith	194	95 (49%) Multiple mod. 7	14 (7.2%) Multiple mod. 3
Total	434	163 (38%)	31 (7%)

the Slavic languages. Germanic languages are largely analytic (isolating), while Slavic languages are inflectional. Finnish belongs to Uralic languages and is agglutinative, heavily relying on suffixal affixation (see, e.g., Skalička 1966). The comparison of grammatical categories across the three language is therefore complex. We will first discuss the translation solutions of the verb itself (Section 10.5.1) and then separately congruent and divergent translation solutions (Sections 10.5.2 and 10.5.3).

10.5.1 *said* and its translations

The translations of the *with*-PP display a variety of possible translation solutions as illustrated in example (18): *said* is translated by its nearest equivalent in both languages (congruent translation), and in Czech, a lexicogrammatically equivalent PP accompanies the reporting *řekla* (18a); in Finnish, *sanoi* is modified by an adverb of manner (18b).

(18) 'I did write it down for you,' she **said, with** a slightly forced cheeriness. (Galbraith)

>   (18a) CZ: 'Napsala jsem Vám to,' **řekla s** poněkud nuceným veselím.
>   ("I wrote it for you,' she **said, with** a slightly forced cheeriness.')
>   (18b) FI: 'Laitoin sinulle siitä muistilapun,' hän **sanoi** hieman väkinäisen **pirteästi**.
>   ("I gave you a note on this,' she **said** slightly artificially **cheerfully**.')

Example (19) illustrates occurrences in which the translators opt for a different solution than using the direct equivalent of *said* (divergent translations). In Czech (19a), the translator opts for a lexical blend and does not use a reporting verb at all, instead, uses a verb describing the speaker's body language (*pokrčit rameny* (shrug one's shoulders)), a meaning which is in English expressed within the *with*-PP (*with a shrug*). The semantics is thus preserved but there is a lexicogrammatical shift. It needs to be noted that speech reporting by other than reporting verbs is not unusual in Czech. By blending the reporting verb with the meaning of the PP, the Czech example points to a possible interpretation of the English pattern by the Czech translator as one lexical unit. The 'blending' solution at the same time presents an elegant way of avoiding repetition (see also note 6). In Finnish (19b), the translator uses instead of the neutral verb *sanoi* the verb *sivuutti* (commented) and the PP is conveyed by a nominal phrase in adessive case. Adessive case has a variety of functions – in English, it may correspond to prepositions *on* and *with*. In comparison to English and Czech, Finnish relies on its complex case system to express meanings that would be conveyed in Indo-European languages through prepositional phrases. This solution (19b) semantically enriches the source text by using a more expressive reporting verb.

(19) 'Yeah, well,' **said** Strike **with** a shrug. (Galbraith)

 (19a) CZ: 'No, jo,' **pokrčil** Strike rameny.
 ("Yeah, well,' shrugged Strike his shoulders.')
 (19b) FI: 'No, joo,' **sivuutti** Strike olankohautuksella.
 ("Yeah, well,' Strike commented with a shoulder shrugging_ADESSIVE.')

As discussed above, we have first classified the translations based on the translation of *said:* the translations are congruent when the translators render the English *said* with its direct equivalent *řekl/řekla* and *sanoi* respectively and divergent if other solution is used (see Figure 10.1).

Figure 10.1 clearly shows differences in congruency between Czech and Finnish translations. While Czech translators use a divergent solution, that is, verbs other than *řekl/řekla*, in 65 per cent of cases, in Finnish, the majority of the translations are verb congruent (78 per cent); there are only thirty-six instances of verb-divergent translations, of which twenty-nine occur in Galbraith's translation. In terms of the types of verbs used in the divergent translations, two-thirds of them are discourse structuring (e.g. *vastasi* (answered), *kysyi* (asked)) (for verb typology see Section 10.2; Caldas-Coulthard (1987)). In Czech, Galbraith's and Grisham's translations are fairly balanced between the congruent and divergent categories, while Ishiguro's translator Hanuš opts exclusively for

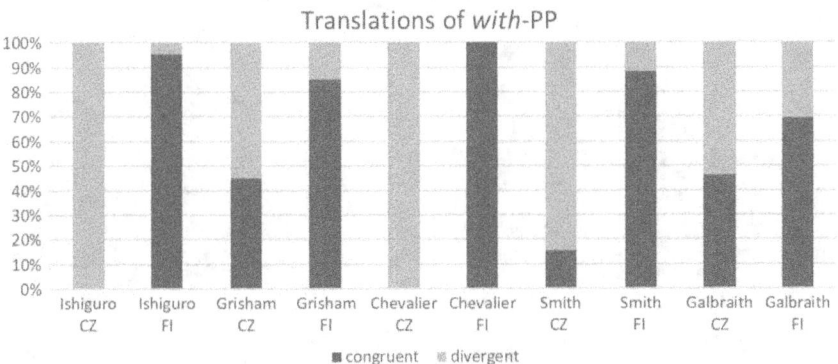

Figure 10.1 *With*-PP: Congruency of verb translations (Czech and Finnish).

divergent translations. Similarly, Smith's translator Diestlerová opts for divergent translations in the majority of cases (85 per cent). Both Galbraith and Grisham represent the genre of fast-paced detective story/thriller and this could possibly be one of the contributing factors. Figure 10.2 shows similar differences in verb congruency between Czech and Finnish in cases where the English source text contains the negative variant: *without*-PP. Apart from three instances, all the occurrences are congruent in Finnish, while 61 per cent of the Czech translations are divergent.

10.5.2 *With*- and *without*-PP: Verb congruent translations

10.5.2.1 Czech

The Czech translators clearly prefer translation solutions with verb variation, but they often opt for congruent translation of the *with*-PP with the main equivalent being the corresponding *s*-PP (see example 20). Galbraith's translator Šenkyřík, in addition, tends to use *a*-clauses ('and'-clauses), see example (21), and occasionally (9 per cent) opts for an adverb. The verb congruent translations are absent in Ishiguro and less frequent in Smith; Smith's translator Diestlerová opts apart from the above mentioned for several other solutions, e. g., *řekla tónem* (said in a tone) with instrumental case, which essentially carries the semantics of 'with' (see also 19).

(20) 'In five minutes,' Chard **said with** a smile. (Galbraith)
    (20a) 'Za pět minut,' **řekl** Chard **s** úsměvem.
    ("In five minutes,' **said** Chard **with** a smile_INSTRUM.')

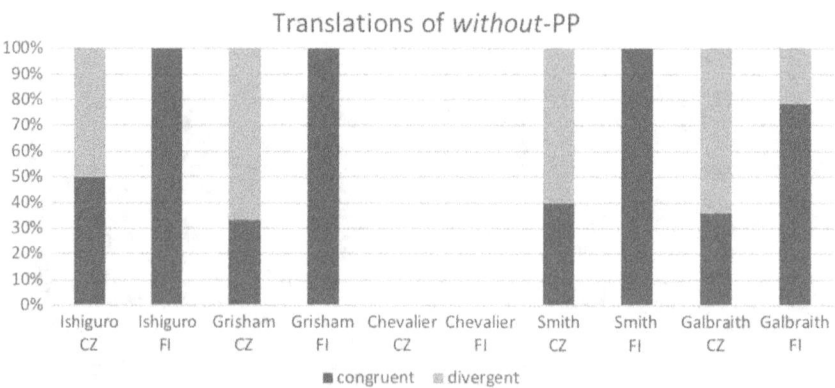

Figure 10.2 *Without*-PP: Congruency of verb translations (Czech and Finnish).

(21) 'Well, she thought she did know,' Strike **said with a shrug**. (Galbraith)

(21a) 'Ona si ale opravdu myslela, že ví, kam jde,' **řekl** Strike **a pokrčil rameny.**

("But she really thought she knew where she was going,' **said** Strike **and shrugged his shoulders.'**)

W*ithout*-PP corresponds mostly to *bez*-PP and semantically equivalent *aniž*-clause (see example 22).

(22) 'You're lying,' he **said without** moving his lips. (Grisham)

(22a) 'Ty lžeš,' **řekl, aniž** pohnul rty.

(" You're lying,' he **said, not/without moving**_3RD_PERSON_PAST_TENSE his lips.')

The analysis shows that when congruent verb *řekl/řekla* is used, Czech translators tend to keep the closest lexicogrammatical equivalents (see Tables 10.6 and 10.7): in the case of *with-PP* in 61 per cent of instances and in the case of *without*-PP in 75 per cent of cases.

Table 10.6 Translation solutions of *with-PP* in verb congruent translations (Czech)

	s	*a*-clause	ADV	Other	Total
Ishiguro	0	0	0	0	0
Grisham	7	2	0	0	9
Chevalier	0	0	0	0	0
Smith	2	0	2	1	4
Galbraith	26	10	5	3	44
Total	35	12	4	4	57

Table 10.7 Translation solutions of *without-PP* in verb congruent translations (Czech)

	aniž-clause (without + VERB)	*bez* (without)	Other	Total
Ishiguro	2	0	1	3
Grisham	1	1	0	2
Chevalier	0	0	0	0
Smith	0	1	1	2
Galbraith	2	2	1	5
Total	5	4	3	12

10.5.2.2 Finnish

As discussed in Section 10.3, Finnish is typologically distant both from English and Czech. The most frequent lexicogrammatical constructions corresponding in Finnish to the English *with*-PP are E-infinitives (in instructive case), essives, *-sti* manner adverbs, and, similarly as in Czech, *ja*-clauses ('and'-clauses) expressing simultaneity. E-infinitive is used to express manner and/or simultaneity of action (see example (23)) (VISK § 516). Essive, which expresses the status of the subject (see 24), may sometimes be close to manner adverbials (in Finnish, typically ending in *-sti*); the *-sti* adverbials may indicate the actions as intentional (animate subjects), but the essive characterizes the state of the subject (VISK § 975). It is worth noting that all of these constructions, except adverbs, represent lexicogrammatical means that tend to emphasize simultaneity in line with the semantics of the source *with*-PP and *without*-PP.

(23) 'Is that so,' I **said, with** a laugh. (Ishiguro)
  (23b) 'Onko niin?' minä **sanoin** naura**en**.
  ("Is that so?' I said laughing_E-INFINITIVE_INSTRUCTIVE')
(24) 'You read that, did you?' **said** Fancourt, **with** vaguely flattered surprise. (Galbraith)
  (24b) 'Vai luitte sen,' **sanoi** Fancourt hieman **imarreltuna** ja hämmästystä äänessään.
  ('... said Fancourt a bit flattered_ESSIVE and surprise_PARTITIVE in his voice_INESSIVE.')

The detailed analysis of the Finnish translations (see Table 10.8) shows that E-infinitive is the most preferred translation solution overall. However, while it is heavily used by Ishiguro's translator Bützow, it does not occur at all in Ruuska's translation of Smith. Ruuska seems to favour adverbs, which are the second-most frequent translation solution overall. It may be worth noticing that Smith

Table 10.8 Translation solutions of *with*-PP in verb congruent translations (Finnish)

	E-inf	Essive	ADV	*ja*-clause	Other	Total
Ishiguro	18	0	1	1	0	20
Grisham	5	0	4	7	0	17
Chevalier	0	0	0	1	0	1
Smith	0	2	16	0	4	23
Galbraith	24	6	19	10	5	66
Total	**47**	**8**	**40**	18	9	127

Table 10.9 Translation solutions of *without*-PP in verb congruent translations (Finnish)

	MA-inf ABE	ilman/vailla ('without')	ADV	E-inf	Other	Total
Ishiguro	6	0	0	0	0	6
Grisham	4	1	1	0	0	6
Chevalier	0	0	0	0	0	0
Smith	3	2	0	0	0	5
Galbraith	4	3	1	2	1	11
Total	17	6	2	2	1	28

herself uses a great variety of adverbs, which may have influenced the translation (see Table 10.4 in Section 10.4).

Finnish has various specific lexicogrammatical means that express absence, which are also reflected in the translations of *without*-PP. The most frequent translation solutions are MA-infinitives in abessive case, *ilman*-PP (without-PP) and *vailla* postposition (without). MA-infinitive in abessive case is the most frequent and is used to express absence (the abessive case itself indicates that something is missing) (VISK § 494), see (25). Table 10.9 shows the distribution of these patterns across the Finnish translations.

(25) 'You're lying,' he **said without** moving his lips. (Grisham)

    (25b) 'Valehtelet', hän **sanoi** huuliaan liikuMAtta.
    ("'You're lying,' he said his lips not moving MA-INFINITIVE-ABESSIVE.')

In both languages, the translators tend to emphasize, by their lexical and grammatical choices, simultaneity of the speech and 'something else happening'. In addition to making use of the corresponding specific lexicogrammatical repertoire in each of the languages, both in Czech and Finnish, we find among the translation solutions *and*-clauses (*a* and *ja* respectively). At the beginning of our pattern classification, we initially excluded *and*-clauses together with other clauses (see Sections 10.3 and 10.4 for discussion), as we felt they were not sufficiently syntactically integrated. The occurrence of *and*-clauses among the translations, makes a case for re-evaluating the status of clauses within the pattern typology of patterns frequently occurring with the verb *said*.[7]

10.5.3 With- and *without*-PP: Divergent translations

In the case of divergent translations, we are interested both in what other verbs are being used to replace *řekl/a* and *sanoi* and the translation solutions of the *with*- and *without*-PPs. In addition to various verbs of speaking, translators also use other verbs. The most varied category is descriptive verbs. They frequently participate in constructions, which we term 'blending'. We use the label 'blending' for translation solutions, in which the meaning of the verb and PP blend as in example (19a) – *said with a shrug* being translated as 'shrugged his shoulders' without further reporting verb.

The PP may sometimes be included in the translation solution as in (26a), where it amplifies the meaning of the source, but more frequently the meaning is captured only by the verb as in (27a). In (26), Robin is angry and the narrator highlights her state of mind within the *with*-PP. Šenkyřík (26a), on the other hand, lets the reader know of Robin's anger already in the choice of the verb. In (27a), Hanuš omits the reporting verb and uses 'blending' solution (*with a laugh* occurs in Ishiguro nine times and it is translated in this way eight times). Blending occurs most frequently in Ishiguro's translation (65 per cent of the verb incongruent translations), Galbraith (22 per cent) and Smith (17 per cent). It does not occur in Kříž's translation of Grisham.

(26) 'You know, there's pride, and then there's stupidity,' **said** Robin, **with one of the first flashes of real temper...** (Galbraith)
   (26a) 'Víte, jedna věc je hrdost a druhá je hloupost,' **odbyla** ho Robin **s prvním zábleskem skutečného hněvu...**
   ("You know, one thing is pride and the other stupidity,' Robin **brushed** him **off with** a first flash of real anger...')
(27) 'I doubt that,' I **said, with a laugh**. (Ishiguro)
   (27a) 'Pochybuji,' **zasmál jsem se.**
   ("I doubt that,' I **laughed**.')

Blending is much more common in the Czech translations than in Finnish, where divergent translations of *said* are overall less frequent, see Table 10.10. In addition to blending, notably in Ishiguro's and Galbraith's translations (and not present at all in Grisham's and Chevalier's translations), other patterns include various 'speaking' verbs (*verba dicendi*) accompanied by the same lexicogrammatical patterns that occur with congruent translations (see Section 10.5.2.1). There are only nineteen occurrences of '*said without*-PP' with verb-divergent translations. The most frequent translation solution here is various verbs of speaking followed by *aniž*-clause.

Table 10.10 Translation solutions of *with-PP* in verb-divergent translations (Czech)

	Blend	Dicendi s	Dicendi ADV	Dicendi a-clause	Omission	Total
Ishiguro	12	4	0	0	0	21
Grisham	0	7	2	2	0	11
Chevalier	0	1	0	0	0	1
Smith	3	11	3	0	0	22
Galbraith	18	23	6	3	1	51
Total	38	46	11	5	1	106

As noted earlier, Finnish translators do not choose verb-divergent solutions frequently. There are only thirty-six instances of 'said *with*-PP' translated by verbs other than *sanoi* and only three instances of 'said *without*-PP'. Among these, blending solution occurs only once, the most frequent solutions are 'speaking' verbs followed by E-infinitive (twenty-two cases altogether) and verbs of speaking with ADV (nine cases). Among the 'speaking' verbs, we find mainly (65 per cent) discourse-structuring verbs (e.g. *vastasi* (answered), *kysyi* (asked)), while in Czech, the diversity of divergent verbs is much wider: descriptive verbs are the most frequent (35 per cent), followed by structuring (22 per cent), discourse signalling (14 per cent) and illocutionary (17 per cent).[8]

Considering the substantial variation among the translators, it seems that the translators sometimes interpret 'said + *with*' and 'said + *without*' as a pattern, but frequently not; the translations seem to be driven more by the individual translator style; genre and source text author style are possibly also contributing to the final translation product. Ishiguro and Smith often cluster in terms of the translation solutions together as do Galbraith and Grisham.

10.6 Conclusions

The repetitive nature of the English reporting verb *said* offers an interesting research space when examined through the lens of translation. In this research, we were interested in *said* occurring as part of a pattern, that is, *said* with further semantic modification, hypothesizing that in these cases it may no longer be perceived by the translators as neutral and repetitive. Our analysis was limited due to constraints on the data availability; however, this limitation allowed us to analyse the data in greater depth. The analysis suggests potentially considerable differences in style (both author and translator) and among genres and more research is needed in this respect.

Our case study of five contemporary English novels and their Czech and Finnish translations shows that *said* occurs in fictional texts both as a neutral verb but is also frequently accompanied by various semantic modifications. We have established five dominant lexicogrammatical patterns that regularly accompany *said* in fictional texts. While their frequency varies across the authors – adverbs/adverbials are consistently the most frequently used modification together with -*ing* participles and various prepositional phrases. The semantics of these patterns covers a range of aspects that are relevant for the character speech; what many of these patterns have in common is the emphasis on simultaneity of the speech and something else – for example, the English -*ing* participles emphasizing simultaneity grammatically (*she said, her voice breaking*) or *with*-phrases carrying the inherent semantics of simultaneity (*said with a laugh*).

We were interested to see whether the patterns we have identified in the English data are perceived as patterns by the translators or whether they tend to treat the reporting verb separately from its modification. Our case study of *with/without*-PP has shown very different results for Czech and Finnish respectively. The Czech translators overwhelmingly prefer to vary the reporting verb and avoid using its main equivalent *řekl/a*. This variation was unsurprising and confirmed earlier studies. In some cases, the translation shift is semantically substantial as the main category of verbs being used as translation equivalents are 'descriptive' verbs. The verbs (i.e. the tendency to avoid repetition) thus seem to be the core element driving the translation into Czech. Finnish translators, on the other hand, tend to use the closest equivalent *sanoi* and infrequently resort to other solutions – if they do, they use mainly 'structuring' verbs which are semantically closer to the neutral verb.

The analysis of the translations of *with/without*-PP shows that the dominant translation equivalent in Czech is the corresponding *s/bez*-PP and *aniž*-clause in both verb congruent and divergent translations. These results suggest that the translators perhaps perceive *said* and *with/without*-PP as separate lexical units and not as a pattern. On the other hand, the high number of 'blending' cases points to their interpretation as one lexical unit. Clearly, more data involving more authors, translators and genres is needed. The analysis of the Finnish translations was challenging for establishing the equivalency of the PP due to different language typologies. The translations of the *without*-PP fully exploited the grammatical means that Finnish offers to indicate absence, the translations of *with*-PP displayed a bigger fluctuation of solutions, though most of these primarily exploited the aspect of simultaneity that the semantics of *with*-PP offers, for example, E-infinite and essive were used but also *and*-clauses.

Our small corpus study shows that individual author and translator styles influence the results substantially and genre is possibly also a factor. The case of Finnish shows various translation 'equivalency' routes: lexical as between the reporting verbs, grammatical as between the PPs but also more broad semantic features, such as simultaneity in this case. This takes us to the beginning of the study, where we were delimiting what constitutes a pattern and what will be excluded, as was the case of *and*-clauses. We have excluded *and*-clauses because we felt that syntactically their integration is not sufficient to form a pattern with the verb. However, our study showed that *and*-clauses occur regularly among the translation solutions of *with*-PP into both languages; what they have in common is the simultaneous nature of speaking and something else. This, then, suggests that the pattern around *said* may need to be conceptualized more broadly than its individual lexicogrammatical realizations; this once again reminds us of Stig Johannson's (2007: 1) words:

> It has often been said that, through corpora, we can observe patterns in language which we were unaware of before or only vaguely glimpsed... My claim is that this applies particularly to multilingual corpora. We can see how languages differ, what they share and – perhaps eventually – what characterises language in general.

Acknowledegement

We would like to thank two anonymous reviewers for their invaluable suggestions.

Notes

1   Potentially, there may be differences in rhetoric norms in British and American fiction. However, as we do control for author differences, these will be noted when appropriate.
2   J. K. Rowling is the acclaimed author of the children's fiction *Harry Potter* series.
3   We would like to thank one of the reviewers for pointing us in the direction of Fabricius-Hansen and Haug (2012).
4   This is statistically significant difference at 0.05 (Chi2 test).
5   The PP category is based on purely formal criteria and as we are primarily interested in stylistic effects we do not distinguish between syntactic functions, for example, between adjuncts and complements. This category is thus rather heterogenous and

more nuanced classification is outside the scope of this chapter; we will, however, comment on some differences throughout the chapter.
6 We would like to thank one of the reviewers who had a personal communication with Petra Diestlerová (Smith's translator), who said she prefers 'blended' counterparts as they present an elegant solution to avoid repetition.
7 The same tendency to choose coordinated clauses as Czech translation counterparts of English adverbial participial clauses was reported in Malá and Šaldová (2015).
8 The remaining 12 per cent cover other types and verbs similarly neutral as *said*.

References

Baker, M. (1993), 'Corpus Linguistics and Translation Studies – Implications and Applications', in M. Baker, G. Francis and E. Tognini-Bonelli (eds), *Text and Technology: In Honour of John Sinclair*, 233–50, Amsterdam: John Benjamins.

Blum-Kulka, S. (2004), 'Shift of Cohesion and Coherence in Translation', in L. Venuti (ed.), *Translation Studies Reader*, 2nd edn, 290–305, New York: Routledge.

Bourne, J. (2002), 'Controlling Illocutionary Force in the Translation of Literary Dialogue', *Target*, 14 (2): 241–61.

Caldas-Coulthard, C. R. (1987), 'Reported Speech in Written Narrative Texts', in M. Coulthard (ed.), *Discussing Discourse*, 149–67, Birmingham: University of Birmingham.

Čermák, F. and A. Rosen (2012), 'The Case of InterCorp, a Multilingual Parallel Corpus', *International Journal of Corpus Linguistics*, 17 (3): 411–27.

Cermakova, A. (2015), 'Repetition in John Irving's Novel a Widow for One Year: A corpus Stylistics Approach to Literary Translation', *International Journal of Corpus Linguistics*, 20 (3): 355–77.

Cermakova, A. and M. Mahlberg (2018), 'Translating Fictional Characters – Alice and the Queen from the Wonderland in English and Czech', in A. Cermakova and M. Mahlberg (eds), *The Corpus Linguistics Discourse: In Honour of Wolfgang Teubert*, 223–53, Amsterdam: John Benjamins.

Cermakova, A. and M. Malá (2021), 'Eyes and Speech in English, Finnish and Czech Children's Literature', in A. Cermakova, S. Oksefjell Ebeling, M. Levin and J. Ström Herold (eds), *Analysing Complex Contrastive Data. Bergen Language and Linguistics Studies*, 11 (1): 185–208.

Corness, P. (2010), 'Shifts in Czech Translations of the Reporting Verb *Said* in English Fiction', in F. Čermák, P. Corness and A. Klégr (eds), *InterCorp: Exploring a Multilingual Corpus*, 159–77, Praha: Nakladatelství Lidové noviny.

Eberhardt, M. (2017), 'Gendered Representation through Speech: The Case of the Harry Potter Series', *Language and Literature*, 26 (3): 227–46.

Egbert, J. and M. Mahlberg (2020), 'Fiction–One Register or Two?: Speech and Narration in Novels', *Register Studies*, 2 (1): 72–101.

Fabricius-Hansen, C. and D. Haug (2012), *Big Events, Small Clauses: The Grammar of Elaboration*, Berlin: Walter de Gruyter.

Fárová, L. (2016), 'Uvozovací slovesa v překladech třech různých jazyků', in A. Cermakova, L. Chlumská and M. Malá (eds), *Jazykové paralely*, 145–61, Praha: Nakladatelství Lidové noviny.

Johansson, S. (2007), *Seeing through Multilingual Corpora: On the Use of Corpora in Contrastive Studies*, Amsterdam: John Benjamins.

Lefevere, A. (1992), *Translation, Rewriting, and the Manipulation of Literary Fame*, London: Routledge.

Levý, J. (2011), *The Art of Translation*, trans. P. Corness, Amsterdam: John Benjamins.

Mahlberg, M., V. Wiegand, P. Stockwell and A. Hennessey (2019), 'Speech-Bundles in the 19th-Century English Novel', *Language & Literature*, 28 (4): 326–53.

Malá, M. and P. Šaldová (2015), 'English Non-finite Participial Clauses as seen through their Czech Counterparts', *Nordic Journal of English Studies*, 14 (1): 232–57.

Mastropierro, L. (2020), 'The Translation of Reporting Verbs in Italian. The Case of the *Harry Potter* Series', *International Journal of Corpus Linguistics*, 25 (3): 241–69.

Mastropierro, L. (2024), 'Gendered Voices in Translation. Reporting Verbs in the Italian Translation of the *Harry Potter* Series', in A. Cermakova and M. Mahlberg (eds), *Children's Literature and Childhood Discourses*, London: Bloomsbury.

Nádvorníková, O. (2020), 'Differences in the Lexical Variation of Reporting Verbs in French, English and Czech Fiction and their Impact on Translation', *Languages in Contrast*, 20 (2): 209–34.

Rojo, A. and J. Valenzuela (2001), 'How to Say Things with Words: Ways of Saying in English and Spanish', *Meta*, 46 (3): 467–477.

San Segundo Ruano, P. (2016), 'A Corpus-Stylistic Approach to Dickens' Use of Speech Verbs: Beyond Mere Reporting', *Language & Literature*, 25 (2): 113–29.

San Segundo Ruano, P. (2017), 'Reporting Verbs as a Stylistic Device in the Creation of Fictional Personalities in Literary Texts', *Journal of the Spanish Association of Anglo-American Studies*, 39 (2): 105–24.

San Segundo Ruano, P. (2018), 'An analysis of Charles Dickens's Gender-Based Use of Speech Verbs', *Gender and Language*, 12 (2): 192–217.

Semino, E. and M. Short (2004), *Corpus Stylistics: Speech, Writing and thought Presentation in a Corpus of English Writing*, London: Routledge.

Skalička, V. (1966), 'Ein typologisches Konstrukt', *Travaux du Cercle Linguistique de Prague*, 2: 157–63.

VISK = Hakulinen, A., M. Vilkuna, R. Korhonen, V. Koivisto, T. R. Heinonen and I. Alho (2004), *Iso suomen kielioppi*, Helsinki: Suomalaisen Kirjallisuuden Seura. http://scripta.kotus.fi/visk (accessed 9 March 2023).

Winters, M. (2007), 'F. Scott Fitzgerald's Die Schönen und Verdammten: A Corpus-based Study of Speech-act Report Verbs as a Feature of Translators' Style', *Meta*, 52 (3): 412–25.

11

From Dashes to Dashes? – A Contrastive Corpus Study of Dashes in English, German and Swedish

Jenny Ström Herold and Magnus Levin

11.1 Introduction

Punctuation has long been overlooked in translation studies, which is somewhat unexpected as the appropriate use of punctuation marks is no trivial matter for translators (Shiyab 2017: 93–101). However, recent years have seen a growing interest overall in different languages (e.g. Wollin 2018; Frankenberg-Garcia 2019; Rössler, Besl and Saller 2021). The present study focuses on frequencies, forms and functions of dash-introduced text from an English-German-Swedish perspective, based on nonfiction data from our own parallel corpus LEGS, which is described in Section 11.2. This paper is our third investigation on punctuation in contrast, where previously colons (Ström Herold and Levin 2021) and brackets (Levin and Ström Herold 2021) have been addressed.

Our starting point is the observation that many nonfiction writers have a penchant for dashes. This punctuation mark is often quite prevalent in originals, and when translated it can produce considerable variation, as shown in (1):

(1) Schweigen also, Stille – *'für mich ist das etwas sehr, sehr Schönes'*. Einerseits. Andererseits ist *Merkel geradezu eine Plaudertasche, eine gesellige Vielquatscherin, die eine gute Unterhaltung schätzt.*

So there it was: discretion, silence – 'To me it has great beauty.' This is not always the case – *because Merkel is a sociable person who likes a good natter.*

Wer sie ständig auf Reisen begleiten muss – *ihre Sprecher, die Referenten* –, sollten schon etwas mehr zum Leben beizutragen haben als lediglich Fachwissen: Fußball, Musik, Oper, Kunst, Geschichte – *Merkel schätzt gebildete Menschen, die ihren Grips stimulieren.* Aber es gibt Unterschiede im Umgang – *vor allem beim Thema Offenheit.* (LEGS; German original)	Those who travel with her – *her spokesmen and advisers* – need more than just knowledge in their particular field: they need to know about other things, such as football, music, opera, art, history. *Merkel values well-educated people who stimulate her mind.* But her approach varies according to the company, *particularly when it comes to being able to speak openly.* (LEGS; English translation)

The German original contains two clauses and two phrases introduced by dashes. In sentence-final position, single dashes are used, and in medial position (known as parentheticals) pairs of dashes. The text introduced or enclosed by dashes expresses both more subjective ideas, such as Merkel's own assessment in the first sentence, and more neutral, content-oriented elaborations as in: – *ihre Sprecher, die Referenten* –. The English translator, in turn, retains the first two original dashes but adds one in between (– *because Merkel is. . .*), and substitutes the last two dashes with a period and a comma. Direct transfer, that is, retention, is often observed as the primary translation strategy for punctuation marks, sometimes reaching as high as 90 per cent (Wollin 2018), but as the extract above suggests, other competing strategies are also applied.

Using our trilingual data set-up with originals and translations, it is possible to disentangle language-specific preferences and translation-induced changes. The following research questions concerning English, German and Swedish originals and translations will be addressed:

- What are the frequencies of dashes in nonfiction text?
- What functions, forms and sentence positions do dash-introduced text segments take?
- How are dashes rendered in translations in terms of being, for example, retained, added or omitted, and what other punctuation marks are used as correspondences?
- To what extent do translations adhere to the target-language norms and/or to what extent does source-text usage 'shine through' in translations?

As for the structure of this chapter, Section 11.2 gives an overview of the LEGS corpus and our search procedures, and Section 11.3 presents previous studies on punctuation in general and dashes in particular. Section 11.4 starts with the results for originals and then moves on to the patterns observed in translations.

11.2 Material and method

This study is based on LEGS, the Linnaeus University English-German-Swedish corpus (Levin and Ström Herold 2021). This parallel corpus enables comparisons across three original languages and translations into each of the two other languages, which makes it an excellent resource in both contrastive and translation-based studies. The texts included in the corpus can be said to belong to popular nonfiction, including both narrative genres such as popular science texts, biographies and history, and instructive texts such as books on cooking and personal training. The genres are fairly evenly represented, but with English originals having a slightly lower proportion of instructive texts. Moreover, it should be noted that individual texts are not homogeneous – popular science texts typically contain (auto)biographical sections apart from the scientific parts, and instructive texts are not only operative but are also very technical in their narratives.

The English and Swedish originals comprise eleven texts each and the German nine. Since several books were co-translated, this study is based on the output of more than one hundred authors or translators. Each author and translator is represented only once, thereby minimizing the influence of author- and translator-specific preferences. The overall structure of the corpus is visualized in Figure 11.1.

Our study covers almost 4.5 million words broken down into the proportions per the sub-corpus shown in Table 11.1.

When digitizing and aligning the texts for the corpus, we consistently rendered all dashes as the short en dash (–), in spite of some texts[1] originally having the longer em dash (—) (for guidelines on em dashes, see *New Hart's Rules: The Oxford Style Guide* 2014: 87–8). Using our custom-made LEGS interface, we searched for dashes in originals, retrieving these with the corresponding segments from the translations. We also retrieved target-text segments containing dashes where there was no dash in the corresponding original text segment. For all instances, we determined manually if the dashes

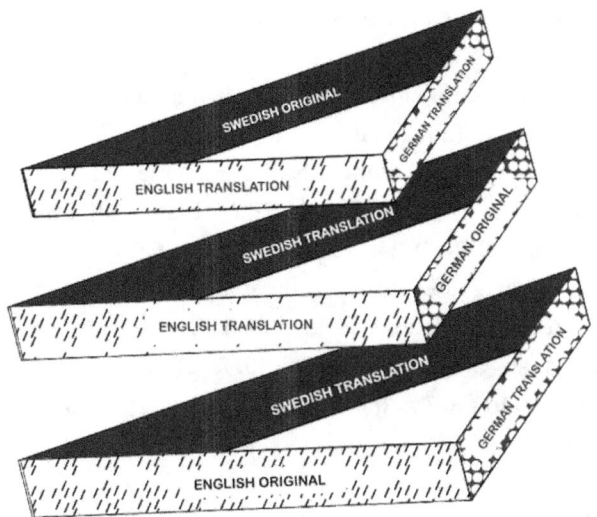

Figure 11.1 The structure of the Linnaeus University English-German-Swedish corpus (LEGS).

Table 11.1 Word counts for the LEGS sub-corpora

		English translation	German translation	Swedish translation
English originals	591,000	*	575,000	573,000
German originals	385,000	445,000	*	392,000
Swedish originals	471,000	516,000	462,000	*

in the original and the translation matched each other. We also classified the dash-introduced text according to form, sentence position (medial or final) and function (interpersonal or content-oriented). In all, more than 13,500 dashes and almost 6,200 non-dashes were identified and classified.

11.3 Dashes and related punctuation marks in monolingual and contrastive studies

As mentioned above, our previous punctuation studies have so far addressed colons (Ström Herold and Levin 2021) and brackets (Levin and Ström Herold 2021). Of these, brackets, as correlative marks, would seem to share the most functions with dashes, as in their use to indicate parentheticals (see example

(1) above). Therefore, the present findings will mainly be contrasted with our results on brackets. As will be discussed below, style guides often address these two punctuation marks in close proximity, highlighting both similarities and differences in terms of functional or stylistic qualities. However, usage guides and standard grammars also mention their (quasi-)interchangeability with other punctuation marks, in particular commas, and, occasionally, colons (Quirk et al. 1985: 1629; Leech et al. 2009: 245; Crystal 2015: 85–6, 158).

Comparing usage guides from the three languages, we notice that similar functions and recommendations are identified and given for dashes (*Guidelines from The Language Council of Sweden* 2017: 214ff; German Duden (*RgD*) 1997: 292ff; *New Hart's Rules: The Oxford Style Guide* 2014: 86ff). These can be summarized as follows:

- Dashes are used for symbolizing a pause, building 'suspense'.
- Dashes are used for parenthetical insertions or final additions which may contain an explanation, a summary or a constraint.
- Dashes are used to set off a clause or phrase from the rest of the sentence – a dash 'visually isolates a word or a phrase' (Lauchman 2010: 114).
- Dashes should not be overused.

Dashes thus serve similar functions across languages, but the distribution of a particular punctuation mark may nevertheless differ greatly depending on language and 'local conventions and traditions' (Nádvorníková 2020: 30). The colon is a case in point. As shown in Ström Herold and Levin (2021), colons are more common in German than in English and Swedish nonfiction, both in originals and translations. Albeit lacking statistical evidence, Eskesen and Fuglsang (1998) suggest a similar colon affinity in French, compared to Danish.

Dashes are used in pairs (as correlative marks) or as single instances, the former enclosing a medial, parenthetical insertion, the latter introducing a final addition, as already illustrated in (1). Particularly for medial usage, style guides and grammars highlight the interchangeability of dashes with brackets and commas. However, it is also repeatedly stressed that dashes and brackets differ in terms of their stylistic value, dashes having a more informal, dramatic flair than both brackets and commas (Quirk et al. 1985: 1629; Leech et al. 2009: 245; Crystal 2015: 85–6, 158). Lauchman (2010: 114–15) even proposes an 'emphasis hierarchy', where information included in dashes has strong emphasis, information between commas has no emphasis (default case), and bracketed information has low emphasis:

(2) a. The President – *reversing his position* – now opposes the legislation. (strong emphasis)
b. The President, *reversing his position*, now opposes the legislation. (no emphasis/default)
c. The President (*reversing his position*) now opposes the legislation. (weak emphasis)

The recommendation that dashes should not be overused might thus be connected with this assumed informal or 'marked' value. This air of informality may be contrasted with brackets, which, in Leech et al.'s (2009: 245–6) words, are typical for 'serious written style'. Interestingly, they also note that dashes appear to be decreasing in use in British English.

The versatility and multifunctionality of punctuation marks were also observed in our brackets study (Levin and Ström Herold 2021), which proposes a typology for bracket use. This model will also serve as a basis for the present investigation on dashes. Two primary functions were identified: the 'interpersonal' and the 'content-oriented' one. These labels were inspired by House's (e.g. 1997, 2011) seminal work on communicative styles in English and German, English writing supposedly being more interpersonal, whereas German is more content-oriented. We noticed that bracketed text may hold factual elaborations on previous content, as in (3), or material where the author expresses their own opinions or, as in (4), addresses the reader (Levin and Ström Herold 2021: 128):

(3) Imperial Oil *(of which Exxon owns a majority share)* sank [...]. (LEGS; English original; content-oriented)
(4) [...] while the bees are visiting your bee-friendly *plants (if you haven't got any, I hope you'll plant some next spring)* [...]. (LEGS; English original; interpersonal)

We found that in all three languages, content-oriented brackets are more common than interpersonal brackets, accounting for around three-quarters of all tokens. Assuming that dashes would have an informal air and strong emphasis, the question is whether we might see a higher frequency of interpersonal use of dashes. Moreover, we noticed that most brackets are retained in translations, retention rates reaching between 75 and 85 per cent in the different language pairs, where Swedish translators retain the most and English the least. This also substantiates the strong tendency for direct transfer found previously for punctuation marks (Wollin 2018; Frankenberg-Garcia 2019: 23; Ström Herold and Levin 2021). Brackets are, however, also added in translation, which makes intuitive sense. Baumgarten, Meyer and Özçetin (2008: 190) suggest that brackets are 'typical sites of translational explicitation' as they are used by translators to clarify information to the target-text reader. Finally, Levin and Ström Herold's (2021) results show that translations partly move towards target-language norms, but some degree of 'translationese' is present, similar to the findings by Rodríguez-Castro (2011) where at least some of the investigated punctuations marks – that is, periods, colons and em dashes – in English-to-Spanish translations produced 'translationese' (for a discussion of the term, see Gellerstam (1986)).

11.4 Quantitative and qualitative findings on dashes

In the following, the quantitative and qualitative results will be presented. Section 11.4.1 starts with the frequencies, functions and positions of dashes in originals, comparing the findings with those for brackets from Levin and Ström Herold (2021). Section 11.4.2 focuses on translations, on how often dashes are retained or changed in translations, and what their translation correspondences are.

11.4.1 Dashes in original texts

11.4.1.1 The frequencies and functions of dashes

First, we will consider the frequencies in the three sub-corpora with originals. These are given in Figure 11.2.

In the LEGS data, German writers use dashes the most and English the least, Swedish taking an intermediate position. The stronger German preference is quite consistent across the different texts in the corpus – the five highest frequencies of dashes were found in German texts, while none of the eight with the lowest scores are German. The English and Swedish data are more evenly distributed in their preferences but with a slightly higher frequency in the latter. A possible reason for the German dash affinity in our material relates to the grammatically determined punctuation principles adhered to in German. In German, a punctuation mark must always be inserted before a subordinate clause (Duden (*RgD*) 1997: 421). The default punctuation mark is the comma, but, as also noted by Neef (2021: 4), other punctuation marks, such as the dash, may serve the same segmentation purpose. This is seen in (5), where the German author chooses the marked dash over the 'default comma' to indicate a pause and

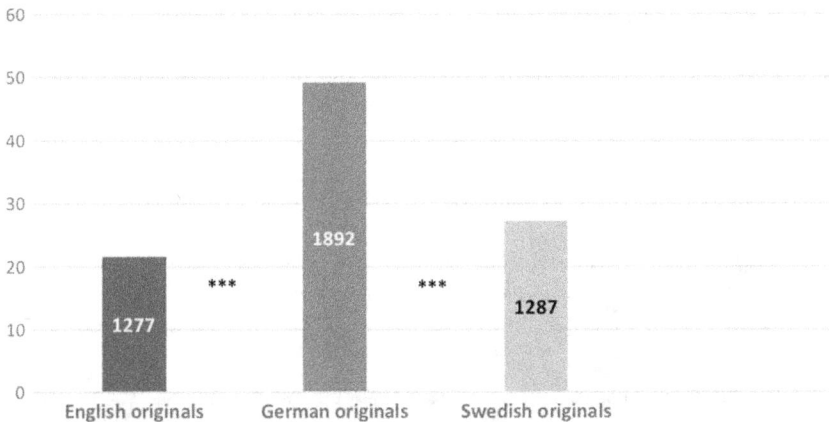

Figure 11.2 Dashes in English, German and Swedish originals in LEGS per 10,000 words.

stronger emphasis. In our material, this is seen repeatedly with the subordinator *weil* (because).

(5) 2012 beschloss man, die Delegationsgespräche simultan und nicht konsekutiv übersetzen zu lassen – *weil es Zeit spare*. (LEGS; German original) (because it saves time).

We will further investigate the reasons for this variation, in particular the observed German fondness for dashes, but at least for now, dashes seem to support Nádvorníková's (2020: 30) observation that different punctuation marks are used to variable extents in different languages.

From a comparison with the frequencies of brackets in Levin and Ström Herold (2021: 124), it is evident that there is cross-linguistic variation in the use of these two punctuation marks. This is illustrated in Figure 11.3.

Dashes are as frequent as brackets in English originals, but two-and-a-half times more frequent than brackets in both German and Swedish. The relatively weaker preference for dashes in English is unexpected in view of the proposed informality of this language (House 1997, 2011). Instead, it is the more content-oriented style of German that in particular relies on dashes (House 1997, 2011). These slightly unexpected findings will be discussed further below.

Our next focus concerns the functions dashes fulfil. As mentioned above, we applied the same classification scheme as for brackets (Levin and Ström Herold 2021: 127–8). In this classification, there are two primary categories:

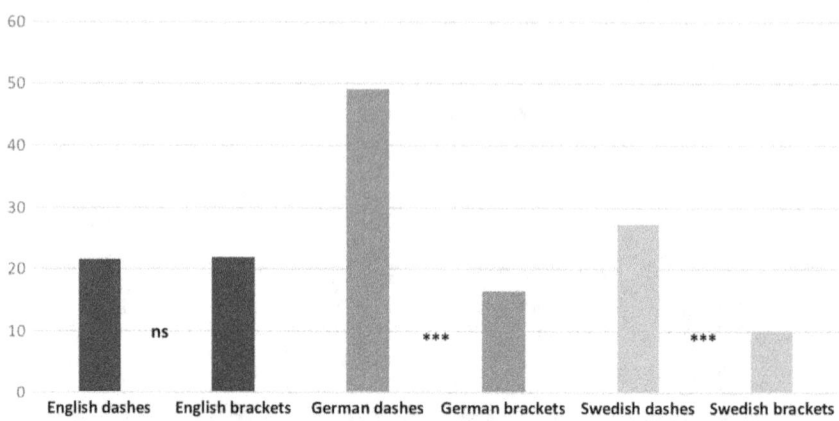

Figure 11.3 Frequencies of dashes and brackets in originals per 10,000 words (partly based on Levin and Ström Herold 2021: 124).

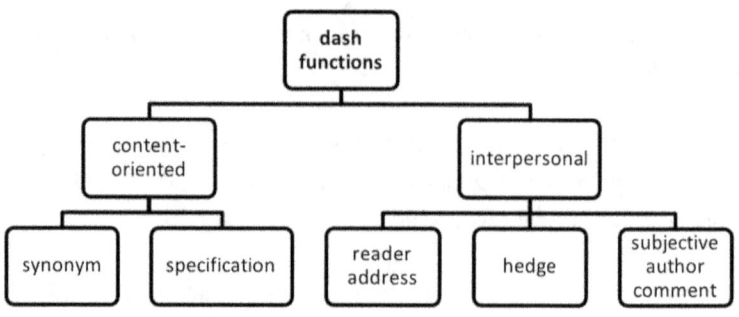

Figure 11.4 Functional categories of dashes in the LEGS material.

content-oriented and interpersonal dashes with five sub-categories as shown in Figure 11.4 and exemplified below.

The sub-category of synonyms includes recurrent types where dashes introduce foreign-language quotes, as in (6), and alternative terms, as in (7). The most prominent sub-category among the content-oriented instances is specification, where writers add factual information to the discourse, as in (8) and (9).

1.1 Content-oriented: synonym

(6) Back in Paris, where the restaurants and cabarets were full, the favourite song was 'J'attendrai' – *'I'll wait'*. (LEGS; English original)

(7) The first time I used psilocybin at sufficiently high doses, the anxiolytic – *anxiety decreasing* – effect lasted 3 to 6 months. (LEGS; English original)

I.II Content-oriented: specification

(8) As he thought about the microprocessor – *a chip that had an entire central processing unit on it* – he had an insight. (LEGS; English original)
(9) That's because the fracking process is leaky – *methane leaks at every stage of production* [. . .]. (LEGS; English original)

The interpersonal category 'reader address' subsumes imperatives and questions directed to readers, as in (10) and (11). In our study on brackets (Levin and Ström Herold 2021: 128), many address instances involve meta-textual comments guiding readers through the text (e.g. *(see Chapter 4)*), but this usage is virtually absent with dashes. The next interpersonal sub-category, the hedge, modifies the truth value of the sentence in which it occurs. Thus, the hedge in (12) restricts the tolerance of affairs to the upper classes, and in (13) the position of the German Chancellor is relativized. Finally, in subjective author comments, writers include their own personal evaluations of the propositions. In (14), the author evaluates the state of affairs with a short sentence-final noun phrase, while in (15), the medial clause includes a discourse marker (*in fact*), a self-reference (*I*), and hyperbole (*always*) apart from evaluative adjectives.

II.I Interpersonal: reader address

(10) You don't have to stick to a once-per-minute regimen – *feel free to rest your mind* [. . .]. (LEGS; English original)
(11) If Assad goes today, a political vacuum emerges – *who will fill it?* (LEGS; English original)

II.II Interpersonal: hedge

(12) By the latter years of the nineteenth century, attitudes to affairs – *at least amongst the upper classes* – were generally tolerant [. . .]. (LEGS; English original)
(13) Israel ist – *für Merkels Verhältnisse* – Emotion pur. (LEGS; German original) (Israel is – by Merkel's standards – pure emotion)

II.III Interpersonal: subjective author comment

(14) Under Roman rule, a large group of nations, [...] were able for a significant period to coexist without fighting one another [...] – *a remarkable achievement*. (LEGS; English original)

(15) Pigeons don't look particularly bright – *in fact I've always felt that they have a rather vacant expression, and they do an awful lot of mindless cooing* – but nonetheless they are capable of truly amazing feats of navigation. (LEGS; English original)

Figures 11.5–11.7 present the distributions of the functions dashes fulfil in originals. Figure 11.5 focuses on the two primary categories, Figure 11.6

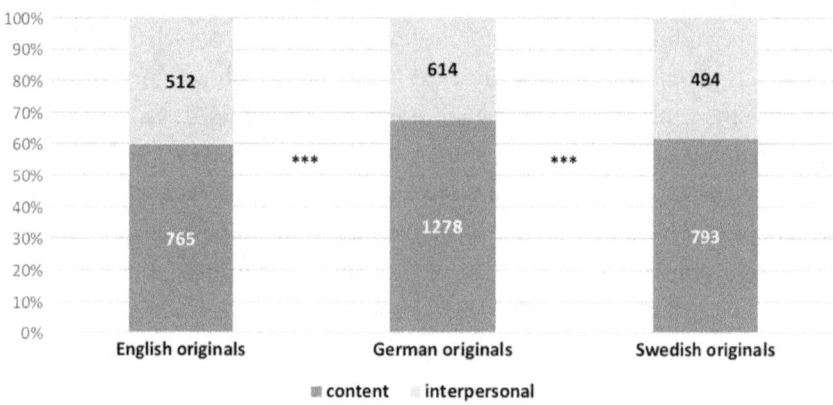

Figure 11.5 Proportions of primary functions of dash-introduced text.

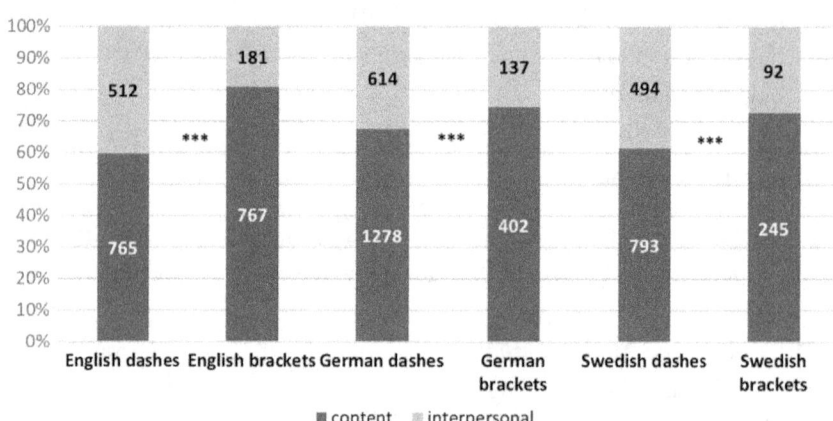

Figure 11.6 Primary functions of dash-introduced versus bracket-introduced text.

compares these to those of brackets and Figure 11.7 breaks down the data into the five subtypes.

Figure 11.5 shows that German uses significantly more content-oriented dashes than English and Swedish, which in turn are very similar to each other.[2] With dashes, German has a lower proportion of interpersonal instances than English, a finding that supports House's (e.g. 1997, 2011) conclusions regarding English communicative style being more interpersonal than German.

As a further elucidation of the usage of dashes, we compared the primary functions with those of brackets in Levin and Ström Herold (2021: 129). The combined results support the idea of dashes being more associated with informality or subjectivity than the more information-based brackets. For all three languages, dashes have a higher proportion of interpersonal uses than brackets, as shown in Figure 11.6,[3] though there are no extreme differences in view of both punctuation marks being associated with the content function in most instances.

Moving on to the five sub-categories, Figure 11.7 gives the frequencies in originals. In all three originals, most dashes introduce specifications, which means that dashes are mainly used for factual information, as is also the case for brackets (Levin and Ström Herold 2021). The frequencies of subjective author comments, the second-most common category in both English and German, nevertheless indicate that a sizeable proportion of dashes involves subjective evaluations. Reader address is the second-most common function in Swedish and is relatively frequent also in German while being very rare in the English data. This latter point is likely due to the less instructive nature of the texts in the English sub-corpus. Hedges and, in particular, synonyms are very rare with

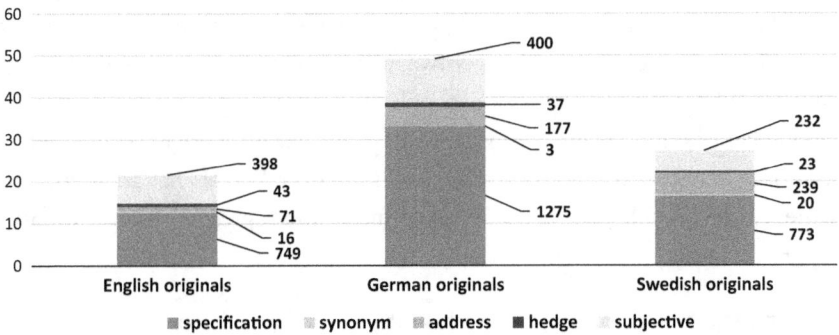

Figure 11.7 Sub-categories of content-oriented and interpersonal functions of dash-introduced text per 10,000 words.

dashes. In the three original corpora, synonyms are much more rarely placed after a dash – less than once in a hundred dashes – than in brackets, where it is one in six. Thus, the two studies indicate that synonyms and hedges are conventionally associated with brackets. Examples include measurements (*311 ounces (100 milliliters)*) and name variants (*near Kolozsvár (Cluj)*). The fact that synonyms are more likely to appear in brackets can be attributed to Lauchman's (2010: 114–15) proposal of weak emphasis being associated with brackets. The dash would be too marked to introduce many synonyms, as synonyms by definition involve strictly factual additions.

11.4.1.2 The forms and positions of dash-introduced text

In the following, form relates to whether the dash-introduced text constitutes a clause as in (9), or a phrase, as in (8). We distinguish two positions: medial parenthetical pairs of dashes and sentence-final single-dash occurrences. For brackets, Levin and Ström Herold (2021: 129–30) found notable differences between the languages in these respects. All three languages mainly put phrases – rather than clauses – in brackets, but this tendency is significantly stronger in German. This German predilection for phrases was attributed to a previously observed avoidance of verb-final subordinate clauses (cf. Becher 2011) and to a general preference for nominal style. Levin and Ström Herold (2021: 127) also note tendencies for different positions of brackets: most brackets occur in the medial position, but German has the strongest preference for this and Swedish the weakest.

Figure 11.8 shows that there are both similarities and differences between the source languages regarding positions and forms of dash-introduced text. In all the languages, sentence-final clauses are the most common uses, and sentence-medial clauses are the least frequent. German and Swedish originals are very similar regarding form and position, while English differs significantly from these languages.[4] In the former two, phrases also favour the final position, whereas in English the two positions for phrases are used equally. Beginning with the medial position for phrases, English in particular seems to have a tendency for listing items between dashes, as in (16). Moreover, English has an affinity for sentence-medial full clauses. In (17), the full clause represents a digression in reported speech.

(16) In most of the stories based on his interviews that day – *in Time, Business Week, the Wall Street Journal, and Fortune* – the Macintosh was mentioned. (LEGS; English original)

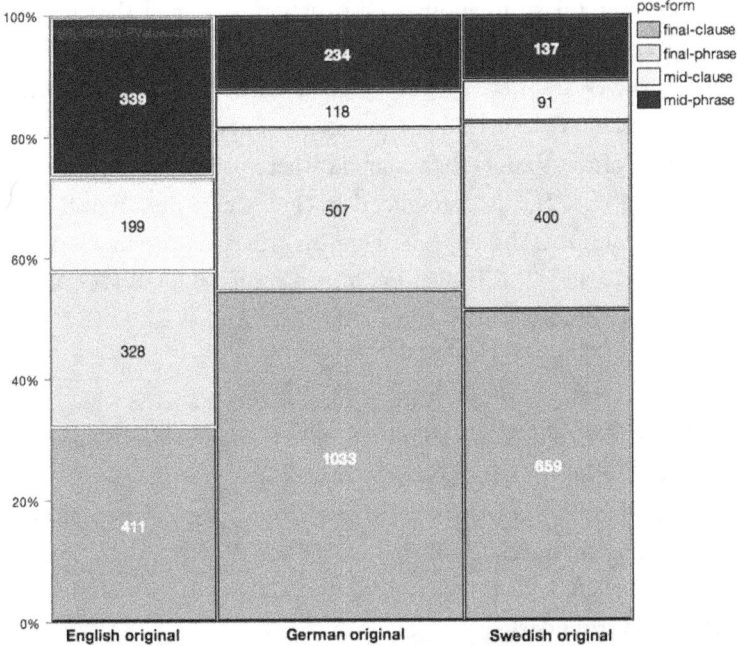

Figure 11.8 The positions of clauses and phrases introduced by dashes.

(17) In fact, one of the earliest, best CrossFit workouts – *I think it's called 'Nancy'* – is run 400 meters, and then overhead squat 95 pounds 15 times. (LEGS; English original)

Overall, most dashes occur in final position, but this preference is significantly higher in German and Swedish than in English. The high frequencies of sentence-final clauses largely explain why there are more dashes in the German and Swedish data than in the English.

Concluding the results on the form, position and function of the two punctuation marks, English writers more often put phrases after dashes, while German writers instead often put phrases in brackets. German and Swedish writers typically use dashes to place clauses in sentence-final position, and dashes are more interpersonal than brackets (cf. Levin and Ström Herold 2021). The remaining parts of this study are devoted to how dashes are rendered in translations.

11.4.2 Dashes in translations

11.4.2.1 Congruent and noncongruent translations of dashes

This sub-section compares the frequencies in originals and translations, distinguishing three different correspondence types: (I) retention, (II) replacement *from* a dash to another punctuation mark and (III) replacement *to* a dash from another punctuation mark. The most straightforward strategy, retention, involves transferring the original dashes to the translation (i.e. congruent translation), as in (18). The noncongruent strategies involve two subcases. The first of these concerns instances where original dashes are replaced with something else. This is exemplified in (19), where the English translator has opted for commas. The opposite happens when other punctuation marks are replaced by dashes. This is seen in (20), where the translator exchanges the original commas for dashes.

I Retention

(18) Auch Brasilien und Indien stünden – *neben China und Russland* – auf der Seite der Skeptiker. (LEGS; German original)
Brazil and India – *as well as China and Russia* – were also sceptical. (LEGS; English translation)

II Replacement from dash

(19) Im August 1940 – *einen Monat nach der deutschen Besetzung von Paris* – notiert er: [...] (LEGS; German original) (one month after the German occupation of Paris)
In August 1940, *two months after Paris was occupied*, he noted: [...]. (LEGS; English translation)

III Replacement to dash

(20) They believed they could do it, *and they did.* (LEGS; English original)
Sie glaubten, sie könnten es schaffen – *und sie schafften es.* (LEGS; German translation) (and they made it)

Regarding the translation of punctuation, Levin and Ström Herold (2021: 131–3) identified two competing forces. On the one hand, translators moved towards target-language conventions and, on the other, they added information for a more explicit target text, most typically in the form of short synonyms, for example, in the spelling-out of an acronym *the RSPB > die RSPB (Königliche Gesellschaft für Vogelschutz)* (Levin and Ström Herold 2021: 135). Most translations, regardless of language pairs, adhered to both these tendencies. For dashes, there is less evidence for the latter trend, one reason being that dashes are seldom used to include clarifying information such as synonyms (see Figure 11.7).

Figure 11.9 shows that these two forces go a long way towards explaining the trends for dashes as well, but that there are exceptions.[5]

The translations from English and German show the same trend of moving towards target-text norms: the German and Swedish translations from English, the source language with the fewest dashes, contain higher frequencies than their English originals, while English and Swedish translations from German use fewer dashes than the German source texts. For the latter language pairs (GE > EN/SW), the translations still contain far more than their respective source-language corpora, so that, for instance, English translations from German have 1.8 times more dashes than the English originals. The source-text preferences thus 'shine through' in the translations, as also found in Rodríguez-Castro's English-Spanish data (2011). The translations from the Swedish originals, however, do not move towards target-language norms, which is a puzzling finding.[6] The translations of dashes and brackets thus seem to follow slightly different principles. For both, movement towards target-language norms is important. For brackets, textual explicitation is also central, something which is rarely seen with dashes.

Several studies have shown that punctuation marks are usually retained to a very high extent in translations, an example being the 75–85 per cent retention rate of brackets in Levin and Ström Herold (2021: 134). Figure 11.10 shows there is more variation in the proportions of retained dashes, all three pairs of translations producing significant differences.[7] Once again, the translations from Swedish diverge in that the English translators retain more dashes than the German do.[8]

Compared to brackets, dashes seem to invite more scope for variation to translators. With dashes, the retention rates range from 87 per cent (EN > SW) to

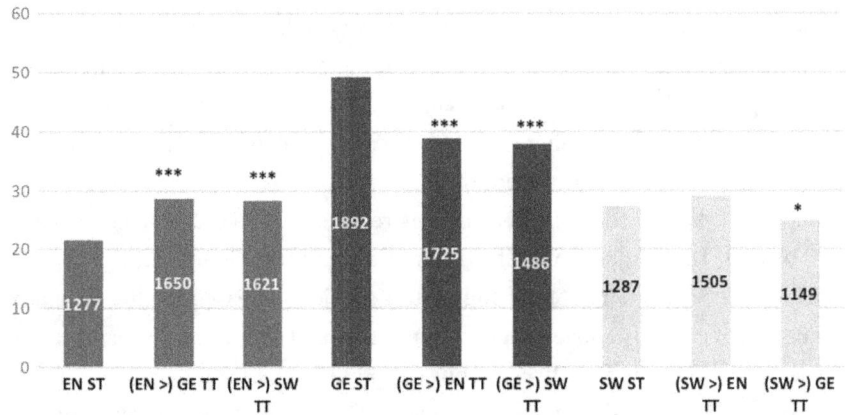

Figure 11.9 Frequencies per 10,000 words of dashes in originals and translations.

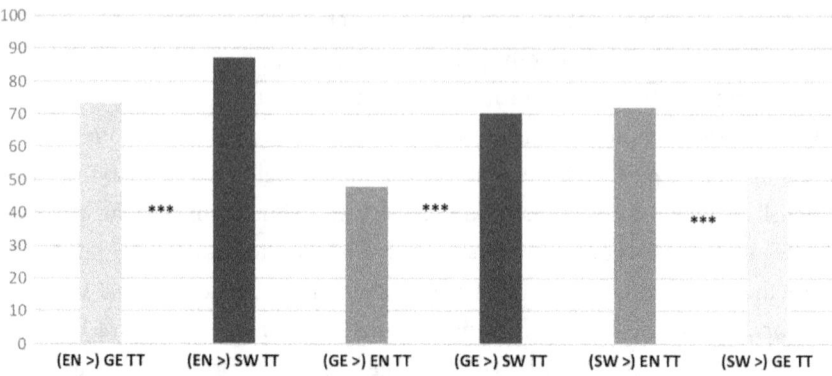

Figure 11.10 Proportions of retained dashes in translations.

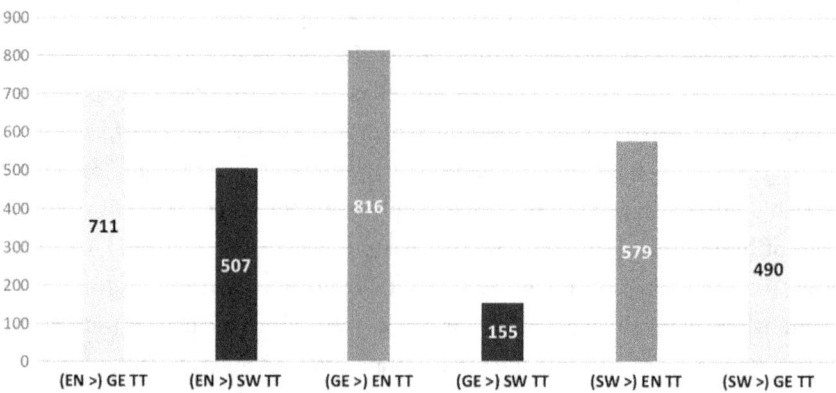

Figure 11.11 Real numbers for added dashes.

48 per cent (GE > EN). We can only speculate as to why English translators tend to change the least and Swedish translators the most. But, in accordance with our previous studies on punctuation, this might be explained by status differences: since English is the only truly global language, translators into 'minor' languages would be more likely to adhere to English patterns than the other way around. These different 'degrees of freedom' in translations are also reflected in the 'addition' of dashes, that is, when there is replacement to a dash (see (25) and (26) below). The numbers of such additions are given in Figure 11.11.

Here the results consistently follow the predictions based on the language status considerations above: English translators add the most dashes, Swedish the least and German in between. Thus, the LEGS translation data indicate that the frequencies of dashes generally move towards target-text conventions and that English translators are the most likely to change punctuation marks.

A closer look at text segments where dashes are either replaced or removed reveals some interesting patterns. As noted by Englund Dimitrova (2014: 96), translators often tone down punctuation marks that they perceive as 'overused' in originals. This is seen in (21), where the unusual occurrence of two pairs of dashes in a single sentence is reduced to only one in the German translation, commas replacing the first pair.

(21) 'In fact, an Islamic revival – *already abetted from the outside not only by Iran but also by Saudi Arabia* – is likely to become the mobilizing impulse for the increasingly pervasive new nationalisms, determined to oppose any reintegration under Russian – and hence infidel – control.' (LEGS; English original)

'Eine islamische Wiedererweckung, *die bereits von außen her vom Iran, aber auch von Saudi-Arabien Unterstützung erfährt,* wird wahrscheinlich aggressive Nationalismen beflügeln, die jeglicher Reintegration unter russischer – und mithin ungläubiger Herrschaft entschiedenen Widerstand entgegensetzen.' (German translation)

Conversely, in (22), dashes are introduced in the target text to clarify segmentation and sentence structure. The dashes make the listed items visually clearly separated from the rest of the text. Arguably, the repeated use of commas in the original is less optimal for segmentation.

(22) Jeder Verbrecher könnte Eigentümer einer dieser Firmen sein, *Mörder, Mafiosi oder Diktatoren*. Mossfon würde ihnen professionell zu Diensten sein – und weiter keine Fragen stellen. (LEGS; German original)

These companies could be owned by any manner of criminal – *murderers, mafiosi, dictators* – and Mossfon is glad to be at their service. (English translation)

The next section takes a closer look at the 'non-dash' punctuation marks in noncongruent translations. As already hinted at, the comma is a prominent alternative to the dash.

11.4.2.2 Punctuation marks in noncongruent translations

For noncongruent translations, we identified five major options: the three punctuation marks colon, comma and period, and the omission or addition of either a dash or a complete text segment introduced by a dash. In (23), the dash is removed from the translation, while the text is kept. In (24), the dash and the text are omitted altogether. In contrast, the translation in (25) adds a dash where there is no original punctuation, and (26) adds a segment introduced by a dash, summarizing information from preceding paragraphs.

Replacement from dash: punctuation omission

(23) She had a beautiful healthy baby boy – *she was unassailable*. (LEGS; English original)

Als Mutter eines bildhübschen, gesunden kleinen Jungen *war sie unanfechtbar*. (LEGS; German translation) (as (a) mother of . . . she was unassailable)

Replacement from dash: text omission

(24) De kan se ut hur som helst – *och gör det också*. (LEGS; Swedish original) (they can look whatever way – and do it too)

They can look completely different to one another. (LEGS; English translation)

Replacement to dash: punctuation addition

(25) Man kan samla nästan vad som helst på nätterna *utom flugor*. (LEGS; Swedish original)

You can collect almost anything at night – *except flies*. (LEGS; English translation)

Replacement to dash: text addition

(26) Alla tre lobbyorganisationerna har kvinnliga VD. (LEGS; Swedish original) (all three lobby organizations have female CEOs)

These three lobby organizations – *in Australia, the UK and USA* – have female CEOs. (LEGS; English translation)

In all four instances, the translators' choices have considerable impact on the message: in (23), the content of the second clause is backgrounded, while in (24) the final restriction is instead highlighted. The omission of the pleonastic clause in (25) does not hinder comprehension but arguably makes the translation less emphatic. The added clarification in (26) makes the translation more explicit. The proportions of the different alternatives are given in Figures 11.12 and 11.13.[9]

Commas are the most frequent noncongruent correspondent in all twelve translation directions in Figures 11.12 and 11.13, while punctuation omission/addition is the second-most frequent in eleven of the twelve cases.[10] Thus, as with both colons (Ström Herold and Levin 2021) and brackets (Levin and Ström Herold 2021), commas and punctuation omission/addition are the most

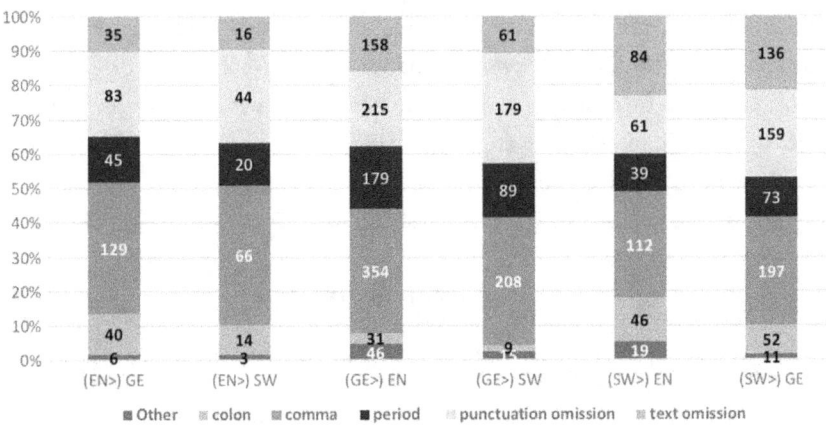

Figure 11.12 Replacements from dashes: proportions of 'non-dash' correspondences in translations.

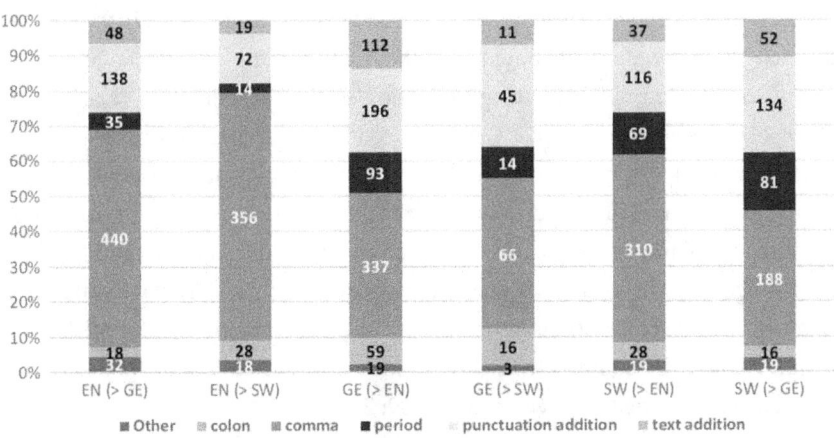

Figure 11.13 Replacements into dashes: proportions of 'non-dash' correspondences in originals.

common noncongruent alternatives with dashes. So, translators mainly change from or into the less 'marked' punctuation choices comma or no punctuation, rather than translating between two marked punctuation marks such as between brackets and dashes. Considering translation universals such as standardization (Baker 1996: 180), it could be surmised that translators would rather change dashes into commas than vice versa. However, this only holds true for German translations into Swedish, while the opposite applies to three translation directions: EN > GE, EN > SW and SW > EN. This result indicates that there is another stronger force involved, that is, adherence to target-language norms.

A final notable observation relates to the omission and addition of text in connection with punctuation. While brackets are more likely to be used by translators to include clarifying information not present in the original, the opposite applies to dashes – text introduced by dashes is more likely to be omitted than added. Alluding to Baumgarten, Meyer and Özçetin (2008: 190), dashes are *not* 'typical sites of translational explicitation'.

11.5 Conclusions

This contribution on punctuation in English-German-Swedish nonfiction has revealed new findings on formal and functional features of dashes. The results are partly in line with our two previous studies of punctuation marks, but there are also features and patterns specific to dashes. The language most prone to using the dash is German. The fewest dashes are found in English texts, which instead contain the most brackets (Levin and Ström Herold 2021). In view of the different stylistic values attributed to dashes and brackets – dashes having an air of informality and brackets being typical of 'serious written style' (Leech et al. 2009: 245) – we did not expect German texts to use so many more dashes than English. A likely explanation is the German prescriptive principles requiring a punctuation mark before and/or after dependent clauses – which quite often is in the form of a dash, as discussed in connection with Figure 11.2. In addition, the cross-linguistic advice against overusing dashes may possibly have influenced English writing conventions more than those in German and Swedish. This would explain the comparatively low numbers in our data and the decreasing frequencies identified by Leech et al. (2009: 246).

Drawing on our functional typology of brackets, we observe that dashes also mainly introduce content-related material, elaborating on objective information in the previous text. Still, dashes do this to a significantly lower degree than brackets. Instead, dashes have more subjective components such as introducing text segments addressing readers (e.g. *The biggest obstacles are social and political – what you need is the will to do it.*). German and Swedish have a particularly strong preference for using dashes to introduce sentence-final clauses, while English has a relatively higher preference for parenthetical sentence-medial use.

Previous studies (e.g. Wollin 2018; Frankenberg-Garcia 2019) have observed that direct transfer is a very common strategy when translating punctuation marks, and Levin and Ström Herold (2021) on brackets was no different. With dashes, however, there is considerable variation in retention rates, depending on language pairs reaching as high as almost 90 per cent and dropping as low as below 50 per cent. As with brackets, the retention rates largely correlate with the status of the languages. Translators into the relatively 'minor' Swedish are most likely to carry over the English and German source-text usage patterns into their target language. The most common non-dash correspondences are commas and zero punctuation, irrespective of translation direction. Replacing a dash with a comma is an expected scenario in view of both the Lauchman's emphasis hierarchy (2010) and the trend towards standardization in translation (Baker 1996). An important factor here is also the tendency for translations to move towards target-language norms.

The relationships between dashes and other punctuation marks require further exploration, not only in popular nonfiction but also more specialized genres. In particular, contrastive diachronic studies would be called for. If the frequencies of dashes (and brackets) are changing in English (Leech et al. 2009: 246), what is the situation like in German and Swedish, not least considering the widespread prescriptive opposition to the overuse of dashes? Thus, our study highlights the need for further investigations into punctuation.

Notes

1. In the LEGS originals, the em dash is restricted to American editions, irrespective of whether the author is American or not.
2. English vs. German, $X^2 = 19.1$, df = 1, $p = ***$, phi = 0.08; English vs. Swedish, $X^2 = 0.72$, df = 1, $p = $ ns, phi = 0.01; German vs. Swedish, $X^2 = 11.6$, df = 1, $p = ***$, phi = 0.06.
3. English dashes vs. brackets, $X^2 = 107.8$, df = 1, $p = ***$, phi = 0.22; German dashes vs. brackets, $X^2 = 9.4$, df = 1, $p = ***$, phi = 0.06; Swedish dashes vs. brackets, $X^2 = 13.7$, df = 1, $p = ***$, phi = 0.09.

4   Form: EN ST vs. GE ST X^2 = 52.2, df = 1, p = ***, V = 0.12; EN ST vs. SW ST X^2 = 27.9, df = 1, p = ***, V = 0.10; GE ST vs. SW ST X^2 = 1.98, df = 1, p = ns, V = 0.02. Position: EN ST vs. GE ST X^2 = 208.5, df = 1, p = ***, V = 0.25; EN ST vs. SW ST X^2 = 181.8, df = 1, p = ***, V = 0.26; GE ST vs. SW ST X^2 = 0.35, df = 1, p = ns, V = 0.01.

5   EN ST vs. EN->GE LL = 58.3, p = ***, OR = 1.32; EN ST vs. EN->SW LL = 52.5, p = ***, OR = 1.31; GE ST vs. GE->ENLL = 51.0, p = ***, OR = 0.78; GE ST vs. GE->SW LL = 57.0, p = ***, OR = 0.77; SW ST vs. SW->EN LL = 2.93, p = ns, OR = 1.06; SW ST vs. SW->GE LL = 5.40, p = *, OR = 0.91. We did not notice any particular differences between individual translators into either of the three target languages.

6   The unexpected pattern is not the result of any aberrant individual text. In both translation directions, about half the corpus texts contain more dashes and about half fewer than the Swedish originals.

7   EN ST: X^2 = 75.4, df = 1, p = ***, phi = 0.17; GE ST: X^2 = 193.9, df = 1, p = ***, phi = 0.22; SW ST: X^2 = 116, df = 1, p = ***, phi = 0.21.

8   This is also substantiated by text-by-text comparisons: six German texts retain fewer dashes as compared to four English texts and one with equal numbers.

9   The 'other' category comprises punctuation marks not exceeding 4 per cent in any sub-corpus: brackets, exclamation marks, question marks and semicolons.

10 The exception being Swedish-to-English replacements from dashes where text omission is more frequent.

References

Baker, M. (1996), 'Corpus-based Translation Studies: The Challenges that Lie Ahead', in H. Somers (ed.), *Terminology, LSP and Translation: Studies in Language Engineering in Honour of Juan C. Sager*, 175–86, Amsterdam: John Benjamins.

Baumgarten, N., B. Meyer and D. Özçetin (2008), 'Explicitness in Translation and Interpreting: A Critical Review and Some Empirical Evidence (of an Elusive Concept)', *Across Languages and Cultures*, 9 (2): 177–203.

Becher, V. (2011), 'Von der Hypotaxe zur Parataxe: Ein Wandel im Ausdruck von Konzessivität in neueren populärwissenschaftlichen Texten', in E. Breindl, G. Ferraresi and A. Volodina (eds), *Satzverknüpfungen. Zur Interaktion von Form, Bedeutung und Diskursfunktion*, 181–209, Berlin: De Gruyter.

Crystal, D. (2015), *Making a Point: The Pernickety Story of English Punctuation*, London: Profile Books.

Duden. Band 9. Richtiges und gutes Deutsch. Zweifelsfälle der deutschen Sprache von A bis Z. (1997), 4th edn, Berlin: Dudenverlag.

Englund Dimitrova, B. (2014), 'Till punkt och pricka? Översättarstil, normer och interpunktion vid översättning från bulgariska till svenska', *Slovo. Journal of Slavic Languages, Literatures and Cultures*, 55: 77–99.

Eskesen, H. and H. Fuglsang (1998), 'Kolon: Den oversete konnektor', *HERMES - Journal of Language and Communication in Business*, 11 (21): 151–79. https://doi.org/10.7146/hjlcb.v11i21.25481

Frankenberg-Garcia, A. (2019), 'A *Corpus Study* of Splitting and Joining Sentences in Translation', *Corpora*, 14 (1): 1–30.

Gellerstam, M. (1986), 'Translationese in Swedish Novels Translated from English', in L. Wollin and H. Lindquist (eds), *Translation Studies in Scandinavia*, 88–95, Lund: CWK Gleerup.

House, J. (1997), *Translation Quality Assessment: A Model Revisited*, Tübingen: Gunter Narr Verlag.

House, J. (2011), 'Using Translation and Parallel Text Corpora to Investigate the Influence of Global English on Textual Norms in Other Languages', in A. Kruger, K. Wallmach and J. Munday (eds), *Corpus-based Translation Studies*, 187–208, London: Bloomsbury.

Lauchman, R. (2010), *Punctuation at Work: Simple Principles for Achieving Clarity and Good Style*, Amacom.

Leech, G., M. Hundt, C. Mair and N. Smith (2009), *Change in Contemporary English. A Grammatical Study*, Cambridge: Cambridge University Press.

Levin, M. and J. Ström Herold (2021), 'On Brackets in Translation (or How to Elaborate in Brackets)', in A. Čermáková, S. Oksefjell Ebeling, M. Levin and J. Ström Herold (eds), *Crossing the Borders: Analysing Complex Contrastive Data*, Bergen Language and Linguistics Studies, 11 (1): 121–44.

Nádvorníková, O. (2020), 'The Use of English, Czech and French Punctuation Marks in Reference, Parallel and Comparable Web Corpora: A Question of Methodology', *Linguistica Pragensia*, 30 (1): 30–50.

Neef, M. (2021), 'Zur Kommasetzung im Deutschen. Eine Analyse mittels dreier orthographischer Bedingungen', in P. Rössler, P. Besl and A. Saller (eds), *Comparative Punctuation – Vergleichende Interpunktion*, 3–24, Berlin: De Gruyter.

New Hart's Rules: The Oxford Style Guide (2014), Oxford: Oxford University Press.

Quirk, R., S. Greenbaum, G. Leech and J. Svartvik (1985), *A Comprehensive Grammar of the English Language*, London: Longman.

Rodríguez-Castro, M. (2011), 'Translationese and Punctuation. An Empirical Study of Translated and Non-translated International Newspaper Articles (English and Spanish)', *Journal of Translation and Interpreting Studies*, 16 (1): 40–61.

Rössler, P., P. Besl and A. Saller, eds (2021), *Comparative Punctuation – Vergleichende Interpunktion*, Berlin: De Gruyter.

Shiyab, S. M. (2017), *Translation: Concepts and Critical Issues*, Antwerp: Garant Publishers.

Ström Herold, J. and M. Levin (2021), 'The Colon in English, German and Swedish: A Contrastive Corpus-based Study', in P. Rössler, P. Besl and A. Saller (eds), *Comparative Punctuation – Vergleichende Interpunktion*, 237–61, Berlin: De Gruyter.

Wollin, L. (2018), 'Punctuation: Providing the Setting for Translation?', *Studia Neophilologica*, 90 (1): 37–49.

Index

aboutness 115
additive 209, 214–16, 228
adjectives 82, 120, 123, 185, 244, 269
adverbial 42–5, 51, 56 n.18, 91, 185, 214, 241, 244, 247, 252, 256
adverbs 15–16, 120, 124, 184, 204, 213, 227, 241, 244–5, 248, 250, 252–3, 256
adversative relations 209–12
animacy 5, 63–5, 68, 70–4, 76–80, 82, 83 n.9
annotation 20–2, 68, 138
AntGram 137, 139–40
Arabic 132, 136, 138–45, 147
aspectual 160, 167–72, 176
audiovisual customization 6, 158–9

bidirectional translation corpus 35–6, 66, 75, 187
blending 248, 254–6
body, *also* body part 64–5, 70–1, 73, 77, 79–80
body language 246–8
brackets 260, 263–73, 275, 279–81, 282 n.9

can/could 6, 157, 159–60, 163, 165–72, 176
causal 209, 214–16, 225
caused motion 103, 105
Chinese 132, 136–45, 149
cognate 5, 29–32, 35–6, 41, 49–50, 52–4, 87–9, 92–105
coherence 7, 11, 16, 109, 159, 204, 205, 207–14, 217–18, 228–9
cohesive (marker, relation) 33, 162, 211
collocate, *see* collocation
collocation 115, 118–28, 129 nn.13–14, 17, 135
colon 260, 263–4, 266, 277, 279
comma 261, 264, 266, 274, 277, 279–81

comparable corpus 4–5, 7, 12–18, 22, 31, 36, 110, 204–7, 211, 215, 217
complementation 34–5, 41–6, 51, 53, 112, 114, 117, 124
concordance 67–8, 70, 213
congruence (in translation) 5, 68, 74–8, 82, 217
connective(s) 7, 15, 22, 204, 210–11, 214–15, 217, 228
contrastive 209, 214–16
contrastive pragmatics 4, 14, 20, 21
conversation 17, 19–21, 44, 139, 157–9, 187, 190–1, 214, 222, 225, 227–8
Czech 16, 18, 108–12, 114–22, 125–7, 128 n.2, 238–40, 246–51, 255–6
Czech National Corpus 112, 128 n.5, 239

dash 260–82
dative 87, 89, 90, 92, 94–100, 105
deixis 161, 174–5, 177
deontic (modality) 221
determiner 63, 78, 114, 117
diachronic development 210, 219, 229
dialogue 30, 35, 37–49, 53, 55 nn.6, 13, 16, 56 nn.17, 25, 158, 162, 174, 177, 187–8, 206
direct speech 37, 237, 242
discourse marker 14, 16, 33, 35, 46, 48, 50, 52, 157, 159, 269
dislocation 16–17
ditransitive, *see* double object construction
double object construction 87–105
dubbese 157, 159, 167–9, 171–2, 174–5

English-Norwegian Parallel Corpus (ENPC) 14, 29–30, 36–8, 61, 66, 72, 83, 83 n.1, 87, 90, 183, 186–8, 199–200
ENPC, *see* English-Norwegian Parallel Corpus

entropy   113, 136, 139, 141–2
epistemic (modality)   3, 221
Europarl Corpus   13, 16
evaluation   18–20, 22, 125–6, 213, 237, 269, 271
evaluative prosody, *see* semantic prosody
explicitation   238, 266, 275, 280

fiction   4, 5, 7, 29, 35, 36, 41, 44–6, 48, 54, 62, 63, 70, 71, 77, 169, 187, 236, 237, 241
Finnish   237, 239–40, 248–9, 252–3, 255–7
football match reports   16, 30, 35–6, 38, 41, 54
formulaicity   133–6
French   204–35

genitive alternation   62, 64–5, 67, 79
genitive, *see* periphrastic genitive; *s*-genitive
genre   13, 16–22, 36, 105, 134–7, 146, 169, 177, 204–6, 211–13, 215, 217, 225, 228–9, 239, 240, 250, 255–7, 262
genre analysis   17–20
German   17, 21, 238, 260–81
grammaticalization   14–15, 67, 82, 218, 229

hedging   15, 19–20, 22, 185, 200, 214, 269, 272

idiomaticity   81, 146
imperative   37–40, 48–9, 185, 191–2, 194–200, 268–70
implicitation   96
incongruence, *see* congruence
infinitive   37–40, 44, 49–50, 160, 167, 186, 194, 252, 253, 255
interpersonal function   14, 17, 184, 263, 265

journalism, *see* newspaper discourse

kinship   65, 68, 70–1, 73, 76, 80–2

learners   134, 136, 186

LEGS corpus, *see* Linnaeus University English-German-Swedish corpus
lemma   37, 38, 50, 52, 90, 112
lemmatized, lemmatization   110, 111, 118, 126–7
lexical bundle   135–6
Linnaeus University English-German-Swedish corpus (LEGS)   260, 262–3, 266–78, 281 n.1
lip-syncing   157, 159
literary translation   237–8, 246, 255
locative   80, 82, 116

Malay   132, 136–46, 151
match reports   30, 35–6, 38, 41–2, 44–50, 53–4, 55 n.16, 56 n.22
meaning units, *see* units of meaning
mental cognition   30, 32–5, 46–52
mental perception   30, 32–5, 46–52
modal (auxiliary, verb)   15–16, 40, 50, 55 n.15, 157, 159, 160, 165, 167, 197
multifunctional(ity)   14, 17, 218, 219, 265
multimodal corpora   16–17, 22
mutual correspondence   3, 75, 101, 103–4

narrative   29–30, 35–49, 53, 237, 242, 262
newspaper discourse   19, 109–12, 125–7, 137
n-grams   108, 110–18, 125–7, 128 nn.5, 7, 129 n.11, 137
non-fiction   62, 66, 69–75, 78, 80, 82–3, 90, 169, 187, 260–2, 264, 280–1
Norwegian   29–86, 87–107, 183–206
noun phrase (NP)   16, 42–5, 65, 78, 83, 87, 114, 117, 126, 244, 269

of-genitive, *see* periphrastic genitive
overuse   112, 158, 165, 168–9, 172–7, 264–5, 277

parallel corpus   1, 12–16, 18, 22, 29, 36, 66, 87, 160, 163, 166, 183, 187, 205, 239, 260, 262
participle   38–9, 186, 244, 256
period   261, 266, 270, 277

periphery 16, 222, 224
periphrastic genitive 62–7, 69–70, 74–6, 78–82
p-frame 132, 133, 135–46
phrase frame 132, 134
phraseological units 108–9, 132–6, 143, 145–6
phraseology 108–10, 125, 127, 132–47
pied-piping 97
please 183–201
poder + infinitive 160, 167
politeness marker 184–6, 188, 190–1, 193, 200
polysemy 14, 29, 218, 223, 227
possession 65–6, 80–2, 89–90
possessor 63–5, 67–8, 70–4, 76–80, 82, 83 n.9
postmodifier/postmodification 62, 78, 114, 241, 244
pragmatic function 15, 139, 145
pragmatic marker 4, 11–18, 22
pragmaticalization 14–15
pragmatics 11, 21–2, 92, 183
predictability 133, 135–6, 138–46, 217
prefabricated orality 157–9, 165, 176
premodifier/premodification 78, 82, 241, 247
prepositional patterns 108–27, 128 n.2
prepositions 63–4, 67–8, 70, 78, 80–2, 108–27, 231, 244, 249
process types 32, 47
pronoun 63, 95, 97, 99, 118, 126, 157–77
pull factor 93–4
punctuation 110, 114, 117, 126, 127, 137, 207, 209, 240, 260–82
push factor 93

recipient 17, 87, 89–91, 94, 96–7, 99–100, 102–3, 184, 197
register 4–6, 29–31, 35–6, 38, 41–50, 52–4, 55 n.3, 62, 65, 71, 82–3, 89, 94, 104, 108–9, 112, 116, 125–7, 134–6, 162, 206, 217, 237
repetition 236, 238, 248, 256, 258 n.6
reporting verbs 7, 236–8, 241, 248, 254–7
request marker 184, 186, 188, 190–1, 195, 197, 200

ritual frame indicating expression (RFIE) 184–5, 188, 190–1, 196–200

see/se 29–54
semantic change 49, 210, 218, 225
semantic map 218, 229
semantic preference 108–9, 119–22, 125–7
semantic prosody 108–9, 119–21, 123–6
s-genitive 5, 62–8, 78–83
simultaneity 241–2, 245, 252–3, 256–7
source language influence 159, 187, 266
Spanish 15–17, 19, 157–77, 211–12, 238, 266, 275
speech act 15, 20–2, 214
statistical significance 6, 38, 91, 104, 140, 142–3, 146, 159, 165, 169, 172, 257 n.4
style 7, 63, 65, 71, 109, 127, 227, 242, 246, 255, 257, 264–5, 267, 271–2, 280
subject pronouns 6, 157, 159–61, 165, 173–5, 177
subordinate clause 266, 272
subordinator 110, 118, 267
subtitling 13, 17–18
suffix 62–3, 127, 248
Swahili 4, 6, 132, 136, 138–44, 146, 152
Swedish 3–4, 14, 17, 33–4, 183, 186, 197, 198, 215, 260–82
synonym 120, 268, 272, 274
synchronization 167–8, 170–1, 176–7
Systemic-Functional Grammar (SFG) 32–3, 35, 41, 47

temporal (expressions, relations) 116–17, 204, 209, 213, 214, 218–21, 224–9, 241
tertium comparationis 12, 21, 35–6, 132, 162, 174, 205, 211–12
theme 87, 89–90, 94, 96, 98, 100, 102–5
transfer 5, 6, 87, 89, 91, 94–5, 102–3, 105, 157, 159–60, 169, 172, 176–7, 200, 261, 265, 274, 281
translation 12–18, 22, 105, 106 n.2, 110, 117, 125, 128 n.3, 143, 157–60,

163–5, 172, 174, 177, 183, 186–7, 190, 193–9, 205, 210–12, 217, 236–9, 246–57, 260–6, 273–81, 282 n.6
typology   33, 108, 111, 117, 127, 133, 137, 145–6, 211, 237–9, 247, 252–3, 256

underspecification   13, 15–16, 22
underuse   165, 168–9, 172–7, 186

units of meaning   6, 132–3, 136–7, 139, 145

variability   133, 135–6, 138–43, 145–6
visual phonetics   157, 159

word order   133, 137, 145

zero (correspondence)   15, 68, 74, 75, 95, 96, 97, 98, 100

www.ingramcontent.com/pod-product-compliance
Lightning Source LLC
Chambersburg PA
CBHW071805300426
44116CB00009B/1205